INTEGRATING
KNOWLEDGE
AND PRACTICE

INTEGRATING KNOWLEDGE AND PRACTICE

The Case of Social Work and Social Science

Edited by
David J. Tucker,
Charles Garvin,
and Rosemary Sarri

Westport, Connecticut
London

HV
40
.I 54
1997
June 1998

Library of Congress Cataloging-in-Publication Data

Integrating knowledge and practice : the case of social work and
  social science / edited by David J. Tucker, Charles Garvin, and
  Rosemary Sarri.
        p.   cm.
    Includes bibliographical references and index.
    ISBN 0–275–94967–2 (alk. paper)
    1. Social work.   2. Social service—Philosophy.   3. Social
sciences—Philosophy.   I. Tucker, David J. (David John), 1943– .
II. Garvin, Charles, 1929– .   III. Sarri, Rosemary C.
HV40.I54   1997
361.3—DC21   96–50324

British Library Cataloguing in Publication Data is available.

Library of Congress Catalog Card Number: 96–50324
ISBN: 0–275–94967–2

First published in 1997

Praeger Publishers, 88 Post Road West, Westport, CT 06881
An imprint of Greenwood Publishing Group, Inc.

Printed in the United States of America

The paper used in this book complies with the
Permanent Paper Standard issued by the National
Information Standards Organization (Z39.48–1984).

10 9 8 7 6 5 4 3 2 1

Contents

Part II: Social Science to Social Work

Part III: Social Work to Social Science

Part IV: Themes and Perspectives

Part V: A History of Educational Integration in One Program

Illustrations

Tables

Figures

Introduction: Evolution and Change in the Relationship between Social Work and Social Science

David J. Tucker, Charles Garvin, and Rosemary Sarri

Accounting for change in the social organization of science is an important problem in the sociology of knowledge. Patterns of scientific organization have crucial implications not only for the production and validation of scientific knowledge but also for the control of future research directions. Traditionally, scholars have approached this problem by focusing on the development of scientific communities in order to identify the processes underlying the emergence of new specializations and disciplines. The reason for adopting this focus is a view of science as composed of sets of loosely connected groupings of producers and consumers of knowledge formed around particular knowledge goals. Because these groupings, or communities, tend to follow a similar pattern of knowledge development once they are established, scientific change is most likely to happen in their formative stages. Hence, if we are to understand how scientific knowledge changes, it is plausible to concentrate on the founding processes of new scientific communities.

Observers have criticized this view of the origin of scientific change as modeled mainly on the development of a single science, namely physics. Thus, it does not acknowledge the diversity and plurality of patterns of change and development across the natural and social sciences. Moreover, it does not take into account the effects of the university context or other more immediate circumstances and conditions on scientists' goals and decisions. One approach to overcoming these deficiencies involves treating the sciences as *reputational organizations* (Whitley, 1982). Incorporated into various employment organizations (mainly universities), reputational organizations are systems of work in which practitioners seek reputations by selecting tasks and pursuing knowledge goals in light of the particular beliefs and purposes of the reputational community of which they are members (Whitley, 1982, 315). However, the extent to which reputational organizations are dominated by their respective reputational communities varies, depending on such factors as the professionalization and the autonomy of various fields, as well as their relations with employment organizations and the munificence and structure of funding sources. Considered from this perspective, it is plausiable to examine changes in the patterns of knowledge development of a given science by analyzing how that science is affected by changes in its connections to various dimensions of the environment in which it is embedded.

We use this approach here to examine relations between the social sciences and social work. In order to create a context for understanding its current status, we begin by focusing on the historical background of this connection, documenting the various phases through which it has passed since its inception in the mid-1800s. Next, we ask how contemporaneous changes in knowledge development processes in the social sciences have affected current social work knowledge perspectives. Our central assumption is that to the extent that there is a plurality of knowledge perspectives in social work, this plurality strongly reflects the developments in the social sciences in the post-World War II era. Finally, we move to contextualize the relationship between social work and social science more fully by conceptualizing them as a single reputational organization, examining how both together are likely to be affected in the future by the all-encompassing process of globalization.

HISTORICAL BACKGROUND

The issue of defining the relationship between social work and social science has persisted since the earliest days of the profession. As early as 1879, the leaders of the newly developing fields of organized charities and corrections declared their interests to be different from those of the developing social sciences. By the midpoint of the twentieth century, however, leading social work academics and practitioners were calling for a closer relationship between the two spheres, arguing both that social work should incorporate social science knowledge and research findings into its knowledge base, and that social scientists in turn should become more involved in the resolution of social problems. Underlying this change has been an ongoing debate over the knowledge base of social work. "What do social workers need to know to perform the tasks required of them competently?" and "Does the abstract knowledge of the social sciences contribute to the development of social work practice methods and helping processes?" Clearly, the answer to these questions changed between the late 1800s and the mid 1900s.

This section will briefly review the evolution of debate regarding the proper knowledge base of the profession from its earliest days to the 1970s. While we acknowledge that there has never been a consensus about the issues in this debate, we identify four periods that were marked by differing views concerning the relationship between social work and social science: a period of *nondifferentiation* from 1865 to 1879, in which the two were intertwined; a period of *peaceful differentiation* from 1880 to 1900, in which the two developed separately; a period of *conflicted differentiation* from 1900 to 1950, in which they continued a largely separate existence, but in which social work experienced pressures and tensions around the advisability or necessity of reaffirming a relationship; and a period of *integration and development* after

1950, in which social work fully embraced both the knowledge and the methods of the social sciences.

Nondifferentiation: 1865 to early 1880

By the midpoint of the nineteenth century, academic and civic leaders in the U.S. were seriously concerned with questions of how best to understand and address the emerging problems of poverty, crime, and mental illness. Imbued with an optimistic faith in science and organization, states had begun to appoint Boards of Charities and Corrections to oversee the growing numbers of state institutions charged with the care of the poor, insane, and criminal classes, and to advise government and citizens about the best methods for curing and preventing such social problems. To this end, members of the State Boards, along with the administrators of their institutions, began meeting annually with members of the fledgling American Social Science Association (ASSA), an organization composed of academics who shared their concerns. Formed in 1865, the Association intended

to aid in the development of social science and to guide the public mind to the best practical means of promoting the amendment of laws, the advancement of education, the prevention and repression of crime, the reformation of criminals, and the progress of public morality, the adoption of sanitary regulations, and the diffusion of sound principles on the questions of economy, trade, and finance. It will give attention to pauperism, and the topics related thereto; including the responsibility of the well-endowed and successful, the wise and educated, the honest and respectable, for the failures of others. It will aim to bring together the various societies and individuals now interested in these objects, for the purpose of obtaining, by discussion, the real elements of truth; by which doubts are removed, conflicting opinions harmonized, and a common ground afforded for treating wisely the great social problems of the day (Sanborn, 1876).

Academics, administrators, and government advisors gathered together annually, attending first the conference of the ASSA and, immediately following, the conference of the State Boards of Charities and Corrections. By 1879, however, it was clear that the interests of the two organizations had begun to diverge. The academics in the newly developing social sciences were focusing increasingly on developing theory and conducting research, while the administrators and State Board members were primarily concerned with the material problems and conditions faced by institutional administrators and workers. Hence, in 1879, the Conference of State Boards and Charities ceased to function as a section of the ASSA and formed a separate organization, the National Conference of Charities and Corrections (NCCC), which first met in 1880.

Peaceful Differentiation: 1880 to 1900[1]

Both the ASSA and the NCCC continued to meet separately throughout the remainder of the century, though published proceedings indicate that members of each organization would occasionally participate in the conference of the other. Within the ASSA, the more academic of the two organizations, most scholars viewed the developing spheres of social work and social science as separate but complementary; for them, the task of social science was to "discover the general laws and principles governing human intercourse; [of] charity, to furnish the data, to test the principles, and to attend to the practical, day-by-day work of amelioration and prevention" (Bruno, 1957, 134). Furthermore, ASSA members regarded the data assembled at by the NCCC as "excellent source material for college courses in charity and corrections" (Bruno, 1957, 134).

The NCCC, on the other hand, reaffirmed its pragmatic focus after 1880, when members of private sector organizations (charity organization societies, children institutions, settlement houses) were invited to attend the meetings. This focus expanded from the mainly organizational and programmatic concerns of state institutions to include the more direct service interests of "friendly visitors," child welfare investigators, and settlement workers. Indeed, it is generally conceded that by 1900 the concerns of the private sector groups came to dominate the concerns of the public sector groups at NCCC meetings. This resulted in a shift in the focus of debates from examinations of the causes of social problems to questions about their proper management—notably, which organizational auspice (public or private) and which method (settlement or casework) were superior.

The nature of the debates around methods revealed underlying conflicts in the developing social work community that were due in part to differing beliefs about the role of social science knowledge. While the majority of settlement workers had university training in the social sciences, this was less often the case with charity organization workers, especially those involved in direct service work. The educational backgrounds of Jane Addams, the leader of the settlement movement, and Mary Richmond, a leader of the charity organization movement, typify this difference. Addams graduated from Rockford College and went on to medical school, although she subsequently had to leave because of poor health. Richmond, on the other hand, was a high school graduate who worked her way into a leadership position in the charity organization society movement after originally being hired as a clerk (Franklin, 1986, 510). Given their educational backgrounds and the focus of their change efforts, settlement workers like Jane Addams were inclined to favor a closer connection with the social sciences, while charity organization workers such as Mary Richmond adopted a more applied approach. Thus it was common for the settlements to have close working relationships with local social science departments and to serve as "social laboratories" in which students honed their skills in researching social problems.

Despite these differing orientations regarding the value of social science knowledge, there does not appear to have been open debate in this period about the comparative merits of the abstract knowledge of the social sciences as opposed to the pragmatic orientation of applied philanthropy. However, with the development of the formal training programs for social workers in the early twentieth century, this issue was forced into the open.

1900 to 1950: Period of Conflicted Differentiation

Early efforts at training social workers came from within both the settlements and the charity organization societies. The first full-time school, the New York School of Philanthropy, opened in 1904 and was affiliated with the New York Charity Organization Society. Reflecting Mary Richmond's influence, the curriculum emphasized practical work rather than academic subjects (Bruno, 1957, 138–144). By 1915, the U.S. had five independent schools and two programs with university affiliations. As the schools were "free to develop [their] own curriculum unfettered by academic rules," these early university affiliations have subsequently been characterized as "tenuous" and "platonic" (Bruno, 1957, 142–144). Like the New York School, most of the newly formed schools were connected in some way with private charitable organizations that "wanted especially to rationalize the methods of their own friendly visitors" (Muncy, 1991, 68). The valued knowledge in such programs was heavily methods-oriented, providing the "how tos" for such things as family needs assessments, record keeping, and efficient service delivery.

After a beginning similar in orientation, the Chicago School of Civics and Philanthropy proved to be a battle-ground for the debate on the value of applied versus abstract knowledge. Affiliated with the city's settlements, the Chicago School originally began as a single course on philanthropy run by Graham Taylor, a settlement leader who eschewed abstract knowledge in favor of the value of experience and the guidance of religion. Expanding quickly to a full program that provided general knowledge in community welfare as well as a "more technical preparation" for those interested in professional and voluntary service, the school initially focused on transforming "the nineteenth century's friendly visitors into the twentieth century's caseworkers" (Muncy, 1991, 68–74). With the aid of a grant from the Russell Sage Foundation in 1907, the Chicago School quickly expanded to include its own research department "for social investigation on a scientific basis" (Muncy, 1991, 68). Though several other schools, including New York, received similar grants, Chicago's decision to hire Sophonisba Breckinridge and Edith Abbott set that school's program on a different path. Breckinridge, with a Ph.D. in political science, and Abbott, with a Ph.D. in economics, took command of the research department and turned it into a program for the study of the extent and causes of social problems and conditions. Over the ensuing years, the school gained considerable expertise and a reputation for its research, with Breckinridge and Abbott collaborating frequently with social science researchers from the University of Chicago. By 1920, over the objections of Taylor, Breckinridge and Abbot successfully negotiated for the absorption of the school by the University of Chicago, and renamed it the School of Social Service Administration. Equating the role and training of caseworkers in other schools of social work with that of technicians, Breckinridge and Abbott announced a different intention: to create an academic discipline in which the goal was the "collection of a body of authoritative data upon which programs for social reform and recommendations for changes in social legislation may be based" (Muncy, 1991, 76). Their program would not turn out technician caseworkers; rather, their graduates would become administrators and policy makers whose training was based on social science theories and incorporated social science research methods.

Although the tensions between social reformers and caseworkers and between abstract and craft knowledge were clearly evident in the formation of the Chicago School, they were less volatile in other training programs that were more inclined to incorporate both casework and settlement methods. Although tolerance for diversity of aims and methods had the advantage of giving the nascent field of social work a large membership base, it also proved to be a major stumbling block, as its leaders sought to raise the status of their craft to that of such acknowledged professions as law and medicine. In 1915, the desire for professional status led the National Conference of Charities and Corrections to invite Abraham Flexner to deliver his controversial paper, "Is Social Work a Profession?" Claiming that social work lacked "specificity of aim" and could claim no technical skill or specialized knowledge, Flexner answered his own question with a definite no (Flexner, 1915). Dismayed by Flexner's analysis, social work academics and practitioners increased their efforts to establish a unique professional identity for social work. For most teachers and leaders of social work, this did not mean aligning themselves with the abstract knowledge of social sciences. Instead, it meant compiling and consolidating the experiential knowledge of the casework method in a more scientific way.

Mary Richmond's classic book *Social Diagnosis*, published in 1917, was the first systematic effort to develop a practice model that was recognized as countering Flexner's criticisms. Outlining and advocating scientific methods of observation, data collection, and interpretation, Richmond articulated a model of social casework that involved providing a careful assessment of client's experiences in coping with adverse social conditions and offering a "treatment" that involved interventions with agencies in the environment as much as change within the individual client. The abstract social sciences, while not a focus of Richmond's concerns, provided a means for understanding the social conditions and problems seen to contribute to the client's problems. Thus, in this earliest systematic model of casework, the social sciences—especially sociology—played a secondary role to practice methods. At the National Conference of Social Work in 1918, the year after Richmond's book was published, Charles Ellwood called for an even more extensive reliance on the social sciences, urging social work "to use modern scientific methods to accumulate bodies of social facts, to study the processes and movements in community life, and to link its efforts with the social sciences" (Ellwood, 1919, 687).

By the early 1920s, however, Richmond's sociological approach to casework was being challenged by the psychoanalytic approach, drawn particularly from the works of Freud. This development had the effect of largely removing the social sciences from the supporting role they held in Richmond's casework model. Social workers were directed by psychoanalytical theory to focus less on social context and more on the personality formation and dynamics of individual clients to explain and address the problems they experienced. At the same time, the settlements had declined in significance and power, resulting in a concomitant decline in the significance of settlement methods in social work training. The overall effect was that a more psychologically-oriented casework became the dominant social work method, which was taught and practiced in a manner that distanced it from much of social science. The one connection that social work did retain with the social sciences was its use of scientific methods. Hence, the primary link between the two became one not of abstract knowledge, but of technique and procedure. It was not unusual, therefore, to see academics such as Ernest W. Burgess, the distinguished sociologist at the University of Chicago, address social workers on such matters as to how to be more scientific and rigorous in the recording of data on cases (Burgess, 1927, 191–193). Social work casework researchers themselves began borrowing the data collection and measurement procedures of social scientists, and adapting them to meet their own needs. For example, in 1926, Sophie Hardy urged other social workers to follow her lead after she developed instruments to measure both the child-training habits of a mother and the marital habits of a husband and father that were related to Watson's behaviorism and to Thomas's translation of wishes to habits (Orcutt, 1990, 140).

Social work's concern with technique and its separation from reform efforts and the abstract knowledge of the social sciences reached their apex in the late 1920s. Epitomizing the search for method, Porter Lee, the director of the New York School of Social Work, in his well-known speech "Social Work: Cause and Function," argued that social work must disassociate itself from the cause of reform and attend to its function in promoting "well-organized community life" (Lee, 1930). Lee's call to focus on function, or method, was echoed by other social work academics who believed that though the profession had developed to the point of being able to provide a good assessment of a client's problems, it was substantially behind in its ability to treat them (Ehrenreich, 1985, 71–72). The focus of the profession for the 1930s was thus established as the pursuit of method.

The separation of social work and the social sciences, however, was not one-sided. Just as social work had begun to distance itself from social science, the social sciences began to distance themselves from the concerns of social workers. As social science continued to develop from its early stages, it had its own fight to gain legitimacy in universities where the physical and biological sciences were already established. One way it did so was by demonstrating its scientific rigor and lack of bias in the examination and analysis of data. This required that social science separate itself from its ideological commitment to work on behalf of the poor and other disadvantaged populations. No less a figure than Charlotte Towle, a pioneer of the development of casework theory, later pointed to the results of the social scientists' disengagement from the poor and vulnerable when she criticized a fictional sociologist in a novel by Richard Wright. This sociologist, she explains,

typifies many of our experiences, in which the social scientist befriended the delinquent boy in order to observe him and sat by, never lifting a wrist to put him in helping hands while he watched him proceed to the electric chair. The Clifford Shaw group of sociologists sat by and wrote "Jack Roller" accounts and were loath to refer individuals for help lest they interfere with their research findings. Unlike the medical group they separated study and treatment and did not use social caseworkers to treat individuals in their hour of need. Instead they were focused on eventually making social ills known in order that broadside program planning might occur. . . . Inevitably social caseworkers saw them as ruthless and perceived that in hobnobbing with individuals to study them, they were exploiting them and often affording a corruptible relationship to those who confided in them. (Towle, 1958, 4)

Although most social workers remained wedded to casework, it became impossible to view the problems of poverty and desertion in individual terms with the onset of the depression of the 1930s. Moreover, casework could hardly be the solution for the millions of Americans whose lives were devastated by the grinding poverty of the depression years. By 1934, even Porter Lee acknowledged that the "most congenial area for discussion among most social workers is not that of professional competence, but it is rather that of the promotion of social change" (Ehrenreich, 1985, 116). Thus the depression opened social work to the importance of the abstract knowledge of the social sciences in understanding and addressing complex and troubling social and economic conditions.

The depression also shook social work's claims to professional status. To dispense relief to the millions of applicants and to administer the rights-based programs of the New Deal, thousands of untrained personnel were drawn into the ranks of the social services. Despite the lack of formal training, such workers were nevertheless given the title of "social worker"; additionally, many sought to join the professional association. Others, notably those who joined the rank-and-file movement, decried the elitism of the professional association, championed social legislation and social reform, and declared casework to be largely irrelevant. Though the assault of the rank-and-filers on the existing professional model dissipated by the latter stages of the depression, it had nevertheless provided social work leaders with additional motivation to rethink their profession. Needing to rethink the basis of social work to incorporate thousands of would-be professionals into their ranks and to take into account new social, economic, and political realities, leading social work academics and practitioners were again faced with the questions: "What is relevant knowledge in social work education?" and "How can the abstract knowledge of the social sciences fit into social work helping process?"

Sullied by the events of the depression, casework nevertheless emerged from the 1930s as the dominant method in social work practice and education. The psychoanalytic model of the 1920s, however, fell out of favor as social workers sought new models that reintroduced the significance of social and economic conditions in understanding and working with clients. Despite the sometimes bitter disputes between advocates of the major competing schools of functional and diagnostic casework and the many differences in their approach to the helping process, both models incorporated a role for social science. Speaking for the functional school, Jessie Taft argued that "it is necessary to know and appreciate the economic, the cultural and immediate social setting of those who constitute our clientele, it is essential to understand and accept tolerantly, but without evasion, the human psychology that is common to worker and client in our culture." Nevertheless, she concluded that though the understanding of social workers must be based on knowledge drawn from the social sciences, social work could not be considered a "science," as it must always subordinate the development of abstract knowledge to the requirements of implementing the helping process (Ehrenreich, 1985, 128). Gordon Hamilton argued the diagnostic position "that the base of social work is potentially scientific; that the social sciences allied with the physical sciences must increasingly throw light on social needs and social improvement; that the organic and psychogenetic theory of personality is fundamental" (Ehrenreich, 1985, 131). Thus, according to both schools of thought, the social sciences offered important contributions to understanding the social conditions that confronted clients, though it remained less clear how they contributed to the solutions of problems.

During the 1940s, therefore, social workers became increasingly aware of the social sciences as possessing knowledge relevant to problems of interest to them. In addition, they began to develop increased competence in selected aspects of social science, in part as a consequence of altered master's curricula and increased availability of opportunities for advanced study. These changes contributed both to their capacity to borrow knowledge more judiciously from social science, as well as to engage in their own original research (Brown, 1942). By 1950, therefore, the stage was set for the appearance of a new and different relationship between social work and social science (Community Service Society of New York, 1949).

Integration and Development: The 1950s and Beyond

The intent of social work to re-embrace the social sciences was clear at the outset of the mid-century period. The January 1950 issue of *Social Work Journal* carried an advertisement announcing a competition for the best article on the contribution of the human sciences to social work practice. The human sciences were defined as including "anthropology, psychology, sociology, economics, and political science, with such other disciplines as legal science, education, human geography, demography, and public administration on the periphery." The purpose of the contest was "to focus attention on the need for a closer working relationship between the human sciences and social work practice." The winner of the contest was to receive a prize of seventy-five dollars, and the winning paper would be published in *Social Work Journal*.

There was a strong response to the announcement. Six months later, a paper by Henry Maas, entitled "Collaboration between Social Work and the Social Sciences," was announced as the winner. In his paper, Maas argued that if social work was to progress scientifically, both social science and social work needed to explore ways to facilitate the incorporation of social science theory and findings into social work practice. In addition, he chided the editors for framing the competition in a manner that minimized social work's contribution to the human sciences.[2] However, the most relevant point in many ways was the fact of the competition itself. In sponsoring this competition, the editors of the journal were signaling the emergence of a new phase in the historic relationship between social work and social science—one that has come to be characterized by strong advances in social science, with social work becoming increasingly interested in borrowing ideas and methods from social science while seeking to interest social scientists in focusing their attention on issues and problems relevant to social work and social welfare.

With such a positive view of the importance of the links between social work and social science, it was not long before the social work establishment sought to formalize and institutionalize the relationship. In 1956, the Russell Sage Foundation awarded funds to the social work schools at both Columbia University and the University of Michigan to strengthen social science training for social work doctoral students. In a summary of this development, Meyer, Litwak, Thomas, and Vinter stated:

With the additions of social scientists to their faculties and with fellowships made available to students, Columbia offered a special concentration in social science within its existing Doctor of Social Work program and Michigan established an interdepartmental Doctoral Program in Social Work and Social Science. The University of California at Berkeley soon thereafter embarked on an advanced program with similar emphasis (Meyer, Litwak, Thomas, and Vinter, 1967, 183).

A more comprehensive treatment of the significance of this action can be found in this book in the concluding chapter by Sarri and Vinter on the history of the interdisciplinary doctoral program at Michigan.

Committed to the integration of social work and social science, social workers became concerned with the problem of how to disseminate relevant social science knowledge in sufficient depth to enough scholars to ensure that there would be theoretical continuity in the lines of investigation underway in social work. An important event addressing this issue was an institute held in June 1959, sponsored by the research section of the National Association of Social Workers. Its purpose was to examine the relationship between social science theory and social work research, and many of the social scientists and social workers who were most concerned with the issues of research, knowledge development, and dissemination participated. Three bodies of social science theory were the focus of the discussions: role and reference group theory, organization theory, and small group theory. The papers and discussions of this institute were published the following year; it included social scientists such as Edgar Borgatta and Alvin Gouldner, who worked closely with social workers, and social workers such as Martin Loeb, Alfred J. Kahn, Herman Stein, Edwin Thomas, and Robert Vinter, who were sophisticated in the social sciences (Kogan, 1960).

In 1967, Meyer and his colleagues made another important contribution to the integration of social work and social science with their analysis of how social work utilized sociological theory. While sociology was the social science on which they focused, their concept of "levels" of social work practice and theory (interpersonal, agency, community, societal), of activities (obtaining information, processing information, evaluation), and their use of such concepts as "treatment organizations" established a structure on which many branches of social science could build.

Since these works of the 1950s and 1960s, social workers have drawn increasingly on many types of social science knowledge to advance their understanding of social problems and their solution. This book, in fact, presents a rich array of such contemporary efforts. There are numerous other examples, including Frank Turner's *Social Work Treatment: Interlocking Theoretical Perspectives* (Turner, 1986), which reports no fewer than twenty-two theoretical perspectives on clinical social work alone, with most of the identified perspectives coming directly from social science. Also, two edited volume's on state-of-the-art quantitative and qualitative research methodologies in social work (Gillespie & Glisson, 1992; Riessman, 1994) report a wide range of studies based mainly on advances initiated in the social sciences. By the same token, by the 1970s we also find the beginnings of a more contemporary change in the relationship between social work and social science. The unity-of-method hypothesis, dominant in social science since its earliest days, came under serious questioning by feminists and postmodernists, and the face of social science began to change in some quite remarkable ways. We turn now to a description of these changes and to a consideration of their implications for knowledge development processes in social work.

THE CHANGING FACE OF SOCIAL SCIENCE

The social sciences have been marked by significant social and intellectual changes over the past three decades. Interestingly, the most prominent changes seem contradictory, or at least conflictual, in nature, with indications of an increased heterogeneity of emphasis, as shown by increasing numbers of specializations and the emergence of new traditions of intellectual inquiry, occurring side by side with indications of an increased homogeneity of emphasis, as shown by the considerable growth in interdisciplinary forms of endeavor. At another level, however, these changes move in the same direction. While social science's conceptual map clearly has become more complex, it is also true that there is still something distinctive, both individually and collectively, about those activities designated "the social sciences." For example, sociology is still sufficiently bounded in its knowledge claims as not to be confused with economics, psychology, or political science; and we continue to give the terms "the humanities," "the social sciences," and "the natural sciences" unique meanings. Hence, although there have been important tensions and changes in the social sciences over the past few decades, there also has been stability.

No doubt one important reason for this stability is that, at its heart, social science continues to be heavily influenced by positivism, with individual disciplines having accumulated large enough bodies of knowledge within this research tradition to justify their continued separate existences. This is not to deny, however, that there has been a growing theoretical and methodological pluralism within social sciences' positivistic tradition, reflecting a deeper appreciation of the complexity of social life and human behavior as well as refinements in the interests and preoccupations of researchers, scholars, and practitioners. One visible consequence of this pluralism has already been mentioned, that is, the increased concern over the excessive compartmentalization of knowledge, resulting in the wide-scale promotion of interdisciplinary forms of study and action. A second, more subtle consequence has been a change in how the overall research process itself is viewed. Earlier conceptualizations viewed social research in unidimensional terms, rank-ordering the scientific merit of various methodological strategies in terms of how closely they approximated the experimental ideal. In contrast, the research process now is viewed as a series of interlocking choices about how to maximize the conflicting research desiderata of generalizabilty, precision in the control and measurement of variables, and realism of context. Because, in principle, there is no way to maximize all three research desiderata simultaneously, the process of devising and implementing research strategies is no longer regarded as involving a set of problems to be "solved." Instead, it is seen as a set of dilemmas to be endured because the choices made in devising a strategy inevitably sacrifice on some desiderata and maximize others.

Viewing knowledge development as founded not on conformity with a set of "objective" rules but on a complex, multilevel process of choice and dilemma has resulted in a more conscious, as well as a more public, awareness of the limits of social science. Though it is still possible to find arguments that the only "real" knowledge is that which results from the rigorous and repeated applications of traditional scientific methods, such "a confident and blinkered positivism" now carries less authority than it once did. In light of this, Collini's (Collini, 1993, xlvi) observation about the change in the natural sciences is equally applicable to the social sciences: "it has become more widely accepted that different forms of intellectual enquiry quite properly furnish us with a variety of kinds of knowledge and understanding, no one of which constitutes *the* model to which all the others should seek to conform."

In terms of impact on research and knowledge development in social science, feminism and postmoderism have probably been the most significant new forms of inquiry, creating not only new subjects of knowledge but also generating fundamental critiques of the practice of social science itself. Feminism refers to ideas produced mainly by women from the perspective of viewing women as a distinct social group. It interprets the evolution of women's roles in society as social and political in origin, based on the argument that relations between men and women in their various shared spheres such as work and family reflect socially imposed patterns of gender inequality. Although humans are born as male or female, gender differences between men and women are socially produced and have the strong effect of establishing and maintaining male dominance. That is to say, the gender order is a hierarchical one, with male spheres consistently having dominance. Moreover, like any privileged group with power, men work in various ways and use various strategies to maintain their position of dominance. To the extent that the substance and practice of science has been invoked in debates about "the proper role of women" in society, feminists have proposed the scientific ideals of control and impersonality as gender-specific and have argued that the conception of rationality dominant in science enshrines a strong "masculinist" bias. By asserting an ideology that separates knowledge from values, social science seeks to conceal its involvement with the politics of gender and its role in perpetuating oppressive cultural stereotypes of women (Rose, 1983).

Postmodernism is an enormously diverse and enigmatic topic, comprised more of a stream of loosely related ideas and critiques than of a readily recognizable system of inquiry built around commonly accepted methods and an integrated set of questions. While it does share certain features with other longer standing traditions of inquiry, such as the Marxist distrust of face-value presentations and its emphasis on the centrality of the role of power as well as the prominence afforded cultural beliefs and symbolic processes by the new institutionalists, its critique is much more challenging. Postmoderism rejects the assumption that there is an external social reality that exists independent of our minds, knowable by means of objective observation and measurement. Similarly, it denies the possibility of explaining this reality based on overarching theoretical laws formulated as a result of repeated empirical observations of regularized patterns of human activity. Instead, the postmodern conception views reality as both socially constructed and highly fragmented and as resulting from the operation of autonomous, highly interactive social processes, or discourses, accepted as normal in specific local contexts (Bauman, 1988; Rosenau, 1992; Parusnikova, 1992; Murphy, 1990). Because historical eras and local discourses differ from each other not only in terms of what people think, but also in terms of what is thinkable (Swindler & Arditi, 1994, 314), accounting for people's behavior requires understanding the meaning it had for them at the time they acted it out (Stauch, 1992; Agger, 1991). Seen from this perspective, knowledge about human behavior is neither unitary nor cumulative (Agger, 1991, 117); nor is it defined by rigid disciplinary boundaries between the various social sciences or between the social sciences and other fields of human endeavor (Rosenau, 1992, 6). Instead, there is a plurality of knowledges framed by the multiplicity of discourses and practices constituting peoples' experiences at a given historical time. Located in this plurality, social science cannot claim superior status over others in its capacity to reflect social reality faithfully (Lepenies, 1989, 65). It merely constitutes "one set of cultural activities among others, as much an expression of a society's orientation toward the world as its art or religion, and equally inseparable from fundamental issues of politics and morality" (Collini, 1993, xlix).

Although feminism and postmodernism currently are the most prominent new knowledge orientations in American social science, they are by no means the only additions (Seidman, 1994, ch. 7). Over the past decade and a half, Afrocentrism and gay and lesbian theory have emerged to offer related perspectives on the shortcomings of positivism, as well as new ways of theorizing and studying aspects of contemporary society. Afrocentrism argues that the scientific disciplines in American and European societies have imposed "Eurocentric" paradigms of knowledge development as universal, resulting in the exclusion of social perspectives that reflect African values and traditions or that value people's particular social experiences as a criterion for determining the nature and validity of knowledge claims. Gay and lesbian theory, like feminism and Afrocentrism, contests positivism's propensity to separate knowledge from values and politics. Its unique contribution lies in its analysis of how a normative heterosexuality affects the structuring of cultural order in society. Overall, the emergence of these new knowledge orientations, combined with changes emanating from a more diverse and less authoritative positivism, have helped produce an expanded, more complex, and more fluid social science than existed three decades ago. We now briefly consider the association of this "new social science" with the nature and structuring of knowledge processes in social work.

Plurality and Knowledge Development in Social Work

There is no shortage of reviews and assessments of the nature and state of knowledge development in social work (Tucker, 1996). Prior to the early 1980s, nearly all reflected an uncritical acceptance of the positivistic "unity-of-method" conception of knowledge development; that is, the quality of the knowledge produced by social work researchers was judged mainly by how rigorously it conformed to the canons of scientific inquiry imported from the natural sciences by way of the social sciences (Roth, 1987).[3] Beginning in the early 1980s, however, there was a sharp change, with most reviews and assessments being written by persons intending either to critique positivistic methods or to put their own special stamp on a contentious and polarized debate about the methodological propriety of alternative approaches to knowledge development in social work.[4]

We do not intend here to review the substance of this debate or to add our own particular viewpoints. For that, the interested reader is referred elsewhere. Rather, the relevant concern is to understand the origin of the change signified by the aforementioned debate; that is to say, what factor or factors account for social work's movement away from a taken-for-granted acceptance of the unity-of-method thesis, with its central positivist tenet that to be meaningful, statements about the world must be either logically true or empirically testable, to a clear acknowledgment of the principle that there are many possible ways of knowing the world and that use of sophisticated methods of empirical verification and analysis is just one particular way-of-knowing in this society?

In conformity with our earlier arguments about professions and disciplines as reputational organizations heavily influenced by their relations with their larger contexts, our working hypothesis is that the transition in social work to a broader acceptance of methodological pluralism has been strongly influenced by its embeddedness in a context in which social science is a dominant influence. The rationale comes from ideas in institutional theory that isomorphism with rationalized frameworks in the environment enhances the legitimacy of an organization. This enhanced legitimacy facilitates access to resources, thereby contributing to the organization's prospects for survival and growth (Meyer & Rowan, 1977; DiMaggio & Powell, 1983). Applied to the relationship between social work and social science, this argument implies that because of social work's strong dependence on social sciences for its formal knowledge and research methods, it will be constrained to resemble social science in the frameworks it applies to its own internal knowledge development activities. To do otherwise would be to entertain the prospect of decreased legitimacy with internal and external academic and research bodies whose decisions about resource allocations are influenced by social science norms regarding acceptable approaches to the development of knowledge. Hence, to the extent that methodological pluralism has found a place in social science (and the discussion in the preceding section suggests it has) it is plausible to expect that, in time, social work would undergo a parallel change.

Although it is not possible to inquire fully into the validity of this hypothesis in the space of this chapter, we believe that most observers would give it some modicum of credibility. Differences in interpretation, we suspect, would concern questions of causal direction, depth and pace of change, or comprehensiveness of explanation. On the basis of research findings showing the long-term presence of diverse approaches to knowledge development in social work literature (Fraser, Taylor, Jackson, and O'Jack, 1991) or philosophical arguments that differing cognitive interests by researchers and practitioners about practice lead to differences, but not inequalities, in knowledge claims (Kondrat, 1992), some might argue that social work's knowledge development processes have always been pluralistic. Hence, it is really a matter of social science starting to emulate social work as opposed to the reverse. We are not persuaded by this argument. Available studies of cross-citation patterns between social work and social science (Simpson, 1978; Cheung, 1990), as well as a close reading of the reference sections in social work literature on methodological pluralism, simply do not support a view of social science as tending to borrow knowledge on an a priori basis from social work; instead, the reverse pattern is clearly the dominant one at this point.

The second argument is that social work has not been much affected by the emergence of methodological pluarlism in social science. Scratching beneath the surface of "the many ways of knowing" rhetoric currently making the rounds results in a view of social work scholarship as still strongly dominated by the positivistic unity-of-method thesis (Riessman, 1994). Suggested reasons for this include the propensity to inertia characteristic of most forms of organization (Hannan & John Freeman, 1984; Hannan & Freeman, 1989), complicated in social work's case by its relatively insecure professional status, which constrains it to approach change even more cautiously than other more established disciplines and professions (Riessman, 1994, x). Here, we would remind the reader that inertia, or the propensity for organizations to resist change, is generally conceded to be a relative rather than an absolute condition of organizational life (Hannan & Freeman, 1989, 66). It is not that organizations do not change but that change, planned or otherwise, cannot be timed to coincide with the pace of change in the environment (Hannan & Freeman, 1989, 66). Hence, while we would accept as plausible the view that currently methodological pluralism has not penetrated social work to the same extent it has social science, we propose that it is entirely premature to conclude that matters will remain this way. Change is not a cross-sectional process but a longitudinal one. Gauging its nature and extent is one of those issues that requires the passage of a meaningful span of time. Viewed from this perspective, we believe that, at a minimum, most would agree that this argument does not invalidate our hypothesis. Instead, it simply affirms that in the case of social work and methodological pluralism, the jury is still out.

A third argument that might be made raised regarding the validity of our view of methodological pluralism emerging in social work as a function of its earlier emergence in social science is that as an explanation it is underspecified, particularly in its exclusion of the effects of factors internal to social work. For example, it might be argued that social work has experienced tremendous growth over the past three decades. Because the norm of originality dominates in knowledge-development work, this growth is likely to have pressured scholars and researchers to show increased differentiation of approaches and tasks in order to demonstrate the uniqueness of their contributions so as to obtain resources and recognition (Whitley, 1982, 330). Thus, if social work is indeed becoming more methodologically diverse, it could be due to the effects of change in its institutional context as well as to the effects of increasing size mediated by internal structural change. In our view, this hypothesis does not undermine our main argument but instead enriches it. Indeed, it highlights the importance of developing a more complete theory of knowledge for social work.

THINKING ABOUT GLOBALIZATION

As we move to the close of the twentieth century, the world faces major challenges. Global influences in the economy, polity, environment, as well as in the social sphere are now at unprecedented levels. Rapid developments in technology, communications, and transportation, combined with the development of new economic power blocks, the emergence of newly industrialized countries, and pervasive shifts toward market economics have recast the world as a true global village. At the same time that we are witnessing these astonishing changes, however, we are also witnessing the emergence of major social problems—rapid population growth, particularly in impoverished developing countries in the southern hemisphere, growing resource inequality between the developed and developing nations, the internationalization of refugee problems, drugs, racism, sexism, violence and terrorism, and increasing conflict and instability associated with the breakup of the former Soviet Union and its allies (Brecher and Costello, 1994; Dasgupta, 1993). Ironically, just when social benefits are increasingly important for the health, education, and general well-being of peoples, we see a decline in the influence of the nation state, which has been the primary guarantor of such benefits. The growth of international capitalism and trade has not produced corresponding improvements in the well-being of people, as the 1995 United Nations Human Development Report documents (Corcoran, 1995). Welfare statism was a major outgrowth of the nation state's development, although its development varied widely among nations. Currently, there is no substitute for the nation state as a mechanism of social benefit development and distribution, and the United Nations has been greatly weakened in recent years with respect to its role in social development. The decline in the influence of the nation state, combined with the lack of international mechanisms of social development, may be an important factor exacerbating the growing inequality between developed and developing countries and between the northern and southern hemispheres.[5]

The rapidity and extent of global social change will no doubt have important consequences for the interactions between social work and social science. One possible effect is that this change may draw social science and social work further apart, recreating the more differentiated pattern of interaction we identified earlier as extant in the first half of the century. Because of its applied nature and historic involvement with disadvantaged groups, social work may be called on to assist in the development or restructuring of social welfare systems in various areas of the world. Indeed, it may be that it is only by undertaking such activity that social work will be able to retain its status as a relevant helping profession in the world of the twenty-first century (Specht & Courtney, 1994). Social science, on the other hand, may become more isolated from the impact of these changes, at least in the short run, because its emphasis is more clearly on the pursuit of knowledge for its own sake than on the development and implementation of intervention and control strategies. Accepting these arguments, the implication is that the utility of social science knowledge to social work could fall as a result of the transformations associated with globalization, leading to a more distant relationship between the two spheres than has been the case for the past few decades.

In 1987, Russell Jacoby indicted social scientists and other academics on the grounds that much of their research is irrelevant to the needs and problems of contemporary society. His criticism is not an isolated one but part of a growing critique of the relevance of the academy and its scientists at a time when global social problems and change demand careful analysis of alternatives and new strategies for resolving global problems. In the past, the academy has been looked to by many for ways of thinking about and addressing social problems. Currently its assistance appears more needed than ever. Unfortunately, the response has been minimal with respect to critical analysis of alternatives to the assumptions of capitalist society. Too often it appears that academics assess the contribution of their research and knowledge development mainly in terms of peer reviews by discipline-specific colleagues rather than seeking out external evaluation that might present other views. For example, research on social problems in natural settings usually does not permit the types of research design and controls that are necessary if one utilizes traditional experimental design. Thus, such research may not be undertaken for fear of unfavorable assessment by discipline colleagues rather than the value of or need for the research (Kilty & Meenaghan, 1995).

A the same time, however, the presence of countervailing forces should not be ignored. Because the federal government funds a great deal of social science research, it could demand that funded social research be conducted on specified problems in ways that directly consider implications for change and action. Some of the discussions about National Science Foundation funding by the U.S. House of Representatives suggest that they wish to have a more active role in establishing priorities for research (Congressional Quarterly, March 1995). By the same token, it is important to be aware of how calls for a more applied social science are framed. Contemporary policy makers may have a greater willingness to fund research that emphasizes individual responsibility than research that examines social structural factors as predictors of behavior. Analyses of federal funding priorities in the 1970s and 1980s provides some support for this interpretation (Specht & Courtney, 1994). The implication of this is well known but still worth repeating: the relationship between knowledge and action is not ideological neutral. Hence, and as feminists, postmodernists, and others have argued, care must be taken in differentiating between research that works to maintain the status quo and research that works to change it.

Changes are also occuring in various locations and under various auspices that have implications for the future relationship between social work and social science. There is growing interest and activity in the development of new approaches to social welfare and social work in the nations of the former Soviet Union, in East and South Asia, and in some countries in southern Africa. The collaborative work of the National Association of Social Workers with the Association of Social Pedagogues and Social Workers in Russia illustrates what is being accomplished at local community levels in several countries. Several community projects have been established that have trained staff in the development and delivery of social services.

Another positive sign of the development of mechanisms to aid the collaboration of human service professionals and scientists can be found in United Nations International Conferences, such as the one in Cairo in 1994 on Population Growth and the one in Copenhagen in 1995 on Social Development. Equally important developments resulted from the fourth International Conference on Women held in Beijing in 1995. The International Social Development Conference in particular illustrates the opportunities for policy makers to work with social and natural scientists as well as with human service and environmental professionals toward enhanced global social development. This summit conference brought together one hundred and eighteen heads of state and representatives of 2,400 different organizations representing civil society worldwide. The Conference Declaration and Program of Action offers benchmarks for measuring progress at the local, regional, and international levels. By proposing a plan of action with provisions dealing with such issues as the eradication of poverty, full employment, equality and equity between the sexes, and universal access to education and health care services, it offers both a framework and a challenge to social workers and social scientists to be actively and collaboratively involved in the perpetration and evaluation of social and economic progress, not merely to be observers or naysayers.

CONCLUSION

In suggesting that social work and social science can be treated as reputational organizations, we have tried to show how similarities, changes, and differences in the interactions between them can be understood in terms of variation in the nature of the context in which they were embedded. The initial undifferentiated nature of the relations between social work and social science in the ninetheeth century meant that, because they were so entwined, it was inevitable that change in one would cause change in the other. Subsequent developments in the professionalization of social science that linked jobs and status more to intellectual than to activist reputations helped produce the differentiated pattern of interaction found in the first half of this century. As social work diversified into a wider variety of organizational and institutional settings, including universities, there was increased emphasis on the importance of using abstract knowledge to help solve problems, as well on producing knowledge that was specific to the realization of social work's purposes. With the concomitant ascendancy of the "scientific method" as the essential means of producing social knowledge, it was inevitable that the relationship between social work and social science would again become close. However, the dynamic of that relationship was unlike that associated with earlier forms of interaction because of, among other things, the more dominant position of social science in the overall system of professions and disciplines. Knowledge developmental processes in social work were now more directly determined by social science norms and actions, and the relationship became a more dependent one. At the same time, mutually determined problems persisted as evidenced, for example, by increased tension in both social work and social science about whether status and rewards should be allocated mainly on the basis of intellectual or activist reputation. It is unclear whether current patterns of interaction between social work and social science will persist into the future, given the emergence of the turbulence and uncertainty of globalization. Regardless, viewing them as reputational organizations that vary in their structures, emphases, and relations based on changes in their environments seems a more useful approach than treating them as autonomous, self-governing groups whose futures are primarily determined internally.

All of the contributions to this volume deal with the relationship between social work and social science, providing a more detailed sense of where it came from, where it stands now, how it works, what problems it is experiencing, and how it is likely to look in the future. Part I contains chapters by Gambrill, Price, Rein and Laws, Boettcher, and Jamrozik, each dealing critically with questions about factors that affect the viability of maintaining working connections between social work and social science, as well as with questions about the nature and effects of such connections. Overall, these chapters remind us that the relationship between social work and social science can take unexpected forms and have unexpected effects. They also make clear that we should not take our understanding of the dynamics of the relationship for granted. Part II has a more instrumental orientation, with chapters by Brower and Nurius, Gorin, Viswanathan, and Arje, Lambert, Berstein, Goodman, and Epstein, and Mace illustrating how theory and methods from social science can be used to advance understanding and to suggest actions across a number of topic areas relevant to social work. Although Part III also has an instrumental orientation, it has an opposing emphasis, with chapters by Ramon, Abramovitz, Longres, Lauffer, Jamrozik, Kaplan-Vinokur, and Gutierrez producing findings and insights relevant to social science through the examination of issues and problems central to social work practice. The general significance of the chapters in Parts II and III is that they show how knowledge-development tasks can be coordinated between social work and social science in a manner that is relevant to the goals of both communities. Part IV contains a single chapter by Edwin Thomas. It provides an analytic overview not only of all preceding papers in this volume but also of all the papers presented at the conference from which this volume is derived. In addition, it provides ideas for the development of a newer more comprehensive model of integration between social work and social science. Finally, Part V comprises a single chapter by Rosemary Sarri and Robert. It reports a history of the joint doctoral program in social work and social science at the University of Michigan. Among other things, Sarri and Vinter show that Michigan faculty and graduates have made impressive contributions to both social science and social work, thereby providing strong evidence of the fruitfulness and viability of interdisciplinary, or cross-reputational, study and research.

NOTES

1. Frank Bruno (1957) calls this period of the interrelatedness between theory and practice the "honeymoon period."

2. The editor responded by announcing a competition for papers dealing with the contribution of social work to the human sciences. However, there was no cash prize for this competition. In addition, examination of subsequent issues of Social Work Journal did not uncover an announcement that a winner of this competition had been chosen and a paper would be published.

3. Fischer presents a clear example of "unity-of-method" thinking in his well-known 1981 article on the emergence of empirically based practice in social work. Following a description of how empirical methods are being applied in social work, he notes, "This specificity in spelling out these methods of knowledge development has major implications for social work. It means that social workers can begin to harness the technologies of the social and physical sciences to build a greater degree of systematization, objectification, and precision into their selection of knowledge for practice." See Fischer, Joel. 1981. "The Social Work Revolution" *Social Work* 26: 199–207. For additional discussion of this same point, see Weick, Ann. 1987. "Reconceptualizing the Philosophical Perspective of Social Work." *Social Service Review* 61: 218–230.

4. It is interesting that there appears to be a fair time lag between change in the nature of knowledge development activity in social science and the take-up of the change in social work literature. Others also have noted this lag (e.g., Reitmeier, 1989). How to account for this apparently slow rate of diffusion is a topic worth addressing in its own right.

5. There are other arguments concerning how globalization has affected people's well-being. For example, Mohan (1995) argues that the end of the Cold War resulted in developments in free market economics that have contributed to a "corporate" rather than a "global" perspective on welfare, resulting in further deterioration of people's well-being.

Part I

PROMISES AND PROBLEMS

Introduction: Progress and Problems in the Integration of Knowledge and Practice

David J. Tucker

Louis Pasteur observed over a century ago that "There are not two sciences. There is only one science and its application, and these two activities are linked as the fruit is to the tree." This integrative view of the relationship between the development of scientific knowledge and its application has made such good sense that it has achieved an almost taken-for-granted status. We have become accustomed to viewing most forms of scientific investigation as justified not only as ends in themselves but also because of the practical benefits they convey. This faith, shared by the public and the scientific community alike, is an optimistic faith and persists even when the scientific study of a problem does not produce the desired improvements. Failure is usually explained in terms of the need to refine research methods or by resource inadequacies. We are much less likely to explain failure by questioning the validity of the underlying premise of the sciences' inherent potential to contribute to social and material progress.

While social science has come to share natural science's aura of being a force for social and material progress, it has not been as free from criticism of its fundamental underlying premises. As various scholars have pointed out, there are good reasons for questioning whether the better understanding of social conditions promised by social science has contributed to their improvement. These reasons span a broad spectrum, ranging from populist, anti-intellectual arguments made on the basis of illustrative cases where reliance on social science knowledge seems not to have contributed to the resolution of social problems to broad philosophical treatises questioning the validity of presuming the possibility of a science of human behavior, particularly when that science is built upon the tenets of logical positivist empiricism.

In Part I, we explore some of the issues that arise when efforts are made to forge links between social science and social action. Our purpose is not to condemn the application of social science knowledge and expertise to social problems as *ipso facto* inconsequential or misleading. By the same token, neither do we argue that adopting an integrative view of social science and social action is inherently positive. Instead, we seek to clarify that arguing either the usefulness or the uselessness of associating social science and social action involves confronting certain "awkward realizations" about the basis and consequences of such arguments (Rule, 1978). Most critics would not claim that associating social science and social action has done more harm than good. Neither would they be likely to endorse actions that would reduce the amount of resources directed at such endeavors. Similarly, advocates would probably acknowledge that their rationales for an integrative view of social science and social action invoke assumptions about a variety of phenomena, such as the nature of the processes underlying the diffusion of ideas or the relationship among values, knowledge, and action, that require serious analysis in their own right. Finally, both critics and advocates are likely to be disquieted by the implication that a clear conclusion cannot be drawn about the overall usefulness to society of associating social science and social action.

The chapters in Part I address some of the "awkward realizations" that surface when purposeful attempts are made to apply an integrative view of the relationship between social knowledge and social action. The focus is mainly on social work and social science because ambitious efforts have been made over the past number of years to create and maintain a working relationship between the development of knowledge, as envisaged by social science, and the requirements of action, as envisaged by social work. Eileen Gambrill opens the discussion, arguing that the infusion of the everyday practice of social work with valid knowledge from the social sciences is fundamental to the successful realization of social work's purpose of helping clients attain outcomes they value. Achieving such diffusion, however, is a daunting task, requiring, among other things, an appreciation of the complexity of the decision processes underlying the development and use of scientific knowledge, as well as concerted efforts by both academics and practitioners to consider critically and subsequently to overcome barriers to diffusion posed by current practices and misunderstandings. Overall, Gambrill is strongly supportive of increased integration of social work and social science, providing such integration is built on knowledge about facts and not on conjecture or uncritically held beliefs.

The next two chapters take a different analytic tack, raising questions about assumptions and presumptions that underlie how we usually think about the relationship between knowledge and action. Richard Price points out that it should not be assumed that a better understanding of social and community life is automatically or necessarily linked to improved social conditions. Instead, that link is a proposition that merits critical analysis in its own right. He subsequently examines how alternative models of the way society works give rise to conflicting interpretations of the connection between knowledge and action because of differing assumptions and ideas about the origin and use of knowledge, as well as about who the beneficiaries of change should be. An important implication of Price's chapter is that it reminds us that most often social knowledge is uncertain knowledge, and that includes our understanding of the relationship between thought and action.

David Laws and Martin Rein also begin by questioning the validity of the dominant view that disciplinary theory and research provide insights that have direct applicability to social problems, leading to social improvements. Indeed, their review of the literature, combined with analysis of specific cases, leads them to conclude that the relationship is highly problematic for all parties. Processes contributing to this problem include *neglect*, resulting from the dominance of research concerns over practice concerns, *crowding out*, resulting from the inability to reconcile research concerns with those of practice, and *capture*, resulting from the dominance of the practice orientation over weak research standards. The authors move on to illustrate a triadic model of the relationship between knowledge and action that potentially provides a framework for useful collaboration between scholars and practitioners because it helps to expose, and to hold up for analysis and consideration, the issues and tensions inherent in such efforts.

In his chapter, Richard Boettcher addresses a long-standing concern for social work, namely, its capacity to use theory and methods from social science to build its own unique knowledge base. To this end, he undertakes a longitudinal analysis of a selected number of completed doctoral dissertations, examining such key considerations as their use of theory, the rigorousness of their research designs, and their contribution to a cumulative knowledge development process. Overall, he concludes, the findings are disappointing, with dissertations tending to be atheoretical with weak logical designs. Equally disappointing is the fact that these findings replicate those of other earlier studies. One question raised by these findings might be how to account for this apparent lack of change. Future researchers may find it fruitful to explore whether it reflects the effects of Laws and Rein's capture or neglect processes as described in their chapter.

The final chapter in Part I is by Adam Jamrozik, a social policy scholar from Australia. He analyzes the effects on the knowledge-action link of two recent trends in most western societies—the emergence of governments as dominant institutional supporters and consumers of research and the increasingly hegemonic position of economic thought in framing and analyzing social problems. By changing who is in control of asking questions about social circumstances and conditions, these trends have helped produced, among other things, a *retreat from social explanation*, or a tendency of scholars and practitioners alike to describe problems rather than to explain their origins and to avoid critical analyses of the relationship between the social organization of a society and its social problems. An important implication of this change is that social research has overtly become less a vehicle for informing social action than an after-the-fact means of justifying it. Similar, then, to other chapters in Part I, Jamrozik's chapter reminds us that the connection between knowledge and action—or, more specifically, between the scholar and the practitioner—is strongly influenced by the material and ideational context in which it is embedded.

2

Making Decisions about Integration

Eileen Gambrill

An emphasis on the integration of social work and social science is a hallmark of the doctoral program in social work at the University of Michigan. By integration I mean the infusion of knowledge from related disciplines and professions into the everyday practice of social work and the construction of social welfare policies and institutions. By knowledge I mean information that reduces uncertainty about how to attain a given outcome (Nickerson, 1986). I assume that the purpose of integration in the professions is to help clients attain outcomes they value and to help society prevent and mitigate social problems. In a nutshell my argument is as follows: clients have real-life problems; professionals are mandated by society to help clients; integration of knowledge from different sources is valuable in attaining outcomes clients value; and science provides methods of unique value to test knowledge claims critically.

KINDS OF DECISIONS INVOLVED

Decisions about what to include and how to include it are basic to integration. Questions include: Which theories should be considered? What research should be considered? Which disciplines and fields should be reviewed in relation to the preceding concerns? Which criteria should be used to make such decisions? What can be done to encourage integration of helpful attitudes, values, knowledge, and skills into everyday practice? Integration involves deciding what to read, to whom to speak, which environments to observe, what material to enter into a computer, and which references to note. Decisions about integration are made at many different levels. The decision makers include line staff, who make decisions about which assessment, intervention, and evaluation methods to use with clients in their day-to-day work; supervisors, who offer advice to staff and select criteria with which to evaluate staff; administrators, who make decisions about which programs to implement; and planners and policy analysts, who make decisions about programs and policies. Decisions are made about what knowledge to consider in planning a program, which criteria to use to select knowledge, and which criteria to use to determine if a method or policy has been successful. Scholars and researchers make decisions about integration as they go about their daily work (e.g., which theories to draw on; when to stop looking). Social work educators make decisions about what content to include and what teaching methods to rely on. Decisions are influenced by ease of access to relevant material, professional and organizational norms and values, time constraints, educational background, preferred practice theories, and personal beliefs about knowledge (what it is and how it can be gained).

THE CHALLENGES OF INTEGRATION

Integration requires knowledge of diverse frameworks and levels of analysis, as well as translation skills for understanding the logic of different perspectives. Gerald Patterson's research is a model of such analysis (Patterson, Reid, and Dishion, 1992). He and his colleagues have explored interaction patterns among family members as well as environmental factors that influence them, such as poverty (Patterson, Reid, and Dishion, 1992). Another example of a scholarly contribution reflecting integration is *The Social Causes of Psychological Distress* (Mirowsky & Ross, 1989), which integrates information from the fields of psychology and sociology as applied to psychological distress. Developmental models include integration of knowledge from a variety of sources as a key component of their practice (Rothman & Thomas, 1994). The greater the need for integrating diverse perspectives and databases, the more challenging the task. The range of disciplines and professions related to social work is large, and the range of problems of concern is broad. Integration requires sharing credit with others. It requires effort and time. It requires virtues related to critical thinking such as intellectual empathy (accurate understanding of other perspectives) and intellectual humility (recognition of the limits of one's own knowledge) (Paul, 1993). Integration requires an understanding of how different disciplines approach a problem. Questions asked include: What is unique about how a sociologist or an anthropologist approaches a problem? What kinds of questions does each discipline ask, and why does it ask them? What kind of data does it collect? Different disciplines and professions have different content as well as different ways of approaching topics of concern. They have different languages. These differences may seem foreign, even jarring, to those in other disciplines or professions, and they may encourage misunderstandings that get in the way of exploring possible contributions. Valuable content may be rejected because of misunderstandings based on superficial knowledge. Consider, for example, the many misunderstandings of radical behaviorism.

Integration requires a willingness to look beyond favored theories, methods, and levels of analysis, as well as an appreciation for what both qualitative and quantitative methods have to offer (Phillips, 1990a). Linkages between different views must be explored, and decisions about how to integrate different kinds of data must be made. Not only must successful integrationists understand different views and accurately weigh the current evidentiary base for each within a discipline, but they must do this across disciplines and related professions as well.

ASSESSING INTEGRATION

We could design an integration index reflecting the percentage of knowledge related to a topic that is drawn from other sources. Components of such an index might include knowledge, untested speculations, irrelevant content, or content that contradicts well-established knowledge. Working within this framework, we might ask, "What percentage of knowledge is brought to bear on a question with what effect?" For example, research may show that certain assessment methods are more likely than others to help social workers and clients select effective intervention methods. If an author claims to offer a systematic decision-making guide to case planning for children based on relevant theory and research, we can examine what is offered to determine the proportion of tested theory and related integrated research compared to the proportion of untested speculations and misleading or irrelevant data. We can see if favored points of view are compatible with what is known about behavior.

IS LACK OF INTEGRATION A PROBLEM?

The consequences of a lack of integration can be judged only in relation to the goals and potential of integration. Only if integration enhances the likelihood that clients attain outcomes they value is lack of integration of concern. If the goal is to increase the likelihood that people attain outcomes they value, criteria to evaluate success are readily at hand. Do clients attain needed housing, locate day care for elderly relatives, or communicate more effectively with family members? Do staff in residential settings rely on positive rather than punitive methods? Are social work students more successful in helping clients attain valued goals if certain educational formats are used and content covered?

Integration can go wrong by omitting helpful perspectives and data as well as by including misleading material. Irrelevant material may be focused on. We can view knowledge related to a topic as a store. Not only may individual items in given sections of the store be ignored, but entire departments may be overlooked. Consider one of my students, who was using play therapy with a six-year-old child referred for misbehavior at home and at school. This child came to the attention of the agency because the boy's father was concerned about complaints on the part of his son's teacher that the child would not follow instructions. Moreover, the child was not following instructions from the father's live-in partner. This family had immigrated from Hong Kong a year before. The boy's biological mother had died two years earlier. Assessment revealed that this father and his live-in partner were eager to participate in any way they could. No other problems seemed to be present. When asked why she had decided to use play therapy, the student said, "That's what my agency offers." In this example, we see that practice-related knowledge was ignored. There is extensive literature available on helping teachers and parents to alter the behavior of children (Dangel & Polster, 1984; Gardner et al., 1994; Patterson, Reid, and Dishion, 1992; Wierson & Forehand, 1994). By ignoring this literature, my student deprived this family of a choice of methods that maximized opportunities to remove complaints. In this example, lack of integration involved ignoring relevant material.

Psychologists as well as social workers have been faulted for not keeping up with practice-related research (Cohen, Sargent, and Sechrest, 1986; Kirk, 1979; DeMartini & Whitbeck, 1987; Morrow-Bradley & Elliot, 1986; O'Donohue, Fisher, Plaud, and Curtis, 1990). Studies in the field of medicine suggest that the published literature may have little influence on medical practice. Methods that have survived critical tests are often ingnored in favor of methods that are based on a client's testimonial or on a colleague's description of a single case (Banta, 1984). Methods that have been found to be useless or inferior to others may be recommended (Gabbay, 1982). In social work, you might pick up a textbook on a problem solving approach to social work practice and find no references to the extensive research on problem solving. You can pick up a book on case planning for children in foster care and find no mention of current research describing interaction patterns in families in which maltreatment is a concern. You can pick up articles, chapters, and books that discuss behavior with no mention of basic behavioral principles. In a recent book on integration in psychotherapy, there is no mention of research and theory in the experimental analysis of behavior and applied behavior analysis (Goldfried, Castonguay, and Safran, 1992). This omission highlights lack of integration on the part of members of a society devoted to integration.

Lack of integration in social work education can be seen in the content included and omitted, in the instructional formats used and ignored, and in the fragmentation of the curriculum. Students may be offered practice guidelines based on unsupported personal opinions rather than on the results of research that critically tests claims of effectiveness. Teachers may focus on reviewing a variety of untested theories rather than focusing on tested theories—those that have been found to help clients attain outcomes they value. Students often confront a fragmented curriculum and a smorgasbord of theories, and they may be encouraged to embrace a relativistic view of knowledge in which all beliefs are viewed as equally sound. Students may receive conflicting theories and data in different courses—or even in the same course—with no instruction about how to review the content critically, to integrate the material, or to acquire needed translation skills. Material taught in human development courses may not be integrated with content in practice courses. Research courses are given separately from practice courses.

Educational practices in social work are usually not based on research findings about the conditions of learning (Gagne, 1985; Gagne, 1987). Some claim that student values, knowledge, and skills are cultivated and evaluated in the field. Are they? Field instructors often rely on indirect methods to evaluate the quality of a student's work, such as reports in case conferences and supervisory sessions. Such methods may not reflect knowledge, skills, or outcomes attained with clients. Feedback is frequently untimely and unsystematic. Doctoral students are often not required to learn about the conditions of learning even when they fully expect to become educators. There may be an "anything goes" attitude as long as the politically correct words are used (e.g., empowerment, diversity). Students may not learn to look beyond politically correct words such as "empowerment" to see if valued real-life changes occur.

Research is needed to determine whether integration is useful in helping clients and in preventing harm in the process; if so, what kind, and under what circumstances? For example, we can ask: Are administrators who use content knowledge and performance skills related to contingency analysis more effective in encouraging staff to use methods found to be effective compared to those who do not (controlling for factors such as client population and quality of interpersonal skills) (Malott, Whaley, and Malott, 1993)? Does integration influence the success of programs and policies designed by policy planners and analysts? Is learning enhanced as educational programs are integrated with data concerning how we learn? Do those who search for and acquire an accurate understanding of different views related to a question develop frameworks that yield more successful intervention research than those who do not? Are social workers who have a working knowledge of basic behavioral principles more or less effective in helping clients achieve valued outcomes than those who do not? Do clients receive real-life benefits?

SCIENCE AS A GUIDE

The very concept of integration highlights the need to identify criteria for evaluating knowledge claims. Social work is known for valuing many ways of knowing. I suggest that science—defined broadly as critical testing of claims—provides methods of unique value for evaluating knowledge claims—including the belief that integration of social science knowledge into professions is valuable. Science is a way of thinking and a way of investigating the accuracy of beliefs. It encourages us to guess and test rather than to guess and guess again. Science encourages us to make rigorous attempts to falsify even our cherished beliefs. In no other enterprise is objectivity so questioned. Observation is assumed to be theory laden. Questions asked include, Has this claim been critically tested? How critically? What tests were used? What were the results? Far from reinforcing myths about reality, science is likely to do the opposite: to question them. Critical thinking and scientific thinking share many similarities, such as an openness to new ideas and "the most skeptical scrutiny of all hypotheses" (Sagan, 1987, 47). Discarding critical tests as a guide to evaluating the accuracy of claims suggests that there is a better alternative (O'Donohue, Fisher, Plaud, and Curtis, 1990; O'Donohue & Szymanski, 1994). What is this better alternative? Research shows that intuition does not stand up well compared to actuarial methods (Dawes, 1994; Dawes, Faust, and Meehl, 1989). If we do not depend on scientific methods to provide knowledge (i.e., rigorous testing of claims), on what will we rely?

James Rule (Rule, 1978) argues that social problems really reflect political conflicts in which vested interests are primary. "Social science can narrow the range of positions which seem reasonable, and no doubt increase the quality of debate over such positions. But ultimatley choice among such positions—with all the sweeping effects that this implies [not necessarily true]—must turn on at least some assumptions which are empirical in principle, but which remain highly resistant to resolution through debate on 'the facts'" (p. 171). He argues that there is no way to gain universal agreement on what a social problem is. Isn't insistence on agreement among everyone a strawman argument? What about faith? James Rule argues that "What matters most when one is making decisions about solutions to social and political controversies is one's 'non-rational' faith or beliefs" (p. 169). Is this a sound alternative?

Even writers who emphasize the politics of problem definition such as James Rule note the value of science. In *Insight and Social Betterment* he writes, "Only empirical inquiry and reasoned debate can promise to yield any conclusions about them" [the nature of forces that shape human welfare] (p. 98); "But our discussions of politics and society do embody assertions and assumptions about matters of fact, and about cause-effect relations, which are in principle empirically verifiable" (p. 81). Integration of knowledge from different sources can help us to define and describe problems. Consider poverty. We can draw on related knowledge from the social sciences to describe the kinds and extent of poverty as well as the misery it may create. Popper (1961) believes that problems that need resolution are clear (e.g., some people live in poverty) and that science provides a method to evaluate which programs (and related beliefs about causes) may be valuable in preventing and decreasing them. In a critique of *Insight and Social Betterment*, Gomory (Gomory, 1994) notes that the definition of poverty as having an income that falls below a certain level is agreed to by all regardless of political and ideological beliefs. Gomory (1994) argues that Rule seems to confuse the existence of problems with the variety of solutions that might be offered to resolve them. Consider also drug abuse and crime. Data from the social sciences can help us to define the extent of the problem and to sift out sense and nonsense (Walker, 1994). Karl Popper argues that it is clear that there is misery in the world and that we should conduct small-scale tests to decrease this. Rule (Rule, 1978) agrees that "The preservation of life and the alleviation of suffering represent relatively easy values to agree upon. Serious disputes there may be over the value of this or that form of treatment, but these are debates over technique, over the most efficacious means to agreed-upon ends" (p. 17). James Rule (1978) suggests bold experiments of a wide-ranging nature to search for "social betterment" on the grounds that an incremental approach overlooks interrelated structural factors related to problems. Rule severely criticizes Popper (Popper, 1961) for preferring an incremental approach to testing of guesses. He assumes that small-scale changes cannot be effective in removing human misery. These beliefs require testing. The collapse of communism in the former USSR is one strike against large-scale change. Popper argues that the danger with bold experiments is that wide ranging changes will require imposing unwanted changes on many citizens and may have serious unanticipated negative consequences. The claim by Rule (1978) that Popper "does not have much to say explicitly about the role of social scientists" (p. 88) is false, as can be seen by a review of his many writings on social science (e.g., Popper, 1961, p. 1).

OBSTACLES

If the degree of integration is not what we would like, we must ask why. Discovering obstacles will require digging beneath the surface of everyday activities. Background values may be especially hard to identify because they are part and parcel of the society in which we live, or the profession of which we are a part, and therefore may not be questioned or even recognized. They are part of what Ellul (Ellul, 1965) refers to as sociological propaganda. Competing political and economic interests may limit agreement on the steps that should be taken (Rule, 1978). Obscure rather than clear writing as well as fragmented accounts of problems in which facts are presented out of context can mystify problems. Burnham (Burnham, 1987) argues that journalists and educators encourage superstition by presenting fragmented bits and pieces unrelated to the "big picture." Twelve interrelated obstacles are suggested in the next section.

Different Views about What Knowledge Is and How to Get It

People use different criteria to review the accuracy of claims and the wisdom of actions. A definition of knowledge as information that decreases uncertainty about how to attain a given outcome seems uniquely well-suited for professions such as social work. However, this criterion may be discarded in favor of questionable criteria such as popularity, tradition, authority, and testimonials. Milton Rothman (Rothman, 1989, 26) argues "that much of what passes for logical argumentation consists of the repetition of certain clichés that are believed to be true by large numbers of people." Some argue that basing practice decisions on related research cannot be done because there are so many conflicting findings.[1] Only when specific goals are considered can we assess the fruitfulness of different ways of knowing in yielding information that decreases uncertainty about how to attain a certain outcome. Asking "Is social work helpful?" is not a useful question. This is like asking "Is medicine effective?" Only when specific outcomes are considered can the success of different approaches be reviewed. Nongoal-centered debates distract from critically testing specific claims about what is helpful.

Lack of Understanding of and Misrepresentation of Science

Lack of understanding of and misrepresentation of science is a key obstacle to integration. Surveys show that most people do not understand the basic characteristics of science (Miller, 1987). It has become increasingly fashionable to attack science as antifeminist, patriarchal, and culture-based (Gross & Levitt, 1994). Many of these attacks confuse logical positivism and current-day science. Phillips (Phillips, 1992) describes fabled threats to and defenses of naturalistic social inquiry in his recent book, *A Social Scientist's Bestiary*. Many writers confuse values internal to science (e.g., rigorous testing) with values external to science (how findings should be used) (Phillips, 1992). Discussions of "different ways of knowing in the social work literature often misrepresent science" (Gambrill, 1994). Science bashing, or presenting an incorrect view of science and then attacking it, as well as scientism, or glorifying what science can offer, can make it difficult for the average person to understand the value of science. It is true that some professional literature gives the illusion of a base in scientific thinking through its inclusion of the "trappings" of science. It is true that the number of quantitative research reports has increased in social work journals. However, quantitative research is not synonymous with scientific reasoning.

Incorrect descriptions of science deprive clients of the products of careful investigation. Such descriptions increase the likelihood that researchers will pursue unpromising paths to answering questions and that educational programs will misinform rather than inform students. Because of misunderstanding, methods uniquely designed to test claims rigorously may be discarded in favor of questionable criteria (e.g., "what sounds right," or newness). Misrepresentations of scientific thinking perpetuate dysfunctional arguments about the value of practice wisdom and empirical investigation. These two should go hand in hand. Conjectures based on experience can be "put to the test" in systematic investigations (Popper, 1963).

How We Search For and Process Information

We tend to think within points of view rather than about them (Popper, 1992). The influence of preconceptions on our behavior is one of the more rigorous findings over the past forty years of research in psychology (Nisbett & Ross, 1980). We seek data consistent with our preferred theories and preconceptions and tend to disregard contradictory data (Snyder & Thompson, 1988). We tend to search for data that justify our claims rather than search for ways to falsify them. The problems with a justification approach to knowledge development have been well described by Karl Popper as well as others (Bartley, 1990). We are also influenced by representativeness, or how closely an event or concept resembles something that we have experienced in the past. This similarity may be misleading rather than informative. Generalization of critical thinking skills is a major problem. For example, we rely on different criteria when making decisions about clients than when making personal decisions. Biases influence acceptance of manuscripts in the professional literature (Bornstein, 1990; Mahoney, 1977). A number of books are available to help us to avoid cognitive biases (Dawes, 1988; Gambrill, 1990; Gibbs, 1991; Turk & Salovey, 1988).

Poor Scholarship

Poor scholarship is an obstacle to integration. I think most people would agree on many of the components of good scholarship, such as correctly representing different points of view, citing prior work, presenting data against as well as for favored views, and quoting others accurately. A call for increasing the quality of scholarship has been made in many fields. For example, Levis (Levis, 1990, 10) argues that "We must stop extensive use of misleading references, inaccurate references, misleading definitions of the problem and critical omissions of relevant literature." It is not uncommon to read an article, book, or chapter in which key terms are not defined or unpopular positions are misrepresented (Catania, 1991; Todd & Morris, 1983). Phillips (Phillips, 1987) suggests that many who write about "different ways of knowing" have not been thorough in their research. "The fact of the matter is that many of the social science and educational researchers have been selective in their philosophical reading. They have not done their homework and they naively suppose that because a well-known author (like Kuhn) asserts something then that makes it true" (Phillips, 1987, 90; Phillips, 1990b; Phillips, 1992).

Incorrect appraisal of knowledge is not uncommon. Some claim that little if anything is known about how to help clients. This is true for some problems, but not for all (Giles, 1993). Because nothing is known for sure does not mean nothing is known. Isaac Asimov (Asimov, 1989) points out that it is probably unlikely that we will discover that the earth is a cube during the next century and is a doughnut shape the century following. Insisting on a criterion of proof and saying that, if this is absent, there is no usable knowledge is neither descriptive of what is known nor useful in discovering knowledge. What we need is information that decreases uncertainty about how to attain certain outcomes. Underestimating available knowledge encourages others to falsely believe that it is not possible to obtain information that decreases uncertainty, with the result that integration opportunities are lost, and clients are deprived of effective services. Both overestimating and underestimating the effectiveness of a given practice may have negative effects on clients. While overestimating at least takes advantage of the placebo effect, underestimating encourages a negative placebo effect on both practitioners and clients. However, the (incorrect) belief that nothing is known, and that all voices are equally valid does have a payoff for social workers: If nothing is known, they do have to spend time acquiring related content and procedural knowledge.

Propagandistic Styles of Discourse and Scholasticism

People differ in preferred styles of talking, listening, writing, and reading. The goal of scholarship should be to move closer to an accurate account of whatever topic is under discussion. It should not be to be right, to show how much one knows, to hide areas of ignorance, or to win a discussion by appealing to informal fallacies such as ad hominum arguments and appeals to unfounded authority. The goal of propaganda is to encourage belief and action with the least thought possible (Ellul, 1965). Scholarly and propagandistic styles can be distinguished in many ways (Gambrill, 1992). For example, presenting inaccurate descriptions of disliked points of view, appealing to self-interest to encourage beliefs, and simply asserting that other points of view are wrong are propagandistic styles. Use of these styles by instructors can be demoralizing to students, many of whom recognize their inappropriateness in an educational setting. We are surrounded by propaganda on a daily basis (Ellul, 1965; Pratkanis & Aronson, 1991), which makes it difficult to resist its lures. The same critiques that Karl Popper has made of philosophical writing could be made of some of the literature in social work and the social sciences. "Scholasticism, in the worst sense of the term, abounds; all great ideas are buried in a flood of words. At the same time, a certain arrogance and rudeness seem to be accepted by the editors of many of the journals as a proof of boldness of thought and originality" (Popper, 1992, 185).

Conflicting Values and Goals

Many values and goals compete with the goal of helping clients achieve outcomes they value. Goals of enhancing personal status and resources may compete with integration. Once a laboratory is set up to peruse a certain methodology such as surveys, gearing up to use other methodologies can have a high cost. Given the learning time and the loss of expertise involved with change, it is often easier to overlook the limits of one's own specialty, as well as the potential benefits of other methods. Interdisciplinary work requires sharing with others. One of my colleagues told me that there was a norm against sharing in his previous department. The attitude there was, "We worked hard to develop this course outline, so why should we give it to others?" Some may view giving proper credit to others as lessening their contribution in the eyes of others.

Integration may pose a danger to current social, political, and economic interests. Professional newsletters illustrate the intense struggles among practitioners in increasing and maintaining professional turf. We cannot assume that the main goal of a publisher is to inform the public or the profession as a whole. Profit making may override this goal. Nor can we assume that the sole goal of editors is to inform their readers; rather, their primary goal may be to appear "in step with the times." There is a relentless pressure to come up with new paradigms, to keep in step, to satisfy the grounds for rewards in the social sciences that may not be those that advance knowledge (Sperber, 1990). Expectations for productivity have increased over the past years, resulting in a flood of publications (Lasson, 1990). A focus on goals such as publication may result in hasty efforts at integration, which impede effective use of knowledge and skills. Problems may be incorrectly structured, resulting in harm or failure to help. The reward system in higher education supports hasty publication. By this, I refer to published material in which theories and approaches are misrepresented, relevant empirical research is omitted or misrepresented, unwarranted conclusions are drawn (e.g., regarding practice prescriptions), weak appeals are relied on to persuade readers (e.g., testimonials, case examples), or key terms are not defined. Vague, obscure writing may be valued over clear, straightforward descriptions to create an illusion of profoundness and to hide ignorance. Inclusion of potentially valuable content (e.g., use of single case designs) may be advocated in an overly zealous manner that alienates potential consumers. Doors may be closed that are hard to open.

As long as academics are divided by spurious controversies, they are unlikely to pose a danger to economic, political, and social circumstances that foster social problems. Continued controversy makes it easier for the government to avoid implementing policies that help its citizens. A government may encourage contentious debate to give the illusion that change is really possible (Ellul, 1964). "If we teach everybody, let's say high school students, the habit of being skeptical, perhaps they will not restrict their skepticism to aspirin commercials and 35,000 year old channelers (or channelees). Maybe they'll start asking awkward questions about economic or social, or political, or religious institutions" (Sagan, 1987, 41). Pettigrew (Pettigrew, 1985) argues that funding agencies deliberately insist on an "either-or" framing of research questions ("Does it work or not?") because this provides easier guidelines for policy decisions. They can then say either that Headstart works or that it does not, rather than having to consider that a program may work to different degrees in different settings with different people. The discovery and implementation of knowledge within such a complex framework can be messy and costly. It is easier to pronounce that something simply does not work, because people may then believe that the government has looked into a program and made a reasonable decision not to implement it. If research suggests that a program is effective, the controversies that surround any claim can be used to delay implementation—especially when a great deal of money is involved. Controversy that befuddles and confuses is not helpful and is often at clients' expense.

Political correctness may be used as the criterion to select content. Do titles have the right buzzwords? Current buzzwords include "multicultural," "empowerment," and "diversity." Politically correct language is not necessarily correlated with content designed to fulfill the very spirit of the buzzword used, that is, to offer the outcomes alluded to by the language. If key terms such as "empowerment" are not defined, what is discussed or done may have an effect contrary to that desired; it may disempower rather than empower clients. It may refer to methods that limit rather than expand options to enhance the quality of one's life.

Time and Effort

Integration and scholarship take time and effort. Time must be taken to understand different points of view, to check secondary sources, to understand research methods used, to review the appropriateness of statistical analyses, and to assess conclusions and recommendations based on data reported. Scholars from different disciplines must take the time to understand colleagues in different fields. Researchers and practitioners must work hard to understand views that may seem odd or even distasteful. Developmental, integrative, and experimental research programs designed to discover intervention knowledge related to a problem require years of work. Isn't it easier to do a survey—to ask people what they think is effective?

Seduction by Theory

Many people think with theories rather than think about how to test them critically and what critical tests have been made. They think within a framework rather than about it (Popper, 1994). Baer (Baer, 1991) argues that lack of success in eliminating client complaints is often followed by too much guessing and too little testing. Theory should be an aid to critical inquiry, not an obstacle. Is a theory helpful in yielding knowledge that decreases uncertainty about how to attain a certain outcome? The criterion of usefulness in discovering intervention knowledge is not always accepted. Other criteria may assume priority such as interest or entertainment value or an apparent astuteness unrelated to testability and evidentiary base. Emphasis may be on explanation and interpretation unrelated to prediction and influence. Only if theories are explicit can they be critically tested. Only if they are not viewed as dogma will they be reviewed critically. Whatever theory is developed should be compatible with current empirical findings about behavior.

Specialization

Specialization strains against a systems view (Burnham, 1987). The more specialized one becomes, the less likely one may be to see the whole picture. Some universities have recognized the benefits of multidisciplinary work and have provided communication channels across professions and disciplines. The joint program in social science and social work at the University of Michigan is one such example; however, further steps could be taken even here. Even here, someone who selects social work and psychology may graduate without understanding how a sociologist or an anthropologist may approach a problem. Shouldn't all doctoral graduates accurately understand how people in other related fields approach problems and how their methods differ? Shouldn't they understand what other perspectives have to offer?

Misuse of Technology

As with any technological product such as the car or the steam engine, we can examine uses and abuses of technology in the professions. Possible abuses of technologies are just as important to examine as possible uses, although the history of technology indicates that, even with careful planning and analysis, neither is necessarily predictable (Pacey, 1986). Computer-based data analysis methods may be used more to lend an aura of credibility to data than to describe the data candidly. Assessment instruments may be used even when they do not provide data that decrease uncertainty about how to help clients attain outcomes they value.

The Search for a Unique Knowledge Base

The search for a unique knowledge base has been encouraged by social work's historical concern for professional status. For some, this seems to imply that social work should have a knowledge base that has no overlap with other professions and disciplines. The cost of insistence on a state of uniqueness that is not present cuts off social work from other sources of knowledge that can inform its practice.

Prevalence of Pathologies of Science

Social science and professional journals contain research reports that are irrelevant to or distorting of the events under investigation (Chubin, 1989; Colman, 1987; Lipton & Hershaft, 1985; Skrabanek, 1990). Practitioners are not immune to the influences of mass media, nor are researchers or academics. The marketing of "pop psychology" in all its various forms (books, magazine and newspaper articles, workshops, and talk shows) oozes into all areas of life. Fragmentation is a hallmark of media presentations (Burnham, 1987). Proselytizers of many sorts cloak empty claims in the trappings of science. For every appeal to scientific criteria, we are subjected to scores of pseudoscientific appeals in advertisements, newscasts, films, TV, newspapers, and professional sources, making it a challenge to resist their lures (Jensen, 1989). The classification of clients into psychiatric categories lends an aura of scientific credibility to this practice, even though it is unwarranted (Kirk & Kutchins, 1992). Scientific ideology is used to reaffirm and maintain current definitions of problems and service delivery systems that may harm rather than help clients (Scheper-Hughes & Lovell, 1987; Szasz, 1994). This does not mean that the scientific process is not useful. It indicates that, like anything else, it can be appropriately or inappropriately applied.

IN SUMMARY

A key purpose of social work is to help clients prevent and remove complaints. Empirical investigation is necessary to discover whether drawing on knowledge from the social sciences and other professions forwards this goal and, if so, what kinds of knowledge are most useful in what circumstances. Why not critically test the accuracy of different accounts that flow from different points of view? Differences of opinion make a field vital and growth-oriented if handled in constructive ways. The attitudes, knowledge, and skills involved in critical thinking offer a way to discuss differences constructively. We should care enough to test as well as to guess, rather than simply guessing and guessing again. Predictions can be tested as to whether they are accurate. Does a point of view yield knowledge that decreases uncertainty about how to help clients attain outcomes they value? Doesn't the guess-and-test method of science allow us to see if certain beliefs offer leverage in achieving outcomes clients value? Isn't a key purpose of social work to help clients prevent and resolve problems?

Potential benefits of integration should be explored in all areas of social work. We can draw on empirical research describing how behavior is influenced by the environment to discover ways to forward integration (Malott, Whaley, and Malott, 1993). A multilevel contingency analysis will reveal consequences that work against as well as for an integration that benefits clients. It will highlight the conflicting interests involved in different views of social problems and how to approach them (Kunkel, 1970). It will help us to see who benefits and who loses from an integration that helps clients achieve outcomes they value. A multilevel contingency analysis can be used to identify relevant behaviors, as well as the setting events, cues, and consequences that influence them. Valuable behaviors may include reading widely (not only in one's discipline or profession, but in others as well), seeking evidence against as well as for favored views, developing an accurate understanding of other views, and talking to people with different views.

We could probably agree on and immediately implement some common practices that would improve the value of the professional literature. For example, we could insist that authors define key terms and avoid the use of propagandistic devices such as omitting data that do not support favored positions, ad hominem attacks, and misrepresentations of other positions. Editors and publishers could select reviewers who are familiar with a topic and require authors to test claims critically rather than appeal to a personal authority or anecdotal experience. Scholars, educators, researchers, journal editors, and publishers have a heavy responsibility in their role as gatekeepers of knowledge. The challenges of integration place unique responsibilities on educators who groom the next generation of social workers. Practitioners are often blamed by researchers and academics for not basing practice decisions on related research findings. However, practitioners cannot integrate knowledge if they do not know about it. Integration requires renaissance practitioners, educators, researchers, and scholars—those who understand the need for and value of casting a wide net in the search for helpful content, those who know how and are committed to fearlessly critiquing views—especially favored ones, those who take the time needed to understand different perspectives, those who question accepted views, those who provide arguments and evidence for claims made, those who are committed to helping clients achieve outcomes they value as reflected in deeds as well as words. Integration requires people who are willing to say their view may be wrong; let's critically test it.

NOTE

1. For a critique of this and other beliefs that interfere with knowledge use, see O'Donohue and Szymanski, (1994).

3

Mechanism, Conflict, and Cultural Symbol: Three Views of the Relationship between Social Insight and Social Transformation

Richard H. Price

The broad theme of this book is the relationship between the way social scientists study social conditions and efforts to improve them. In short, the topic is what James Rule (Rule, 1978) calls the relationship between "insight and social betterment." The fundamental question is whether (or even *if*) a better understanding of social and community life actually can bring about improved social conditions. How does one (or *can* one) go about translating social insights derived from research and scholarship into improved conditions for families, organizations, and communities? I do not assume that social understanding and social betterment are automatically or necessarily linked. The proposition deserves analysis and argument, and that is what this chapter is about.

To begin the argument, we need a close and critical analysis of the underlying assumptions of social thinkers who have considered the question of the relationship between social knowledge and social betterment. Let me begin by describing two underlying "models of relevance" or paradigms describing the relationship between social understanding and the improvement of community life (Rule, 1978). By examining these models and making their underlying assumptions explicit, we may find one that is satisfactory. If not, we may still ask what ideas and assumptions we can use to guide our actions as scientists or advocates.

These alternative models are actually models of how society works as it attempts to transform social science knowledge into improved social conditions. That is, these models present an organized set of assumptions about where social science knowledge should come from, how it should be used in the interest of social change, and who the beneficiaries of knowledge and change should be. Moreover, each of these models also offers alternative role prescriptions for us as social scientists and provides directives about what effective action might be.

SOCIETY AS MACHINE: SOCIAL SCIENTISTS AS REPAIR AGENTS

A dominant conceptual model, one particularly appealing to professionals, has been proposed by social theorists and philosophers in a variety of forms (Rule, 1978). The most familiar names include Robert Merton (Merton & Nisbett, 1971) and Karl Popper (Popper, 1963). This model sees the insights gleaned from our research and theory as directly applicable to social problems and as leading to social improvement. For example, Merton begins by arguing that it ought to be possible to identify social problems or difficulties in social relations that would be in everyone's best interest to solve. Presumably, Merton believes that there are core conditions such as violent crime, poverty, or epidemics where social betterment would come about if solutions to these problems could be identified. Merton argues that problems of this sort represent a major discrepancy between agreed-upon social standards and actual conditions of social life. His definition of social problems assumes that a single, unified, underlying set of values exists in our society (or, for that matter, in any society) and that a value consensus can allow us to develop shared social standards about what actually constitutes a problem and how to solve it. It is certainly true that such a list of social conditions could be developed; however, the meaning of a particular social problem, its significance, and what would be an improvement are matters where agreement is very difficult, as Rule (Rule, 1978) has pointed out.

Merton's model compares society to an organism or a machine and sees the solution of social problems in terms of functional analysis. Our job as social scientists, according to this view, is to make technical adjustments in the social system. But this prescription for technical change in the machine of society fails to contend effectively with the problem of consensus about the nature of social problems and, indeed, with what constitutes an agreed-upon course of action for doing something about the problem. The underlying belief here is that it is the agencies of the state who should receive our social knowledge and engage in enlightened action. This position, of course, makes the critical assumption that our government—or the state in general—is committed to the eradication of offending social conditions.

Another aspect of this model that deserves at least a brief discussion is the implicit political tone of the piecemeal social engineering orientation. Advocates of this point of view, such as Popper (Popper, 1963), are made very uneasy by more ideological approaches to change. They express a strong discomfort with sweeping indictments of our current social system and object to fundamental propositions for social change. They view this kind of thinking as "ideological" and, therefore, doctrinaire and closed-minded. Instead, Popper argues for what he calls piecemeal social engineering. It is the most rational approach, from his point of view, because he believes that we do not yet understand enough for large-scale sweeping reform. Therefore, he explains that such large-scale efforts are impossible to evaluate in terms of success or failure.

Weick (Weick, 1984) has made a more elaborate argument of the same kind, arguing for "small wins," noting their workability, the momentum they generate, and their attractiveness in not challenging basic value positions. Popper and his more modern counterparts warn against sweeping utopian plans and argue instead for the elimination of concrete problems. Unfortunately, Popper's and

Merton's analyses leave ambiguous the response to the question of which concrete problems can be agreed upon consensually.

This model of the relations between social science knowledge and practice calls up role images that are familiar to all of us. A model that sees direct links between gains in social understanding and improvements in human well-being is one that sees the social scientist as a seeker of truth, someone eager to uncover the facts or someone who wants to unlock the social puzzle. This role model also offers us a clear idea of how to get the knowledge we need. The image usually involves the construction of an elaborate empirical research project that will yield data for prescriptions to policy makers based on knowledge hard won from painstaking analyses (Price, 1989).

SOCIETY AS AN ARENA OF CONFLICT: SOCIAL SCIENTISTS AS POLITICAL ADVOCATES

However, there are compelling arguments to make us skeptical of this incremental, social engineering perspective (Rule, 1978). For example, Banfield and Wilson, in their book, *City Politics* (Banfield & Wilson, 1963), make a sophisticated argument against the relevance of social science knowledge to social improvement. They argue that knowledge cannot play a real role in the solution of social problems because we are actually held back by disagreements among interested parties rather than by a lack of knowledge. Banfield and Wilson summarize their argument with an analogy, saying, "[t]hinking that a general increase in the level of knowledge (about politics) will promote better and faster solutions of social problems is something like thinking that a general increase in the skill of chess players will lead to shorter games or to a 'solution to the problems of chess'" (p. 3). In other words, in this skeptical view, the contending actors may be able to deploy social science knowledge in the service of their interests, but the problems will not be solved any more quickly.

This second model, then, views society as an arena of conflict and has enjoyed widespread popularity among social thinkers. As an advocacy approach, it accepts from the beginning the idea that what we call social problems are actually the result of conflicts between contending interests in society. It argues that we as social scientists should take sides, identifying special constituencies within society who would best benefit from whatever social insights we may generate.

Of course, the most famous proponent of this view was Karl Marx (Marx and Engels, 1959). For Marx, the special constituency to benefit from his social insights was the proletariat. He believed that we (and, by extension, we as social scientists) should explicitly identify ourselves with a particular set of interests in society. In other words, our job is to communicate insights about the workings of the social world to this constituency. Marx believed, ultimately, that the proletariat would become free of the coercion of a capitalist state. The program for accomplishing this goal was nothing less than revolution.

More recently, this constituency-oriented model has been expanded to identify new consumers of social insight who are, potentially, special beneficiaries. They include racial minorities, the poor, and socially stigmatized groups that can represent special constituencies for the insights of social scientists. Unlike Marx's approach, this most recent version of the conflict model does not argue that it is critical social insights that fuel social change. Rather, the constituency-oriented model argues that it is our job as social scientists to dramatize the discrepancies between what society asserts as its social values and our actual practices with these groups. This is clearly an activist approach, but one that, as James Rule (Rule, 1978) observes, does not guarantee that our portrayal of these discrepancies will be received sympathetically by most people. Furthermore, this view does not specify how the consumers of these insights can act effectively to produce social change.

In this view, social problems are not technical problems, but evidence of fundamental social conflict. As Seymour Sarason (Sarason, 1978) points out, social problems are not like arithmetic problems. However, if social problems are not like arithmetic problems, what are they like? Is there an alternative conception of social problems, and if so, what is its implication for action? Rule (Rule, 1978) has argued that attempts at rational technocratic social problem solving may actually disguise social conflict and competing efforts to control desirable resources in society. According to this view, we do not have a "racial problem." Instead, what we call "racial problems" are actually symptoms of a conflict between supporters and opponents of more opportunity in society for people of color. Similarly, we do not have an "unemployment problem." Instead, we have workers who have become too old or too expensive, which has led corporate owners to close plants and hire younger, cheaper workers elsewhere.

This view of social problems argues that there is no definition of a social problem that is devoid of political judgments and parties in conflict. Moreover, there are no solutions to such problems without conflict among social actors. This view of social problems counsels us not to look for a "fix" of the problem, but instead to identify the contestants and to take sides.

C. Wright Mills offers a similar prescription, arguing that it is our job as social scientists to hold those in power responsible for their decisions. He explains that we should educate those who are unaware of the consequences of those decisions and communicate the insight we have about the ways in which "personal troubles of the individual are actually connected with larger public issues" (Mills, 1959, 186).

The role image for social scientists offered here is familiar to all of us. In this view, the social scientist is a seeker of justice and an attacker of oppression. Invariably, social scientists acting in this role must have a clear idea of who the victim is and who the oppressor is. The methodology is also well known. Community organizing and political advocacy are the recommended tools. The advocacy model calls up a vision of liberation of the oppressed through struggle where, ultimately, the oppressor is vanquished.

Weaknesses of Mechanistic and Political Views

Only a moment's reflection is required to recognize that the mechanistic view that sees society as a machine in need of repair ignores the problems of power. But the political view of society as an arena of conflict is also limited in part because it has little to say about the real technical uncertainties faced by political regimes that succeed in bringing about change. It is not enough to declare oneself a market economy, for example. There are real technical demands that accompany social transformation. And, while the political conflict view is clearly attuned to power as a central dynamic, it is often silent on what it is that establishes a legitimate claim to power. Both the mechanistic and the political conflict views actually share a weakness, however: they ignore the symbolic and the cultural as basic constituents of social reality.

SOCIETY AS A SYSTEM OF CULTURAL SYMBOLS: SOCIAL SCIENTISTS AS CULTURAL TOOL USERS

There is a third view of society. It is a view that sees society as a system of cultural symbols, some of them conflicting or in fundamental contradiction. It is this system of conflicting cultural symbols that, in turn, shapes our social institutions and organizations. Often, so this argument goes, we are unreflective about how cultural symbols shape and constitute our social reality. Instead, we take the norms and rules that emerge in society and culture as "given." We assume we know what is meant, for example, by "motherhood" or "family values."

Nevertheless, I want to argue that institutional actors often use these symbols in instrumental ways as tools to create leverage for social change. This third view of society both expands and replaces the mechanistic and political views, offering perhaps a less deterministic view of social change, but one that is more in keeping with the social world we know, where symbols can have dramatic potency in fueling change.

Barley and Knight (Barley and Knight, 1991) suggest that both anthropologists and semioticians would claim that culture can be thought of as a system of symbols (Turner, 1967; Geertz, 1983). Furthermore, this line of argument contends that the most powerful cultural symbols acquire a considerable part of their meaning and potency as a result of oppositional contrast (Jacobson, 1978). For example, Turner (Turner, 1967) suggests that societies are characterized by a few dominant symbols that both point to and attempt to reconcile contradictions and conflicts that may exist in the way that a society views the world. The conflicts are often deeply embedded in the society and involve polarities such as equality versus inequality, individualism versus collective action, or stability versus change. Levi-Strauss (1963) has argued that such symbols stand for deep cultural structures that often involve cognitions that are fundamentally opposed to each other. Similarly, Geertz (Geertz, 1983) suggests that members of a society cope with contradictory forces by developing dominant ideologies that incorporate contradictory polarities and themes.

To appreciate how a single term can take on such power and embody emotional tensions, here an example is offered by Barley and Knight (Barley and Knight, 1991):

Consider the symbolic trappings of the term, "welfare program." "Welfare program's" denotation is notably mundane: state support for the poor. However, since the 1960's, "welfare program" has become an emotionally charged term precisely because it has come to symbolize a central contradiction in our cultural understanding of poverty

(Edelman, 1977). On one hand, poverty is a recognized result of social forces over which individuals have no control, yet failure to escape poverty is also widely thought to reflect indolence. Hence, "welfare program" has become an expression that connotes our culture's ambivalence about the role that voluntarism and determinism play in shaping a person's station in life (p. 13).

One could easily identify other terms freighted with powerful symbolic meaning and embodying tensions and conflict, such as, for example, "affirmative action," where equality and inequality is a pivotal polarity.

According to the argument that society is comprised of cultural symbols, even those symbols that contain contradictions or conflicting impulses are often incorporated into laws, administrative arrangements, and organizational rules (Scott, 1987; Zucker, 1987). The rules resemble what Meyer and Rowan (Meyer & Rowan, 1977) have called "rational myths" that prescribe what is right and proper to do. They are "rational" because they seem to make sense, and they are "myths" because they are untested beliefs about means-ends relationships. In any case, cultural symbols may be transformed into laws or rules that attempt to incorporate conflicting values. In their official capacity, they may produce conflicting or contradictory organizational practices and unanticipated organizational or economic consequences. These contradictions may appear either when the rules or laws are first formulated or when environmental conditions change (Meyer, Scott, and Strang, 1987; Powell, 1987) and bring the contradictions to the surface.

To return to our welfare program example, consider rules requiring means testing to qualify for assistance. Means testing for welfare recipients may reflect a cultural ambivalence about the "deserving poor" and the degree to which welfare recipients are involuntary victims of external forces or are capable of commanding control over their own fate. Means testing assures qualification for an entitlement, to be sure, but it also reveals a deep ambivalence about what it means to be a member of the "deserving poor," a cultural symbol that sends contradictory signals about whether poverty is a voluntary or involuntary status.

However, once these conflicting cultural symbols are hardened into procedural rules or laws, how constraining are they? Some authors have argued that we are captured and constrained by such rules. DiMaggio and Powell (DiMaggio & Powell, 1983) and, of course, Weber (Weber, 1947) before them suggest that institutional norms and administrative or legal rules can become an "iron cage" both governing and constraining organizational behavior of the government, labor, employers, and the professions—an "iron cage" that in turn shapes institutional beliefs and norms.

Other theorists have criticized this view because it ignores the role of organizational interests and active agency (Covaleski & Dirsmith, 1988; DiMaggio, 1988; Perrow, 1985; Powell, 1985). Institutional actors may not just respond to various laws and demands in the organizational environment with passive conformity (DiMaggio & Powell, 1983; Meyer & Rowan, 1977; Powell & DiMaggio, 1991); rather, as Oliver (Oliver, 1991) argues, institutional actors may actually use cultural beliefs as tools and counterarguments to advance their own interests. Since many of the most powerful cultural beliefs have conflicting or contradictory aspects, social entrepreneurs (Goffman, 1959; Goffman, 1974) may be able to seize on one aspect or another of the belief or rule to pursue his or her ends. One advocate may emphasize a particular family configuration as reflecting "family values" to justify qualification for welfare payments, while another may emphasize the importance of a committed relationship in the name of those same values.

Seen in this way, cultural symbols not only confer legitimacy on actions taken by various institutional actors (Meyer & Rowan, 1977; D'Aunno, Sutton, and Price, 1991) but can also be used to justify actions taken in pursuit of valued material and symbolic resources. This suggests that institutional beliefs and norms do not just constrain organizational behavior. Organizations and organizational actors can use "taken for granted" beliefs as tools to achieve their own goals and interests. Indeed, social policies and laws that reflect conflicting institutional beliefs may represent especially promising tools for organizational action.

What, then, is the role prescription for social scientists and practitioners implied by this third view of society as a system of conflicting cultural symbols? It suggests that, as social diagnosticians, we become readers of symbols. Symbols are not "merely symbolic." They are, instead, powerfully packed with assumptions and directives for action. Therefore, when we consider action or prescriptions for action, we ignore this symbolic freight at our own peril. Embedded in the language and symbolism we use to characterize social groups, statuses, and professions is kinetic energy that can fuel social action.

CONCLUSION

Implicit in my argument has been the idea that we cannot ask coherent questions about the relationship between social science knowledge and social practice unless we first establish a framework of assumptions. The assumptions must be about the nature of society and, by extension, the nature of knowledge useful in both diagnostic and corrective remedy.

Mechanistic views are appealing because they suggest that social problems really can be solved like arithmetic problems—that there is a calculus of definition and solution. Uncomfortable questions of power, justice, and oppression can be set aside. "Win-win" solutions are available, this mechanistic view argues, if only we could identify and implement them.

Political conflict views, on the other hand, gain credence when we reflect that, all too often, it is not the technically correct solution to social problems that is implemented, but the one that is the favorite of those in power. This view often seems to counsel that our diagnostic and intervention skills as social scientists ought to be placed in the hands of those needing justice—if only we could unambiguously identify who they are and be comfortable that countervailing claims lack validity. However, thoughtful people are often ambivalent about who the beneficiaries should be, at least in the broad range of cases, and are skeptical about reassurances that new found power will not be abused.

While neither the mechanistic or political views are satisfactory, it may be not because they are wrong, but rather because they are incomplete. A third view argues that we live in a world of cultural symbols, and societies actually incorporate and bind some of their most fundamental conflicts in those symbols. These cultural symbols, in turn, inform and shape our institutional practices and organizational arrangements in powerful ways. However, we are not passive recipients of these rational myths and cultural symbols. Cultural symbols may actually be the tools of social entrepreneurs (Goffman, 1959; Goffman, 1974) who use them to shape our understandings of who the beneficiaries of our social ministrations should be.

Our use of symbolic tools in the continuing debate among various contending groups in society is perhaps that which distinguishes our species from others most clearly. This is not a retreat from either the technical or the political views of insight and social betterment. It is, instead, a recognition that, as social scientists, we are part of, not apart from, a continuing cultural dialogue struggling with fundamental conflicts that are folded into the fabric of society.

4

Knowledge for Policy and Practice

David Laws and Martin Rein

A common view of the relationship between knowledge and action assumes that integration is possible, desirable, and unidirectional. This view fits many descriptions of applied social science that anticipate a sequentially integrated process, where insight derived from theory is tested and refined by research and used to guide intervention. The model of a policy-making process in which agenda setting is followed by program design, implementation, and evaluation draws on similar assumptions. Policies, which reflect insights derived from research, are implemented in practice and evaluated through research, which informs a second round of policy decisionmaking.

It is second nature to expect that someone will want to acquire knowledge before taking action; informed action goes hand-in-hand with ideas about reasonable and rational action. The view that knowledge will be relevant for and guide action makes a number of assumptions. First, it assumes that consensual goals exist and that they will be sufficient to resolve any conflict that may encountered. Such a resolution may be accomplished analytically, through a transitive ordering indexed to these goals, or procedurally, through a discussion mediated by reference to them. Second, the view also assumes that questions are both asked and answered in a rough sequence. Finally, it assumes that there is enough of a common language to permit meaningful translation between stages.

As entrenched as these assumptions are, it can be unsettling to read about efforts, knowledge, and practices that point to problems, frustrations, and unfulfilled expectations. Such accounts are especially unsettling if they seem to point not to correctable faults, but to central characteristics that systematically affect attempts to integrate knowledge with practice. In this essay, we review several accounts of this relationship between knowledge and action and offer some suggestions as to what they say about integration. Our sample is not exhaustive or even necessarily representative. We feel, however, that it is sufficient to prompt reconsideration of some common expectations that shape efforts to carry out research or to use it to illuminate and shape practice.

In the sections that follow, we examine accounts of attempts to integrate knowledge and practice through the use of the products of disciplinary research and accounts of efforts to bring researchers and practitioners together in practice-oriented programs, in evaluation research, and in two policy-reform efforts. In the concluding section, we try to suggest some implications of our review.

NEGLECT BY DISCIPLINARY RESEARCH

Several reviews of the relationship between disciplinary research and practice suggest that disciplinary research on its own is unlikely to produce findings that are of more than tangential interest to practitioners working in associated fields. In a thoughtful analysis of the role of practice in schools of education, David Cohen has shown that, although scholars from Dewey to Piaget have developed theories of learning, the serious study of teaching has been neglected.

Theorists who seek to reform the practice of teaching write nearly exclusively about the practice of learning rather than of teaching. Dewey, Bruyner, and others offered extended accounts of how children learn, or should learn, but they gave little attention to how teachers teach, to how they should teach, or to the nature of teaching practice.

Lloyd Rodwin has suggested that much the same relationship has held for a long time between the practice of urban or city planning and adjacent social science disciplines. In a review of the outcome of an effort by planners to attract attention to common problems, Rodwin describes how

even in the mid-sixties, when the interest in urban affairs reached its crest, urban and regional questions appeared to have only a minor bearing on the central problems of the different social sciences as well as law and civil engineering. At best, social-science departments might arrange for faculty appointments, and perhaps even disciplinary specializations, in urban economics, urban sociology, and urban politics. And from time to time, one could expect cities and regions to serve as the occasional laboratory for illustrating or testing general problems of interest to these social scientists. This situation was much better than the egregious neglect of these questions in the past, but it was most unlikely that the problems of the city and region would receive sustained careful attention except from programs which had a *central, long-term* concern with these matters. (Rodwin, 1981, 269, emphasis his)

Donald Schon and his colleague Chris Argyris have pointed to similar difficulties. In a recent paper, Schon described their views as follows: "Argyris and I believe that the results of normal social science research fail, even in the long term, to provide knowledge usable by practitioners in the everyday world of organizations. The reasons for this failure are inherent in the normal science conception of causality and causal inferences." In their view, there is a mismatch between the particular kind of rigor reflected in research standards and methods and the "practitioner's demand for knowledge that is usable under the pressured and often confusing conditions of everyday practice" (Argyris &

Schon, n.d.,4). This mismatch is significant enough to call for a redefinition of the relationship between social science and practice.[1]

These observations suggest that the integration of research and practice is unlikely to proceed without problems. In many professions, there are conferences and workshops that explicitly try to bring research and practice closer together and presumably try to respond to the problems of integration. Sheldon White sketched some "critical events" at an education conference of this kind (White, 1992). His comments suggest that the problems may require bringing research and practice even closer together.

The conference White discusses was built on assumptions similar to those discussed above: "Knowledge made in laboratories will be transmitted to practitioners in education, who will translate theory into practice" (p. 20). The critical events that he describes, however, run counter to these assumptions. The first followed a presentation of recent research on word perception, when a participant asked, "Why are you telling me this? What does any of this have to do with the classroom?" (p. 2). White describes the "immediate impact" of the question: "As soon as it was asked, you suddenly did wonder about what, exactly, teachers were supposed to get from a blow-by-blow portrayal of the technicalities of cognitive research. The question was aimed at a specific speaker, but it went towards a major assumption governing the meeting as a whole." He suggests that such "blunt, confronting questions" may be rare because they hit too close to home, and just the fact of asking them may burst the bubble of deeply held assumptions (p. 2).

The second critical event that White describes raises this question even more explicitly. White focuses on a presentation by Frank Smith, who "said flatly that he has some real skepticism about whether theory can be translated into practice in any genuine way. He pointed out that attempts to translate theory into practice usually rest upon 'forced and oversimplified reasoning,' 'egregious over-generalization,' 'the overlooking of important issues,' and 'the confusing of causes with consequences.' As White relays the conversation, Smith argued "that if we examine many of the advertised linkages between research and practice we will often find that they are unreal. The translation is invalid on the research side, on the educational side or both." This was enough to cause White to wonder whether there is "an alive and vital connection between research and practice in education" (p. 3).

White takes the gulf identified by these "critical events" seriously. In his view, it is also noticeable in the failure of "academic proposals and prescriptions for the betterment of education," which flounder "because they are based on simplistic stereotypes; they are irrelevant, incompetent, and immaterial with respect to complex reality." He suggests that the isolation of researchers from the world of practice may be responsible. The gap between the worlds and activities of the researcher and the practitioner impairs efforts to perceive problems and to take corrective action.[2]

These examples suggest that, even with effort, the interaction between research and practice may be best described as a pattern of neglect.[3] The experiences of researchers and practitioners may overlap very little, if at all. The problems that researchers focus on are not necessarily those most likely to interest or aid practitioners. The methods and standards of research will not necessarily lead to answers that practitioners find relevant. The standards of one activity may conflict with those of the other. The ties between research and practice may be much more tenuous and problematic than suggested by common assumptions; indeed, there is, in many cases, a significant gap between research and practice.

CROWDING OUT AND OTHER TENSIONS IN UNIVERSITY PROGRAMS

In practice- or problem-oriented fields, recognition of neglect has led to efforts to bridge the gap in university programs of instruction. Some city planning and social work departments have treated the gap between disciplinary research and practice as an opportunity for interchange that could be addressed by bringing together social science researchers and practitioners in one program.

The Department of Planning at MIT decided in the 1960s that the best way to build the sustained effort necessary to address urban problems and to intellectually invigorate both its faculty and the planners it was educating was to bring in social scientists from other disciplines, especially economics.[4] The rationale was that an exchange of views would create an intellectual environment that would raise the quality of planning education. Researchers interested in the problems of the urban environment would deal with the theoretical and conceptual issues in a somewhat different way than would planning practitioners. The discourse between the social scientists and the practitioners would stimulate and enrich the intellectual grounding of the practice.

A second, compatible rationale for this approach was provided by the existence of a wide range of specialists working in the same areas as the planners. These urban sociologists and urban economists were themselves practitioners in the sense that they worked not only in the university but also in government agencies, applying social science knowledge and methods to urban questions. If these social science practitioners could work together with the physical planners, the two types of practitioners could form an alliance that would deepen the field.

Schools of social work also turned to social science knowledge to enrich their practice. At first, they brought social scientists to the faculty to teach research methods and sociological and psychological theory. Many schools began to develop their own doctoral programs to train practitioners to become social scientists themselves. Presumably, many of these graduates would go on to educate future generations of practitioners; the knowledge they would draw upon would be grounded in both social science and practice. The University of Michigan developed a bold program of training practitioners in the social sciences under the assumption that social science knowledge would enrich and strengthen professional practice.

The outcome of these efforts was to reproduce the tension between research and practice within the boundaries of the program. This was not entirely unproductive. In planning, the effort did attract some social scientists to the ranks of the planning department and make some headway in getting social science departments to devote more time and resources to questions that planning practitioners shared. The social scientists also "questioned and often discredited some basic ideas of city planners" (Rodwin, 1981, 261). Collaborative research and teaching have occurred where individuals have managed the tension creatively.

Yet the focus on acquiring a disciplinary background and mastering formal research methods tends to crowd practice questions out of the research part of the program. This is felt most explicitly in Ph.D. programs, where faculty expectations, competition for funding, and the specters of publishing and eventually tenure review push students towards a more conventional social science approach. At the same time, however, concern about the relevance of dissertation topics to the profession persists among planning faculty.

This tendency to crowd practice out of the curriculum met with more resistance in other areas of the planning program. The practitioners on the faculty did not always accept the power relationships implied by the applied social science model. Instead, "there is little evidence that the design-based faculty found itself redundant, or that the disciplinary specialists initially brought into the city-planning departments either outranked the city planners or were regarded by themselves or by the city planners as superior in status." Instead they met with skepticism about "how much they could contribute to the analysis to the professionals (who compared themselves to architects, doctors, or lawyers and not to "mere" applied social scientists)" given the "fuzzy state of social science knowledge" (Rodwin, 1981, 261).[5]

RESEARCH CAPTURED BY PRACTICE

Many schools of public policy took an almost opposite tack to bridging the gap between research and practice. They acknowledged the problem of neglect and extended it with the recognition

that restricting scholarship to the protocols of normal social science is a plainly unacceptable strategy for fulfilling our professional mission. Given the inadequacy of available methods with respect to the complexity of the reality we seek to understand, the result of such a restriction would be, at best, trivial "truths" of little value in "improving practice wisdom."

These schools tried to develop new programs of teaching and research that would shake off "the dead hand of social science" and use a practice orientation to "pursue a deeper, more socially significant, and more resonant truth" (Lynn, 1992, 91).[6]

This effort to accumulate "new intellectual capita" drew its inspiration from business schools with their emphasis on the executive function, strategy, decisions, and best practice. The appropriate research strategy, therefore, would be to accumulate cases on public management problems and practices—a case development program had already been established at the Kennedy School; identify better and worse practices; promote systematic comparative research; and link intellectual development to the training of manager. (Lynn, 1992, 10–11)

This perspective, Lynn suggests, "has been strong and consistent within the public policy community ever since" (p. 11).[7]

In Lynn's view, the emphasis on practice in public policy research has come "at the expense of conceptual clarity and analytic rigor" (p. 14). For all that may have been done to enrich the discussion of practice, Lynn argues that the output of these research efforts has been one or another kind of "homiletics"; statements that derive from biographically-rich descriptions to increase their relevance have resulted in knowledge that is noncumulative and nongeneralizable and, as such, is of limited value. With all the research emphasis placed on practice and little or none on an internal research agenda around issues such as research design (which could produce careful comparisons) or the use and development of theory (which could produce statements that could be tested against experience), the resulting knowledge has suffered.

No simple explanation is sufficient to account for these outcomes, although the stature practitioners enjoyed in public policy schools doubtlessly contributed.[8] This and other factors contributed to a situation in which there was no independent research perspective that could pose questions of research design and theory building. Nor were researchers led to develop and describe their work in relation to a body of theory or to develop general propositions or general prescriptive suggestions from their work. The outcome was that instead of informing practice, research was captured by it.

Each of these vignettes—the *neglect* of practice in disciplinary social science research, the *crowding out* that occurred with the introduction of social scientists into practice oriented planning and social work departments, and the *capture* of research by a strong practice-policy orientation in public management research— point to imbalances that have impaired efforts to integrate research and practice. *Neglect* can be seen as the dominance of research concerns with knowledge accumulation over either practice concerns that offer prescriptive advice for taking action or policy concerns for setting objectives and accountability. Crowding out and polarization can be understood as stemming from an inability to reconcile research concerns with those of practice. Capture can be understood as a complementary problem arising out of the dominance of the practice orientation (at least in part as a response to the problem of neglect) over weak research standards.

Recognition of these and other difficulties has not settled the issue of research for practice. There have been and still are sustained efforts to reduce neglect and crowding out and to avoid capture by developing a program of research that is both rigorous and relevant. Chris Argyris and Donald Schon's work is notable for its effort to develop a balanced and productive relationship between the two activities. It is based on the recognition that included in what practitioners know is a limited, but not negligible, capability to carry out research on their own practice. Thus, in those cases where practitioners get stuck, what is called for is a form of collaborative inquiry that can produce systematic reflection on what practitioners know and do and can get at the underlying assumptions, implicit frames, and methods of inquiry. In this approach, the practical application of knowledge can be used as a test of its validity and an occasion for its continuing development.[9]

Charles Lindblom's *Theory of Impaired Inquiry* is another attempt to address the problem of integration.[10] He emphasizes the importance of inquiry and collaboration in "probing" important problems and the need for different kinds of knowledge—including, but not limited to, social science knowledge. Carol Weiss, David Cohen, and Janet Weiss, whose work we cite at length here, are others who have attempted to understand and respond to these difficulties.

We have chosen to focus on the problems of neglect, crowding out, and capture because they are common and related and because they call into question some central assumptions about the integration of knowledge and practice. Up to this point, we have concentrated on efforts to integrate research with practice in universities. This is not the only place in which there has been an effort to integrate research with action. A great deal of activity has also taken place in the context of public policy. We turn now to some examples to examine whether similar problems are encountered in policy and what they might add to our understanding of the problem.

KNOWLEDGE FOR POLICY IN EVALUATION RESEARCH

While much policy research is free standing and directed at critical policy analysis, a considerable amount is commissioned by oversight agencies concerned with monitoring practice. Evaluation research, with oversight agencies as a willing partner, has responded to the need for oversight by developing and applying a set of tools that can provide the information needed for accountability.

This research reveals three characteristic problems. First, the criterion problem highlights the question of how the output of a program is related to its intention or goals. This question is problematic in the world of practice where goals are vague, multiple, conflicting, and continuously evolving. The second problem involves input and suggests that a program cannot be treated as a black box or a given. This would avoid critical questions about the nature, quality, and consistency over time of the programmatic inputs. The third problem concerns design rationality and the logic or theory embedded in the design of a program. How precisely is a program expected to realize its intentions? Are there resources in place to achieve each stage that the logic of the program requires? In the practice of putting a program into place, a step is often left out. The elision of qualitative research that could have responded to these problems left researchers with results that suggested programs were not working, but no basis on which to say why or what should be done.

Given these problems, it is not surprising that commissioned evaluation research has won the reputation of being a "killer" because the results almost uniformly undermine the programmatic assumptions the effort set out to judge. Taken together, the effect of these evaluation problems have reinforced a loss of faith in government capability and led to a pessimistic view that "nothing works" —a finding that has been used politically to discredit policies and to disclaim professional expertise.[11]

Hugh England has described a similar evolution in social work practice in the United Kingdom (England, 1986). The profession in the 1990s is besieged by external attack, internal doubt, and low morale, which is a dramatic shift from the 1970s, when the Seebohn report recognized the potential value and integrity of social work. Social workers in the United Kingdom, fearful of public criticism, are increasingly unwilling to take risks, for fear of being maligned in the press. They have turned to a "defensive practice" designed largely to protect themselves against public criticism. England suggests that this threat to the profession is tied to its inability to form an adequate model of what social work actually does and the kind of outcomes that are achievable. This agenda would require a constructive relationship between research and practice.

This outcome is also not so surprising when we consider that evaluation research is sponsored by oversight agencies asking a different question than that of the practitioners they are evaluating. These agencies face policy concerns about how to allocate scarce resources among different strategies for dealing with a problem. This is very different from the practice question of how to make a particular strategy work. Where practice asks how to act and how best to fix a program within the limits of what you know, what you have, and what you can get agreement on, policy asks whether it is worth supporting the program at all.

Moreover, as is clear in the experience of evaluation research, policy concerns are often inseparable from practice. From this brief account of efforts to integrate research and policy, we conclude that at least some of the difficulties arise because of the neglect of practice. Efforts to integrate research and policy frequently demand knowledge of practice. Thus three distinct perspectives can be identified: *practice*, focused on actionability and client needs; *policy*, concerned with defining problems, setting expectations, and accountability; and *research*, concerned with internal standards of validity and developing knowledge that is cumulative or generalizable in addition to being useful. More common than a pattern of independent dyads—research for policy or research for practice—is for these perspectives to be knit together in a triad of research, policy, and practice.

We propose a triadic model of the relationship between knowledge and action. This approach exposes a set of key issues that must be addressed if actors working within the triad are to develop a collaborative framework that will permit them to perceive tensions inherent in their work environment and the transactional effects of their activity on other actors.[12]

External influences can generate tensions within the triad. Knowledge for policy is not only different from knowledge for practice, but potentially conflicting.[13] Practitioners may be likely to see the story of the close alliance between policy makers and researchers as a threat that reinforces the threat of negative evaluation. Policy makers, on the other hand, may focus on the need to be accountable for expenditures of public funds and to demonstrate results to win continuing support for a program. Researchers might focus on the difficulty of making comparisons across different cases or upholding research standards when faced with multiple and conflicting objectives. Accounts of these internal tensions are likely to vary according to the reference actor within a particular constellation of interactions.

Tensions may also be generated by the internal constraints faced by each class of actors. Practitioners are tied to the clientele they serve, policy makers to the political process and the need for accountability, and researchers to peer review and funding systems. Research, policy, and practice are pulled in different directions by the demands of these different audiences.

These tensions and conflicting perspectives can undermine the possibility of integration. An evaluation of the type described above might, for instance, lead to protectiveness and hostility on the part of practitioners and erosion of support or frustration on the part of policy makers. When examined from the perspective of the triad, however, such a scenario is not about which perspective is right, but about the tensions and imbalances that shape the set of relationships. The elision of practice from evaluation research can be seen as the result of the close ties forged between research and policy that dominate the research agenda.

THE INTERACTION OF RESEARCH, POLICY, AND PRACTICE

Discussions or descriptions of interactions between research, policy, and practice are not abundant. In this section, we turn to two stories of policy reform to give a more detailed portrait of the triad and how it can help illuminate efforts to integrate knowledge and action. The first, studied by Janet Weiss and David Cohen, is one of the few accounts we know of that tries to examine research, policy, and practice perspectives simultaneously and to analyze how their interaction shaped the outcome of a reform effort (Weiss & Cohen, 1991). The second example illustrates another kind of interaction common in the politics of policy reform.

Reforming Reading Policy and Practice in Michigan

In the mid-1980s, during a period of intense scrutiny in U.S. education when "[c]riticism of teachers and public schools had become fierce [and] many national groups were pressing fundamental reform," the state of Michigan undertook an extensive reform of the way reading was taught and of the way the performance of students was evaluated. The origins of the reform effort were serendipitous, instigated by an interaction between research and policy.

The instructional specialist in the Michigan Education Assessment Program who was given the job of revising the reading objectives for the statewide exam was fresh out of Michigan State University and familiar with recent research on reading.[14] She saw this "relatively routine" exercise as an opportunity to introduce recent research into educational policy and practice in the state and overhaul outdated objectives (p. 13).

To initiate reform, she convened a group of researchers and specialists. They focused on the definition of reading used in the state's performance objectives. This group derived a new definition of reading that was more consistent with the current theory of how people read.[15] This definition was endorsed by the Michigan Reading Association, "a professional organization of school reading specialists" (p. 10). It "rendered the existing state assessment in reading obsolete, and had implications for other aspects of state policy, such as curriculum guidelines and professional development for teachers" (pp. 10–11).

The magnitude of the change in the objectives did not sit well initially with the elected state Board of Education, who demanded evidence that practitioners understood and supported the changes (p. 11). In response, "state officials launched conferences, regional meetings, and informal consultations reaching 3,500 educators to spread the news about the new perspective on reading (Wixson and Weiss, 11). The state instructional specialists also "recruited dozens of volunteer teachers and local administrators to help turn the definition into concrete, feasible curriculum objectives" and "developed suggestions for implementing the new definition in the classroom (Weiss & Cohen, 1991, 11). These efforts eventually led to approval of the revised "Essential Goals and Objectives for Reading Education" by the State Board of Education.

The story at this point sounds like a model for the integration of research with policy and practice. New research on reading was translated into new policy goals and objectives, which would subsequently be incorporated into practice. The outcome should be new policy and teaching practice that reflects the new understanding of reading. However, when Weiss, Cohen, and the researchers they worked with went into classrooms and observed teachers, they found something different. The new policy objectives and guidelines did affect practice, but not in the broad and significant ways suggested by the reorientation in research and in the policy objectives.

One group of teachers taught, or was moving in the direction of teaching, reading in keeping with the revised state policy. This group included teachers who had been teaching reading according to newly recommended strategies for some time and saw that "conformity with the policy required no changes in their work." It also included teachers "whose practice was changing in directions that were roughly consistent with the policy," but who "reported they saw few connections between the changes in their classrooms and the policy" (Weiss & Cohen, 1991, 17). These teachers attributed the change to their own frustration with past practice, contact with researchers, or reading books on instruction. Still other teachers attributed their practice to recent university training. [16]

Another group of teachers "reported that they had learned from the policy and related research and that their practice had changed in consequence" (Weiss & Cohen, 1991, 18). Self assessments of the degree of change in practice prompted by the new policy ranged from "helpful" to "fundamental." In their classroom observations, Weiss and Cohen found modest refinements in practice but not much more, even among those practitioners who reported "an enormous influence." While "[s]ome elements in these classrooms seemed consistent with the new ideas about reading," the practice "was in most respects still quite traditional" (Weiss & Cohen, 1991, 18–20).

An explanation for this disparity can be found in the interaction of research, policy, and practice. Relatively few teachers met with researchers; a few more heard researchers give talks at professional meetings. Teachers were not given the opportunity to discuss issues raised for practice with researchers. Instead they "heard or read summaries given by administrators, or in brief handouts, or in flip charts used in meetings" (Weiss & Cohen, 1991, 16). They may also have learned about the research from reading educational magazines or participating in continuing education. Direct interaction with researchers seems to have been rare and limited. The variety of conferences and workshops organized by the state policy specialists seem to have sought to disseminate the new ideas about reading by spreading the news and offering suggestions for implementation, rather than by discussing potential problems or implications.

In terms of the triad, the close ties forged between research and policy seem to have led to the elision of practice, at least in terms of any substantive contribution, from the reform effort. Practice was hitched on as a concern for implementation. The process was dominated by the connection of new research ideas with revised policy goals and objectives.

The research driving these revisions focused on learning rather than teaching practice. The core of the new definition of reading and policy objectives was a cognitive account that stressed the active role of the reader in constructing meaning from a text. While research on teaching practice is mentioned in the account, the research seems to have evaluated practice relative to a theoretical account of reading rather than through an attempt to understand practice. The research on classrooms cited in Weiss and Cohen's description was evaluative, suggesting that practice needed to be revised to be more in keeping with current research understanding. There was little appreciation for problems or efforts at innovation from the world of practice.

Practitioners were involved throughout the process, but always following a strong lead established by research and policy. The reform started with social science research findings. Policy played the role of codifying the implications of the research and then "spreading the news" to teachers. Practitioners' participation was limited to approving the new definition or suggesting ways to implement it. Practitioners were not part of the conversation when the objectives were being debated, and their protests were portrayed as reactionary rather than reasoned responses. The close ties between research and policy created an environment that was indifferent or hostile to practice. In response, practitioners seem to have ignored large parts of the policy innovation.

We do not mean to suggest that there is anything pernicious about research or policy concerns or that the parties involved acted in anything but good faith. However, the imbalance created when practice was hitched on to a change initiated by policy and practice created an environment that at best failed to engage practitioners and at worst was hostile. The advocates of reform failed to find the practitioners who were most sympathetic to their goals and who might have been able to contribute to the substantive development of the new program. Their involvement might have led to a clearer diagnosis of the problems practitioners face and a policy more responsive to the world of the practitioner.

Again, we want to emphasize that close ties between one dyad led to the neglect of the third element of the triad. Another version of the story might have found close ties between the policy and practice communities, crowding researchers out of the policy conversation. New theories about reading might have been ignored as policy tried to respond to the demands of the electoral process and the problems presented by practitioners. This type of interaction is best exemplified by the effort to form a policy for homelessness in Massachusetts in the 1980s.

A Policy for Homelessness in Massachusetts[17]

We move now to a brief discussion of three critical turns in the interaction of research, policy, and practice that shaped the development of homelessness policy in Massachusetts in the 1980s. The first was the forging of ties during the 1984 gubernatorial election between former Governor Michael Dukakis, and the Massachusetts Coalition for the Homeless, the broader social services coalition, and, particularly, the advocates for the homeless. After his reelection, Dukakis remained tied to a group committed to an agenda based on a right to housing and resistant to conflicting views such as homelessness as pathology.

Second, continuing political pressure and legislative maneuvering forced Dukakis' new administration to accept a comprehensive program of housing and social services before an analysis of the problem could be completed. Third, the governor's decision to provide new services for the homeless through the existing framework of social service agencies created persistent interagency conflicts over action, and willingness to be involved administratively in the homelessness problem. This resulted in ongoing struggles over power and resources and led to a fateful decision to let homeless families jump the queue for housing vouchers.

Early efforts to address the problem took place in an environment of political necessity. The "camp meeting"[18] atmosphere left little room for critical policy research to intrude. The commitment to compassion and action displaced inquiry. Research that reinforced this commitment could be accepted. However, research that was distant or critical found little opportunity to enter a discourse already crowded with the demands of advocates and the conflicting arguments of state agencies.

In this environment, resistance even included explicit efforts to limit the influx of new ideas and information. Ellen Bassuk, a psychiatrist who had done independent research on the homeless in Massachusetts shelters, developed a view that most of the homeless were "mentally disabled and isolated from the support that might help to reintegrate them into society."[19] Her research suggested that the state was not responding to the problem that existed—one tied closely to mental illness and the unfulfilled promises of the community mental health movement.[20]

When her findings became public, advocates saw them as a threat to their effort to frame homelessness around the right to shelter. Her position may also have conflicted with their experience. Whatever their reasons, they vigorously disputed Bassuk's findings and appealed through the political process to exclude them from the discussion. Some advocates even accused members of the state agencies of "setting Bassuk against them" to "diffuse their pressure on the state to provide affordable housing for the poor."[21]

The design of the statewide program attempted to grasp and build on the growing body of experience. It offered a new definition that emphasized the multiple causes and dimensions of homelessness and differentiated the "economic" homeless from the "situational" and "chronic" populations. This mandated a complex policy that provided both housing and social services and responded to emergency, transitional, and long-term needs.

Implementation of the new program brought political and practical conflicts that, again, monopolized attention. There was little opportunity to test the program's assumptions or examine the interactive effects of newly created relationships. When a perverse incentive was discovered that actually encouraged marginal families to make themselves homeless, the finding became the focus of a new policy crisis, another effort to "blitz the problem," and yet another reappraisal of the problem.[22] There was no way to separate thought and action, and no mechanism for combining them. Only later, when the political and economic environment shifted and the political commitment to compassion faded, were practitioners able to reflect on previous experience and reshape the program's design.

CONCLUSION

These stories do not demonstrate much learning. The most recent and sophisticated attempt we know of to address the relationship between practice, policy, and research is the SSRC and Rockefeller Foundation project on the urban underclass. This program isolated social science research from both policy and practice. After an extended period of research, a new agenda emerged; research, policy, and practice cannot be separated. This led in turn to the renaming of the problem and the foundation's recent Conference on Persistent Urban Poverty.

The interaction of researchers, policy makers, and practitioners raised tensions and antagonisms. These were recognized but not focused on at the conference, and an attempt was made to synthesize what could be agreed on across perspectives. While there is nothing wrong with codifying agreement, we think efforts of this kind cannot proceed without recognizing and attempting to cope with the tensions among research, policy, and practice.

The idea of a divided profession may offer a productive way to examine these tensions. This approach builds on the metaphor of a divided self, which recognizes the tensions that often characterize an individual's beliefs and desires and the problem this presents for rational action.[23] The divided profession recognizes that research, policy, and practice must be seen as distinct and valid, but interdependent, perspectives.

Bringing research, policy, and practice together is not likely to be an easy task. It will mean accepting and trying to understand conflicts and tensions in the way problems are perceived, knowledge is needed, and outcomes are desired. Institutional grounding, gaps in language, and communication, and habits of practice are likely to add another layer of problems. Integration will have to be seen as a process of balancing tensions and bridging differences.

As difficult as these problems may seem, we feel that working on them is likely to be more productive than the approach of separating research, policy, and practice. The metaphor of a divided profession needs to be developed, as do its implications for integrating research, policy, and practice. We close with it in the hope that it offers a beginning for further and productive work.

ACKNOWLEDGMENTS

We would like to thank our colleagues with whom we have discussed the argument in detail for their help and suggestions. Donald Schon and Langley Keyes provided a sounding board at several critical points. David Cohen, as one of the few people we know who is working on the interaction of research, policy, and practice, offered helpful discussion and insights. Sheldon White provided us with many stimulating and evocative metaphors and helped us to lay out the field in a suggestive way. Monika Wohlrad-Sahr provided helpful comments. Finally, special thanks go to Carol Weiss for her insights and her help in disciplining our thoughts and for connecting us to an expanding body of relevant literature.

NOTES

1. Donald Schon, personal communication.

2. This criticism is echoed by other researchers concerned with practice. Donald Schon has reached similar conclusions with respect to the study of organizations. White goes on to suggest that researchers move out of the laboratory and into the "functioning educational system" in order to address the deficiencies in current relationships and to "pass beyond the legendary and stereotypic."

3. Practice may also neglect research. Sheldon White discusses two presentations that focused on how research that is successful and has implications for practice, including some that was evaluated positively, often fails to have any effect on practice. For a related view in psychotherapy, see John A. Lindon, "Does Technique Require Theory?" *Bulletin of the Menniner Clinic: A Journal of the Mental Health Professions* (Lindon, 1991). Lindon argues, inter alia, that what is crucial for good practice isn't the theory that guides it, but the ability of the analyst to "be attuned to the patient's central effects states." This is part of a more general argument that research and practice are distinct activities.

4. This built on the experience of the Joint Center for Urban Studies of MIT and Harvard, which was organized in 1959. Part of the rationale for the center was to "push for a broader and more direct involvement on the part of the social sciences in urban and regional studies" (Rodwin, 1981, 268).

5. Institutional factors such as a shortage of courses which pushes students to become involved in disciplinary departments, or the need to compete for sources of funding, which favor traditional social science approaches. See also Judith Innes et al., "Report to the Commission on the Doctorate in Planning to the Association of Collegiate Schools of Planning, 1992" (Innes et al., 1992), and Bish Sanyal, "Some Tentative Interpretations about Students' Comments on Ph.D. Education in Planning" (Sanyal, n.d.). Professor Sanyal was on the Commission on the Doctorate in Planning. The commission's report noted that "From the faculty viewpoint, common weaknesses of the students lie in their difficulties in framing researchable questions, [and] in their preparation in formal methodologies" (p. 15). The commission tried to classify dissertation topics in a sample of 311 dissertations from planning departments in the 1980s as to whether they were "theoretical or practice-related, academic or policy-oriented." This attempt was inconclusive because they "could agree neither on the categories nor on how to classify individual abstracts within categories." Their comments are instructive, however. "Our problem mirrors the dilemma of the field and is an indicator of how we as faculty have difficulty advising students about appropriate research topics. It also suggests that concerns of faculty about the 'relevance' of dissertations may mean different things to departments or individuals" (p. 18).

6. It is somewhat ironic that this movement occurred in public policy schools that originally differentiated themselves from the practice-oriented schools of public administration, which, in turn, had been established in reaction to the way practice was

taught in political science departments. The schools of public administration sought more practical and applied knowledge than was being offered in traditional disciplinary departments. Over the years, the teaching of public administration languished largely because it was unable to develop a more general theory and was simply a weak program. Schools of public policy began to replace the programs in public administration. The analytic knowledge base became essentially applied microeconomics analysis, while the policy making component focused on the process of public decision-making. The dominant theme, however, was policy analysis, and the more the analytic framework was developed the less the program became relevant for practitioners. In some cases, practice reasserted itself, and a struggle between administration and the newly developed field of policy analysis emerged in the schools of public policy. The outcome was that some schools, such as the Kennedy School at Harvard, were renamed schools of public policy and administration. The tension between the two forms of knowledge persisted, now within the same school, polarized into those concerned with practice and those concerned with research and theory building.

7. Lawrence Lynn (1992) cites comments by Eugene Bardach: "How can the systematic scholarly study of public management be made to serve the needs of practicing managers? By articulating, refining, and circumscribing the knowledge about management that the wise and experienced already have"; by Robert Behn: "The task of the public management scholar is to analyze specific examples of public management, to extract principles from them and to examine why and when these principles apply"; by Alan Altshuler: "The most fruitful path to public management theory is to observe practice closely, and, more specifically, the best way scholars can help improve public management is to search out, observe, and think hard about 'best practices'" among others as evidence of the support this view has enjoyed in the public policy community.

8. Donald Schon and Martin Rein (Schon & Rein, 1993) point out the contrast between the stature of practitioners and the relative stature enjoyed by disciplinary researchers in Glazer's (1974) description of the "minor professions."

9. See, for instance, Chris Argyris's (1993) discussion of the problem of "actionability" in *On Organizational Learning*. Cambridge, MA: Blackwell

10. See, in particular, Charles Lindblom. (1990) *Inquiry and Change: The Troubled Attempt to Understand and Shape Society.*

11. This is one of the "reactionary rhetorics" that Albert Hirschman has described in *The Rhetoric of Reason.*

12. We recognize that actors will often find themselves in roles that span or merge two or more of the perspectives we identify in the triad. We readily accept this ambiguity; it seems to us a strength that the model can explain tensions felt by individual actors as well as impairment and tension experienced in broader communities.

13. We thank Carol Weiss for this insight.

14. MEAP is the branch of the Michigan Department of Education concerned with statewide testing and assessment.

15. The old definition defined reading as "the process of transforming the visual representation of language into meaning. Thus an idea is being transferred from the written page to the reader's mind." The revised definition described reading as "the process of constructing meaning through the dynamic interaction among the reader's existing knowledge, the information suggested by the written language, and the context of the reading situation" (Wixson and Peters, 1984, in Weiss and Cohen, 10).

16. Weiss and Cohen point out that the policy changes were not irrelevant to these teachers. The policy changes "legitimated what these teachers were trying to do." Some felt they gained enhanced respect and all "felt vindicated by their exposure to research" (p. 18).

17. This account is derived from "Homeless in Massachusetts," Chapter 6 in Schon and Rein, earlier versions of the case, and discussions with those authors and with Langley Keyes. Keyes is a professor at MIT who was on leave and working with the Executive Office of Community Development during the effort to develop a policy on homelessness.

18. This description was given by Langley Keyes in Schon and Rein, page 136.

19. Ellen Bassuk, (1984) "The Homelessness Problem," *Scientific American* 251: 40–45.

20. Schon and Rein, page139.

21. Ibid., page139

22. Ibid. pp. 153–154 and note 25. The flaw occurred because of the policy of giving priority for housing vouchers to families in emergency shelters. This created an incentive for families in marginal housing situations to make themselves homeless in order to get access to benefits and improve their situation in the long run. This strategy was recognized by families, advocates and social workers, and even landlords. New York and other states later encountered similar problems. The rising number of families in emergency shelters was troubling to Dukakis, who was already contemplating a run for the presidency. He ordered agency heads to "get the numbers down."

23. See, for instance, Thomas Schelling, (1984) "Self-Command in Practice, in Policy, and in a Theory of Rational Choice" *American Economic Review* 74: 1–11.

5

Content Analysis of Social Work Dissertation Papers: Epistemological Implications

Richard E. Boettcher

A recurrent theme among the writings of those who analyze the nature and structure of the professions is the significance accorded to a profession's claim to specialized knowledge. From Flexner (Flexner, 1915) to Abbott (Abbott, 1988), we are reminded that the conveyance of professional status to any occupational group is strongly dependent on the group's claim to specialized knowledge that is systematic, educationally transmissible, and continually expandable through scholarship and research. Fraser (Fraser, 1994) refers to a profession's capacity both to generate and to transmit knowledge about practice as a defining element of that profession.

Since the beginning of the twentieth century, professions have relied increasingly on universities as the source of new knowledge through research. This observation is most certainly true for the profession of social work and for those who serve the profession in its academic arenas. As the emphasis on knowledge development through the professoriate has taken root and expanded in this century, there has been correlated growth in doctoral education in the schools of social work in North America (Orcutt, 1990). Under the close supervision of faculty experienced in research, doctoral students are expected to make a significant contribution to the knowledge base of the profession and to become committed to the habits of scholarly productivity. Thus, it is assumed that doctoral research is a very significant link in the intellectual food chain that nourishes the profession.

The purpose of this chapter is to report on a study of social work dissertations presented over a period of five years at a national symposium, organized by the College of Social Work of the Ohio State University, that focuses on doctoral research and its linkage to social work practice. A basic assumption behind this study is that doctoral research is a rich source of new information that may be highly significant to the development of the profession's knowledge base, which in turn undergirds the practice of social work. This position is close to the view of Orcutt (Orcutt, 1990), who argues that doctoral education in social work should prepare students for social scientific theory development and research, with a specific emphasis on its application to social work practice settings. The overarching purpose of this study is to determine the extent to which my underlying assumptions concerning the significance of dissertation research to professional knowledge development are supported by the dissertations themselves.

BACKGROUND AND CONCEPTUAL FRAMEWORK

The present study was guided by three questions; the first, epistemological,[1] and the second and third are methodological. First, I was interested in determining the types of knowledge generated by social work dissertations. Different disciplines and professions rely on different "ways of knowing," with the "scientific way of knowing" predominating in western thought. In this study, I assess the types of knowledge generated by the dissertations by using Greenwood's (Greenwood, 1957) framework for classifying social work research. This framework is summarized in Table 5.1.

According to Greenwood's typology, social work research consists of two main classes: operational research and basic social work research. *Operational research* refers to descriptions and enumerations of the characteristics and attributes of organizational operations, client groups, cohorts, and populations. Such characteristics include the group's environment, as well as the nature of the social work job performed in an organizational context. *Basic social work research* is always applied research. It differs from operational research in its predication on theoretical foundations that are directly related to social work history, philosophy, culture, or practice. According to Greenwood's theory, basic social work research has greater potential for contributing to the knowledge of the profession than operational research. Greenwood includes humanistic, scientific, and philosophical "types of knowledge" under the rubric of basic social work research. By doing so, his typology acknowledges that inquiries into these three areas may contribute significantly to the knowledge base of the profession.

The second question guiding my study of dissertations concerns the types of research designs employed. For the purposes of classifying the dissertation studies according to research design, I employed the taxonomy of research design developed by Tripodi (Tripodi, 1981), and presented here in Table 5.2. The advantage of Tripodi's taxonomy over other possible choices is that the various designs are shown to be related to types and levels of knowledge associated with the designs.

The types of knowledge objectives presented in Table 5.2 are on a continuum in terms of their potential contribution to the goals of scientific research, namely, explanation and prediction. The lowest level knowledge objective involves the development of concepts, variables, and hypotheses and is termed hypothetical-developmental. Reasearch aimed at this objective produces virtutally no explanatory or predictive information.

The highest level knowledge objective for social work research is cause/effect knowledge. The pursuit of this objective through research seeks to produce information that may confirm or disconfirm theories that hypothesize cause and effect relationships between variables. The goals of explanation and prediction are best served by cause and effect knowledge objectives.

Table 5.1
Greenwood's Conceptions of Operational and Basic Social Work Research

A. Operational Social Work Research	
1. Descriptive statistics	Simple fact gathering, service, auditing, accounting.
2. Planning information	Enumeration and facts gathered to help plan services, define problems.
3. Administrative information	Enumeration and data collection relevant to the efficient operations of social services.
B. Basic Social Work Research	
1. Historico-sociological knowledge	Qualitative interpretations of trends, values, and cultural motifs affecting the profession and society.
a. Social work history	The evolution and trends of the profession and its institutions.
b. Social work philosophy	The value bases and moral premises of the profession and its institutions.
c. Social work culture	The social organization of the profession and its institutions.
2. Measurement theory	Construction and utilization of measuring devices used in social work practice.
3. Practice theory	Organized body of principles that guide social work practice.
a. Diagnostic	Propositions that enable the assessment principles practitioner to classify and understand the gestalt of the practice situation.
b. Treatment or intervention	Propositions that guide practitioner principles choice in designing and effecting interventions.

The highest level of knowledge objective for social work research is cause/effect knowledge. The pursuit of this objective through research seeks to produce information that may confirm or disconfirm theories that hypothesize cause and effect relationships between variables. The goals of explanation and prediction are best served by cause and effect knowledge objectives.

Quantitative-descriptive and associational knowledge are ranked second and third, respectively, on the continuum of research objectives. Quantitative knowledge deals with facts that distinguish one set of phenomena from another (e.g., men and women; ethnic groups; occupations), but this type of knowledge offers no explanation for the observed differences. Associational knowledge both demonstrates and suggests explanations of observed relationships and differences.

Finally, the continuum of knowledge objectives in Table 5.2 is related to a similar continuum of standard research designs that serve as the frameworks of research studies. Low-order designs (e.g., cross-sectional or longitudinal case studies) yield low levels of knowledge. Higher order designs (e.g., classical experimental or interrupted time series) are intended to yield high levels of knowledge.

The third question I explored was the extent to which the dissertation studies were guided by *a priori* theoretical formulations, and the ways in which these theories were applicable to social work knowledge. Associated with this emphasis on the use of theory were the additional considerations of the quality of the data, the base on which the research was developed, and the question of how systematically the design was implemented (Kerlinger, 1973).

Table 5.2

Tripodi's Taxonomy of Research Designs and Related Knowledge Objectives

Research Design	Knowledge Objective
1a. Cross-sectional case study	Hypothetical-Developmental
1b. Longitudinal case study	
1c. Purposive cohort exploratory study	
2a. Cross-sectional survey	Quantitative-Descriptive
2b. Replicated cross-sectional survey	
3a. One group pretest-posttest	Associational
3b. Static group comparison	
4a. Classical experiment	Cause/Effect
4b. Posttest only control group	
4c. Nonequivalent group comparison	
4d. Interrupted time series	

DATA SOURCES AND METHODS

Since 1985, the College of Social Work of the Ohio State University has sponsored a conference featuring social work doctoral dissertation research.[2] Recent graduates of social work doctoral programs from across the country are invited to submit scholarly papers derived from their completed dissertations. One purpose for the conference is to provide doctorates with a forum for the presentation of their research. A second and equally important goal is to promote a dialogue between the researchers and social work practitioners. To this end, panels of social work practitioners, administrators, and policy analysts are assembled to react to and comment on the dissertation research presentations. The present study examines the dissertations presented from 1985 to 1989.

A total of 103 papers were presented at the five conferences. The papers were written in accordance with a common format required of all presenters and published in an annual conference proceeding. Table 5.3 provides a breakdown by year of the numbers of paper submissions, selected presentations, conference papers published, and the total number of dissertations completed in social work nationally. The table is largely self-explanatory; however, it is worth clarifying that only 72 of the 103 presented papers were published, because of the presenters' failure to submit final manuscripts in time to meet printing deadlines.

The published papers, 72 in number, constitute a purposive sample of doctoral dissertations completed during the period of 1985–89. The published papers represent 8 percent of all social work dissertations completed during that time frame. This is neither a randomly selected sample; nor is it a large sample. The representativeness of this body of work cannot be easily estimated since the submitters were initially self-selected, and those papers ultimately presented were selected by competitive, blind review. Taken as a whole, the 72 papers reflect how some students, advisors, and faculty regard the purposes, functions, scope, and methodologies of doctoral research in social work. Whether the conclusions drawn from this content analysis of dissertation papers are representative of the body of work done in the name of doctoral research in social work for the time period 1985–89 can only be approximated by comparisons with other studies of a similar nature, and is a question awaiting fuller investigation.

Table 5.3
Dissertation Papers Submitted, Selected, and Published by OSU Conference 1985–89, and Social Work Dissertations Completed 1984–88

	1985	1986	1987	1988	1989	Totals	Ratios[b]
Papers submitted	50	40	38	44	42	214	24.6%
Papers selected and presented	26	13	18	27	19	103	11.9%
Papers published	9	11	16	22	14	72	8.3%
Social work dissertations completed 1984–88[a]	162	191	171	174	171	869	

[a]From Dissertation Abstracts

[b]The percentage of the total of 869 dissertations completed from 1984 to 1988.

The schools and universities represented by the dissertations presented at the conferences are shown in Table 5.4. About three-fifths (32 of 54) of the social work doctoral programs are represented in the five-year cohort. All sections of the country are represented.

Two persons independently read and classified each dissertation paper according to the Greenwood taxonomy for types of studies and the Tripodi schema for research designs, and assessed their theoretical underpinnings. Greenwood's typology of epistemology and Tripodi's typology of research design proved adequate except in the following circumstances. When difficulties were encountered in differentiating between operational planning studies and basic social work practice theory studies, classification was determined on the basis of whether the investigator was attempting to confirm either a social work or a social science theory through the investigation. If either social science or social work theory was evident, we classified the study as a basic practice theory study, provided that the author made explicit applications to social work. In the absence of theory, or if applications to social work were not evident, the study was classified as operational. On the whole, the Tripodi typology, presented in Table 5.2, satisfactorily embraced the range of designs found in the dissertation studies except for the need to add one subtype, namely, the "purposive cohort exploratory study," designated 1c in Table 5.2. This design subtype applies to that research in which the investigator purposively selects a very small number of subjects or cases to study in an exploratory way. Hence, it is differentiated from the case study design because it involves more than one subject, and it is differentiated from the higher order cross-sectional design because it does not involve random selection.

Theory documentation was straightforward and descriptive in form. The various theoretical constructs and propositions articulated by the dissertation authors were enumerated, and the authors' labels were employed. If an author indicated that the study employed exchange theory as a conceptual backdrop and discussed this theory in relation to the study findings, then we credited the study with employing exchange theory. Some authors employed more than a single theoretical frame of reference. Therefore, the types of theories employed outnumber the studies in which theories were found.

FINDINGS

From Table 5.5, it may be noted that 41 of the 72 studies (57%) are illustrative of operational social work research. As such, according to Greenwood's "types of studies," these dissertations probably make only a limited contribution to the social work knowledge base. A total of 23 (32%) are classified as practice theory studies, indicating more fundamental contributions.

As shown in Table 5.6, the cross-sectional survey design was the modal type employed by the dissertation researchers. When combined with the "purposive cohort exploratory study," which also employs cross-sectional observational methods, the survey design accounts for 39 of the 72 studies. Cumulatively, 53 of the 72 studies (74%) in the sample are associated with Tripodi's hypothetical-developmental or quantitative-descriptive knowledge objectives; 26% are at the associational knowledge level or beyond.

It is worthy of note that there are six experiments and two quasi-experiments. From this it would appear that the most rigorous forms of research design have not penetrated doctoral research to a significant degree.

The most notable observation reported in Table 5.7 is that 28 of the studies are atheoretical. That is, the authors of these studies make no reference to any theories, perspectives, or analytic frameworks that may be said to guide and direct the inquiry. These studies are about questions or issues which the authors attempt to answer by data collection without reference to explicit hypotheses or theoretical constructs.

Sixteen studies employed some type of theory related to the systems' family; nine were related to stress, crisis, and social support; seven employed theories about organizations. Nine studies employed seven distinct theories of human growth and development. These results show a lack of unifying theoretical focus in recent doctoral research as the dissertations reflect a wide range of theories that extend in diverse directions across several cognitive maps.

Table 5.4
Universities Represented by Doctoral Dissertation Papers
Published by OSU Conference Proceedings, 1985–89 (N=32)

University	Papers Presented
Adelphi University	1
Barry University	1
Bryn Mawr College	1
Case Western Reserve	4
Columbia University	3
Florida State University	1
Howard University	5
St. Louis University	1
University of Southern California	2
Tulane University	1
Catholic University of America	5
University of Alabama	3
University of Illinois (Chicago)	4
The Ohio State University	9
University of California/Berkeley	2
University of California/L.A.	2
University of Chicago	2
University of Denver	1
University of Kansas	1
University of Maryland	1
University of Michigan	3
University of Minnesota	1
University of Pittsburgh	3
University of Pennsylvania	2
University of Texas (Arlington)	2
University of Texas (Austin)	2
University of Utah	1
University of Washington	1
University of Wisconsin (Madison)	1
University of Wisconsin (Milwaukee)	1
Virginia Commonwealth University	3
Hunter College	1
Total	72

All of the dissertation papers reviewed in this study approach their objective of knowledge development by employing the canons of science. None is an example of either the philosophical or the humanistic ways of knowing. Even the "qualitative" studies are, in reality, examples of quantitative pilot research rather than case studies. Furthermore, those studies that attempt to contribute to historico-sociological knowledge employ questionnaire survey methods rather than traditional methods of historical or philosophical research. Given that these dissertation papers reflect the scientific approach to knowledge building, they were evaluated for their adherence to some of the characteristics of the scientific approach to knowledge building.

Table 5.5

Types of Social Work Research according to Greenwood Typology Represented by Dissertation Papers Published in OSU Conference Proceedings 1985–89 (N=72)[a]

Classification	1985	1986	1987	1988	1989	Total	%
A. Operational Social Work Research							
1. Planning information	4	6	9	10	7	36	(50.0)
2. Administrative information	1		1	2	1	5	(6.9)
B. Basic Social Work Research							
1. Historico-sociological knowledge							
a. Social work history	1		2			3	(4.1)
b. Social work philosophy					2	2	(2.8)
c. Social work culture	1		1			2	(2.8)
2. Measurement theory				1		1	(1.4)
3. Practice theory							
a Assessment principles	1	3	1	5	2	12	(16.7)
b. Intervention principles	1	2	2	4	2	11	(15.3)
Total	9	11	16	22	14	72	(100.0)

[a] Figures in parenthesis are precentages of the total number of papers presented.

DISCUSSION

Systematic Methodology

The dissertations demonstrate a wide range of techniques and methods employed to reduce observer and subject bias. Standardized instrumentation is employed in order to encourage higher levels of reliability and validity in observation and measurement. With respect to standardization of instrumentation, the dissertation papers reflect a close allegiance to the principles of scientific measurement and methodology.

In terms of the underlying logical designs of the studies, there is a rather high reliance on a single methodology, namely, the survey method employed in both the purposive cohort exploratory studies (1c) and the cross-sectional studies (2a). The survey method of research design is employed in 39 of the 72 studies. According to the typology offered by Tripodi, this methodology is associated with hypothetical-developmental or quantitative-descriptive knowledge.

As such, this design produces information that is unlikely to have a significant influence on the propositional thinking of practicing social workers and thus could be considered a methodological weakness.

Table 5.6
Research Designs according to Tripodi Typology Found in Dissertation Papers Published in OSU Conference Proceedings, 1985–89 (N=72)[a]

Research Design	1985	1986	1987	1988	1989	Total	%
1. a. Cross-sectional case study			1	6	6	13	(18.0)
b. Longitudinal case study			1			1	(1.4)
c. Purposive cohort exploratory study	2	2	3	4		11	(15.3)
2. a. Cross-sectional survey	5	9	8	3	3	28	(38.9)
3. a. One group pretest-posttest				1	1	2	(2.8)
b. Static group comparison	1		1	4	3	9	(12.5)
4. a. Classical experiment	1		1	3		5	(6.9)
b. Posttest only				1		1	(1.4)
c. Nonequivalent group comparison			1		1	2	(2.8)
Total	9	11	16	22	14	72	(100.0)

[a] Figures in parenthesis are precentages of the total number of papers presented.

A second weakness of the dissertation papers is limited use of random sampling. The studies mainly rely on convenience or purposive samples. This approach to knowledge building places serious limits on the type of knowledge generated by the investigation. Such sampling falls short of reaching the level of knowledge development in which inference can be employed.

Theory Directed
The use of theory to guide and direct inquiry was evidenced by the broadest of definitions in only 44 of the 72 dissertations; 28 of them were atheoretical. According to Kerlinger (Kerlinger, 1973, 8), the "basic aim of science is theory." While 61 percent of the dissertations employed some kind of theoretical framework, the range and breadth of territory covered by these cognitive maps

would suggest that there is very little intellectual communication and linkage between the students and the profession at large. One grows accustomed to acknowledging that social work is a very broad profession; however, from the point of view of scientific knowledge building, it would be advantageous to witness greater linkage among studies that deal with the same class of phenomena

Table 5.7
Theoretical Frameworks Employed in Doctoral Dissertation Papers Published by OSU Conference Proceedings, 1985–89

	Theories	Total
A.	*Systems Theories*	
	Social system theory	6
	Role theory	6
	Family system theory	2
	Ecological theory	2
B.	*Organization Theories*	
	Organizational dynamics	1
	Organizational exchange/balance	2
	Leadership theory	1
	Decision-making theory	3
C.	*Human Development Theories*	
	Ego psychology	2
	Life satisfaction theory	1
	Personal adjustment theory	1
	Psychosocial development theory	1
	Social development (socialization)	1
	Self-concept theory	2
	Adult life theory	1
D.	*Sturm und Drang Theories*	
	Stress theory	5
	Crisis theory	1
	Social support theory	3
E.	*Symbolic Interaction*	1
	Neurolinguistic theory	
F.	*Social Learning Theory/Behavior Modification*	4
G.	*Political Theories*	
	Feminist theory	1
	Gender discrimination theory	1
	Diffusion of innovation theory	1
	Value theory	1
H.	*Other*	
	Family acceptance/rejection of mental health patients	1
	Family development/family stress	1
	Therapeutic communication	1
	Total theories employed:	54
	No theory employed:	28

as well as greater linkage with antecedent investigations. Moreover, even though 44 of the 72 studies reflected a theoretical base, it often appeared to be window-dressing, rather than a compass for the voyage.

The failure to actually use theory gives rise to a high percentage of operational research as compared with basic social work research. Fully 41 (57% of the dissertations were classified as operational studies. This means either that they are atheoretical (28) or that they do not translate their a priori framework into some form of basic social work questions or hypotheses.

Greenwood observed in his 1957 article that the "monopoly of operational research in social work had come to an end"; however, these papers rebut Greenwood's conclusion. Among the dissertations studied, operational research remains a prevalent mode of research, widely accepted by dissertation advisors and their students. It is perhaps sufficient to say that until we embrace the notion that scientific inquiry must be directed by theory, we shall not be in a position to make significant contributions to the knowledge base of the profession through dissertation research.

Empirical

Almost all of the dissertations reviewed for this paper appear to subscribe to the principle that there is a reality outside of the observer's selfhood that may be understood through controlled sensory observation. Almost all investigators are interested in connecting two or more variables together in ways that would explain, predict, and potentially control some element of the external world. By virtue of their approaches to measurement and observation, the investigators appear to be acknowledging that social relationships among individuals, families, and communities can be studied objectively and that these phenomena are subject to orderly patterns that can be described and potentially predicted.

Cumulative Principle

It has been observed that knowledge is power. This principle speaks to the idea that through the building up of knowledge bit by bit, idea by idea, association by association, we may achieve a situation in which we can potentially predict the occurrence of events and therefore be in a position to influence or control their occurrence. This reflects the familiar objectives of science, namely, explanation, understanding, prediction, and control. For the cumulative principle to be in effect, there must be focused attention upon an interrelated set of questions or hypotheses concerning some phenomenon as it occurs in nature or, in the case of social work, some social (i.e., human) reality. Judging from the topics and purposes espoused by the dissertations reviewed in this paper, there is little interrelationship occurring in social work dissertation research. Similarly, judging from the array of theories employed to guide these studies, there is a diversity in perspective that is almost as wide as the entire social and behavioral sciences. This absence of consensus on central questions in basic social work research is particularly disturbing insofar as it undermines completely the cumulative principle of science and leads instead to a chaotic array of information that cannot purport to contribute to a scientifically oriented social work practice.

It is interesting to compare the findings of this research with findings from other similar studies. Briar studied the abstracts of 162 social work dissertations completed in 1982–83 (Briar, 1985). He concluded from a reading of these abstracts that 75 percent or 122 of these studies were descriptive and exploratory in nature. Such studies would most closely approximate the category of "operational research" as employed by Greenwood. Briar found that 26 dissertations were related to social work intervention, 6 were historical, 4 dealt with social work education, 3 dealt with clinical judgment, and 1 was an international dissertation focusing on international affairs. Thirty-nine dissertations, or roughly 25 percent, therefore, met the Greenwood criteria for basic social work research. Briar makes a plea for more intervention related social work research, which corresponds to Greenwood's subtype of practice theory.

Fraser, Jensen and Lewis (Fraser, Jensen, and Lewis, 1991), in a study of doctoral education in the United States, report that only about half of the 54 doctoral programs in social work place major emphasis on research scholarship and knowledge generation. Within that half, only a dozen or so programs focus in a highly intensive and rigorous way upon this curriculum objective. This finding offers one possible explanation for why the dissertations examined in this chapter reflect the undeveloped state of the methodologies, designs and theories employed in the studies.

SUMMARY AND CONCLUSIONS

The doctoral dissertations reviewed for this study are flawed in several respects in relation to the canons of a scientific epistemology. Although there are a few notable exceptions, these dissertations as a group tend to employ relatively weak underlying logical designs; very few are based on random sampling; more than half (57%) are operational studies rather than studies designed to contribute, directly or indirectly, to the knowledge base of the profession; many (39%) are overtly atheoretical; and there is a noticeable absence of adherence to the cumulative principle of science in terms of the questions addressed and theories employed.

The present study of dissertations is itself flawed by the purposive nature of its own sampling method. On the other hand, these dissertations were selected for presentation through a competitive evaluation in which the evaluators employed standards for knowledge building. These dissertations were judged to be the "best" among those submitted for presentation. Even if the sampling error for this study was as high as 25 percent, it would still mean that a very large number of Ph.D. dissertations in social work completed between 1985 and 1989 would fail the Greenwood criteria for basic social work research. Other studies, cited in this chapter, tend to support this conclusion.

Social work doctoral research is one of the very few venues available to the profession in which theory-driven, rigorous, and systematic investigations can be conducted. The findings of this study of Ph.D. dissertations in social work suggest that additional research based on a national sample is both warranted and urgently needed.

NOTES

1. Epistemology is the study of the origin, nature, methods and limits of human knowledge (Random House Dictionary, 1987). It is the study of the ways in which it may be said that we "know something" about a subject matter as distinguished from how we may feel about it or what we may believe about it. As a subfield of philosophy, epistemology deals with the ways in which we fix belief about the validity about an idea, phenomenon or occurrence.

2. The conference was not held in 1991 or 1992, but resumed in 1993.

6

Research and Social Policy: Conceptual Frameworks and Social Inequality

Adam Jamrozik

Conceptual frameworks used in social research are not value neutral. From unstated assumptions and formulated hypotheses to methods of investigation and reporting results,values pervade the process of research and influence the selection of issues for investigation, the analysis of data, and the interpretations of findings. Consideration of the values implicit in research is especially important in policy-relevant research, as the prevailing methodological trends that emerged in the 1980s have often served to legitimate social inequalities created by social and economic policies.

This chapter examines the relationship between social research and social policy. It draws on observations of the developments in this area of social activity in Australia and notes two trends in these developments: first, the government's growing interest in, and sponsorship of, policy-relevant research has brought with it greater government control of the research agenda; and, second, the theoretical orientation of policy-relevant research has shifted from sociological concepts and perspectives to economic theories—especially to the theories and concepts of the "neoclassical" economics and economic rationalism. Researchers thus tend to reflect the temper of the times, focusing on research that perceives and interprets social issues in economic perspectives and serves to validate government social policy by the criteria of economic rationality.

In terms of policy-relevant research, the most significant feature of the 1980s was the prominence gained by economists. In contrast to the growing input of policy-relevant research from the field of economics, input of comparable research from the field of sociology decreased, and research from schools of social work and social work practitioners was so rare as to be almost nonexistent. These trends pose some important theoretical and value questions concerning the role of the social sciences in contemporary societies and, in particular, their role in providing data input for social policy formulation. The observed trends pose especially relevant questions concerning the role of social work in the field of the social sciences, in social research, and in policy input and policy implementation through administration of services and service delivery.

The observations and comments presented in this chapter are based on the author's experience in social work education and social research in Australia. Whether or to what extent the observed trends are present in other countries is an open question; nevertheless, the issues raised in this paper have universal implications for the role of the social sciences and social research in social policy.

ASSUMPTIONS AND VALUES IN SOCIAL RESEARCH

Research conducted in the various disciplines of the social sciences has enormous potential for input into social policy. Social scientists, practicing professionals in human services, and especially researchers engaged in social analyses and policy-relevant research all address policy issues in their work and authoritatively define social reality through the interpretation of their findings. For this reason, what social scientists do, how they do it, and why they do it, are important social—and even moral—issues. Whether the researcher deliberately intends it or not, there is always a social effect of some significance emanating from the conducted research, even if the effect is confined only to placing certain issues on public notice. Most social research, however, is conducted with certain aims that influence the selection of the issues for investigation, as well as the method of inquiry and the analysis of data. *Quis custodiet ipsos custodes*— who guards the guardians—is thus a relevant question to ask here.

The fact that no research and no theoretical framework guiding research is value-free is especially true in research concerned with social issues or issues in social policy. As Hugh Stretton has observed, "Values are built into theories and methods in many and various ways" (Stretton, 1976, 138–139). This certainly does not mean that research cannot be conducted with objectivity. However, objectivity can be achieved not by claims of value neutrality, but by the researcher's revelation of his or her value stance and the stated (and, if possible, also the unstated) assumptions on which the research design has been formulated. Unfortunately, such revelations in research monographs are rare.

The reasons for conducting a given research project are equally important. The reason may be only the researcher's endeavor to explain certain phenomena, but it may also be a desire to achieve a certain social purpose; for example, to turn public attention to certain issues or "problems," or to provide data for remedial intervention into such "problems." Sponsors of research, too, will have certain aims, which may not always be stated explicitly or clearly or be identical to the researcher's aims. Yet the notion of value-free science is still held in some quarters. Claims of "value neutrality" in research are still made frequently, even when the aims of the research, the methods used, and the interpretation of data are well-grounded in normative assumptions and beliefs or are clearly related to certain policy issues or objectives.

These issues are important because the results of research activities— presented in books, journals, and conference papers—do have an effect, if not always on policy directly, then certainly on the opinions held in the community at large. The authoritative nature of research findings emanating from known social scientists and research institutes—especially economic researchers and institutes—does have an effect on public opinion, if only by placing an issue in the public arena. Often, the knowledge generated and disseminated by such institutes reaches the public in a mediated form through the mass media, affected by selectivity or bias of interpretation. While the researcher cannot be held responsible for the working of the mass media, there is a need to be aware of the probability of such outcomes.

It is also to be expected that with the developments in the social sciences and in correspondingly more sophisticated methods of economic research, governments would not only want to use research findings to affect, evaluate, or validate policy but would also want to exercise influence over the research agenda, the output of the research, and its dissemination. The government may exercise control over these activities by allocating research funds to certain researchers or research institutes, by appointing "politically reliable" persons to boards of management or advisory committees, and by publicizing certain research activities while discouraging or criticizing others.   Thus, while governments need research for policy formulation, they often use it as *policy validation* or, as Gouldner expressed it some years ago (Gouldner, 1971, 349), as *rhetoric* in support of their policies.

The interests of researchers engaged in policy-relevant research also constitute an important factor in the role the social sciences play in the allocation of resources by governments, thus contributing, directly or indirectly, to policies of equality or inequality. Researchers want to do research that is "worth doing" in relation to a certain purpose, and they do obtain some gratification when they see their findings adopted by policy makers. As Helga Nowotny has observed, "One of the strongest underlying assumptions of social science research has always been that of intended usefulness. The often covert ethical tenet is one of public service, one that dates back to the old wish of serving as adviser to the Prince" (Nowotny & Lambiri-Dimaki, 1985, 7). For these reasons, it is appropriate to consider how the issues discussed so far are reflected in the conceptual frameworks used in social research—especially in policy-relevant research.

CONCEPTUAL FRAMEWORKS IN RESEARCH

Issues of social research are considered here in a comprehensive analytical framework in which the research process is perceived as an integrated system of ideas, values, and principles, which together determine the object of research, the method of inquiry, and the analysis of data. The framework includes:

- The theoretical and normative assumptions on which the process of conceptualization is built,

- The level of conceptualization and formation of research design and its implementation,

- The control of the research agenda and sources of research questions,

- The dissemination of findings,

- The relationship between the researcher and the sponsor of research.

In the light of the observed developments during the 1980s, a brief comment on each of these aspects will illustrate the significance of the issues involved.

First, the process of conceptualization is rarely, if ever, revealed in its entirety in a research monograph. The researcher's failure to make explicit the assumptions, the value base, and the reasons for conducting a given research project gives the impression of a self-evident objectivity and scientific validity. Yet policy-relevant research tends to focus on the so-called problem areas, or "undesirable" conditions such as poverty, unemployment, crime, and single parenthood. In all such research, there is an implied, if not always explicit, "correctionist" stance—namely, that the conduct of research into these "problem areas" indicates a desire to alleviate or eliminate the examined condition. Such an approach to social research does not necessarily lead to policy action aimed at achieving the intended outcome; on the contrary, research of this nature may, and often does, serve to legitimate a lack of action about a given condition, as the research itself is presented to the community as an expression of concern and a form of remedial action.

Second, the level of conceptualization and the investigation and analysis that follow it tend to focus on the symptoms of the underlying social causes rather than on the causes themselves. The symptoms thus acquire an "ontological" existence; that is, a sui generis condition unrelated to the underlying causes. Having been conceptualized as such, the symptoms are related to the characteristics of the affected population and are explained in those terms. Methods of policy response then focus on those characteristics rather than on the policy itself; poverty, unemployment, and family violence are some examples of this approach.

Third, the control of the research agenda and corresponding sources of research questions looms increasingly larger as an ethical and political issue in policy-relevant research. While this issue undoubtedly has always been present to some degree, there is now ample evidence that since the early 1980s, governments of all political persuasions, and certainly the Australian federal government and its bureaucracy, have increased their control over the research agenda as a whole and over policy-relevant research especially. This has been achieved by a range of measures that include the allocation of research funds for specific areas of policy, the commission of specific research projects to selected consultants, the appointment of "politically reliable" persons to advisory committees and boards of management in government-financed research institutes, and the prescription of certain methods of inquiry as a condition of sponsorship.

Fourth, the dissemination of research findings is related to the issue of the ownership of intellectual property. In research institutes funded by the government, decisions about the publication of research findings are now made by government-appointed directors or by boards of management. Research projects commissioned by the government are published only after approval by the minister concerned, and some research reports are never released for publication. Moreover, dissemination of a report may be either wide or restricted. In a broader sphere, efforts are now being made in some quarters to alienate the producers of knowledge and information from their products. For example, the Vice-Chancellors' Committee of Australian universities (AVCC) has advised the universities "to revise their statutes, making clear that they [the universities] hold copyright in a range of educational materials, including lecture notes and tapes" (Wicken, 1991).

Fifth, the researcher/sponsor relationship, which has always been one of the problematics in policy-relevant research, acquired a new significance in the 1980s. Because of conditions imposed in some research grants provided by government bodies, there has been an increasing rapprochement between researchers and policy makers. As a result, policy-relevant research has served increasingly either to validate government policies in a way not necessarily intended by the researcher or to produce rather trivial results, indicating concerns that have already been expressed by the government and are rather "harmless" in their interpretations, conclusions, or suggestions for action. Increasingly, too, research methods in some policy-relevant research have tended to reflect the value position of policy makers, accepting and validating, as it were, the prevalent social policies in which inequality of resource allocation is justified by claims of economic necessity.

IS THIS A CAUSE FOR CONCERN?

At this point it is appropriate to ask: Why should we be concerned about these issues, especially about the issue of inequality? In the light of the earlier observations, at least four reasons may be advanced to substantiate the concern: first is the democratic ideal of equality embedded in the principles of social democracy; second are the ideals and goals of what may still be called "the welfare state," even if that concept has been eroded severely over the past two decades or so; third is the value base of at least some social sciences, especially sociology; and fourth is the expressed value base of the professions such as social work that are engaged in human services and that draw on the knowledge generated by the social sciences. In all four areas, the ideals are, more often than not, exactly that—ideals—but they serve as signposts indicating the direction that the societies claiming to subscribe to these ideals should pursue. It would follow, then, that social scientists and researchers who perform their tasks with societal sanctions should be expected to follow these ideals as well.

As far as sociology is concerned, issues of social inequality were prominent in the work of its founding fathers, and the discipline still claims these issues as its central interests. For example, Bryan Turner observes: "Sociologists have been concerned to understand the nature of social inequality since the origins of sociology itself. Indeed, we can virtually define the core of sociology as an inquiry into the origins, characteristics and consequences of social inequality defined in terms of power, status and class" (Turner, 1986, 30). Moreover, a well-known Australian sociologist, Sol Encel, asserts: "The task of the social sciences, and especially of sociology, begins with the exploration of the social division, cleavage and conflict arising from the tension between natural equality and established social inequality" (Encel, 1970, 6). Does this concern with inequality mean that the value base of sociology is the pursuit of equality, or is it simply an aim to explain the nature of inequality and thus validate, as it were, its existence in society? Views on this issue would, no doubt, differ among sociologists, although most would probably claim that concern with inequality implies that the pursuit of equality is the underlying value base of sociology.

However, sociology is not the only discipline in social science engaged in studies of social and policy-relevant issues. Theoretical assumptions and value positions held by other disciplines lead to different areas of research interests and methods of inquiry. For example, there are significant differences in these aspects between sociology and economics—especially "neoclassical" economics. As Therborn notes, the prevailing position in economics is to examine social issues from the perspective of the accepted theoretical and value position of the capitalist system. Sociology, on the other hand, "developed and became decisively established as an attempt to deal with the social, moral and cultural problems of the capitalist economic order" (Theborn, 1976, 143). Indeed, the two disciplines differ considerably in their assumptions about human nature and about society. *Homo economicus* is perceived to be "a rational, self-interested, instrumental maximizer, with fixed preferences," while *homo sociologicus* is a much more complex being whose actions are influenced by "culturally given values," not solely by a "pure (culture-free) calculation of self-interest" (Hirsch, Michaels, and Friedman, 1987).

It may be expected, therefore, that policy-relevant research emanating from each of the two disciplines is likely to be different in theoretical and value assumptions and consequently different in the conceptualization of issues, in the methods of inquiry, in the analysis of data, and in the interpretations of findings. As noted earlier, policy-relevant research conducted by economists has become much more prominent over recent years in Australia than research from other disciplines. Governments show distinct preference for research conducted in the economic mode because of its "technical" rather than "political" analyses of issues, which provide them with useful data for validating their policies to the public on the grounds of economic feasibility rather than on the grounds of political choice or expediency. Furthermore, as most public officers in the Senior Executive Service (Flexner, 1915) of the federal public administration are now graduates in economics, commerce, or business administration (Pusey, 1991), they see research emanating from similar disciplines to be congruent with their own perspectives on social issues and therefore more useful to their role as technical advisers to government.

The "technical" character of policy-relevant research gives the impression of scientific objectivity, rationality, and value neutrality and is claimed as such by its protagonists. However, the concepts and methods used in the studies of that kind lead to interpretations of findings that serve to legitimize policies of social and economic inequality. I will explore two examples of such studies in the following pages: first, studies of poverty; and second, studies of government allocations of resources to services such as education, health, and welfare that are referred to as "the social wage." In using these examples, I have no intention of ascribing to the researchers any deliberate aims of legitimizing inequality; rather, the examples aim to show how certain conceptual frameworks and research methods can lead to such outcomes.

Studies of Poverty

Books, journal articles, research reports, and conference papers published over the past two decades on the subject of poverty in Australia number in the hundreds (Encel, 1988). Many of these have not been concerned with poverty, per se, but rather with the measurement of poverty. Central to these endeavors has been—and continues to be—the concept of the poverty line. In Australia, this means the Henderson Poverty Line, named after Professor Ronald Henderson, who first used the concept in that country as the basis for calculating the level of income needed by a family or an individual to maintain a minimum acceptable standard of living (Henderson, Harcourt, and Harper, 1970). This concept of the poverty line has been in use now for nearly 25 years. However important Henderson's contribution might have been originally in bringing to the community's notice the existence of poverty among widespread affluence, the use of the concept since then in determining the extent of poverty has produced some detrimental social effects.

One such effect has been the shift from the perception of poverty as a political issue to the perception of poverty as a problem susceptible to a technical solution, which thus effectively removes it from the political agenda. Through the use of the concept of the poverty line as the main or sole criterion in defining the extent of poverty, the issue of poverty has been translated into a problem of measurement, confined to a one-dimensional variable of weekly income. Measurements of poverty focused on the poverty line have become the subject of repetitive research papers in which the details and amounts of statistical data, equivalence scales, and mathematical symbols are exceeded only by their trivial nature. Some researchers using this concept do, in fact, address the question, What is wrong with the poverty line? Nevertheless, they continue to use it, and the search for further refinement of this arbitrarily reified concept continues with the researchers' undiminished dedication and fervor akin to that of the medieval alchemists' search for phlogiston and synthetic gold. For example, two such researchers, in an oft-quoted review of poverty research, question the validity of the concept by saying, "In common with earlier criticisms of Henderson line, it is shown [in their review] that this poverty standard is essentially arbitrary, the method for adjusting for families of different size and composition is of dubious relevance to Australian families, and the method of updating over time is also problematic" (Saunders & Whiteford, 1989, 2). However, having said this, the authors then admonish the critics of the concept by saying, "The onus is on those who reject the Henderson poverty line to provide an alternative poverty standard if their criticisms are to be taken seriously" (Saunders & Whiteford, 1989, 2). The essence of their argument seems to be the concern with the necessity of having a demarcation line that can serve to divide neatly "the poor" from the remainder of the population. Indeed, they argue: "In order to identify those in poverty, it is necessary to have an indicator, or set of indicators, that allow the population as a whole to be ranked on a comparable basis, and *a dividing line that separates the poor from the rest of the population* in terms of the[se] indicator[s]. This dividing line is conveniently referred to as the poverty line" (Saunders & Whiteford, 1989, 3; emphasis added)." Thus the concept of a poverty line, a methodological device that arbitrarily defines the level of poverty by the sole dimension of weekly income, also serves as a basis for social division, and for the exclusion of "the poor" from the societal context. In such a "truncated perspective" on a social and political issue, poverty becomes a sui generis phenomenon and is no longer perceived as the tail-end of inequality generated in the market economy.

However, the detrimental effects of the concept of the poverty line cut more deeply. Such a theoretically flawed "truncated perspective" leads to explanations of poverty in terms of characteristics of the affected population. For example, the notion of an "underclass," which originally was a structural concept, now serves to ascribe to the poor population certain "negative" characteristics that set it apart from the rest of the society. As Michael Katz observes, "Social science reifies social categories, turning poor people (and other groups) into one-dimensional cardboard cutouts neatly stacked and divided from one another" (Katz, 1989, 170). If the poor are portrayed as "different" in their personal characteristics from the rest of the population, their exclusion from the mainstream of social and economic life becomes politically legitimate. Furthermore, any remedial measures aimed at alleviating poverty can then be directed at the poor themselves in the effort to discover and change these "negative" characteristics.

The poor are also studied because of their accessibility. They constitute a captive audience, readily available to those researchers for whom poverty and the poor seem to hold great fascination, as well as a source of data for publishing repetitive research monographs. Such efforts are justified as an expression of concern for the poor, but they also enable the researchers to stay clear from studying those societal arrangements and processes through which inequality and consequent poverty are created and maintained.

Studies of Resource Allocation

It is an assumption of social policy studies that governmental resource allocations in welfare-oriented societies are designed to have a redistributive character, that is, that the allocations tend to favor the lower income sections of the population, thus lessening the inequalities in the distribution of primary market incomes. To achieve this objective, income tax rates increase progressively as income increases, while allocations to services such as education, health, and welfare services are claimed to increase in the opposite direction, thus benefiting the lower-income groups. The principle guiding social policy in these areas is referred to as *vertical equity*, and redistributional allocations that follow this principle are deemed to be *progressive*. They are distinct from allocations working in the opposite direction, that is, those that favor the higher income groups, which are referred to as *regressive*.

Two methods of measurement are in use in studies of governmental resource allocations: *distribution*, or the proportion (e.g., the percentage) of the total allocation received by a social or income group; and *incidence*, or the value received by any such group as a percentage of that group's income before allocation. Both methods are technically correct, but each leads to different and often entirely opposite conclusions about the redistributional effects of a given allocation. The use of the concept of incidence can be quite misleading in the interpretation of whether an allocation is progressive or regressive. The users of the incidence method define its application as follows:

The impact of tax and social security policies is considered to be neutral if those in each income decile receive the same share of benefits as they do of private income. If inequality is reduced by tax and social security programs the redistribution is considered progressive, while if it is increased, the distribution is regressive (Economic Planning Advisory Council, Paper No. 27, April 1987).

The flawed and misleading nature of this reasoning is illustrated by two examples presented in Table 6.1. The first example contains data from a 1988–89 survey of household expenditure in Australia, conducted by the Australian Bureau of Statistics, 1992; the second example draws on the same source of data except for a substitution of a hypothetical, less unequal distribution of the primary income. The allocation of education expenditure across the various income deciles is the same in both examples; however, the allocation measured by the incidence method is shown to be "progressive" in the first example and "regressive" in the second example. It is clear that this apparent incongruity is due to the different distribution of the primary income—the "independent variable" in the equation—which is taken as a "given" in the use of the incidence method.

Table 6.1
Methods of Calculating Government Allocations of Expenditure on Education

A. Actual Allocations 1988-89					
	Disposable Income		Education Expenditure Distribution		Incidence
Household Income Deciles	$	%	$	% of total	% of first column
All households	5,058	100.0	489	100.0	9.7
Lowest 3 deciles	544	10.8	68	13.9	12.5
Low-middle 3 deciles	1,225	24.2	154	31.4	12.6
Middle-high 3 deciles	2,062	40.8	19.5	39.9	9.4
Highest decile	1,227	24.3	72	14.8	5.9

B. Hypothetical Distribution of Disposable Income: Same Allocation of Expenditure					
All households	5,058	100.0	489	100.0	9.7
Lowest 3 deciles	804	15.9	68	13.9	8.5
Low-middle 3 deciles	1,650	32.6	154	31.4	9.3
Middle-high 3 deciles	1,902	37.6	19.5	39.9	10.2
Highest decile	7,02	13.9	72	14.8	10.3

Source: Australian Bureau of Statistics (1992) Household Expenditure Survey, Australia: The Effects of Government Benefits and Taxes on Income, Catalogue No. 6537.0, Australian Bureau Of Statistics, Canberra

Thus, the incidence method, although technically correct, is based on a serious theoretical flaw because it considers allocations out of context, as if government allocations functioned outside of the whole economic system. As a result, the more unequal the distribution of incomes in the market, the more progressive or "downwardly" redistributive the government allocations will appear to be, even if the allocations favor the higher-income groups. Whether intended or not, such flawed methods of measurement serve to validate policies of inequality by presenting them as "progressive" or "redistributive." It must be noted that this problem does not occur with "progressive" income tax rates, as the rates are related to the levels of income; as income levels vary, so do the tax rates, thus maintaining their progressive nature.

SOCIAL WORK AND SOCIAL RESEARCH

As mentioned earlier, research contributions to social policy from schools of social work and social work practitioners have been almost nonexistent in Australia. Yet social work practitioners' daily activities take place at what may be called the "cutting edge" of social issues and social change, and social work teachers are also directly or indirectly in contact with social processes and events of direct relevance to social policy. Both are thus in a position par excellence to observe and collect primary data on the processes and events as they occur and then to translate the results into issues of social policy.

Why, then, are social workers not doing this? A number of explanations may be advanced: It is difficult for social workers in the field to combine their daily tasks of practice with research activities; social work teachers in universities have to give priority to the education and training of students; and social work is a practice-oriented rather than research-oriented profession. Course curricula in social work do have research components, however, in most cases, these constitute only a minor part of the program. The main emphasis in undergraduate social work programs is on methods and skills of intervention in human problems and rarely extends beyond the focus on the individual, the family, or a small social group with particular characteristics. The study of community organization and development now has only a peripheral place in most curricula, as have social science subjects such as sociology. Indeed, the core of studies in most social work courses consists of both training in methods of intervention into the problems of "dependent" or "disadvantaged" individuals and families and the socialization of students into professional attitudes and values. The number of students undertaking higher-degree studies in social work is not large, and higher degrees by course work rather than by research are prevalent.

However, while these features have always been present in social work education in Australia, with the exception of a brief shift to community orientation in the early 1970s, the current focus on the individual in both social work education and practice reflects the "temper of the times," which may be defined as *retreat from social explanations*. As discussed elsewhere (Jamrozik, 1991a), this "retreat" has occurred since the mid-1970s in policy responses to social problems, in professional perceptions and methods of intervention, and in much of social welfare research. In that perspective, certain social phenomena that are considered undesirable and that are the symptoms of underlying social conditions or of economic, political, or legal arrangements have acquired their own ontological existence and are treated as such. The underlying causes are no longer examined or questioned. Thus, there is a great concern about poverty, manifest in the repeated production of statistics without any examination of the social causes of poverty. Researchers demonstrate similar attitudes towards unemployment, family violence, single parenthood, child neglect, and child abuse. The preference for treating symptoms rather than searching for explanations and causes leads to a certain legitimization of these conditions, and policies and services that are introduced to alleviate the conditions may in fact, over a period of time, contribute to their continuation and growth.

In the course of their daily endeavors, social workers come into face-to-face contact mainly, if not exclusively, with the disadvantaged sections of the population. Although it is often claimed that certain problems such as child neglect, child abuse, and family violence occur in all socioeconomic strata, recorded data clearly show that surveillance and intervention activities by public welfare agencies and social workers concentrate on low socioeconomic areas and on low socioeconomic status families (Young, Baker, and Monnone, 1989). Individually focused intervention methods lead to the perception among researchers that the problems experienced by these sections of the population can be explained in terms of their personal characteristics. When the same problems occur in other socioeconomic strata, they tend to be perceived differently and to lead to different methods of intervention—more likely under the label of "health" than "welfare" and more often treated by private (although often publicly funded) agencies where discretion and confidentiality is assured.

Perceptions and explanations of social problems in terms of the personal characteristics of the population experiencing these problems in turn lead to research projects investigating the same sections of the population. Research of this kind yields predictable results and predictable explanations, namely, a direct or inferred relationship between the problems and the characteristics of the investigated population. Such "truncated perspectives" in research on social issues of relevance to social policy serve to reinforce the beliefs of personal inadequacy and other "negative" characteristics of the poor sections of the population. The retreat from social explanations thus continues, validating existing methods of intervention and policies of inequality.

CONCLUDING REMARKS

The aim of this chapter has been to discuss certain trends in social research that have developed in Australia over the past decade or so. Characteristic features of these trends have been a growth of policy-relevant research, much of it sponsored by government, and a corresponding closer association between researchers, research institutes, and government. The outcome of these trends has been an increase of government control over the research agenda and research output that tends to reflect government social policies—often serving as the means of validating these policies. As the federal government in Australia has followed policies influenced by the "neoclassical" economic theories that accept economic and social inequality as an unavoidable feature of an efficient market economy, much of the policy-relevant research sponsored by the government has served, unwittingly perhaps, to legitimize policies of inequality.

Although the discussed issues have been drawn from the Australian experience, there are indications that similar issues have been identified and commented upon in other countries as well. Expressions of concern have been voiced particularly about the increasingly close relationship between social science research and governments and about the likely effect on the integrity of social research and its eventual usefulness for policymakers. For example, Helga Nowotny has observed that: "Too close ties to the political powers of the day turned out to be a disservice to all parties involved and more often than not, tended to be detrimental to the quality of research" (Nowotny & Lambiri-Dimaki, 1985, 13). Similar concerns have been expressed by Weiss (Weiss, 1986, 234), who sees "independence of thought, conceptual sophistication, understanding of policy issues and methodological rigour" as crucial components of social science and policy-relevant research.

The observed retreat from social explanations in social research has particular implications for social work and its relationship with the social sciences. As noted earlier, social work in Australia has contributed very little to social research; moreover, by the prevalence of its perceptions and methods of intervention in social problems, it has served unwittingly to reinforce certain beliefs that lead to policies of inequality.

For social work to reassert its "social" character and its value base, a thorough reassessment of educational programs and methods of social work intervention will be necessary. An integral part of that process will have to be a reassessment of the relationship between social work and social science, so that social work not only will continue to draw on the knowledge generated by the social sciences but will also become an important contributor to that knowledge.

Part II

SOCIAL SCIENCE TO SOCIAL WORK

Introduction: How Social Science Contributes to Social Work

Charles Garvin

In social work, there are two broad questions related to the use of social science knowledge, as well as social science methodologies for building knowledge. The first and most abstract question is the way that social workers select such knowledge and employ it to answer the question at hand. This issue is raised in every section of this book, and we refer to it as a "model of integration." Some theorists employ philosophical and ideological criteria for the selection of social science content, asking such questions as whether it is informed by a feminist perspective, by postmodernist considerations, or through the participation of the individuals and systems of concern, as in action research models. Some identify valid information as that which has been obtained in the most objective and neutral manner possible, while others are more concerned with phenomenological considerations. Still others focus on contextual issues related both to the creation of the social science knowledge as well as to the process of relating such knowledge to the question at hand. Running through each of these positions is the very fundamental question of the nature of data, and each theorist must address the issue of how qualitative and quantitative considerations entered into his or her collection.

The other broad question asks what aspects of the issue under examination can best be illuminated by consciously employing knowledge from the social sciences. We use the word "conscious" because we believe that virtually every effort by a social worker to describe or analyze a social work or social welfare situation employs terms, theories, categories, and concepts that originated with or are used by social scientists. This is not to say that there is nothing in social work other than ideas from the social sciences, but rather that social workers have not been isolated from social scientists. Instead, they have been educated in the same liberal arts, speak the same language, and are affected by the same societal conditions as those that affect social scientists and that expand or limit theorizing about the human condition. Our point, then, is to consider how social workers can expand on the conscious utilization of social science for specified social work purposes.

With respect to the model of integration, we include a chapter by Edwin Thomas in Part IV of this book: "Themes and Perspectives on Integration and Related Models." This chapter also constitutes a summary of the entire conference that produced the papers we have collected here. After examining every paper presented at the conference, Thomas generated a typology of eight integration models into which he classified every paper, as well as other major works that are not represented among the presentations. His categories include some that are very well developed—such as social research on social work and social welfare issues, research utilization, action research and empirical practice—and some that are less well developed—such as ecological, developmental research and sociopolitical change models.

The question as to what aspects of an issue can be illuminated by drawing upon the social sciences is a complex one. One way to examine this issue is to look at various aspects of theory building in social work; another is to examine phases of an intervention or policy creation/implementation process. The chapters in Part II fit with one or another of the models identified by Thomas, but focus on aspects of the intervention/policy process.

An interesting aspect of the works of several of the authors in Part II is that they demonstrate how the use of new, emerging, or developing social science theories can operate in a heuristic manner to suggest new approaches for practice and policy. Thus, the chapters here incorporate the ideas of chaos and complexity theory, grounded theory, social movement theory, and social cognitive theory.

The chapters in this section also illustrate the use of social science theory to understand human behavior involving all levels of social systems. The Brower and Nurius chapter on the use of social cognition theory has implications for interpersonal helping directed at individual change; the Fisher and Kling chapter on community organization and new social movement theory is directed at community change; the Sheinfeld Gorin and Viswanathan chapter on information theory and management decision making, the Lambert chapter on theories of occupational structure and worker well-being, and the Bernstein, Goodman, and Epstein chapter on grounded theory all focus on the level of organizational change. Finally, the Mace chapter on chaos and complexity theory has implications for intervention at all levels.

Each of the authors in this section consider the following questions of research methodology:

- What methodology should be utilized to investigate the nature of individual and systemic behaviors of concern to social workers?

- What methodology should be utilized to investigate the effectiveness of a social intervention?

- What methodology should be utilized to investigate the consequences for relevant systems of intervention programs and social policies?

The Brower and Nurius chapter indicates ways of studying cognitive phenomena; the Sheinfeld Gorin and Viswanathan chapter indicates models for studying management decision making; the Lambert chapter is an example of studying the relationship between organizational behaviors and employee consequences; and the Bernstein, Goodman, and Epstein discussion of grounded theory directly informs us of qualitative approaches for studying organizational phenomena. This latter chapter also has implications for studying the effects of social policies.

Finally, one may break down the intervention or policy formulation or implementation process into the following components. Each provides the occasion to draw upon social science theory:

- Specification of a problem

- Obtaining entry into relevant systems to initiate change

- Development of a working relationship with some part of the system

- Assessment of the relevant systems

- Goal setting

- Selection of a change strategy

- Implementation of a change strategy

- Maintenance of change

The chapters in this section do not bear upon all of these issues but can be located within them. The Sheinfeld Gorin and Viswanathan chapter is highly relevant to selection of a change strategy, in that it portrays alternative models of management decision making. The Lambert chapter is pertinent to specification of a problem and goal settings in that it suggests ways of determining issues in management decision making and how one might create appropriate goals for this process. With its participatory research model, the Bernstein, Goodman, and Epstein chapter has a great deal to say about how to enter and form working alliances during a change effort. The Fisher and Kling chapter has implications for the kinds of problems one may encounter and goals one may establish with relationship to community change efforts. Finally, the Brower and Nurius chapter also suggests new sets of goals and strategies with relationship to individual problems and individual change.

This section is rich with ideas about how social workers may benefit from integrating social science knowledge and methodology into their thinking. As can be seen from some of the topics we have generated in this introduction, there are many gaps in the ways that social science knowledge is drawn upon to enhance our understanding of social work activity. A fuller analysis of these gaps can lead our profession to the profitable retrieval of much knowledge that is likely to be useful to us. This is not to negate the hard task of assessing the effectiveness and utility of the intervention and policy consequences of this retrieval process. Nevertheless, many of the polished or unpolished jewels available in social science must first be mined and brought to light before we can fully examine the issue of utility.

7

Schemas and Niches: Social Cognitive Resources for Contemporary Social Work Practice

Aaron M. Brower and Paula S. Nurius

The linchpin of this volume is the integration of social science and social work in the service of strengthening both. In this part, our mandate is to consider ways in which our own and others' work in social science provide fuel and guidance to future directions in social work. In this chapter, we focus on some core contributions from the social psychological study of social cognition and their potential for better understanding and supporting strategies for coping and striving through social work practice. In light of the need for brevity, we will focus on cognitive schemas and how they bring greater clarity to central, but all too often fuzzy conceptions of practice, such as how people develop personal identities and mental maps of their social world; why people selectively notice and remember some things and not others; and how we draw on our past experiences, anticipate future ones, safeguard what is "known," and rebuild what is shattered.

Specifically, in this chapter we discuss what cognitive schemas are; how they influence perception, interpretation, and action; and how they provide better precision to our measurement and our explanatory models of both normative and problematic behavior. For a more extensive treatment of the concepts discussed here and their implications for social work practice, the following resources should prove useful: Brower and Nurius, 1993; Fiske and Taylor, 1991; and Nurius and Berlin, 1993. The chapter is organized around four points as they pertain first to the self development and normative functioning of the cognitive self system, and then as they bear upon processes of social transaction. These four points can be summarized as follows:

- How the person-in-environment practice concept can be operationalized in terms of "situated" or "working" self- and social-schemas.

- How expectations, hopes, and fears about the future take on a tangible schematic form.

- What factors are needed to develop, gain access to, and effectively draw upon desired self- and social-schemas.

- How schemas can serve as a resource in both reactive coping and proactive striving.

SELF-DEVELOPMENT AND FUNCTIONING OF THE COGNITIVE SELF-SYSTEM

The notion of "the self" tends to be viewed in the social work practice literature as central not only to normal functioning but also to the etiology of many problems in living. However, the self in general, and self-definition in particular, have often been treated with considerable blurriness. This, naturally, has left a lot of room for idiosyncrasy in explaining exactly what "the self" is; how exactly "it" goes about interacting with the social environment; through what demonstrable mechanisms the notions of self-concept and self-esteem exert influence over thought, feelings, and actions; and how it is that we can reconcile the seemingly paradoxical sense of having a stable, coherent sense of identity with the far more variable phenomenological experience of being very different people under different circumstances (for example, the self visiting parents at home for the holidays versus the self enjoying a private romantic interlude versus the self mopping up the red wine just overturned on our dinner host's new white sofa).

Let us consider how social cognitive findings about schemas can assist in diminishing both the blurriness and the sense of paradox and, subsequently, can better inform practice assessment and intervention planning efforts.

How the person-in-environment practice concept can be operationalized in terms of "situated" or "working" self- and social-schemas.

Schemas have been described in the literature on information processing and memory functioning as the mental structures within which information is organized, stored, and manipulated and from which it is later recalled. Schemas can be thought of both as indexing systems of previously experienced knowledge or events and as blueprints for what phenomena and interrelationships to anticipate. Although they do not explain everything, schemas are the physical carriers of our memories, concepts, and representations of ourselves and the world around us (Fiske & Taylor, 1991; Greenwald & Banaji, 1989; Hastie, 1981). It helps to look at the way that we process information in terms of the memory system. That is, information that we take in, store, revise or build upon, and later recall gets stored in both a physical form and an organized format. Figure 7.1 illustrates components and processes of information and memory processing (Anderson, 1983; Nurius, 1993).

As we see here, input from the external environment must first be noticed and encoded or interpreted as a first step to becoming meaningful information. Information that is held in temporary, short-term memory may not necessarily become stored in long-term memory. We may hold a phone number that we just looked up in memory long enough to dial it, but not go through the steps to commit it to long-term memory. There are numerous distinctions we can make about information that does become part of our knowledge or memory base: one is between declarative information (descriptive information about concepts, people, or events) and procedural information (the behavioral guidelines about how one goes about being or doing the phenomena in question).

Figure 7.1
Elaborated Architecture of Memory Functioning

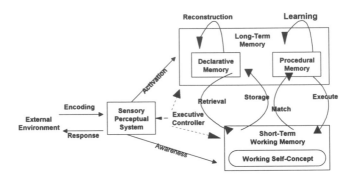

Within this system, let us look at how the person-in-environment notion can be operationalized in terms of a situated, or working, self. Although we have a vast number of schemas stored in long-term memory and therefore *potentially* available to us, we have a very limited number *actually* accessible at any given moment. Our working knowledge is a continually shifting subset of our total repertoire that has been activated for current use. It is held in short term working memory and represents a part of the information that we access, retrieve, and modify that defines the self.

One of the limits of earlier conceptions of the self was the effort to conceive of the self as a single, monolithic "true self" that the individual carried from one situation to the next. This conception fostered assessment approaches that viewed the self-concept as global and relatively fixed, as an entity that was expected to be internally consistent. Seeming incongruities (such as contradictory attributes or behaving one distinctive way in one situation but quite differently in another) were thereby often treated as indications of confusion, inauthenticity, or dysfunction.

We now know that the self-concept is more situationally responsive. Rather than a single self-concept, it is more accurate to think in terms of a working self-concept (Figure 7.2). This refers to the subset of self-schemas that have been cued or activated and are actually at work for the individual in a given moment. Here we can see a translation of social work's person-in-situation as (1) how the self-concept develops and evolves over time and (2) how the individual's prevailing definition of herself or himself is sensitive to differing conditions in the current environment that will activate different self-schema subsets. We spoke earlier, for example, of the personal experience of incongruity, where at times we literally feel as if we are different people under differing contexts. As we look at the information processing basis of differing contexts, we can also see some very tangible differences in the subsets of cognitive schemas (about oneself and the social world) that are activated. These differences thus create importantly different perceptual frameworks out of which the individual will be operating, but that will not be observable to others (Kihlstrom et al., 1988; Markus & Kunda, 1986; Nurius & Markus, 1990).

Figure 7.2
Working Self-Concepts

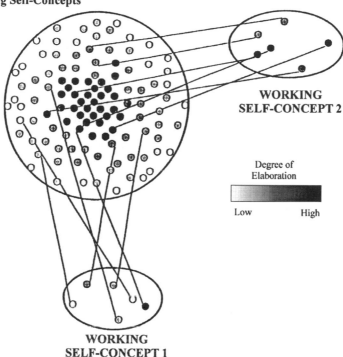

WORKING
SELF-CONCEPT 2

Degree of
Elaboration

Low   High

WORKING
SELF-CONCEPT 1

Because we focus on the self-concept, we are speaking about self-schemas. However, schemas are the organizing physical carriers of social knowledge as well as of self-knowledge. We will later consider how schemas for broader social and physical phenomena are communicated, negotiated, and elaborated among groups (whether they be familial, cultural, religious, or community). At this point, we look at how cognitive schemas help look to the future—how our expectations as well as our individualized goals, hopes, and fears move from being passing thoughts to retrievable pieces of our memory system.

How expectations, hopes, and fears about the future take on a tangible schematic form.

It is easy to see how we build a repertoire of schemas derived from past experiences and the inputs and habits of present life. What is less obvious is the cognitive work we invest in our possible futures. We spend a great deal of time and emotional investment contemplating positive and negative possibilities, as well as thinking about the more humdrum aspects of the future that have to do with our more routine activities. Certainly, some of this thinking about the future takes the form of fleeting fantasy. Yet, much of this activity entails repeatedly running mental simulations of possible futures, which cumulatively give schematic, retrievable form to the possible selves and niches (i.e., situations that we surround ourselves with) that we are envisioning. Some of these possible selves and possible niches may be dramatic, such as the image of making it big in some financial venture, or of finally becoming a body beautiful or, conversely, of becoming seriously injured, ill, or victimized. Other images are linked more to past and present selves and niches, such as when first-year social work students imagine becoming seasoned practitioners and supervisors or when parents envision their young children's inevitable teen years.

In short, these schemas of possible future selves and future niches reside in memory just as schemas of other information do (Hart, Fegley, and Brengelman, 1993; Langan-Fox, 1991; Markus & Nurius, 1986). They can be activated, drawn upon, and elaborated just as other schemas can. There are many ways in which future-oriented schemas can influence social functioning, but here we will restrict our attention to their potential for changing behavior, since that is a primary concern for social work intervention. In this framework, schemas about specific possible selves and niches can be seen as the cognitive road map for getting from here to there. If one's goal is to have a nondrinking self and lifestyle, then future schemas about what a nondrinker is, looks like, does, and does not do are crucially important.

Schemas of what not to be, look like, or do (in this case, schemas of drinking or alcoholism) may be informative, but they do not effectively guide behavior toward desired selves and situations. Similarly, schemas of a nondrinker that include only declarative knowledge are unlikely to be effective, in that they do not include the personalized if-then guidelines about what to do and how to do it. Such guidelines can help a person "see" a high risk condition and galvanize desired behavioral responses rather than his or her more familiar and developed "drinking-self" responses (Higgins, Vookles, and Tykocinski, 1992; Oyserman & Markus, 1990; Ruvolo & Markus, 1992; Segal, 1988).

Thus, as we will discuss, for schemas about possible futures to guide behavior effectively, they need to contain information about what that ultimate destination "looks like," which interim steps are needed to achieve it (or avoid or reduce undesired selves or situations), and what kinds of corrective and reinforcing feedback will help elaborate and strengthen these relatively new and untried knowledge structures (Linville & Clark, 1989; Nurius & Berlin, 1993). An important underlying point here is that for cognitive schemas to influence the person-in-environment effectively, they must not only be available (i.e., exist within the individual's long-term memory), but they must also be accessed (i.e., actually retrieved from storage to become part of the working knowledge and information processing of the moment). Thus, we will next turn to consideration of factors that influence this accessibility.

What factors are needed to develop, gain access to, and effectively draw upon desired self- and social-schemas.

Here we encounter a significant dilemma. Our information processing system is geared toward stability and confirmation of what we know as reality.

Generally, this serves us quite well. We all develop reasonably workable schemas and scripts about who we are and how the world works. These schemas incline us to search for confirmatory information, and we are generally right enough of the time, or enough right, adequately to anticipate events and negotiate our social exchanges. Schemas are known to be tenaciously resistant to challenge, which is an asset in maintaining a sense of coherence and predictability. However, this same confirmation bias is a formidable obstacle to desired change, particularly in those schemas that are central to a person's identity or understanding of social world.

Thus, one of our challenges to effect change in the self-concept (or in other core beliefs, for that matter) is how to circumvent this confirmatory bias without undermining its essential function (because we will want to take advantage of this protectionism of new and changed schemas once they have been adequately established). Let us go back to Figure 7.1 and consider the importance of the sensory/perception system. We mentioned that schemas are continuously cycling in and out of working memory; a set becomes activated and then fades in salience as a new subset takes prominence. Inputs from the sensory/perception system play a large role in this triggering process. That is, the things we see, hear, smell, feel, and even say serve to trigger knowledge structures stored in memory: schemas about what the phenomenon is, what can be expected of it, what is expected of oneself in relation to it, and how to go about operationalizing the appropriate response. Because schemas are organized in associative networks, activation of one structure will tend to activate (or make more easily accessible) those related to it. For example, as we see in Figure 7.3, when a situation has activated schemas involving incompetence, related schemas such as failure, embarrassment, and future self as a lost cause are far more easily accessible in the moment than are competitive schemas related to skillfulness, confidence, and images of future self as proudly successful.

Again, although we are simplifying a complex process, we will quickly review some of the factors important to accessing and effectively using schemas (Anderson, 1983; Brown & Taylor, 1988; Linville & Clark, 1989; Nurius, 1994a):

- Schemas are activated when attached to easily perceived cues. If we want to stimulate a certain reaction, we should not risk subtle cues that can be overlooked or discounted.

- Schemas are activated when attached to cues that are vivid (i.e., novel, emotional, compelling, personally significant), that are nonroutine in positive or negative ways, and that literally "grab" our attention.

- Conversely, schemas are activated when attached to cues that are highly familiar. In our patterned routines of everyday life (i.e., within our niches), we really do not "notice" inputs as we observe social norms in eating a meal, driving a car, or interacting with people in the hallway of our workplace.

- Schemas are activated when they contain procedural knowledge that has been well developed. We may have a lot of knowledge about what something is or looks like in others. But if we have not undertaken a considerable degree of personal enactment—specifically, practice with reinforcing feedback—we are likely to have a keen image and sense of what we would like to do in the moment, but unlikely to have a clear sense of exactly what to do to make that desire happen.

Figure 7.3
Contrasting Self-Schema Repertoires and Networks Related to the Domain of Intimate Relationships

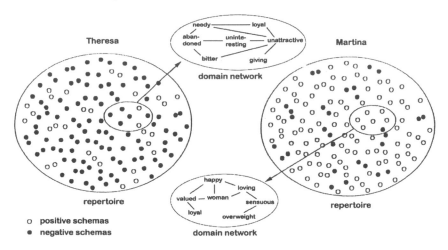

- Schemas are activated when congruence exists among schemas active in working memory. This is one of the difficulties in changing problematic reaction patterns; as an individual works to activate preferred schemas in a given situation, there will initially be at least part of the set of problematic schemas that have become habitually responsive to the situational cues. We then have a competitive framework within working memory of discordant schemas (e.g., of current and future self), which can generate a sense of confusion, ambivalence, and uncertainty in behavioral response.

- Schemas are activated to the degree of their strength and elaboration. Not surprisingly, schemas that are more elaborate (more rich, detailed, complex) will have an advantage in influencing momentary emotional, cognitive, and behavioral action relative to those that are less elaborated. There are several features to consider here. One is that those schemas that are most frequently activated not only tend to become easier to activate but also, as a function of being frequently engaged, contain more autobiographical and social feedback information. This is part of what makes routines and habits difficult to break. Not only do individual schemas become more routinized in their activation under similar circumstances, they also contain more historical content and become interrelated in more complex ways with associated schemas.

Part of the point of examining schemas in such detail is that they are key players in activities important to social workers, such as proactive striving toward goals and more reactive coping with threats and problems in living. Let us now turn to a brief discussion of the role of schemas in coping and striving.

How schemas can serve as a resource in both reactive coping and more proactive striving.

As we have seen, both the composition of schemas that are recruited into working memory and their qualitative nature (e.g., degree of development) are critically important guides to how people respond—in other words, what they think and feel in a given moment as well as how they behave. In practice change efforts, an important question is (a) whether schemas that reflect knowledge of a desired self-image or action are simply not part of the person's knowledge or memory system or (b) whether those desired schemas are actually present in long-term memory but are either impoverished in their degree of development or relatively inaccessible vis-à-vis stronger, more competitive schemas (Nurius, 1994a). The latter situation, of course, gives us something cognitive to build on, whereas the former involves a more thorough educational intervention.

Our work and that of others have indicated that schemas about possible selves and possible niches are potentially valuable resources to reactive coping and to more proactive striving (Carson, Madison, and Santrock, 1987; Markus, Cross, and Wurf, 1990; Nurius & Markus, 1990). In part, this is because they help provide both the motivational incentive as well as the behavioral guidance for how to traverse the distance from "present me" to "desired me," from present scenario to preferred ones. We have also found that focus in practice on possible selves and possible niches helps to reduce the natural resistance to challenge of the self-concept as it is currently "known" by the individual. A client may, understandably, resist the notion that she is worthy or self-sufficient if this contradicts a prevailing and socially reinforced self-schema. But she may well be able to tolerate the claim and image that she may become, or is becoming, worthy and self-sufficient.

As we have stressed repeatedly, this cognitive mediation, in the case of coping and striving, is both an intrapersonal psychological process and an interpersonal social influence process. This duality is reflected in the Figure 7.4. Here we see an abbreviated depiction of the complex social network activities that provide social functions (e.g., social norm construction, social support, social demand) as well as reflected appraisals (e.g., input regarding individuals' identities and attributes and judgments of these). These social processes set the stage for the emergence, development, and use of certain possible selves and working self-concepts, which in turn shape the individuals' individualized coping and striving processes (Heller, Swindle, and Dusenbury, 1986; Nurius, 1991; Hart, Fegley, and Brengelman, 1993; Oosterwegel & Oppenheimer, 1993).

Increasingly, it is becoming evident that individuals vary greatly in both their experience of and response to life transitions and crises. Long-time crisis theorist Moos has noted that these challenges, mediated through an individual's cognitive appraisal of his or her personal significance and meaning, set forth adaptive tasks to which various attributes and skills can be applied. The concept of *assumptive worlds* encompasses beliefs both about one's world and about oneself and one's place in that world. It is these assumptions and the knowledge structures that undergird them that are perhaps the most elemental factors in shaping an individual's sense of meaning and efforts in negotiating in stressful conditions. This theme of the centrality of individuals' assumptive world is repeated in Moos's (Moos, 1977) typology of the major sets of adaptive tasks: (a) preserving a reasonable emotional balance, (b) preserving a satisfactory self-image, (c) preserving relationships with family and friends, and (d) preparing for an uncertain future (Taylor, 1983; Taylor & Brown, 1988; Janoff-Bulman, 1989).

Figure 7.4
Health and Mental Health Outcomes

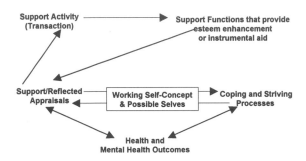

During crises and transitions, individuals must learn and develop new ways of thinking about the world and their place in it. This relearning involves a relinquishing of "old" assumptions and an establishment of "new" ones (Jacobson, 1986). This involves varying degrees of an initial sense of loss and disorganization when old assumptions (schemas) are threatened or perhaps rendered false or impossible (e.g., when one's future as a professional dancer is destroyed by a back injury, or one's capacity as a breadwinner and family head is undermined by unemployment or illness). This initial disorganization is followed by a search for understanding and alternatives. The relative success of this search is greatly contingent upon the prevailing social and physical environment. The extent to which alternative possibilities are expanded or constrained and the availability of models and supports are intimately influenced by the beliefs and expectations of individuals' significant others.

In accomplishing such transitions, the ability to construct, invoke, and sustain schemas of preferred possible selves and situations is a critical determinant in the relearning necessary to successful adaptation as well as to goal attainment. Yet general goals or expectations often do not indicate specific actions or pathways toward achieving these end states. It is through exposure to and experience with others and with situations relevant to desired change that these means-ends connections become elaborated and more competitive self-schemas and social schemas evolve. And it is often through these social conduits that possible selves and possible social niches are reinforced and strengthened as part of the newly emerging assumptive world (Markus, Cross, and Wurf, 1990; Nurius, 1994b).

Thus far, we have focused on the form and function of cognitive schemas primarily in intrapersonal terms. To be sure, self-schemas and other-schemas are social in nature. That is, they both derive from and exert influence on interaction with the social environment. At this point, we will shift to a greater focus on social interaction. Specifically, we will focus on daily life: on the routines, norms, and scripts that provide the landscape of our lives. Within this framework, we will discuss how schemas are communicated from one member to another in a culture and how the processes through which we develop consensually hold perceptions and understandings of ourselves as individuals and of the world around us.

SOCIAL SCHEMAS AND SOCIAL INTERACTION

Exploring the interconnections between people and their environments starts with a discussion of the social niche, which includes the parameters of the environment in which people interact, the patterned ways in which people interact with these environmental components, and how each component within the niche is in a balance with each other component (Brower, 1988). In our daily lives, our niche takes the phenomenological form of establishing and maintaining routines and scripts in our daily behavior: the morning routine of waking up, showering, and getting kids off to school, for example. One's niche is created and sustained through intimate and constant contact with the environment. From a cognitive ecological perspective, "person" and "environment" are inseparable. Gregory Bateson makes this point well in his discussion of evolution: "The horse isn't the thing that evolved. What evolved actually was a *relationship* between horse and grass. The grass changes and the horse changes, and the grass changes and the horse changes, and they change in such a way that the relationship between them may stay constant" (Bateson, 1991). We are intimately tied to our surroundings. We view the world through "schematic filters"—that is, by calling up schemas to make sense of ourselves and our environment and dictating routines for how to lead our lives. It is our contention that every part of our lives is dictated by routine because of the two levels of "filters" that we use to make sense of our surroundings and to direct our social interactions. By looking at Figure 7.1, we see that one filter exists in the sensory perceptual system: we select the cues that we see. The other filter exists through the process of drawing schemas into working knowledge: Our schemas shape how we respond to our internal and external cues. These routines describe the niche in which we live. At times, of course, we encounter events that are both unexpected and unfamiliar. However, even under novel circumstances, we tend to draw upon what we know best, however adaptive or maladaptive that may prove to be in the end. Furthermore, our routines themselves are interconnected and, at least to some degree, dependent on each other.

We can now turn to the four points that were raised earlier in this paper with a new focus on how they relate to schemas and social interaction.

How the person-in-environment notion can be operationalized in terms of "situated" or "working" self- and social-schemas.

The basic premise of the cognitive-ecological approach is that all parts of a system must change and adapt to changes in any other part of the system. Thus, when a person enters a situation, his or her ability to function requires that a "working self" be formed to fit the specific demands of the situation and the specific goals and purposes of the individual within that situation. When this person acts from within the working self, his or her actions are understood in context (i.e., within the consensually held situational cues and structures), allowing others to respond in kind.

If the creation of a working self creates the opportunity for social interaction, sustained interaction is dependent on the extent to which individuals can share their schemas with others. Sharing our schemas through social interaction is the basis of communication and human relationships. We articulate our schemas to each other—either directly, when we have "heart-to-heart" talks to share our life stories, or indirectly, when we observe how others respond in various situations. The depth and strength of our relationships are based on our ability to articulate our schemas to others and to respond to others' schemas by "finding ourselves" in them (that is, finding parts or whole schemas shared by others). When we feel understood by others, we mean that we feel that others understand our schemas—about who we are, how things are, and what is important.

Relationships are built on the process whereby shared schemas are developed. This process begins with each party in the interaction acting on the basis of his or her preexisting schemas. Each will begin to understand the other because each will begin to identify and respond to elements of the other's schema that make sense or are familiar. Then, depending on the extent to which both parties are invested in the interaction, they will begin to develop shared elements that can attach to each other's schema. The extent to which they each are invested in the interaction will dictate the number and salience of the shared elements that they develop. Ultimately, if they interact effectively and over enough time, they will have created together a schema of the situation and of the interaction that they share (Brower, 1989).

This can happen quickly, as when one "clicks" with another after a brief meeting, or it can happen through a laborious and lengthy process. Our investment in the development of shared schemas will be directly proportional to our goals for the interaction. If neither person has a particularly high investment in the interaction, the amount of shared schema needs only to be sufficient to allow one to make the interaction as painless as possible (as when we choose not to argue with others whom we have just met at a party). However, when both parties have high investments, as members of an ongoing neighborhood organization, for example, the development and articulation of a shared schema will necessarily need to be greater.

The extent to which we bend our schemas to others' also depends on our formal and informal roles within the setting; for example, if one party is a senior to the other, it is likely that the junior member will adapt his or her schema to suit the senior member. All of the social psychological principles of group dynamics, of power and influence, will apply here (Nye & Brower, 1994). Note that for this process to create a structural change (i.e., a schema that becomes part of one's permanent store), the interaction between the two people either must be emotionally significant or must endure over a long period of time. This is what we mean when we state that a relationship has left a "mark" on us.

How expectations, hopes, and fears about the future take on tangible schematic form.

From a cognitive-ecological perspective, life goals are given center stage in the understanding of how we process information, interact with others, and lead our lives. We use life goals (or more precisely, possible selves and possible niches) to set the course for our current life decisions and actions. Our decisions, actions, and motivations are based, in part, on our ongoing monitoring of the discrepancies between our current state and our "possible" states, using processes described by a "thermostat" analogy (Lauer & Handel, 1983; Mead, 1938): We act either to decrease distance between our current state and our desired possible selves and niches or to increase distance between our current state and our feared or negative possible selves and niches. We can chart our "life trajectory" on the path between our past life story, our current niche, and our future possible selves and possible niches.

This perspective understands humans as proactively striving towards life goals rather than reactively coping with challenges and problems as they arise in our lives (Emmons, 1986). From a cognitive-ecological perspective, daily life is structured by our thoughts, feelings, and actions that are directed towards the life goals and tasks specified by our possible selves and possible niches (Cantor & Kihlstrom, 1989). Goals and goal striving give our lives meaning, and we use them to define who we are (Brower, 1992; Emmons & King, 1989).

The individual's perceptions regarding what is possible or appropriate stand as powerful personal gatekeepers about what is dreamed and attempted. Nevertheless, goals and their creation are by no means "all in the head." Environments convey different messages about what is appropriate or realistic for different groups and individuals, and environments both constrain and foster access to needed opportunity and supports.

At this point, the reader may be aware of an apparent paradox between the notion of goal-directed, future-oriented behavior, on the one hand, and our inherent inclination to maintain stability and consistency in our niche, on the other. This has been a criticism of "homeostasis" system models of behavior: While a homeostasis model assumes that a system will always react to neutralize or negate the effects of change (either internal to the individual or external in the environment), evolution and mutation create opportunities for growth and development. From a cognitive-ecological perspective, the individual is both social product and social force; changes are viewed as points at which the individual can decide whether one's niche will change in significant ways (i.e., evolve) in response to the change or will instead become more resilient to it (i.e., maintain the status quo). While people seek a balance between predictability and curiosity, we will lean more in one direction than another at different points in our lives. Thus, we often exhibit our dual need to maintain the integrity of our niche and our sense of personal identity with our need for stimulation and the capacity to learn from and evolve with an ever-changing world.

Life goals—or possible selves and possible niches—provide us with ballast, with directional signs and signals that allow us to navigate in a more-or-less purposeful course through life's changes and surprises. Understanding our own and our clients' life goals thus provides keys to understanding our efforts to cope and strive—and to develop our life story and life trajectory.

What factors are needed to develop, gain access to, and effectively draw upon desired self- and social-schemas?

There are numerous points in the schema-development, schema-access process toward which we can direct interventions with clients. We will discuss two such intervention strategies here; others are identified and discussed in Brower and Nurius (Brower & Nurius, 1993).

Figure 7.1 shows that we will access specific schemas when we are attuned to specific internal and external cues. One intervention strategy, then, involves helping clients attune to different cues in their field.

This technique of retraining clients to attend to different environmental and internal cues has been described by cognitive-behaviorists as cognitive reframing (Cormier & Cormier, 1991). However, in traditional reframing, one challenges the client to see how attention to irrational or inappropriate cues causes their irrational or inappropriate responses. From the cognitive ecological framework, one first helps the client see that their responses are understandable, that they "make sense" given the prevailing schemas that are influencing their perceptions and interpretations. After this first step, clients can then be helped to see that they have a choice of cues to attend to and how to interpret them. This intervention is aimed at the perceptual level of functioning; it is aimed at an almost involuntary sensation rather than at a more voluntary level of cognition. One's efforts are not spent convincing clients of the rationality of giving a different interpretation to an event. Instead, one helps them see and recognize other cues, which leads more naturally to other interpretations of events. Joining with the client's already existing perceptual and schema-activation system is a more natural process than retraining the client to use another system entirely.

This intervention assumes, of course, that a client has other appropriate schemas and procedural knowledge stored in memory and has a perceptual and schema-activation system that is intact. Many clients will need help developing additional schemas or alternative ways to view a situation, developing procedural knowledge (that is, how to respond given their perception of a situation), and learning how cues can be put together to create situational interpretations.

It is powerful and empowering for some clients simply to gain a "schematic" view of the world and how one fits into it. When clients do not have such a view, they perceive the world as unpredictable and frightening. It is useful for all clients, particularly those who have difficulty making sense of their surroundings to reinforce the perspective that while everything does not happen for a good (i.e., "just") reason, it is possible to "decode" messages and cues in one's surroundings, and to understand one's own patterns and routines. We have found this to be very effective for schizophrenic clients, who often experience the world as unpredictable. For them, the ability to see routines and develop structure in their lives is particularly important.

A second intervention strategy exists when clients see situations correctly but are not able to respond in ways that brings them closer to their life goals. For this case, the sensory perceptual system is working properly and the appropriate cues are attended to, but either procedural knowledge is lacking for how to respond, or the possible selves and niches—i.e., the life goals—are vague or uncompelling.

Interventions for this case will be of the behavioral training type—to increase procedural knowledge—and of the type to make life goals more clear and compelling. Since ample research and skills-training literature exists, we will instead focus on a discussion of how to help clients develop clear and compelling life goals.

Helping clients enhance their life goals is accomplished by making their goals more clear and "alive," meaning more fully articulated, attached to emotions, and attached to existing procedural knowledge. Clients can be helped to describe their possible selves and possible niches more completely in terms of how they will feel, who they will be with, what they will see, smell, and hear, what they will be wearing, what they will be doing, and what they will have to do to reach their goal state. Life goals are compelling when they come alive for clients and when they have a real sense that they can "get there from here."

From our experience, these discussions are often fun and lively, where clients are imbued with the excitement of possibility. Guidance is given to develop a realistic picture of the possible self and niche and to establish the necessary sequences from cues, to interpretation, to behavior. The more that the new schemas are accessed and acted upon, the greater the likelihood that these new access pathways can compete under a variety of situations. Similarly, the more clients use their "enlivened" possible selves and possible niches in their life course decision-making, the more likely they are to make positive steps towards realizing their goal states and the less likely they are to be distracted by short-term setbacks.

How schemas can serve as a resource in both reactive coping and more proactive striving.

Operationally, possible selves and possible niches provide motivation for clients by presenting them with clear and vivid images of themselves and their surroundings that contain information about how to progress from their current state to this result state. Of course, such a statement assumes that clients' possible selves and niches are clear and vivid; and we have already discussed the importance of helping clients develop their future-oriented self- and other-schemas in terms of their emotional salience and procedural and semantic knowledge.

Note that this approach views us all—clients and social workers alike—as living our lives striving toward life goals. That is, we all strive to achieve desired possible selves and niches and to distance ourselves from undesirable possible selves and niches. This striving approach contrasts with a coping orientation, where humans are seen to react to events that disrupt our status quo. The potential benefits to clients of utilizing a striving perspective is clearest when we look at mainstream work with the elderly and with those suffering from severe mental illnesses (such as schizophrenia). For example, notice how embedded the reactive coping model is in the list of topic headings in the classic book by Lieberman and Tobin (Lieberman & Tobin, 1983), *The Experience of Old Age*: "The impact of threat and loss," "The crisis of environmental change," "The management of threat and loss," and "The maintenance of self-identity." From a reactive coping perspective, elderly clients are seen as having already reached the pinnacle of their lives, with "successful aging" serving to protect oneself against the erosion of physical and cognitive abilities and their concurrent threats to self-esteem. Maintaining the status quo is considered the goal, and work with the elderly is geared towards achieving this goal.

In the field of schizophrenia, a reactive coping perspective is even more entrenched. In 1989, *Schizophrenia Bulletin* published a special issue devoted to the problem of the "person" having become lost in the study and treatment of schizophrenia. As a reaction to the coping perspective, Strauss argued eloquently for viewing the schizophrenic person "as a goal-directed being" with "feelings [that help] drive the phases of disorder and improvement" (Strauss, 1989). Estroff wrote that study of this illness must include "the person, the subject, [and] the self that both *has* and *is* this disorder" (emphasis in the original; Estroff, 1989).

Interestingly, one chapter in Lieberman and Tobin is entitled "Hope and Despair," in which they lament the lack of good research and discussion concerning the role of "hope" in the lives of the elderly. They discuss the importance of maintaining hope, defined as helping clients project themselves into the future rather than allowing them to fall into the depression and despair of solely living in the present, "bereft of both a future and a past, [seemingly] unable to extend themselves in either direction" (p. 313). As Lieberman and Tobin allude to, and as both Strauss and Estroff argue directly, a striving perspective puts into the forefront the notion that people create a life trajectory for themselves that explicitly contains a past, a present, and a future. We all need to see our lives in these progressive terms, regardless of whether we are in the late stages of life, like the elderly, or face frequent environmental and internal disruptions, like those suffering from severe mental illnesses.

CONCLUSION

One's sense of identity, place, and future are essential elements to healthy functioning. The compatibile integration of social cognition and social work highlights these elements. It helps us anchor practice wisdom with conceptual and empirical advances and helps us inform theoretical and research efforts in the direction of neglected populations and poorly understood problems and needs. As social workers, we are committed to supporting individuals' self-determination of social functioning and directed action. As social scientists, we are committed to strengthening the knowledge base upon which these helping efforts are based. Advances in social cognition in general, and in schema operations in particular, hold great promise for further support toward crafting, utilizing, and realizing individuals' possible selves and possible niches in their unfolding life stories.

8

Community Organization, New Social Movement Theory, and the Condition of Postmodernity

Robert Fisher and Joseph Kling

Community organization remains, as Schwartz (Schwartz, 1977) contended, a practice area in search of a theoretical paradigm. Taylor and Roberts (Taylor & Roberts, 1985), in a book devoted to both theory and practice, end up focusing on the fluid nature of organizing theory and the difficulties of developing an effective theory to inform practice. Specht (Specht, 1986) echoes the disappointment of Taylor and Roberts that "there is little theory underlying practice." Most recently radical analysis—structuralist, Frierian, and feminist— has begun to offer theories of empowerment related to community organization, but as of yet these paradigms remain limited in their origins and practice (Carniol, 1992; Weil, 1986; Gutiérrez, GlenMaye, and DeLois, 1992). In order to help counteract the relative absence of explicit use of contemporary social theory in community organization practice, we would like to begin to confront, in this chapter, what community organization as a political practice and theories of new social movements and postmodernism might have to contribute to and learn from each other. We do this because we believe progressive social work needs to be sensitive to the kinds of issues that the paradigms related to postmodern thinking raise.

We do not not consider ourselves "postmodernist," nor do we think that community organization as a political practice needs to "become" postmodern. We do, however, believe that those concerned with the effective mobilization of communities must take into account what new social movement and postmodern theorization have to say about the fragmentation of community and about the new power of cultural symbols in an information- and media-based age. These shifts in the way people experience the social world have much to do to with the nature of domination, resistance, and empowerment that shapes community organization theory and practice.

The first section of this chapter offers an overview of what we understand to be the postmodern perspective and new social movement theory and why we believe them to be central to discussions of contemporary social change. A second section examines the ways in which new social movement and postmodern theory mirror, inform, and are contradicted by past and present community organization practice. The chapter concludes with some strategies for thinking about and dealing with the challenges posed by new social movement theory and postmodern conditions to contemporary organizing.

POSTMODERNISM, NEW SOCIAL MOVEMENT THEORY, AND THE DECENTERED SOCIETY

Postmodern Visions

Social work, let us begin by stating, is an intrinsically modernist undertaking. Historically, its modern origins lie in the social service ideologies of early twentieth-century pragmatism and progressivism, developed most fully and articulately, perhaps, in the ideas and practice of John Dewey (Dewey, 1939) and Jane Addams (Addams, 1902; Addams, 1910). Their work—his based at the University of Chicago, hers at Hull House—was mutually supportive, with shared intellectual roots in the rationalist assumptions of eighteenth-century Enlightenment thought and nineteenth-century social reform. Traditional social work practice, precisely because it is progressive and modernist, therefore, is grounded in a notion of a general public realm that can be shaped by collective action, rationally planned and strategically implemented by a community of actors who are capable of sharing a common discourse.

Under modernist concepts of social action, the public realm, though understood as a social/cultural artifact, is nevertheless assumed to be real and external to the particularist groups who inhabit it. The theoretical key to community and political social work practice is the assumption that, by acting in concert, these groups have the ability to affect and reshape the public realm in accord with the larger historical narratives of democracy, equality, and social justice. In the 1960s and 1970s, most community organization practice also became "emancipatory" in its theory and objectives, committed to personal and collective liberation, empowerment as well as power.[1]

From the early nineteenth century through the end of the World War II, "class" and "citizenship" were accepted as the major organizing identities that could unite varying constituencies of working people to oppose existing conditions of oppression and to challenge unequal access to social opportunities and resources. "Class position"—defined by a common situation in relation to a system of production that exercises power and control over people's lives through the extraction of surplus value—linked subaltern groups across differences of race, ethnicity, gender, and neighborhood. "Citizenship" tied all groups together in a mutual project of exercising common rights against injustice and legitimated the identification of working people with the larger democratic polity. A politics based upon both the primacy of class and the rights of citizenship informed almost all localist movements for change, whether their site was the workplace or the neighborhood and whether their immediate bases of organization were race, ethnicity, or gender (Adamson & Burgos, 1984).

Settlements were initiated by upper-class "reformers" from outside the poor, largely immigrant neighborhoods. Here social settlement workers, at their best, consciously sought to deliver services to and empower the working class while, at the same time, serving as "class mediators" (Fisher, 1994).

Settlement work borrowed more heavily from the functionalist ideas then developing in the work of Max Weber than it did from Marx. For Marx, class identity was oppositional. For Weber, it reflected a symbiotic division of labor. That is, under the right conditions of authority and legitimacy, class politics allowed release of the tensions of a capitalist social order while keeping political and economic conflict within the bounds of negotiation and consensus.

The functionalist model—in a guise consistent with reformist social democracy—eventually came to shape the social work profession. Our larger point is that both Marxist and Weberian models expected that modernist consciousness—framed by the growth of such institutions as industrial production, global markets, nation states, corporate and governmental bureaucracies, and metropolitan centers—would come to see human groupings as structurally connected across cultural and regional difference and moulded by an underlying commonality of experiences, needs and motivations. Rationalist modes of apprehending the world, rather than traditionalist and culturally bound ones, would shape individual choice, collective identity, and political policy. Indeed, modernist thought—whether Marxist or Weberian—had long assumed that the forces of economic, political, and cultural centralization would eventually lead to the disappearance of particularist outlooks and identities and to their replacement by generalized, bureaucratic, and class-oriented ones.

It has not quite worked out that way. "As the modern public expands," Marshall Berman wrote in his seminal work on contemporary life, *All That Is Solid Melts into Air*, "it shatters into a multitude of fragments, speaking incommensurable private languages, the idea of modernity, conceived in numerous fragmentary ways, loses much of its vividness, resonance, and depth, and loses its capacity to organize and give meaning to people's lives" (Berman, 1988, 16–17). The dissolution of social mappings tied to rationalist/universalist understandings of the human condition is no small historical transition. Our suggestion is that, whatever their complexity and abstraction, the contemporary debates about the emergence of a postmodern society and culture all flow over and about the meanings of this transition. It is the collapse of the experience of political and cultural centrality and, in Lyotard's words, "the crisis of narratives" (Lyotard, 1984, xxiii) that are at the root of the debate between modernist and postmodernist sensibilities.

There are at least two aspects to understanding and describing this explosion of publics and the decentering of cultural life that accompanies it. The first looks to the socioeconomic underpinnings of the postmodern condition, its roots in the fragmentation of locality by global capital, in the shift of capital markets, and in the rise of sophisticated communication technologies (Harvey, 1989; Soja, 1990). The second examines its grounding in an era where the mechanical reproduction of images, rather than the direct experience of labor or of deeply felt ties to a physically demarcated place of everyday life, shapes people's understandings of who they are and what is real. This second approach emphasizes the importance of signification and representation to contemporary experience (Barthes, 1972; Baudrillard, 1975; Debord, 1983). Scott Lash attempts to clarify the arguments at issue by suggesting that "modernism conceives of representations as being problematic, whereas postmodernism problematizes reality" (Lash, 1990, 13).

Both these approaches to contemporary experience—the socioeconomic and the representational—are essential. While we will concentrate, in what follows, on the first, we will nevertheless keep an eye continually on the second. It is not that we wish to privilege the socioeconomic over the representational and cultural; it is just that, within the confines of a single article, it is not possible to give both approaches their due. The second deserves a full-length essay of its own.

New Social Movement Theory and Contemporary Resistance

The consequences of a fragmenting socioeconomic world and the decline of the great social narratives that evolved to give meaning to that world are staples of contemporary social existence. With the shift of the classic forms of industrial production from the central cities of advanced capitalist states to peripheral regions and Third World nations, the structural bases for class-oriented mobilizations literally move out from under organized labor. The idea that the world is a rationally ordered place, progressing inevitably towards some sort of universal justice, has been shattered by the uses to which science was put in two world wars, by the threat of nuclear destruction that has hung over humanity for most of the latter part of the century, and by the failure of the two great political narratives of the era—socialism and liberal democracy—to deliver on their promises of equality and rights.

Within the context of such material and ideological changes, social movements related to race, gender, nation, and the protection of localist enclaves have not only found space to emerge but also have become the principal arenas of defense and insurgency. While class remains a mobilizing force in some arenas, it no longer has the political salience or experiential immediacy it did in societies shaped by direct industrial production and informed by narratives of social progress.

New social movement theory offers some critical insights both into this process and into the nature of resistance since World War II—especially since the rise of the Civil Rights Movement. Admittedly, any social theory, particularly one based on a rigid dualism of "old" and "new" social movements, is too simple and too time-bound to do justice to the complexities of our contemporary condition. Nevertheless, the absence of a social theory that can reasonably account for the emergence, persistence, and proliferation of community organizing efforts since World War II and over the past two decades suggests that an explanation of grassroots activism, applicable from place to place, is in order.

Let us step back first to examine what new social movement theory means by the old social movements. In the early twentieth century, social democratic movements and regimes arose in the United States and Western Europe to control the excesses of industrial capitalism. These "old" social movements share critical similarities (Epstein, 1990; Fisher, 1992; Scott, 1990). Workplace-based, the locus of organizing was the industrial factory. Here, unions were organized around class issues. The ideology of the organizers—social democratic or communist—challenged capitalism and proposed a working class vision of the future. They targeted employers, the owners of the means of production. At the same time, they involved themselves in politics, hoping to win state power. Their victories, in the United States and Western Europe, were the foundation of public policy and state action in the West World War II. The more community-based, communitarian, decentralist versions of this politics, such as the social settlements, remained a fringe element, but one that nevertheless shared the old social movement vision and agenda.

Between 1946 and the late 1960s labor-oriented, "old" social movements built a consensus around economic growth, welfare state expenditures, and United States imperial control. The "Fair Deal," "New Frontier," and "Great Society" symbolize this era in the United States, and the C.I.O. stands as a classic example of such old social movement formation (Offe, 1987).

Many factors led to the decline of the old social movements. The increasing globalization of the world economy undermined their ability, and that of their political representatives, to redistribute resources to constituents. As capital flow increasingly superseded state control in the emerging global economy, the welfare state faced increasing fiscal crises. The social democratic state lost support, while those associated with its development and implementation lost credibility. Moreover, the new postindustrial global economy put pressure on two inherent weaknesses in the old social movements. First, those in power developed an increasingly parochial and self-serving agenda. Second, the old social movements may have achieved power as the voice for disadvantaged workers, but they also perpetuated the silence of others such as minorities, women, young people just entering the workforce, and the unskilled. Increasingly these previously quiescent groups began to organize, challenging the liberal democratic leaders and parties that gave only perfunctory attention to their interests and concerns. The opposition—the new social movements— emerged in insurgent grassroots associations over issues of democratic participation, personal liberty, civil rights, and quality of life.

The heirs of the old social movements found themselves hamstrung by a global economy that escaped national regulation and control and under attack from the right—as well as from segments of the left—for "statist" orientations and politics. For the generation that came to political consciousness in the years between 1960 and 1990, the practitioners of such old-style liberal politics devolved into anachronisms (Flacks, 1990).

The New Social Movements

The new social movement opposition to the postwar political economy, while emerging at different places at different times, possesses five characteristics that distinguish it from the old social movements.

First, these movements are community-based in principle; that is, they focus on communities of interest or geography. This is generally in contrast to the way organizing was done in the past, when organizing took place at the site of production against the owners of capital (Offe, 1987). Castells (Castells, 1983) summarizes this difference in bases of organizing as organizing at the site of consumption rather than the site of production.

Second, they are transclass groupings of constituencies and cultural identities such as blacks, ethnics, women, gay men and lesbians, students, ecologists, and peace activists. Labor becomes one constituency among many, not *the* constituency group or even the first among equals. Class becomes part of, not *the*, identity (Brecher & Costello, 1990; Fisher, 1992).

Third, the ideological glue is a neopopulist vision of democracy that rejects all hierarchically based forms of social interaction: in the state, in concepts of leadership, in political parties and organizations, and in the family and personal relationships (Amin, 1990). Their organizational form is sufficiently small, loose, and open to be able to "tap local knowledge and resources, to respond to problems rapidly and creatively, and to maintain the flexibility needed in changing circumstances" (Durning, 1989, 6–7). Some have argued that these movements are "nonideological" because they dismiss the old ideologies of capitalism, communism, and nationalism and because they tend to be without a clear, centered philosophic critique of existing systems. But others argue that ideological congruence is their essence. Their "neopopulist" principles and beliefs are what makes them new (Dalton & Kuechler, 1990; Offe, 1987; Boyte & Riessman, 1986; Fisher & Kling, 1988; Boyte, Booth, and Max, 1986).

Fourth, struggle over culture and social identity play a greater role in community-based movements than in workplace-based efforts of the past. "After the great working class parties surrendered their remaining sense of radical political purpose with the onset of the cold war," Bronner (Bronner, 1990, 161) writes, "new social movements emerged to reformulate the spirit of resistance in broader cultural terms." Feminism. Black Power. Sexual identity. Ethnic nationalism. Victim's rights. Of course, culture and identity—grounded in historical experience, values, social networks, and collective solidarity—have always been central to all social movement formation (Thompson, 1967; Gutman, 1977). But as class becomes fragmented in the postindustrial city and as the locus of workplace organizing declines in significance, the resistances that emerge increasingly do so around cultural and identity bases (Touraine, 1985; Fischer & Kling, 1991).

Fifth, the strategies of the new social movements focus on community self-help and empowerment. Rather than seeking state power, most community-based organizing seeks independence from the state. It relies on a "unitary" conception of democracy, which assumes a predominant concern to promote the common interest, and deemphasizes "adversarial" democracy, which presupposes conflicting interests in the social order (Mansbridge, 1980, 3). As Midgley (Midgley, 1986, 4) points out, central to the rationale of community participation "is a reaction against the centralization, bureaucratization, rigidity, and remoteness of the state. The ideology of community participation is sustained by the belief that the power of the state has extended too far, diminishing the freedoms of ordinary people and their rights to control their own affairs."

While community capacity building becomes the natural focus of new social movement efforts, the most effective new social movement efforts target the public sector. They understand that community capacity building and empowerment are significant but limited strategies. And they realize that the sites of production cannot be leveraged as easily or effectively by the new social movements as they could by the old social movements. Equally important, they recognize that the state is the entity most responsible and vulnerable to new social movement claims and constituencies (Piven & Cloward, 1982; Fisher, 1992).

These are some of the major insights of new social movement theory. Its central linkage with postmodern ideas is a shared explanation and critique of the postwar changes in social and cultural organization: the emergence of global capitalism, the concomitant expansion/fragmentation of citizen resistance into community-based groupings, the decline of a central narrative around which society and, more specifically, community organizing coalesces, and the substitution of the project of individual and collective empowerment for the objective of winning and holding state power (Laclau & Mouffe, 1985).

Postmodernism is really no more than an assortment of perspectives assembled into a somewhat coherent paradigm by modernists primarily interested in and sympathetic to the postmodern critique of culture and society. Indeed, it is a term that those identified as "postmodern" themselves rarely use. The postmodern stance that, in many ways, is rooted in Surrealism and its postwar expression, Situationism, tends to identify with the anarchist impulses in the new social movements (Epstein, 1990, 54; Marcus, 1989). Postmodern thought sees these movements as reflecting the alternative, particularistic values that decenter hegemonic ideology. New social movement theory, on the other hand, is fundamentally a midrange, praxis-oriented theory steeped in neo-Marxism and the modernist goals of emancipation and social justice. It maintains a commitment to the search for univeralist values and the best means for their articulation and fulfillment, and it is in terms of this commitment that the modernist and postmodernist sensibilities clash. Before addressing the contribution that new social movement and postmodern theory might make to the development of practice strategies for community organizations, however, let us first turn to a discussion of the congruence of new social movement and postmodern theory with contemporary community organizing practice.

NEW SOCIAL MOVEMENT THEORY, THE POSTMODERN VISION, AND COMMUNITY ORGANIZATION: SOME COMMON GROUND AND CORRECTIVES

Where do postmodern perspectives and theories of new social movements share common ground with our knowledge of community organization practice? In what ways do the practice on the one hand, and the analytic frameworks on the other, seem to be at odds?

First, as we noted earlier, social work and community organization are contemporary manifestations of the modernist project. As such, they may incorporate certain elements and insights from the postmodern, but they will remain fundamentally at odds with its stance of subjective detachment from structured political formations. This is especially evident in the rationalist, progressive, value-driven nature of community organization and social work.

While social work is based on universalist, modernist values, and the idea of a coherent, acting subject, postmodernism offers a much more relativistic perspective, one that suspects all overriding value systems of imposing on individual choice and autonomy and views the acting self as a subject that can never be quite sure of which identity it wants to wear. Political efficacy, under such a framework, is always understood as limited and time-bound, although in a world where one's life and subjectivity are threatened,collective action—ephemeral as it might be—is understood as a responsible, moral choice. ACT-UP's notion of political struggle as one step removed from guerilla theater, inseparably tied to the assault of subversive images on hegemonic ones, is an almost perfect expression of postmodern activism (Crimp & Ralston, 1990). Although postmodern activism may be inherently limited, it is not necessarily ineffective: Such methods have been quite successful in sharpening AIDS awareness, compelling public discusion of its nature and treatment, and making clear its meaning for the population as a whole.

Despite the clash between social work and postmodernist sensibility, however, the core of postmodern ideas, especially the focus on cultural politics, dominates current discourse and practice related to community organization in particular and social work in general. The postmodern emphasis on "multiculturalism" and "cultural competency" demonstrates the increasing importance and value of a polyvocal discourse. It names those people and groups—women, people of color, gay men and lesbians, the disabled, and so on—whose life-worlds were denied independent and specific recognition by hegemonic narratives and politics. At their worst, however, multiculturalism, cultural competency, and postmodernism in general can lead to a parochial, fragmented politics of culture and identity. It is one of the major challenges to community organizers to build on the newly empowered polyvocal constituencies recognized and named by postmodern analysis and to get them to go beyond their cultural parochialism to include issues and narratives of political economy and class.

Second, the literature on community organization is a splendid antidote to ahistorical notions of "newness" evident in both new social movement and postmodern theories. Their claim that community and identity movements are essentially postwar phenomena does not withstand scrutiny. Especially in the United States, there is a rich history of community-based efforts that goes back as far as the Progressive Era in the years before World War I. As we pointed out earlier, community social work, beginning with Jane Addams and the settlement house movement—itself modeled on methods of working with the urban poor that Addams had learned in England—always drew upon both class and citizenship as bases for collective identity and collective action.

There is more salience to the argument that in the years after World War II, and especially in the 1960s, community/constituency–based forms of resistance replaced class and factory/labor–based organizing as the *dominant* form. In this understanding, community efforts begin their ascendance in the late 1930s, coincident with Saul Alinsky's work in Back of the Yards. Alinsky is a perfect transitional figure, whose practice included elements of both old and new social movement organizing. This period also reveals efforts by the social work profession, in the form of the Lane Report, to focus on community and to move further away from class.

Since then, and particularly in the 1960s, community-based efforts have expanded dramatically, not only within social work but even more outside of the profession. At the same time, the focus of these efforts has had less and less to do with a conscious recognition of the role of class. Unhappily, current social work education has followed these trends, for, here, organizing the poor has taken a back seat, if it continues to hold any seat at all, to emphases on race, gender, sexual preference, locality, and varied interest/identity groupings. In fact, all the central components of the new social movement shift—community-based constituency groupings, neopopulist democratic ideology, struggles over culture and social identity, and the focus on self-help and empowerment—have become key elements in contemporary community organization practice. The problem is that class, while ignored, remains an inseparable part of the problems that structure collective life, and the larger social injustices that people encounter in their day-to-day lives cannot be effectively addressed without recognition of its role. Here, older social work traditions have something significant to contribute to both postmodern and new social movement theories.

Third, seen in this light, new social movement and postmodern theory, whatever their other differences, help explain why, in contrast to much received opinion, community organization is not declining. For, in the fragmenting contemporary world, communities of place and identity do not disappear; rather, they proliferate worldwide, as does community organizing. Their proliferation, in fact, may be one result of global restructuring itself, which dismantles the centralized state and forces resistance onto the grassroots level. A number of recent studies support this conclusion by going beyond an analysis of community organization in the United States and Western Europe to include resistances in Third World and formerly communist nations (Durning, 1989; Lowe, 1986; Touraine, 1985; Castells, 1983; Laclau & Mouffe, 1985; Cocks, 1989; Wallerstein, 1990; Frank & Fuentes, 1990).

The common narratives that could bring and hold these movements together continue to lack salience. Nationalism and ethnicity continue to devastate peoples all over the world, the most horrifying current examples being the conflicts in the former Yugoslavia, Rwanda, and Somalia. But, nevertheless, new social movement theory offers to community organization practictioners the prospect that they may be riding at the edge of a growing swell, rather than trapped in the backwaters of a stagnating tidepool.

Fourth, the impact of the decentering and fragmentation phenomena on both the practice and literature of currrent community organization is an ambivalent one. On the one hand, decentering and diversity have encouraged a much wider polyvocal discourse in the area of community organization. Practice is no longer dominated by male leaders fighting for the working class. Gay, feminist, black nationalist, Latino, and disabled organizers, to name but a few, work with their own constituencies, in their own communities. They build community capacity, focus on empowerment, and expand the scope of organizing to arenas and constituencies never before included or never before included to such a significant degree.

But the new diversity has also tended to fragment contemporary social movements into exclusive, often antagonistic, parochial components. "By politicizing the personal," Kauffman puts it, "feminists, queers, and people of color have privileged difference over commonality, and have splintered movements of opposition" (Kauffman, 1992). Despite their obvious shared characteristics and their affinity for other new social movement groups and causes, they tend to parallel rather than to interact with each other (Fisher & Kling, 1991). The divisive politics of culture is exalted above, and often in opposition to, a politics of political economy.

If the current widespread proliferation and persistence of community organizing is truly to address the causes of community problems, efforts must move beyond the narrow focus of cultural politics. The challenge is to simultaneously encourage grassroots diversity, find commonality in the varied efforts, and tie cultural politics to a politics of political economy. There is not enough theory that addresses the critical issue for community organizing in a postmodern context: How do we continue to support diversity and polyvocal discourse and, simultaneously, to find the commonalities necessary to build efforts capable of fighting for significant power and social change?

PRACTICE IMPLICATIONS

Without question, the self-construction of the new social movements through particularist political identities weakens the possibility for coherently imagined challenges to late-capitalist politics and culture. But to recognize their potential to fragment social struggle is not to critique them. It is to do no more than to name one of the determining conditions of organizing that emerges within the context of the postmodern. After all, the logic of capital accumulation creates, across identity politics, common grievances and experiences of domination and control. These compel some sort of search for connection. The threat to the environment is one such aggregating issue. The needs for day care, for a nationally legislated family leave policy, for more comprehensive support of the elderly, for national health insurance, are others. All fit together as part of a shared experience of, in some way, being subject to domination.

Our argument insists, therefore, that the historical dialectic of domination and resistance must be understood and fashioned in terms of the interplay among class, community, and the search for new cultural orientations. We seek a blending, wherever posible, of insights from old and new social movements and from the modern and postmodern approaches to social restructuring. We offer, therefore, as we have elsewhere, the following two strategies as possible bases for building onto contemporary practice, not only the heritage of community organization but also elements of new social movement and postmodern theory as well (Fisher & Kling, 1988).

First, mobilization in the fragmented metropolis demands that broad coalitions be sought between various constituency groups, to build political bridges between the polyvocal components of the postmodern discourse and the new social movements (Fisher & Kling, 1993).

Second, we must move to a more consciously ideological politics. We must seek, at least, more common programs that can draw the decentered narratives of our time toward a focal point. An organizing ideology for our times needs to combine the new postmodern demands for autonomy and identity with older, modernist ones for social justice, production for human needs rather than profit, and the spirit of connectedness and solidarity among people rather than competition. Day-to-day organizing, if it is to move beyond fragmented values and cultures, still needs to be informed by this sort of centering, oppositional ideology. To continue to open activists and constituencies to broader conceptions of social change remains, we think, the primary responsibility of the organizer in the 1990s. Certain types of new social movement and postmodern theory may remain skeptical of the viability of this approach, but in the hands of community organizers, it seems the one most salient and valuable.

NOTE

1. Empowerment is a hotly contested and ambiguous term, often focusing solely on the empowerment (real or imagined) of individuals. In terms of community practice, however, empowerment at its best means a practice and process of community work that struggles around confronting oppression, understands the structual basis of that oppression, and seeks as its ends not only social justice and equality but also the realization of human potential.

9

The Theory and Practice of Decision Making

Sherri Sheinfeld-Gorin, with Narayan Viswanathan

Fundamental to all human activity are decision making, problem solving, problem finding, and the underlying exercise of information processing. Information processing as a prelude to rational decision making is critical to the work of managers. The literature on information processing in managerial decision making is vast and, particularly in the fields of computer science and artificial intelligence, has grown so rapidly that it is difficult for a scholar in any one discipline to keep abreast of the state-of-the-art developments. The varied approaches to managerial information processing—spanning the fields of economics; developmental, cognitive, organizational, clinical and experimental psychology; sociology; operations research; and statistics—clearly do not fall neatly within the boundaries of any one discipline. Further, the different schools of thought concerned with information processing in management decision-making use different vocabularies; often, they have difficulty communicating with one another. The integration proposed herein seeks to preserve the distinctiveness of each approach while illuminating the nature of their convergent or divergent viewpoints. Last but not least, the aim is to offer an orientation to social work practice based on this integration.

THE INTEGRATIVE DECISION MAKING MATRIX (IDMM)[1]

Information use for decision making within organizations may be explored according to two separate dimensions: the first moving from a concern with the organization qua organization to a concern with the individual decision maker, and the second focusing on the decision process or the decision outcome. While all modern organizational theorists are interested in how behaviors are contingent upon a social context, the primacy accorded the individual decision maker and his/her unique cognitive processes varies by approach. Further, each of the models describes a process. However, as in the case of the decision analyis model, an optimal decision making pattern is prescribed only to predict an outcome.

The IDMM (see Table 9.1) specifies four elements of comparison: major schools of thought, epistemology, algorithm/heuristic/problem-solving model, and descriptive or prescriptive focus. The first of the four elements, school of thought, refers to the particular discipline(s) within which a given approach rests. Epistemology refers to the theory of knowledge; it also implies a method of inquiry. Each approach is characterized by its primary and historical orientation to the generation of knowledge. The algorithm/heuristic/problem-solving model used refers to the manner by which decisions are made. Even the use of these three terms depends upon the assumptions of the model being examined. With more deterministic approches, such as the decision analytic, an algorithm (or a procedure that operates in a sequence of well-defined steps and yields a solution) is an appropriate description of the utility-maximization strategem in use. With other models, such as the strategic choice, a heuristic method (or guide) to the context within which the actor creates meaning out of the choices at hand is described. The fourth element of the IDMM depicts the central aim of each approach: A descriptive model is one that describes a reality of the situation, namely, how decisions are actually made. A prescriptive model, in contrast, is one that determines how decisions should be made.

The four quadrants can be seen as four different angles, or four separate camera lenses, with each viewing the same phenomenon of managerial decision making. Yet, as with a hologram, where a picture recorded on a flat surface yields a three-dimensional image, only when decision making is viewed in its entirety, along each dimension of the IDMM, in conjunction with every other dimension, can the phenomenon be understood more completely.

We interpret the IDMM presented in Table 9.1 by describing the four different angles in each of the four quadrants—control, strategic choice, decision analysis, and cognitive. We use aspects of the sets of information about each angle selectively to illustrate salient points about that angle.

Control School of Thought

The control school of thought derives from the fields of systems engineering and management science and highlights the outcome of a *system* of decision making in the organizational context. Its epistemological bases rest in logical positivism, including: an aim of explanation and prediction through empirical inquiry, the value of neutrality, and the subsumption of individual cases under hypothetically proposed general laws (Abel, 1977, 77–80).

Control may be defined as any process that helps align the actions of individuals with the interests of their employing organization (Tannenbaum, 1968). In the control framework, the manager gathers information about environmental variations and uses technical criteria to examine the consequences of responses to alternative demands (Astley & Van de Ven, 1983). Decision making is rational in that it exhibits goal-directed behavior, with an objective logic of effectiveness based on "technical rationality" (Thompson, 1967, 14). The decision-making process is governed by laws inferred from a cost-benefit calculus and a "logic of cost and efficiency" (Roethlisberger & Dickson, 1939).

Table 9.1
Integrative Decision-Making Matrix (IDMM)

	Control	Strategic Choice
Organization	Major Schools of Thought systems Engineering management science Epistemology logical positivism Algorithm/Heuristic/Problem-Solving 　Model decision-making on the basis of "cost efficiency," using available information on cause and effect Descriptive/Prescriptive Focus prescriptive model, with behavior, input or output specification	Major Schools of Thought sociology social psychology Epistemology phenomenology Algorithm/Heuristic/Problem-Solving 　Model choice of relevant operating constraints, enactment of relevant environmental contingencies Descriptive/Prescriptive Focus descriptive model, with specifications of actors, action, meaning of constraints and choices
	Decision Analysis	**Cognitive**
	Major Schools of Thought operations research statistics computer science (artificial intelligence) Epistemology post positivism Algorithm/Heuristic/Problem-Solving 　Model individual, total utility maximization when decisions are value-laden Descriptive/Prescriptive Focus prescriptive, given specification of values	Major Schools of Thought cognitive, developmental, experimental, social psychology Epistemology logical positivism Algorithm/Heuristic/Problem-Solving 　Model satisficing, additive, dominance, lexicographic, models of individual choice Descriptive/Prescriptive Focus descriptive, linear models used as a basis of decision-making, information processing approach
Individual		

Outcome Focused ⎯⎯⎯⎯⎯⎯⎯⎯⎯⎯⎯⎯⟶ Process Focused

Typically, organizations use a cybernetic system (Boulding, 1956) to model the control process. In bureaucratic terms, this system includes: (1) behavior control, (2) output control, and (3) input control (Snell, 1992; Thompson, 1967;

Ouchi, 1977). Behavior control regulates the transformation process; output control regulates results (Snell, 1992); and input control systems regulate the antecedent conditions of performance, including the knowledge, skills, abilities, values, and motives of employees. The type of control employed is dependent upon the knowledge of cause/effect relationships within the organization (Thompson, 1967), as well as the amount, type, and quality of information available to the manager.

The type of control employed may also depend upon several other factors; for example: (1) the strategic context of the agency, including the degree of breadth and change in the agency's products or markets (Hambrick, 1983; Snow & Hrebiniak, 1980); (2) technology, including work flow integration, and the way work flows between units (Child, 1973; Perrow, 1967; Reeves & Woodward, 1970; Thompson, 1967); and (3) size, with executives in larger organizations facing greater demands than those in small agencies in terms of the amount of information they must process (Galbraith, 1973; Khandwalla, 1974).

By specifying behavior, inputs, or outputs, the control theory prescribes a desired outcome of the decision-making process. The control approach specifies an automatic comparator that matches feedback to the template (or image) and sounds an alarm when discrepancies exceed a given threshold (Mitchell & Beach, 1990). The alarm appears to be largely affective, however, even though its consequences are cognitive. For example, when the current state of affairs fails to match the desired state, the discrepancy is experienced as discomfort, unpleasantness, and aversion (Bandura, 1977; Goodman, Pennings, et al., 1977; Porter & Lawler, 1976). In empirical work on job satisfaction, equity perception, and skill acquisition, the comparator does not seem to operate automatically, as motivation to think about how to correct discrepancies is provided by the negative affect rather than by the discrepancies themselves.

Strategic Choice School of Thought

Borne of the sociological and social psychological schools of thought, the strategic choice perspective rests on the process of framing constraints for individual decision making within the context of the organization. The epistemological foundation of the strategic choice framework derives from phenomenology. Phenomenology, as developed most fully by Husserl, and ethnomethodology, the systematic program of research based upon its premises, aim at the intuitive understanding of the "eidos," or the essence of perceptions and cognitive experiences (Mayrl, 1973, 15). Phenomenology maintains that society can be understood only from the point of view of the individuals who experience it (Mayrl, 1973). With its focus on Schutz's source of meaning in the lived experience or the reflective consciousness of the ego on such experience (Schutz, 1967), it offers a marked contrast to the logical positivist models that subsume individual cases under hypothetically proposed general laws (Abel, 1977). Further, it may be contrasted with the epistemological approach of abduction, seen as a postpositivist approach (Thagard, 1988), that integrates the positivist's use of formal logic to analyze the nature of theories (in algorithmic analyses and logic programming) with the account of how human scientists think.

Heuristic: The strategic choice framework highlights individuals, their interactions, social constructions, autonomy, and choices. The environment and the organization are enacted (Weick, 1976) to embody the meanings and actions of individuals, particularly those in power (Astley & Van de Ven, 1983). Decision making is best seen as a consequence of a series of unfolding events or episodes rather than as a rationally contrived process aimed at the instrumental attainment of organizational goals. Goals themselves may be imaginative reconstructions that impute order and rationality to acts and decisions after they have occurred. Logic may be superimposed on a preexisting decision. Managers seem to choose from their environment what the relevant operating context will be for them. The perception, interpretation, and application of outside contexts is part of a strategic choice and action process (Child, 1972). And, while managers experience constraint, they do so only in the sense that they have chosen what will act as a constraint for them (Astley & Van de Ven, 1983). Managers define and create their own constraints, or "enact" (Weick, 1976) their external conditions (Wamsley & Zald, 1973; Bacharach & Lawler, 1980).

Deriving from the work of Thompson (Thompson, 1967), and Astley and Van de Ven (Astley & Van de Ven, 1983), one criticism of the approach looks at the process of strategic choice from the dual perspectives of the organization alone and as a member of a collectivity and suggests that the manager may be seen as both a "statesman" and a "gamesman." As a statesman, she or he is involved in facilitating mutual adjustment among organizations, thereby enhancing self-interest as well as the collective well-being of others in the environment. When deciding as a gamesman, she or he seeks to play for the "maxmin," by maximizing resource acquisition and concurrently minimizing the loss of autonomy. The process of balancing these two strategies is what Thompson (Thompson, 1967, 48) called the "paradox of administration."

The model may be seen as descriptive, specifying actors and actions, as well as the meaning of constraints and choices.

Decision Analysis School of Thought

Common to the fields of economics, organizational behavior, policy analysis, statistics (especially Bayesian models) and artificial intelligence, decision analysis has long been considered traditional decision theory. The model highlights the optimal decision outcome for the individual, within the given constraints. Relying upon an epistemology developed within the field of artificial intelligence, decision analytic theory is developed using a pattern of reasoning called abduction, which is defined as inference to the best explanation (Falkenhainer, 1990; Charniak, 1988; Josephson, Chandrasekaran, Smith, and Tanner, 1987; Pople, 1973; Reggia, Nau, and Wanf, 1983; Schank, 1986). Explanation is based on the search for similarity between the situation being explained and some previously understood phenomenon (Josephson, Chandrasekaran, Smith, and Tanner, 1987). To explain minute occurrences, backward chaining is used, wherein events to be explained are viewed as queries and general theories and other observations are expressed in terms of rules and facts. Backward chaining attempts to reduce the observations to known facts by way of the rules contained in the theory (O'Rourke, Morris, and Schulenburg, 1989, 206). For more complex models, interpretation and explanation take the form of a best match process, by matching the current situation to hypotheses that could explain it (Falkenhainer, 1990; Josephson, Chandrasekaran, Smith, and Tanner, 1987; Reggia, Nau, and Wanf, 1983).

Algorithm: Using algorithms with data from previous observations, inference is used to obtain probability distributions for variables of interest, typically with the assistance of a computer (Shachter, 1988).

Maximizing Expected Utility: Assuming that there is a single, rational decision maker, and that his or her decisions may be uniquely ordered in time, the results derived from probabilistic influence diagrams, or graphs with nodes for each variable in the model and arcs that indicate the relationships among variables (Miller, Merkhofer, Howard, Matheson, and Rice, 1976; Howard & Matheson, 1984; Olmstead, 1983; Schachter, 1986), may be used to diagram sequential decisions toward objectives. For example, a decision variable that is part of the influence diagram may characterize a value chosen by the decision maker as the maximization of expected utility. If the decision maker does not forget, then any information observed before she or he makes one decision will also be available for all subsequent decisions. To solve problems intrinsic to these models, a decision point (or node) is made deterministic, and its informational predecessors become conditional predecessors. Its deterministic function is then constructed through optimization (Olmstead, 1983). While the data on which the decision analytic model depends are descriptive, the central use of this approach has been in prescribing optimal decision-making strategies to administrators. The focus is the individual decision maker as she or he seeks to maximize the decision outcome of several competing alternatives. This approach has been challenged for not reflecting the actual decision-making process, however, both by a set of experimental results and by the observations of professional decision makers making on-the-job decisions (Hershey & Schoemaker, 1980). Moreover, it has been accused of "overintellectualizing (Johansson, 1991) the cognitive processes people go through when choosing alternative actions" (Schwab, Olian-Gottlieb, and Heneman, 1979, 146). Further, Mintzberg (Mintzberg, 1973) observed decision makers and found that most of their decisions involved only one option rather than many and that the decision rested on whether or not to go with that option rather than to choose among competing alternatives. Not surprisingly, Mintzberg confirmed that few decisions involved either explicit balancing of costs and benefits or probability theory, upon which the model rests (Mitchell & Beach, 1990).

Cognitive School of Thought

Founded primarily in the fields of cognitive and social psychology, as well as in experimental and development psychology, the cognitive approach is descriptive and focuses on how the mind of the individual decision maker works. The approach developed within a logical positivist tradition, and most of the empirical work borne of the approach has rested on that epistemological base.

Problem-Solving Model: One type of schema (a structure that chunks information into useful patterns), the script, has found wide acceptance as a simple, well-structured context for understanding the prose dealing with mundane events (Neisser, 1976; Abelson, 1981; Schank & Abelson, 1977). A script is a coherent sequence of events expected by the individual, involving him or her either as a participant or as an observer (Abelson, 1976, 33).

In a script, the person seeking to understand is hypothesized to possess conceptual representations of a stereotypical event, or sequence of events. Scripts are activated when the decision maker can expect events in the sequence to occur in the text (Abelson, 1981, 715). Script-based theory is anchored in individual cognitive structures that may or may not mesh with the performance expectations of others. Scripts may be organized in higher order knowledge structures, known as memory organization packets (or MOPs) (Schank, 1986); a MOP invoked to understand a present experience may spontaneously activate relevant past episodes (Abelson, 1981).

Satisficing, Additive, Dominance, and Lexicography

Four major linear decision-making models (satisficing, additive, dominance, and lexicography) have been explored empirically as means of explaining cognitive functioning. Each of the four will be examined in brief forthwith.

Satisficing. The satisficing theory of decision making states that individuals do not always attempt to find optimal solutions to problems that confront them. Making an optimal decision would involve such an overload on people's information-processing capacity that attempts at optimizing in personal decision making are almost never made (March & Simon, 1958; Simon, 1976a). According to the satisficing theory, people try to find solutions that are "good enough," rather than finding solutions that are "best."

Additive. The standard additive model assumes that a weight can be attached to each factor, and that factor weights and scores are known. The most valued alternative receives the highest score (Berl, Lewis, and Morrison, 1976).

Dominance. The dominance model assumes that comparisons are made factor-by-factor across each factor and then across all factors. Eventually, an alternative is picked if it dominates all the other options (Berl, Lewis, and Morrison, 1976).

Lexicography. Lexicography concerns the comparison of alternatives across factors, assuming the factors can be ordered, and that one can, in fact, compare the factors of importance (Berl, Lewis, and Morrison, 1976).

The cognitive model is focused on the description of thinking behavior within and among individual decision makers. The satisficing, additive, dominance, and lexicographic models form the bases for the prescriptions found in the decision analytic approach; for example, in the macro-matching of scripts or schema-based models of story understanding (Charniak, 1972; DeJong, 1982; Mooney, 1987; Falkenhainer, 1990, 161). In the cognitive approach, however, while actions are organized according to goals and plans (Graesser, 1981; Galambos, 1986), the aim is the empirical investigation of mental processes; normative issues (and prescription) are of interest only to the extent that they characterize people's *departures* from assumed norms (Nisbett & Ross, 1980;

Thagard, 1988). Further, while empirical studies have demonstrated some support for the dominance and lexicographic models as descriptors of decision-making behavior (Berl, Lewis, and Morrison, 1976), they are less strong predictors than the additive model.

INTEGRATION WITH SOCIAL WORK

Each of the four models can make a contribution to a decision-making model for social work. This model must take into account the unique values and knowledge of social work. The picture that emerges from this orientation includes the two relevant IDMM dimensions, which are (1) a concern for the individual within the organization and (2) a focus on process rather than outcome. The two major social work dimensions are (1) relevance to the unique organizational settings, problems, and populations that are the subjects of decision-making in the field of social work and (2) a focus on a cognitive epistemology founded in the work of Heidegger (Heidegger, 1962) as well as in more recent work in hermeneutics. We will now discuss the resulting model (Table 9.2) in more detail.

Table 9.2
Elements of Social Work and the IDMM

Control	Strategic Choice
Systems Orientation	Value Driven
	Ready-to-Hand Mode
	Phenomenological Epistemology
Decision Analysis	Cognitive
Modeling of Individual Variables	Use of Scripts
Empirical Verification in Varied Contexts	

Being Value-Driven with a Unique Clientele

The strategic choice model highlights the importance of the context within which decision making is performed. As with not-for-profit management in general, social work administrators are guided by the values of a collective mission, philanthropy, altruism, social responsibility, equity, diversity, fairness, and legal propriety (Rubin, Adamski, and Block, 1989). Organizational ideology, including a mission orientation and value-laden means-ends relationships within the agency (Sheinfeld Gorin & Weirich, 1981), may influence the organization's relations to the environment (Pfeffer & Salancik, 1978; Sheinfeld Gorin & Weirich, 1995), its stakeholders, structure, technology (Sheinfeld Gorin & Weirich, 1981), and outcomes (Wernet & Austin, 1991; Austin, 1991). This value orientation, described early by Selznick (Selznick, 1957), characterizes the social work agency and thus the social work decision maker, whose primary actions are those of promoting and protecting the organization's values rather than relentlessly seeking maximal payoffs.

Traditional social work settings—child welfare agencies, social service departments, criminal justice agencies, and health care centers—offer contexts that are unique in the extent to which they are value-driven. Further, recent work by Gitterman (Gitterman, 1991) suggests that social work decision makers working in these settings are most likely to engage with more vulnerable and needy populations, who are most likely to suffer burdensome consequences of agency actions.

A Social Work Epistemology

Based on a phenomenological approach to the epistemology of decision making expressed most fully by Heidegger (Heidegger, 1962), the dimensions of the social work–specific model would imply one of three modes of being-in-the-world: the "ready-to-hand" (*zuhanden*). In this mode, the actor has a holistic view of what she or he is doing, and the accompanying feelings and thoughts focus almost exclusively upon the task. In the discovery, one "lets it be" (Heidegger, 1962, 117; Mitchell & Beach, 1990). Of Heidegger's (Heidegger, 1962) other two modes, the "unready-to-hand" (*unzuhanden*) is engaged when the "ready-to-hand" mode encounters difficulties (Mitchell & Beach, 1990); it involves more attention to the surrounding context and its constraints. The "present-at-hand" (*vorhanden*) mode involves a highly rational, detached, analytic problem-solving approach that is engaged when the other modes fail to cope with the task (Heidegger, 1962, 117).

The "ready-to-hand" mode—wherein a situation is experienced primarily as the actual and the possible, and action in turn is experienced in terms of its fittingness and appropriateness to the task at hand (Packer, 1985, 1086)—reflects a highly dynamic, integrative "person-in-situation" model of social work. This epistemological approach is congruent with one scientific tradition in social work, specifically, its emphasis on the dynamic relationship between the observer and the observed. Further, consonant with the control theory of decision making, Heidegger's "tailored fit" between the holistic image and the actor's interaction with it (Packer, 1985) seems to reflect social work's interest in a systems orientation (in practice, Johnson & Goguen, 1991) and its more humane view of how people's cognitive systems deal with epistemic questions.

CONCLUSIONS

What do decision-making theory and research have to say that is generally important and useful to management practice? Under the rubric of the Integrative Decision Making Matrix, this chapter has tried to provide a synoptic overview of a large, complex body of theory and research on decision making in organizations. This body of knowledge does not offer ready-made solutions or quick fixes for every problem that managers confront. Instead, it offers us ways of thinking about organizations and understanding the managerial problems that they present. In a broad sense, therefore, this body of knowledge provides a foundation for human judgment, reasoning, and cognition.

ACKNOWLEDGMENTS

An earlier version of this chapter was presented to the First Annual Conference on the Integration of Social Work and Social Science, October 30, 1992, Ann Arbor, Michigan. The authors would like to thank Mr. Marc Arje for his assistance in the preparation of this chapter.

NOTE

1. The IDMM was inspired by an earlier unpublished monograph by Dr. Sheinfeld Gorin, entitled "Decision Making in Experimental and Field Contexts: An Attempt at Integration" (1979).

10

Expanding Theories of Occupational Structure: Examining the Relationship between Family-Responsive Policies and Worker Well-Being

Susan Lambert

An increasing number of employers are implementing what are called family-responsive policies, such as employer-supported child care, employee assistance programs, and elder care services. The employers adopting such policies tend to be large companies, which tend to employ a substantial number of women in managerial and professional positions (Galinsky, 1988; Galinsky, Friedman, and Hernandez, 1991; Galinsky, Hughes, and David, 1990). Research on family-responsive policies has followed a similar path, focusing primarily on skilled workers in large organizations—often Fortune 500 companies or hospital complexes. This research often employs a program evaluation approach; that is, it strives to isolate the effects of a particular policy or program. For example, a number of studies examine the extent to which on-site child care improves the recruitment and attendance of skilled female employees working in health care settings (Burud, Aschbacher, and McCroskey, 1984; Berkeley Planning Associates, 1989; Fernandez, 1986; Friedman, 1989; Marshall, 1991).

Moreover, most studies look at these policies from a business perspective. Research focuses either on the cost to employers for ignoring workers' family and personal concerns (Fernandez, 1986; Hughes & Galinsky, 1988) or on the benefits to employers for responding to workers' family and personal responsibilities (Bohen & Viveros-Long, 1981; Burud, Aschbacher, and McCroskey, 1984; Fernandez, 1986; Marshall, 1991; McDonnell Douglas Corporation, 1989). It is usually simply assumed that family-responsive policies benefit workers and their families. The validity of this assumption is suspect, however. Many so-called family-responsive policies operate more as work supports than family supports; that is, many of these policies make it easier for workers to adjust their family life to conform to work requirements rather than altering work requirements to accommodate family responsibilities (Lambert, 1993). It remains an empirical question whether family-responsive policies can help overcome the deleterious effects that poorly designed jobs have on individual and family well-being or whether workers benefit from such policies only when their jobs are designed well.

A program evaluation approach that focuses on a policy in isolation from the larger workplace context is insufficient for identifying the extent to which the effects of family-responsive policies do indeed depend upon the design of workers' jobs. Other approaches are needed that enable us to look at the conditions under which family-responsive policies have certain effects. Moreover, a perspective other than a business perspective is needed if we are fully to understand the role that family-responsive policies play in the lives of workers and their families. A social work perspective draws attention to the lack of focus on the relationship between family-responsive policies and worker and family well-being. It also highlights the need for research on the role these policies play in the lives of lower-level and minority workers, who are disproportionately employed in small organizations.

Thus, the integration of theories of occupational structure with a social work perspective leads to new questions about family-responsive policies in the workplace. In this chapter, I articulate some of these new questions and address them with data from a culturally diverse sample of men and women working at a medium-sized manufacturing firm.[1]

CONCEPTUAL FRAMEWORK

Theories of Occupational Structure

A consistent theme in both organizational sociology and organizational psychology is the importance of two basic dimensions of work: job stress and job challenge.[2] Study after study documents that stressful job conditions interfere with workers' well-being both on and off the job; indeed, stressful job conditions often contribute to health problems that shorten workers' lives. Challenging work, on the other hand, is consistently related to enhanced well-being; challenging work promotes workers' participation in and enjoyment of work, leisure, and family.

One unanticipated consequence of the consistency with which researchers have documented the significance of these key job characteristics is that their importance is often taken for granted. In research on family-responsive policies, basic job conditions are usually ignored or are treated as control variables to be gotten out of the way in order to examine the relationships of principal concern. The older literature and theory on occupational structure has the potential to further understanding of how family-responsive policies affect workers and their families by helping to specify the conditions under which workplace supports may or may not have desired effects.

There are three ways that family-responsive policies may influence worker well-being. One way is that these policies may have a direct effect on well-being; in other words, the more benefits workers use and the more they appreciate those benefits, the better off they may be no matter what the nature of their job. Next, family-supportive policies may actually help compensate for poor job conditions. That is, family-responsive policies may play a greater role in maintaining the well-being of workers in poorly designed jobs as compared to those in well-designed jobs. Finally, it may be that supportive policies can augment well-being only when jobs are designed well. That is, poor job characteristics may override the potentially positive effects of family-responsive policies so that workplace supports promote the well-being of workers in good jobs to a greater extent than they do of workers in poor jobs.

My reading of the organizational literature has led me to conclude that there is more evidence supporting this last form of influence than there is for the first two. As suggested above, studies consistently document the importance of basic job structures in promoting worker well-being both on and off the job. Melvin Kohn and colleagues' classic studies (Kohn, 1977; Kohn & Schooler, 1973; Miller, Schooler, Kohn, and Miller, 1979) are especially relevant to this issue. With both cross-sectional and longitudinal data, these researchers document the overriding importance of basic job conditions in explaining characteristics of workers' personalities and of the relationship between workers and their children. Their research gives little indication that workers can find rewards at home or at leisure that compensate for those lacking in the workplace. By extension, if one's family or leisure activities cannot compensate for the lack of rewarding work, then it is unlikely that family-responsive policies can. Good job designs may be necessary if family-responsive policies are to have desired effects.

Institutional Theory and the Role of Workplace Policies

A program evaluation approach to understanding the effects of family-responsive policies is based on the assumption that what is important is whether workers use a particular support. Certainly, there is every reason to believe that workers who use a particular support benefit more from it than those who do not, but this does not mean that there are no benefits to nonusers. For example, health insurance provides an important sense of security even when one is healthy. Moreover, people's needs change across the life cycle, so that workplace supports, like social security, may contribute to a sense of well-being even among those who have yet to need a particular support. Institutional theory provides a framework for understanding why workers' appreciation of workplace supports may promote their well-being no matter how many benefits they use.

Institutional theory posits that organizations adopt policies and practices for which there may be a good rationale but little evidence of effectiveness in solving problems either internal or external to the organization. These institutionalized practices are characterized in terms of organizational "myths and ceremonies." One of the more obscure premises of institutional theory is that organizational myths and ceremonies can help bind workers together (Meyer & Rowan, 1977). Adopting certain practices, regardless of their effects on organizational functioning, can create a sense of organizational identity of benefit to individual workers. In this spirit, family-responsive policies may send a message to workers that their employer is a responsive one who cares about them personally, and this message, this "myth," may benefit workers whether or not they use or need the supports available to them from their employer. When looked at in this way, the issue of how a particular policy affects workers fades in importance. Instead, the issue becomes how workers are affected by their view of these policies in general.

Variations by Gender

One of the primary rationales for implementing family-responsive policies in the workplace is the assumption that they are particularly useful in helping women to balance work and family responsibilities. Given this assumption, it behooves us to look carefully at how such policies may affect men and women differently. Previous research gives us reason to suspect that the effects of these policies do indeed vary by gender, as may the effects of certain job characteristics.

Research by Greenberger et al. (Greenberger, Goldberg, Hamill, O'Neil, and Payne, 1989) shows that women, both married and single, use significantly more family-related company benefits than men. Moreover, women, regardless of occupation, are more likely than men to change jobs for better child care benefits. Thus, it is not surprising that researchers also report that satisfaction with formal family-responsive policies is more important in explaining women's than men's role strain. These findings suggest the possibility that benefit appreciation is more strongly related to women's than men's well-being.

Although the literature suggests that women and men are similarly affected by challenging work (Lambert, 1991; Miller, Schooler, Kohn, and Miller, 1979), some research indicates that men are both more inundated with and more strongly affected by stressful job conditions (Billings & Moos, 1982; Hughes & Galinsky, 1988; Lambert, 1991). Thus, it is likely that challenging work similarly enhances men's and women's well-being and similarly affects the extent to which men and women benefit from formal workplace supports. On the other hand, it is likely that stressful work detracts more from men's than women's well-being and plays a larger role in determining whether men will reap the benefits of formal workplace supports.

RESEARCH QUESTIONS AND HYPOTHESES

The following research questions and hypotheses summarize the preceding literature review and denote the focus of the current investigation.

Question 1:   How do job characteristics help explain worker well-being?

- Hypothesis 1.1. Job challenge will be positively related to worker well-being; job stress will be negatively related to worker well-being.

- Hypothesis 1.2. Job challenge will be similarly important in explaining men's and women's well-being; job stress will be more important in explaining men's than women's well-being.

Question 2: To what extent does the relationship between benefit appreciation and worker well-being depend on the quality of workers' jobs? Do family-responsive policies help compensate for poorly designed jobs, or do they only augment the beneficial effects of well-designed jobs?

- Hypothesis 2.1. The relationship between benefit appreciation and worker well-being will depend upon the design of workers' jobs and will be consistent with an augmentation rather than a compensatory role for family-responsive policies. Specifically, the more challenging the workers' jobs, the more positive the relationship between benefit appreciation and worker well-being; the more stressful the workers' jobs, the less positive the relationship between benefit appreciation and worker well-being.

- Hypothesis 2.2. Benefit appreciation will be more important in explaining women's well-being than men's, although the form of the interaction will be the same for men and women.

METHODS

The data for this study was collected at Fel-Pro, Inc., an engine-gasket manufacturing firm located in Skokie, Illinois. The family-owned company employs about 2,000 workers and is a nonunion shop. Fel-Pro is nationally known for its extensive employee benefits and progressive family-responsive policies (Levering & Moskowitz, 1993). The data come from self-administered questionnaires, organization records, and in-depth interviews with a subset of workers; the questionnaire data were collected during 1991.

Sample Selection, Response Rate, and Bias

Questionnaires were distributed to a random sample of 882 employees: 665 workers (424 factory workers and 241 office workers) and 217 supervisors. Fel-Pro employees represent a wide range of occupations, from assembly-line workers and clerical workers to engineers and managers. Forty percent of the workforce are women. Fully 35 percent of the workforce are Hispanic, 20 percent are African American, and 40 percent are Caucasian. The sample captured this diversity. Altogether, 599 Fel-Pro employees returned completed questionnaires, of whom 218 were factory workers, 210 were office workers, and 171 were supervisors. The overall response rate to the questionnaire was 67.9 percent. The response bias in the data is described by Lambert et al. (Lambert et al., 1993); in general, the data underrepresent the experiences of African American men and Hispanic men and women who have a low education and who work in the factory.

Measures of Dependent and Independent Variables

Psychosomatic health is adapted from an index from the Quality of Employment Survey (Quinn & Staines, 1979). It averages how often respondents reported that they had experienced fourteen stress-related health problems during the past year, including shortness of breath, sleep problems, bouts of depression or anxiety, and spells of dizziness. Respondents' scores on this index have been reversed so that the higher their score, the better their psychosomatic health.

Partner quality is an index adapted from scales developed by Baruch and Barnett (Baruch & Barnett, 1986). It averages responses to thirteen items asking respondents about several different aspects of their relationship, including how easy their partner is to get along with, whether their partner does his/her fair share of work, whether they communicate well with their partner, whether their partner is a good listener and a good friend, and whether they feel appreciated by their partner.

Benefit appreciation is assessed using a six-item index that we developed for this study. It captures the extent to which workers believe that they could not themselves afford most of the benefits and services that Fel-Pro provides, that the benefits have helped their children do things they would not have been able to do otherwise, that the benefits have helped them through some bad times, that they would not trade their benefits for more profit-sharing, that these benefits are good investments for Fel-Pro, and that the benefits make it easier for them to balance their work and personal life.

Benefit use is measured by summing the number of benefits respondents have used during their tenure at Fel-Pro. Fel-Pro offers many different benefits and programs, including an on-site child-care center, elder-care resource and referral service, emergency dependent care, matching gifts program, tuition reimbursement, a fitness center, legal information service, and—for workers' children—a summer day camp, tutoring, and scholarships. Respondents indicated whether they or anyone in their immediate family had ever used twenty different benefits.

Job challenge is measured by averaging responses to five survey items adapted from the Michigan Assessment of Organizations Questionnaire (MAOQ) (Cammann, Fichman, Jenkins, and Klesh, 1983). These items capture the extent to which workers feel their job is challenging and gives them an opportunity to use their skills and abilities on a variety of tasks.

Job stress is measured by averaging four items adapted from the MAOQ pertaining to work overload, for example, the extent to which workers lack the time to do their tasks well.

Measures of Control Variables

A number of individual and family characteristics are included in the analyses in order to control for additional factors that have been shown to be related to psychosomatic health and marital satisfaction. Control variables include a dichotomous variable that distinguishes workers who work in the factory (coded 1) from workers who work in the office or who are supervisors (coded 0); the number of years respondents have worked at Fel-Pro; two dichotomous variables that identify African-American and Hispanic workers (thus the comparison category is Caucasian workers); the number of years of formal schooling workers had completed at the time of the survey; a dichotomous variable that identifies workers currently living with a spouse or partner (coded 1); a dichotomous variable that differentiates workers whose partner works in paid employment (coded 1) from workers whose partner does not (coded 0);[3] the number of children respondents have ever had, including any stepchildren who live with them or to whom they feel close; a dichotomous variable that differentiates respondents with children 5 or younger (coded 1) from respondents with older children or without children (coded 0); the age of respondents at the time of the survey; and the log of a variable summing the incomes of the respondent and his/her partner when relevant.

Data Analysis

The data are analyzed using multiple regression techniques based on the principle of ordinary least squares. The sample is narrowed to those respondents who were working full-time (35 or more hours) at the time of the survey and for whom responses were missing on three or fewer independent variables (N = 581). Missing data are assigned the mean for the relevant independent variable following procedures described by Cohen and Cohen (Cohen & Cohen, 1983); data are missing on less than 10 percent of the cases with one exception: years of education is missing for 75 (13 percent) of the cases. Because of the severe problems that correlated independent variables can create with the estimation of regression coefficients, steps were taken to avoid problems with multicollinearity.[4] Each case is weighted by the probability of being selected into the sample so that the findings are more representative of the entire Fel-Pro work force; the weighting factor adjusts for the actual number of respondents so that tests of statistical significance remain unbiased. Interaction terms are used to identify the extent to which benefit appreciation interacts with job characteristics in explaining well-being. Interaction terms were created by first centering (subtracting the mean from each respondent's score) the relevant independent variables (e.g., job challenge and benefit appreciation) and then multiplying them. Centering the relevant independent variables reduces their correlation to the interaction term, thus increasing the stability of the regression coefficients (Jaccard, Turrisi, and Wan, 1990).

RESULTS

Question 1 asked: "How do job characteristics help explain worker well-being?" Table 10.1 presents the main effects for the independent and control variables in helping explain workers' psychosomatic health and partner satisfaction. The results provide partial support for the hypothesis (Hypothesis 1.1) that job challenge and lack of job stress are integral to worker well-being. As anticipated, job challenge is positively related to both men's and women's psychosomatic health, while job stress is negatively related. Job challenge does not, however, help explain either men's or women's partner satisfaction, and job stress is negatively related to partner satisfaction among women only. Moreover, the data do not support the hypothesis (Hypothesis 1.2) that job stress detracts more from men's than women's well-being. The fact that job stress is significantly related to the quality of women's but not men's relationships suggests that job stress may be at least as harmful to the women as to the men working at this company.

Question 2 concerned the extent to which the relationship between benefit appreciation and worker well-being depend on the quality of workers' jobs? Also, do family-responsive policies help compensate for poorly designed jobs,

Table 10.1

Explaining Worker Well-being

Independent Variables[b]	Psychosomatic Health				Partner Satisfaction[a]			
	Men (N=367)		Women (N=214)		Men (N=291)		Women (N=133)	
	b	se	b	se	b	se	b	se
Job challenge	.126**	.043	.213**	.076	.076	.054	.115	.097
Job stress	-.282**	.040	-.345**	.063	-.057	.051	-.143*	.074
Number of benefits used	-.021*	.009	.007	.017	-.007	.012	.007	.019
Benefit appreciation	Significant interaction (see Table 10.2)		Significant interaction (see Table 10.2)		Significant interaction (see Table 10.3)		Significant interaction (see Table 10.3)	
Control Variables								
Blue-collar job	.117	.063	-.049	.098	.028	.079	-.163	.113
Age	-.002	.003	-.002	.005	.008*	.004	-.013*	.006
Yrs. of education	.047**	.013	-.017	.020	.026	.015	.001	.023
Lives w/partner	.122	.068	-.138	.112				
Partner works	-.051	.080	-.181	.166	-.148	.092	.164	.166
# of children	-.024	.026	-.058	.043	-.080*	.032	.065	.051
Has preschooler	.115*	.056	-.083	.103	-.043	.066	-.389**	.107
Family income	.154	.088	.034	.129	.154	.111	.397*	.167
African American	.162*	.075	.245*	.101	.050	.102	.067	.126
Hispanic	.182**	.056	.054	.099	.099	.067	.051	.101
Intercept	1.76**	.479	3 19**	.750	1.77**	.674	.96	1.04
F (sig.)	8.60 (<.001)		4 77 (<.001)		4.22 (<.001)		3.86 (<.001)	
R² (adjusted)	26.9%		26.6%		17.6%		31.4%	
	(23.8%)		(21%)		(13.5%)		(23.3%)	

[a] Includes only those respondents living with a spouse or partner at the time of the survey.

[b] There were no significant differences between men and women when comparing the unstandardized regression coefficient for the independent variables

** $p \le .01$; * $p \le .05$.

or do they only augment the beneficial effects of well-designed jobs? Tables 10.2 and 10.3 summarize the significant interactions between workers' appreciation of family-responsive policies and job challenge and job stress in helping explain worker well-being; the coefficients specify the relationship between benefit appreciation when a particular job characteristic is one standard deviation below the mean, at the mean, and one standard deviation above the mean (Jaccard, Turrisi, and Wan, 1990). Overall, the results support the basic hypothesis that the relationship between benefit appreciation and worker well-being depends on the quality of workers' jobs, primarily on the challenge of the job. The nature of this relationship varies by gender, however.

The results for women support the hypothesis (Hypothesis 2.1) that benefit appreciation cannot overcome the effects of poorly designed jobs. Instead, the results suggest that benefit appreciation may actually exacerbate the deleterious effects that unchallenging work has on women's psychosomatic health. As shown in Table 10.2, benefit appreciation is negatively related to women's psychosomatic health among women with little job challenge; the relationship between benefit appreciation and psychosomatic health becomes less negative as job challenge increases.

Our follow-up interviews provided some insight into this relationship. A number of workers told us that because Fel-Pro is better than most other companies in that it provides so many supports for workers and their children, they had expected that jobs there would be better than jobs elsewhere and were disappointed when this was not the case. Thus, it may be that the more workers in unchallenging jobs appreciated Fel-Pro's benefits, the greater the inconsistency they saw between the image of the larger organization and their experience in it. The negative relationship between benefit appreciation and psychosomatic health among women in the least challenging jobs suggests that women's mental health may suffer when this discrepancy is large. It also underscores the importance of challenging work in maintaining women's psychosomatic health and in helping ensure that the effects of family-responsive policies are those desired.

In addition to supporting the contention that benefit appreciation cannot overcome the effects of poorly designed jobs, the results pertaining to women's partner satisfaction support the hypothesis that benefit appreciation serves to augment the beneficial effects of challenging jobs. As shown in Table 10.3, the more challenging women's jobs, the more positive the relationship between benefit appreciation and women's partner satisfaction; benefit appreciation does not contribute to the partner satisfaction of women with the least challenging jobs at Fel-Pro. Thus, the results for women are consistent with the idea that job challenge is essential to worker well-being and provides an important context for understanding the role family-responsive policies play in the lives of workers.

The results for men are less consistent with the notion that family-responsive policies only augment the positive effects of well-designed jobs. As shown in Table 10.2, the less challenging men's jobs, the more positive the relationship between benefit appreciation and men's psychosomatic health. This relationship is consistent with the idea that family-responsive policies can help compensate for the deleterious effects of unchallenging work. On the other hand, the results pertaining to men's partner satisfaction support an augmentation role. As shown in Table 10.3, the relationship between benefit appreciation is most positive when job stress is low; the more stressful men's jobs, the weaker the relationship between benefit appreciation and partner satisfaction.

Table 10.2

Explaining Psychosomatic Health: Significant Interactions Involving Benefit Appreciation[a]

	Relationship between benefit appreciation and psychosomatic health when *job challenge* is:					
	Low[b] (-1 s.d.)		Average (0)		High (+ 1 s.d.)	
	b	se	b	se	b	se
Men	.130*	.067	.044	.049	-.042	.064
Women	-.252**	.099	-.113	.085	.026	.120

[a] Including the interaction term increased explained variance (unadjusted) an additional 1% in men's psychosomatic health and an additional 1..5% in women's psychosomatic health.

[b] The difference in the unstandardized regression coefficients for men and women with low job challenge is significant at $p \leq .01$.

** $p \leq .01$; * $p \leq .05$.

Table 10.3

Explaining Partner Satisfaction: Significant Interactions Involving Benefit Appreciation[a]

	Relationship between benefit appreciation and partner satisfaction when *job stress* is:					
	Low[b] (-1 s.d.)		Average (0)		High (+ 1 s.d.)	
	b	se	b	se	b	se
Men	.465**	.094	.298**	.065	.132*	.071
	Relationship between benefit appreciation and partner satisfaction when *job challenge* is:					
	Low[b] (-1 s.d.)		Average (0)		High (+ 1 s.d.)	
	b	se	b	se	b	se
Women	-.990	.111	.175*	.103	.359**	.133

[a] Including the interaction term increased explained variance (unadjusted) an additional 3.1% in men's psychosomatic health and an additional 4.4% in women's psychosomatic health.

[b] The difference in the unstandardized regression coefficients for men and women with low job challenge is significant at $p \leq .01$.

** $p \leq .01$; * $p \leq .05$; & $p \leq .10$.

In sum, the results support the basic hypothesis (Hypothesis 2.1) that the relationship between benefit appreciation and well-being depends upon the design of workers' jobs; this is true for both men and women. The results do not support the hypothesis (Hypothesis 2.2) that benefit appreciation is more important in explaining women's than men's well-being; in fact, the results for men provide some hope that family-responsive policies may help male workers to overcome the deleterious effects of unchallenging work on their psychosomatic health. Thus, the findings suggest that benefit appreciation is important to both men's and women's well-being, but in slightly different ways.

DISCUSSION

I began by explaining how theories of occupational structure are useful in helping to identify the conditions under which supportive workplace policies affect workers and by noting that a social work perspective draws attention to how these policies contribute to worker wellbeing and not just work performance. I will end by summarizing how I think this study feeds back into social science theory and inquiry as well as into the field of social work.

This study's primary contribution to social science theory and thought is in helping to refine knowledge of the role that occupational structure plays in explaining worker well-being. The findings of this study substantiate prior research indicating that job stress and job challenge are strongly related to worker well-being; the main effects for job challenge and job stress were significant in helping to explain both men's and women's psychosomatic health. What this study contributes is the knowledge that not only are job challenge and job stress important in and of themselves in explaining worker well-being, but that the effects of other workplace conditions—in this case, supportive workplace policies—are likely to depend upon just how challenging or stressful workers find their jobs. For example, although the main effects of job challenge and job stress were not significant in explaining partner satisfaction, the interaction effects indicated that the relationship between benefit appreciation and partner satisfaction depended, among women, on the extent to which workers' jobs were challenging and, among men, on the extent to which they were stressful. Thus, the study suggests that basic job conditions help establish the context for understanding how workers will experience other aspects of the workplace. In doing so, the study helps extend traditional theories of occupational structure by clarifying the expanded role basic job characteristics may play in explaining the well-being of workers in companies providing family-responsive policies. It helps us to better understand the relationship between work and well-being.

This study contributes to the field of social work by helping to clarify the importance of both basic job characteristics and supportive workplace policies in promoting the well-being of not only highly skilled, professional workers but also lower-level workers, minorities, and women.[5] Because lower-level workers—who are disproportionately minority and female in this company and most others—are most likely to have jobs that are both stressful and tedious, these results indicate the importance of taking basic occupational conditions into consideration when developing interventions aimed at improving the well-being of many of social work's traditional client populations. Moreover, the findings suggest that working in a company that provides family-responsive policies is no panacea for all the ills of the workplace; jobs, especially those performed by lower-level workers, may have to be improved if workers are to reap the benefits of family-responsive policies. As I have argued elsewhere (Lambert, 1993), workers might in fact need few formal supportive policies if their jobs were more flexible and their supervisors more supportive.

I am convinced that investigations of family-responsive policies in the workplace are strengthened to the extent that they build on established theories of organizational behavior and consider the well-being of employees as well as employers. The implementation of family-responsive policies provides a unique opportunity to examine basic organizational structures and processes of organizational change. Moreover, by considering the larger organizational context in which family-responsive policies are implemented, we can begin to identify the other changes that may have to occur if these policies are to enhance the well-being of all workers, especially those who may need them most.

ACKNOWLEDGMENTS

My appreciation to the employees of Fel-Pro for their participation in this study. This research was funded by the Fel-Pro/Mecklenburger Foundation and the Lois and Samuel Silberman Fund.

NOTES

1. This chapter was written in the spirit of providing an example of the value of integrating knowledge from the fields of organizational behavior and social work. Because of space limitations, I chose to present a fuller overview of the conceptual issues rather than the methodological ones. As a result, many details pertaining to the methodology and its limitations have been excluded. I am happy to provide interested readers with these details.

2. See Lambert (Lambert, 1990; Lambert, 1993) for a review of the literature on the relationship between job conditions and workers' ability to balance work and family responsibilities.

3. Workers without partners were assigned the mean for this variable. Including a dichotomous variable indicating whether or not the worker had a partner and assigning respondents without partners the mean on this variable allow the effects of "partner works" to apply only to respondents with partners (Cohen and Cohen, 1983).

4. Bivariate correlations between all the independent and control variables were examined for extreme values ($r > 0.7$). The multicollinearity diagnostics output by SPSS 5.0 were also examined. The stability of the findings was estimated by systematically adding and deleting variables from the regression analyses. None of these revealed multicollinearity problems severe enough to render the regression coefficients unstable.

5. I looked separately at subsamples of African-American and Hispanic respondents and found similar relationships to those reported here. Please note, however, that the analyses presented in this chapter do not take into account the sample selection bias resulting from non-response to the survey. Thus, the results may be inaccurate to the extent that response to the survey was related to workers' psychosomatic health and

partner satisfaction. The truncated relationships that we may be observing because of this selection bias may be especially problematic when interpreting the results pertaining to minority workers because they were least likely to respond to the survey. Most notably, it is possible that the positive relationship between being African American or Hispanic and psychosomatic health (see Table 10.1) may be at least partly due to self-selection; minority workers may have been more likely to respond the better their psychosomatic health was.

11

Grounded Theory: A Methodology for Integrating Social Work and Social Science Theory

Susan Bernstein, Harriet Goodman, and Irwin Epstein

The central assumption leading to the "discovery" of "grounded theory" was that qualitative and quantitative data could be used to generate, as well as to verify, social science theory (Glaser & Strauss, 1967). However, Glaser and Strauss's emphasis, and that of others adopting their approach, has been to formulate procedures for inductively developing social science theory from qualitative data generated from open-ended, unstructured interviews and participant observation (Gerson, 1991; Strauss & Corbin, 1990; Strauss, 1987). In this sociological tradition, little attention has been given to the relationship between "grounded" and "formal" (deductively generated) social science theory.

Recently, social work researchers have "rediscovered" grounded theory, employing it to derive the ethical assumptions in social work practice (Holland & Kirkpatrick, 1991), to generate hypotheses regarding child sexual abuse (Gilgun, 1992), and as an analogue for administrative practice (Bernstein & Epstein, 1991). In this chapter, this rediscovery is extended and applied to the integration of social work practice and social science theory. Two qualitative research studies are used to illustrate how a grounded theory research approach to social work practice can be used to generate principles and strategies for integration.

The ardent debate about the appropriate relationship of practice and theory in social work has been conceptualized elsewhere (Kondrat, 1992, 238; Fraser, Taylor, Jackson, and O'Jack, 1991, 7–9; Reid, 1991; Tyson, 1992). From our perspective, their complete integration requires that competent practice is conceptualized as theory and that theory reflects and promotes competent practice. Successful integration is dependent on two assumptions. First, there is an integration of theory and practice—of knowledge and action—which is inherent in all professional practice (Argyris & Schon, 1974; Schon, 1983). Second, for social science to access and impact practice effectively, the practitioner and researcher roles need to be integrated, with practice driving the research agenda.

In other words, the process of integration, as Schon argues, must be "turned upside down" by "taking as its point of departure the competence and artistry already embedded in skillful practice—especially, the reflection-in-action (the 'thinking what they are doing while they are doing it') that practitioners sometimes bring to situations of uncertainty, uniqueness, and conflict" (Schon, 1987, xi, 12–13; Schon, 1983). Competent social workers do not merely apply a single theory in their practice. Instead, they reflectively integrate multiple theories and values with each of their actions in different, complex, changing contexts, "where any given situation can be many different things at once" (Morgan, 1986, 343). Ultimately and phenomenologically, theories and values are manifest only in practice. Recognizing the existence of this integrated "practice knowledge" and "studying precisely how practitioners construct knowledge and decisions in action," should be our agenda (Kondrat, 1992, 242, 238, 252).

The "reflective practitioner" is, by definition, a practitioner/researcher (Schon, 1983, 236–266, 308), and some within the profession indeed have conceptualized social workers as practitioner/researchers (Grinnell, 1985, 20–22; Weissman, Epstein, and Savage, 1983, 262–299; Briar, 1980, 35–36). This articulation of roles is critical for the integration of practice and social work/social science theory. Only thus will the practitioner/researcher have intellectual access to the decision-making dynamics of practice.

In the quest for a full integration of social work practice and social work/social science theory, grounded theory methodology is particularly appropriate. Even its apparently oxymoronic name reflects the complicated task: "a way of wrestling with that which joins the visible ground with the invisible abstraction" (Starr, 1991, 270). The practice relevance of grounded theory methodology is its potential to produce a grounded social science that "fits, works, and is relevant" (Glaser, 1991, 15).

Because its objective is "an elegant form of integrated conceptualization inducted from systematic research," grounded theory methodology yields multiple possibilities for integration (Glaser, 1991, 12). The complexities of practice require that theory be taken into account from the beginning to the end of the research process. By contrast, Gerson comments, "The core objection to verificationist thinking was that restricting research to hypothesis testing was *insufficiently* rigorous; that verificationism is an absurdly restricted and inadequate vision of research" (Gerson, 1991, 300). Indeed, the methodology of grounded theory stands on its own; it is not a prelude to hypothesis testing, nor is it "doomed as foreplay to the real sociological act" (Burawoy, 1991, 275). Nonetheless, even some who have labelled their methodology grounded theory maintain a traditional research approach. Gilgun (Gilgun, 1992), for example, conceptualizes her task as generating hypotheses for others to test rather than viewing it as a different kind of testing of hypotheses.

There are many questions in social work practice for which the most viable methodology is grounded theory, both for answering the questions and integrating practice with theory. For the understanding of processes, the sine qua non of practice, this methodology can capture the complexity in ways that testing of discrete hypotheses cannot (Merton, 1988, xi).

In two recent studies—one on managing contracted services and the other on responses of health care professionals to the dying patient—the grounded theory methodology was used to integrate social work practice and social science theory. The integration of practice with theory in each study occurred at four levels of conceptualization: the study itself, the data, the theoretical implications, and the practice implications. In this process of integration, conceptualization involved moving from the particular to the general inductively and from the general to the particular deductively. It involved an ongoing process of testing general theoretical assumptions with qualitative data. All of this occurred in a less sequential, more iterative way than even our discussion indicates.

EXAMPLE 1: THE MANAGEMENT OF CONTRACTED SERVICES

The purpose of this study was to understand how administrators in nonprofit agencies manage the inherent complexities of contracted services (Bernstein, 1991; Bernstein, 1989). As both the provider and purchaser of contracted services, the practitioner/researcher (P/R) had been a manager for several nonprofit agencies. She wanted this study of contracting to reflect managers' passion, their "hot cognition," about the process: what they do and why they say they do it (Janis & Mann, 1977, cited in McCall and Kaplan, 1978, 28).

Although contracting is a primary method for the financing and delivery of human services in the United States, there was little empirical research regarding this process. And, although being accountable to a government agency creates profound administrative, ethical, and political dilemmas for the administrator responsible for delivering a service, there was little empirical research to determine how administrators conceptualize and manage these dilemmas.

Also, while the theoretical literature stresses the administrator's responsibility for successfully managing such issues (or the trade-offs, contingencies, exchanges, or tensions), there are only a handful of studies of this aspect of management in the social work administration literature. As a result, few guidelines or theoretical frameworks have been developed to inform, explain, or teach this crucial administrative behavior.

There have also been rudimentary efforts to distinguish management of human services from the management of other enterprises. The primacy of the clients' interest is hypothesized as a unique driving principle in the work life of the social work administrator (Slavin, 1980, 16–18). However, evidence of whether and/or how this principle guides administrators' issue management behavior is rarely cited.

From her experience and knowledge of the literature, the P/R assumed that administrators' experiences managing the issues of contracted services have generic elements, unrelated to agency position, field of service, type and size of agency, funding source, or type of contract. Therefore, since the focus of the study was issues management, the sample was selected for diversity on each of these dimensions, although each manager had substantial contract management responsibilities.

In accordance with these criteria, three categories of social work administrators were identified to focus the sample selection: program directors of contracted services in multiservice agencies; executive directors of primarily smaller, single-service agencies; and compliance coordinators in child welfare and mental health agencies. The sample size was 18. Data were collected through focused interviews conducted by the P/R in 1987. The interviews were taped. The analysis was conducted with the assistance of a computer software program, *The Ethnograph* (The Ethnograph, 1988).

In the initial conceptualization of the study, the P/R surveyed the limited available literature on contracted services (Bernstein, 1989, 20–43). Relying on practice experience and the few empirical studies and theoretical papers available, she developed a structured interview schedule with six major areas of inquiry. Following the pilot interviews, however, she learned that more meaningful findings emerged when the interview was allowed to proceed organically from the exploration of the respondent's major areas of interest rather than from the structured questions. Staying with the issues raised by the managers was critical.

With the transcripts completed, the P/R began to conceptualize the data. The integration of practice and theory during this process was a long, iterative, painstakingly complex and creative process of conceptualization and reconceptualization. Significantly, during the coding of the transcripts, a new category emerged that was not an area of inquiry on the original interview schedule: "Reaction to Problems." As a result, the focus of the study shifted from the problems themselves to the attempt to understand the experience of these managers. The most striking imagery in their descriptions was of *game playing*, a concept that had not been considered in the conceptualization of the study. The concept of cognitive maps, also new, seemed to capture the managers' perspectives on playing the game of contracted services. As a result, the game metaphor became the primary vehicle for analyzing the data.

Immersion in the "reaction to problems" data files confirmed that the 18 managers, despite differences in their agencies, positions, and backgrounds, shared remarkably similar verbal pictures of what it was like for them to be managing these services. Describing experiences of enormous variety and complexity, as well as their efforts to deal with them, these managers used many of the same words and evoked multiple images and metaphors with the same meaning.

The unifying metaphor was of contracted services as a *game*, and management of them as game playing. Fourteen of the 18 managers made specific reference to the game aspect of their work. All used the language of games in their descriptions when, for example, they referred to rules and strategies and to what they found to be challenging and fun about their jobs.

During this period of qualitative verification of the game metaphor, the P/R reviewed literature on metaphor (Embler, 1966) as well as the work of a number of authors using the game metaphor (Keidel, 1988; Keidel, 1985; Smith, 1988; Burst & Schlesinger, 1987; Harragan, 1977; Maccoby, 1976; Korda, 1975). Emanating from this immersion in the data and the related literature were considerations of the function and dynamics of the game metaphor and the importance of describing the game being played. It became much clearer how to think about the data and begin to organize it.

While they spoke of contracted services as a game, all managers, using an array of synonyms, talked of the "craziness" of the game. The word *game* implies a semblance of order and predictability when skill is exercised in playing it. Therefore, the talk of craziness, of things being ridiculous, a catch-22, making no sense, or being amazing, absurd, and mind-boggling was a seeming paradox. This paradoxical quality also pervaded managers' descriptions of issues and how they felt about and reacted to them. After consideration of this reverberating paradox, the P/R began to conceptualize what it is that makes the game of contracted services "crazy" and how the game metaphor keeps managers from succumbing to "craziness."

At this point in the data analytic process, however, the P/R noted that despite the game-like quality, craziness, and paradoxical nature of the experience of contracted services, there was a clarity of purpose in the managers' descriptions of how they managed professionally and personally in their jobs. To understand this clarity and its significance as these managers struggled with administrative, ethical, and political issues, it became apparent that it was necessary to analyze their perceptions of government funding organizations, nonprofit agencies, and their jobs. From her immersion in some qualitative management research at the time (McCall & Kaplan, 1985, 105–106), the P/R recognized these perceptions to be cognitive maps, the maps that enable managers to cope with the complexity of contracted services.

The conceptualization of the data continued with the writing of the findings. Before beginning each chapter, the P/R sought out any relevant literature for assistance in framing and reinforcing the discussion (e.g., regarding ethical decision making, or the accountability structures in administration). In the process of writing every chapter, new and/or clearer analytic ideas emerged, which resulted in major changes.

The integration of theory and practice continued in the conceptualization of the theoretical implications of the study. From managers' strategies for effecting compliance, change, and ethical accountability regarding government contracts, theoretical concepts for administrative practice emerged (Bernstein, 1991). For the first time, it was determined that the rather extensive game theory literature (Myerson, 1991; Brams, 1985; Muzzio, 1982; Brams, 1978) might be significant for understanding and informing social work administrative practice. The study also validated emerging management theory regarding the value of metaphor in organizational theory and management practice (Morgan, 1986). Moreover, it supported the emerging conceptualization of management research as a process of determining how managers' thinking influences their actions (Bernstein, 1989, 6–20).

In the conceptualization of the practice implications of the study, there were unique opportunities for the integration of theory and practice. The game metaphor gives managers and prospective managers a way of thinking about their work, of analyzing problems, and of identifying possible solutions. The metaphor encourages managers to consider the dynamics of the contracted services game, the skills involved in playing effectively, and the cognitive maps that affect their game. By encouraging consideration of dynamics, skills, and maps, the game metaphor can assist managers in becoming more conscious of the theory, the metaphor, governing their practice (Morgan, 1986, 336).

EXAMPLE 2: STAFF RESPONSES TO CARE OF TERMINALLY ILL

The purpose of this study was to understand the responses of doctors, nurses, and social workers to their work with terminally ill patients—especially those who are management problems—in an acute care hospital (Goodman, 1990). The P/R wanted to know how these staff function in hospitals where the structure and culture support cure and rehabilitation rather than death work.

In order to understand their work realities, the P/R wanted to capture the professionals' practice from their perspective, in their own language. Health care staff are socialized to act in ways that force negative and ambivalent responses underground into informal interactions, which are kept closely guarded from the outsider. The P/R is an experienced clinician, "an insider," who had worked both in a hospital with the dying and in a community agency with the disabled.

The study was conducted during the mid-1980s in "East End Hospital," a large, urban, tertiary and acute care teaching hospital. During the study period, the P/R was a member of the Supportive Care Services (SCS) team, a consultation service offered through the Division of Clinical Pharmacology and the Department of Medicine for patients with psychosocial and medication problems associated with end-stage cancer and AIDS. SCS was established to introduce and teach hospice concepts of care, such as aggressive pain control regimes, to the staff of an acute care hospital. The P/R was a research assistant for the team and had excellent access to terminally ill patients and their caregivers.

Following Feifel's (Feifel, 1959) *The Meaning of Death*, an intense interest in death and dying developed among psychologists, sociologists, and medical personnel, as well as the general public. Subsequent studies focused on the psychological processes of dying and grief, or the manner in which the health care system cared for dying patients (Kubler-Ross, 1969; Saunders, 1960). Whether health care personnel avoided dying patients or openly discussed death with them, how a patient's social value affected efforts by medical personnel, and what was proper care for dying patients were explored in a new scholarly field, "thanatology" (Goodman, 1990, 3–21).

While the scholarly and lay interest in dying patients grew, relatively little attention was given to the impact of work with dying patients on health care professionals and the stress these workers experience (Goodman, 1990, 21–24). Only Mauksch (Mauksch, 1975) attempted to describe the experience of caring for dying patients from the point of view of the health care worker or considered the relationship of systemic variables, such as the context of work, to providing terminal care. With the advent of AIDS, early studies of health care professionals considered patient abandonment, refusal to treat patients, and fears of contagion among medical staff. Several surveys attempted to determine the responses of medical and nursing personnel to work with stigmatized patient groups. The limited study of the impact of AIDS on the work lives of health care professionals focused on the psychological dimension of AIDS work: feelings of helplessness and corresponding anger (Goodman, 1990, 24–39).

For this study, the grounded-theory methods used were participant observation and focused interviews with doctors, nurses, and social workers about dying patients whom they identified as "difficult to manage." Dying patients were defined as those with a prognosis of less than six months to live. During the study period, of the 47 patients referred to the SCS, 38 met the criterion.

Field notes were maintained on staff interactions, conversations with professionals, and observations of staff. Numerous opportunities were available to observe the health care workers' responses to dying patients, including formal teaching and SCS rounds, interdisciplinary meetings, formal and informal interactions between professionals, and contacts with SCS patients. Observations logged early in the study were very broad, but became more focused as they began to yield issues of theoretical interest and as the P/R began to draw on existing social science theory to organize the data.

Informants for focused interviews were solicited from caregivers for dying patients whom health care workers identified as "difficult patients." Responses of the three professional groups were sought regarding a single patient. Of the 15 patients suggested for the study, nine were patients with metastatic cancer and six were patients with AIDS. Eight physicians, ten nurses, and thirteen social workers were interviewed for the study. All interviews were taped. Data analysis was done manually, using index cards to transcribe vignettes from interviews and field log entries to transcribe patient/professional engagements or professional opinions about the patient.

When data showed that hospital workers were extremely preoccupied with "toxic" patients, Goodman consulted the sociological literature to refine the conceptualization of the central study question. Medical sociologists have described "exceptional" patients as patients who present more than "routine" problems for their caregivers. Ordinary patients are rarely commented on by caregivers, who are preoccupied with patients who are either extraordinarily good or extraordinarily bad (Friedson, 1973). Sociologists who examined "bad" or "deviant" patients had considered the functions of informal labels and the contextual and interactive aspects of patient care as expressed by medical personnel (Liederman & Grisso, 1985; Jeffrey, 1979; Lorber, 1975). The theoretical work of these medical sociologists, in concert with the early observations recorded in the study, focused the research on health care professionals' definition of "toxic" and "ideal" patients.

Conceptualization of the data focused on the interactive nature of the patient/practitioner engagement. The data was translated into an original "Typology of Terminally Ill Patient Types: Ideal, Routine and Toxic Patients." Informants suggested patients were, in most instances, simply routine. The exceptional patients were described as "ideal" or "toxic," using the terminology of the informants. The typology expanded upon previous studies that had primarily considered "bad" patients and, to a lesser degree, "good" or "ordinary" patients. Unlike previous studies that considered only doctors or nurses, this study also included social workers. And, unlike previous work, this study focused on a specific patient group—dying patients.

There were numerous revisions in the typology as data from the interviews accumulated. Through an iterative process of moving back and forth between tentative typologies and the substance of the interviews, the P/R eventually found an inclusive structure for conceptualizing the data. At this point, examples of the categories in vignettes from interviews and observations fit easily into the typology, which became the organizing rubric for the study data.

In the conceptualization of the theoretical implications of this study, the integration of practice and theory was particularly striking. Many of the responses of hospital workers contradicted the image of acceptable professional behavior, as well as the stated ethical codes of all three professional groups. Health care practitioners avoided dying patients, were often bureaucratic in their responses, and used pejorative terms to refer to patients they could not manage. These behaviors, which seemed paradoxical to caring, in fact enabled the caregivers to proceed with their work.

In discussions of the meaning of the data in this study with others, an alternative emerged to burnout as a theoretical model for understanding how hospital workers cope with failure to meet the socially approved goal of curing patients. Merton's theory (Merton, 1968) of anomie proved an exceptionally apt concept applicable to health care workers' responses to thwarted goal achievement.

According to this theory, when people are able to reach socially valued goals, they can conform to the usual socially approved methods of goal attainment. When they cannot reach these goals, they experience "anomie," or normlessness. In contemporary hospital care, conformity can take place where a technical intervention can be identified and applied in the service of the social good, or "cure." When health care workers cannot cure patients, they cannot achieve this goal, and their behavior is modified. Innovation, retreatism, ritualism, and rebellion are responses to anomie.

With this theoretical understanding, health care workers' behaviors that seemed antithetical to professional values could be understood as efforts to deal with frustration. Those who avoided patients by limiting contact were practicing retreatism; those absorbed in administrative details at the expense of humane practice were practicing ritualism.

However, "deviant" responses were not necessarily negative, either for patient care or worker enthusiasm. For example, rebellion provided a creative avenue for many who were able to revise their goals and change their means for achieving them. The entire concept of the SCS, in fact, was a form of collective rebellion since the service not only changed the usual goal of "cure" to "care" but, by advocating hospice methods of care, altered the means as well.

In conceptualizing the practice implications for health care workers, anomie theory provided an important alternative to burnout as a rubric for understanding how some staff provide exceptionally fine care in unresponsive and unsupportive systems with patients who will not be cured through their interventions (Goodman, 1990, 195–198). The most immediate possibility for improving care to dying patients in acute care hospitals is to help social workers develop adaptive strategies. Past efforts have relied on teaching social workers about the psychological and social responses to death and dying or about stress management techniques from variables identified with burnout.

However, Merton's anomie formulation suggests a different model of intervention. It describes patterns of responses to the anomie generated by work with the dying. Some of these responses produce good patient outcomes and a sense of satisfaction for the social worker in successfully reaching their redefined goals. Helping social workers will involve identifying a set of skills that can be analyzed and taught. Merton's concept of anomie can be used to teach supervisors about the various responses to difficult dying patients and about supervisory methods to encourage more productive workers' strategies.

PRINCIPLES AND STRATEGIES FOR INTEGRATION

From the two studies, principles and strategies emerge for the qualitative use of grounded theory methodology to integrate social work practice and social work/social science theory. These are applicable for the practitioner/researcher who is using grounded theory as a qualitative methodology to study a practice question, as well as for the reflective practitioner who is thinking systematically about her practice. Other, more recently articulated principles and strategies for grounded theory are couched in excessively complicated terms, perhaps reflecting a perceived need to legitimate this alternative methodology (Strauss & Corbin, 1990; Corbin & Strauss, 1990; Gerson, 1991; Strauss, 1987). Those we propose are simple and, we hope, therefore more accessible, explicit, and understandable. In the qualitative use of grounded theory, the complexity should reflect the richness of the data rather than add to the complexity of the methodology. Two major principles promote theory/practice integration. First, grounding must be pursued continuously. Second, the research product must be true to the complexity and reality of the practice. As with deductive methodologies, violation of these principles risks reification of practice and/or theory.

To pursue qualitative grounding, which is really to pursue the integration of practice with theory, is to seek continuously to understand what one is doing or what others are doing, both inductively and deductively. The links (or lack of those links) between practice and existing theory are to be sought consistently.

To be true to the complexity and reality of the practice is the real test of practice/research integration. Do the findings fit, illuminate, and help to further understand practice? If not, why not? Is there a problem with the inductively or deductively derived theory? Does it need to be modified? If so, how?

Five major strategies emerge for using qualitative grounded theory methodology to integrate practice and theory:

- Start with a point of view regarding the practice problem and the related theory; then suspend it. To frame the initial questions, it is essential to immerse oneself in the most apparent, deductively generated theory regarding the problem. However, having made conscious the cognitive map, one should then put it aside.

- Stay with the data; do not impose concepts on it. Trust that sampling leads, metaphors, concepts, and/or theories will emerge from the data.

- While staying with the data, search for analogues to understand it. Look for similar patterns and concepts, for similarities in different patterns and concepts, or for metaphors.

- Use a colleague(s), grounded in practice and/or theory, to help reflect on the data. Someone not immersed in the study itself can sometimes see and/or validate analogues the practitioner/researcher cannot.

- Persist. Resist the temptation for premature closure. Live with the complexity. Integration is a lengthy, nonlinear, iterative process.

12

Introduction of Chaos and Complexity Theory to Social Work

James Patrick Mace

Over the past 20 years, there has been a fundamental change in the way many physical scientists have been looking at the world. This new way of studying and conceptualizing the real world has created a new science of "chaos," in which the complexity of nature is open for observation and analysis. This new paradigm and its underlying mathematics have produced useful models for researchers working in several fields, including astronomy, biology, chemistry, economics, electronics, geology, medicine (cardiology, hematology, and neurology), meteorology, and physics. It has allowed them to conceptualize the problems in their respective fields in very new and different ways.

Chaos theory (also called complexity theory or nonlinear dynamics) has as its basis the underlying assumption that most natural phenomena are *dynamically nonlinear*. The elements of a natural system do not follow simple linear relationships. A natural system is often incredibly complex. These complexities are compounded by the functioning of the system as a gestalt. Each part affects every other part in iterative processes. As a complex system changes over time, its elements interact with each other. One part impacts on a second part and produces a change. In the next cycle, the change in the second part impacts on the first part and produces a change. Thus, the elements engage in a process of feedback to each other that cycles repeatedly. In many instances, the system maintains an equilibrium, and predicting relationships and outcomes is straightforward. However, the system may change abruptly into a state of chaos, given certain conditions. Simply defined, this chaos is a highly complex nonrandom state in which casual factors are difficult or impossible to determine. Chaos theory provides conceptual and mathematical tools for the analysis of these chaotic states and the phase transitions into them.

Social scientists have done very little work with this new scientific paradigm. However, the implications for social work and other social science professions are enormous. Human beings are very complex organisms. Within each individual and surrounding all of them is a complex system of biological, psychological, and social elements. An individual human being occupies a small, seemingly insignificant, finite space within the universe, but each person has an infinite depth of complexity within that universe.

For the most part, we have studied people by ignoring their complexity. We typically choose a finite number of variables as the focus of our research and ignore everything else, thinking that the impact of extraneous variables is of little importance. However, the work done with chaos theory shows that small changes produced by the extraneous variables in the initial conditions of a system can have tremendous impact on the future behavior of the system. With complexity theory we have a mathematical proof that minor events can produce significant differences. The theory can give us a tool for studying how family systems can suddenly become chaotic, and then re-establish harmony just as easily. To some extent, chaos theory can impact on the social sciences as it has on the physical sciences.

This chapter introduces social work researchers to the concepts of chaos and complexity theory. These concepts include iterative processes, nonlinear dynamics, the butterfly effect, period-doubling bifurcation, fractal geometry, strong and weak chaos, turbulence and strange attractors, self-organized critical and catastrophe theory, and the limits of knowing. Chaos and complexity theory are placed within the context of human development and human systems.

SOCIAL WORK AND SCIENCE: AN UNEASY RELATIONSHIP

Social workers and other helping professionals are often frustrated with information obtained from research. Much research offers little help with the day-to-day decisions made when working with people in practice settings. This problem is due, in part, to the way most of the research simplifies human beings to a point that the data is not very helpful for decision making regarding an individual client. For example, there is a sizeable amount of research that focuses on domestic violence and how to treat individuals who are victims, but no article will tell the practitioner what to do with the abused spouse who is also alcoholic, dyslexic, and pregnant, who has children failing at school, whose mother is terminally ill, and whose family finances do not meet basic needs. Our research ignores the total complexity of the person. We are stymied by our inability to make predictions even for our clients' simplest behaviors.

As researchers, we have followed the model of the physical sciences to reduce the phenomena we study into a few variables for actual study, while discounting the effect of the large number of variables we have chosen to ignore. The physical sciences use this reduction to great advantage. Using these methods, it put human beings on the moon. The Apollo mission did have a great deal of complexity to it, but for the most part scientists were able to reduce this complexity into separate components. Problems were isolated and corrected. Bad or worn parts could be replaced.

On the other hand, human systems are much different. People cannot easily be broken down into their components. Many of our difficulties and problems are difficult to isolate and correct. Human beings are much more complex than anything that we have ever engineered.

This complexity is due to an almost infinite number of elements that affect people and the social systems in which they live. Various scientific disciplines and professions study human phenomena; each offers its own perspective and solutions. Some explanations from one approach contradict those from another. Unlike the physical sciences, the human sciences have not been able to develop underlying unifying principles regarding the nature of humans and human society.

For example, all the physical sciences accept atomic theory as a useful construct for formulating other ideas and concepts. They may argue about the finer points of the theory, but no one challenges the idea that the construct of the atom is a useful model on which to base fundamental understandings of physics and chemistry. These ideas are the bases of all the physical sciences, as well as of biology and medicine. Many similarly accepted and well-acknowledged conceptions form the underlying structure of the physical sciences.

The human and social sciences have produced no similar set of widely accepted constructs about human behavior. There is little agreement about the nature of people. There is much conflict and controversy. Scientific research has not produced an underlying core of theoretical constructs in the social sciences as it has in the physical sciences; rather, it has produced a plethora of conflicting and confusing ideas that have made the understanding of human behavior a difficult and bewildering experience. Underlying this is an obvious fact. Human beings are incredibility complex organisms existing in an even more complex environment. This is a major difficulty for the profession of social work.

Social work is unique in its development. Most of the theoretical basis of social work lies in thought and research developed by other human sciences. Much of this thinking is conflictual. For example, Francis Turner (Turner, 1986), a noted social work educator, has indexed more than twenty theoretical approaches taken from the social sciences and now in use by social workers in their practice. Each approach is based on a different conception of what motivates human behavior and what the important elements are. Social workers are expected to understand and apply at least a portion of these theoretical ideas in their work of helping people and society. Often, theory and research do little to help guide our decisions about our clients, and we rely instead on our personal experience. Most practicing social workers give this "practice knowledge" a high value.

One difficulty is the nature of social research. Most of our empirical research patterns itself on various physical science models. We have placed a high value on models that are verifiable using statistical calculation. When the probabilities are unique, then we accept the findings. When we do statistical analysis on our data, we make a mathematical assumption about the nature of the variables under study. The most common assumption is that the relationship between the variables is linear. This is a rather simple linkage. It is a basic assumption of many of our statistical tests, including the "General Linear Model." If linearity is violated, then we must make compensations (transformations) to the data to use the statistics accurately.

Most quantitative social scientists collect data from single samples at single points in time. The nature of academic life and research funding does not allow many scholars to conduct longitudinal research. Following the physical sciences, a few variables are chosen for study at a single point in time. All other variables (and there are many) are considered uninteresting and are ignored.

Interest focuses only on the effects of the chosen variables. This kind of research produces information at a very specialized level. The variables under study typically account for only a small portion of the overall variation in the model.

CHAOS AND COMPLEXITY THEORY

Some ideas from chaos/complexity theory that have application to human behavior are outlined below.

Iterative Systems

As stated above, complex systems are iterative. This means that the current state of the system is dependent on previous states of the system. Likewise, future states of the system depend on the current state. This is a description of historical processes. It is also a very good description of human processes.

The Butterfly Effect: Nonlinear Systems Have a Sensitive Dependence on Initial Conditions

Edward N. Lorenz (Lorenz, 1963a; Lorenz, 1963b; Lorenz, 1964), an atmospheric scientist working on long-range weather prediction, discovered while attempting to model a weather system on a computer that small changes in the initial numbers of the model produced very significant differences in the outcome. He found that minute differences (even in order of one ten-thousandth), would produce drastically different results in the outcomes of his computerized weather systems if given time. For the real world outside the model, this meant that the lack of precision in measuring the initial conditions of the system would make it impossible to predict long-range outcomes. Thus, Lorenz made the analogy that the turbulence produced by a butterfly flapping its wings in China could cause differences in weather systems in North America at some point in the future (hence the name "the butterfly effect").

If we consider people as dynamic nonlinear systems, this suggests that small changes in life, which for the most part go unnoticed, can result in major differences later on. For example, I had a first-grade teacher who taught me to like to read. That change in the *initial conditions* of my life produced the first college graduate and the only doctoral degree from my family. At the time, the teacher's work went unnoticed. Now, it is obvious that her work was of pivotal importance in my life.

Period-Doubling Bifurcation: How the Dynamics of Systems Change from Simple to Complex to Chaotic

Nonlinear mathematical models show interesting properties when the values of the model are varied. At certain values, the model will operate quite simply, but at other values the model will become more complex. The route from simple operation to complex operation is a process of *period-doubling bifurcation* (Ruelle, 1989). Ruelle uses the example of a boiling pot of water. At phase one the water is still, unmoving, and the dynamics of the system are uncomplicated. Then the heat begins to produce a gentle roll in the water as convection currents are established. The system has made a phase change to a higher level of complexity. Further along is a phase change to small bubbles of steam making their way to the top of the water. As time progresses, the dynamics of the water in the pot become more and more complex, eventually becoming chaotic (hence, displaying chaos theory). This is the bifurcation process as a dynamic system gains greater complexity. This idea can be applied to human behavior.

Take a married couple who usually get along amicably. They are sitting at home in a state of relative quiet watching television. As a system, there is very little occurring. Imagine that one spouse grows slightly irritated by the other's comment regarding the television show. The dynamics of the situation gain an element of greater complexity. A comment is made regarding the irritation. Again, the state of the couple gains more complexity. The bifurcation process may continue until the dynamics of the situation, like the boiling water, reach a state of chaos with enormous complexity, in which much of the couple's individual and collective past history and present state of emotional arousal come into play. People are sometimes murdered in such situations.

Weak Chaos and Self-Organized Criticality: "The Straw That Breaks the Camel's Back"

Bak and Chen (Bak & Chen, 1991) demonstrate that "large complex systems naturally evolve to a critical state in which minor events can cause chain reactions of many sizes." This conceptual model provides another property of complex systems and a model for catastrophic change in those systems. This idea builds on the nonlinear systems' sensitivity to initial conditions. The model provides insight into a number of natural phenomena. The authors model systems that have "millions and millions" of interactive elements. They create sandpiles. Using an apparatus for creating sandpiles, they demonstrate these principles. As each grain of sand is added to the pile, the system becomes more and more complex. When the system reaches a critical state, small and large avalanches of sand occur. The sandpile moves to a less critical state. It simplifies itself. The system moves toward complexity and chaos but limits itself before it gets there.

The human behavior analogy is summarized by the metaphor of "the straw that breaks the camel's back." There are critical points in complex systems that help drive the system back to a simpler state. Take a large family with multiple problems. Each member of the family has a complex set of problems that relate to all the other problems in the family. As the members interact, the family system becomes more complex, and overall stress increases. The family develops a state of severe strain where it cannot maintain the level of complexity. Something has to give. Someone has to break or be broken. Therefore, someone gives in, or a parent goes off to treatment/jail, or a child is removed/sent away from the home. The overall system has reduced its complexity. Most families reduce their complexity themselves. Others have outside interventions either invited or imposed upon them.

Fractal Geometry: The Geometry of Natural Systems

Traditional science, engineering and much of what is taught in basic math courses is based on Euclidean geometry. This is the geometry of pure reason. Lines are straight, squares have 90° corners, planes are perfectly flat, and circles are perfectly round. This geometry has proven very useful to humankind. We have built our civilization upon it. However, Euclidean geometry is not the geometry of nature. To paraphrase Beniot Mandelbrot (Mandelbrot, 1983), a hill is not a pyramid, lakes are not squares or circles, and clouds are not spheres. Nature is not linear. Nature's geometry is "fractal." Mandelbrot (Mandelbrot, 1983) coined this idea to help him deal with the complexities of natural geometry. He surmised that natural objects have "fractional dimension."

This is a difficult concept to understand because we have all been taught Euclidean geometry. Objects exist in space; space has three dimensions. Mathematical abstractions can have one, two, three, or more dimensions, but how can anything have a fractional dimension? This concept can be illustrated by imagining a flat piece of paper. For all intents and purposes, it is two dimensional. However, what are its dimensions if it is crumpled into a ball? If we are standing far away from it, it may seem to be a point, a one-dimensional object. As we move closer, it would define itself into a ball, a three-dimensional object. Closer still, we would discern that even though it is crumpled into a ball it has a two-dimensional surface. Points on the surface could be specified using Cartesian coordinates. However, it is not quite flat, nor is it a sphere. Is it a two- or three-dimensional object? One could say that it is neither. The ball of crumpled paper has a fractional dimension of perhaps 2.25 if it is loosely crumpled or 2.85 if it is tightly compressed. Objects with fractional dimension are referred to as "fractals." They have special properties.

One of these properties is complexity. One of the interesting and artistic developments in this field is the generation of computer graphical images of fractals (Dewdney, 1985; Peitgen & Richter, 1986; Stevens, 1989). By using the calculating and the visual imaging capabilities of computers, fractal geometry has been made visible for analysis. The Mandelbrot set (Mandelbrot, 1983; Petzold, 1990) is a fractal that is generated by iterating (using the results of one computation as the input for the next computation) the equation $Z^2 + c$. Yet this simple equation generates a mathematical object of incredible complexity. According to the makers of Fractal Magic (a computer program for generating and studying fractals), if every human being on the earth had a computer it would take several billion years for all parts of the Mandelbrot set to be viewed and explored.

These conceptualizations can be applied to all objects with irregular shapes, and much work is being done with this by Mandelbrot and other mathematicians. Computer programs have been created using fractal geometry that produce realistic-looking mountains, trees, and plants. They can also create patterns that produce interesting and colorful images on a computer screen. Fractal programs are even used to add realism to the special effects enjoyed in our motion pictures. Fractal geometry is applied in medicine, where it is used to study the structure of the lungs, the cardiovascular system, and the neural pathways of the brain. Most natural objects have fractal dimension. As much of the natural world and our physiology is fractal, it can be argued that perhaps some of our behavior patterns may also be fractal. The assertion can be made that human beings have a fractal nature. People are very deep in the sense that they are very complex.

My own interest in chaos theory was sparked by a simple curiosity about these complex geometrical objects called "fractals." What I found interesting about the Mandelbrot set was that I could explore these images for hours without finding duplicated patterns. I could expand the images and delve as deeply as I wished and not find the same image twice. This process struck a cord in me.

I have practiced clinical social work for over 15 years and have had contact with thousands of clients in various settings. Searching the fractal patterns felt very much like looking into the inner workings of people. In my practice, I could expand on a certain detail of the individual ad infinitum, just as I could with the fractal program. Like the images generated by the computer program, people are as deep as one wants to look, and their complexity can be studied in incredible detail. In exploring the fractal images, patterns would be similar to each other but never quite the same. Just like fractals, people have many commonalities, but each of us is unique.

What started as a diversion became more and more interesting as I discovered what the physical scientists were doing with this new set of mathematics. They were inventing a science of complexity. Its application to human behavior is obvious. Human beings are the most complex phenomena in existence. Complexity/chaos theory should apply to human beings most of all.

IMPLICATIONS FOR CONCEPTUALIZING HUMAN SYSTEMS

The implications for social work and other social science professions are enormous. Human beings are very complex organisms. Although a person can be counted and descriptively coded according to various schemes and designs, he or she is unique and incredibly complicated with aspects that are not collected as data. An individual occupies a finite space but has infinite depth. There is literally no end to what we can study regarding the physical, psychological, and social nature of any single human being.

In the past, we have studied people by ignoring their complexity. We typically choose a finite number of variables as the focus of our research and ignore everything else thinking that the impact of extraneous variables is of little importance. However, from the initial work done with complexity theory, it has been shown that the small changes produced by the extraneous variables in the initial conditions of a system can have tremendous impact on the future behavior of the system. With complexity theory we have a mathematical proof that minor events in a person's life can produce significant differences farther along in that person's life. It may give us tools for studying how people, families, and social systems can suddenly become chaotic, and then just as easily reestablish equilibrium. It undoubtedly will provide us with a different paradigm for explaining the complexities of human behavior.

Limits to Our Knowledge

There is one implication of considerable importance. Complexity theory places limitations on our ability to predict future events. The butterfly effect shows us that these nonlinear systems are very sensitive to initial conditions. Imprecision in measuring the initial conditions of a system builds a compounding error into any prediction of future behavior of the system. The error will become larger as the system iterates. This means that long-term prediction of the future of any nonlinear system is quite beyond our abilities. Whether it is the weather or a single person makes no difference. Our ability to know the future is limited. These point of view are reflected by a number of other authors. David Steenberg (Steenberg, 1991) presents a good nonmathematical review of chaos theory and the ramifications it has for the basic problems of modern philosophy. However, a more extensive exploration of the philosophical problems created by chaos theory is presented by Stephen H. Kellert (Kellert, 1993). Kellert argues that chaos theory in combination with quantum theory severely restricts the concept of determinism and seriously undermines the certainty of our knowledge.

A SHORT LITERATURE REVIEW

This literature review is incomplete. Most of the research into complexity theory is being conducted in the physical sciences and is published in physical sciences journals. I am a social worker/social scientist. Much of the explanations are in high-level mathematical terms, and it has been many years since I studied differential equations. However, there are a few authors who have struggled to try to explain these concepts to the non–physical scientist public.

Among these authors, most notable is James Gleick, who wrote *Chaos: The Making of a New Science* (Gleick, 1987). This best seller can be understood by most people and still gives enough detail to be useful. Most of the book focuses on the historical development of the ideas. In similar vein, in *Turbulent Mirror*, Briggs and Peat (Briggs & Peat, 1989) strive to explain the concepts of complexity theory and chaos to nonscientist readers. Ruelle (Ruelle, 1991) in *Chance and Chaos* explains complexity, chaos, and randomness in nonmathematical terms. In *Does God Play Dice: The Mathematics of Chaos*, Stewart (Stewart, 1989) goes a step further and provides a lucid description of the mathematics involved. Petersen (Petersen, 1988) provides chapters on fractal geometry (a key to understanding chaos theory) and chaos itself. Casti (Casti, 1990) and Burrows (Burrows, 1991) present the nonlinear arguments for the limits to our ability to make predictions of future behavior of complex systems. Pickover (Pickover, 1990) provides an illuminating view of fractal images and art that has some math but also explanatory text. All of the above authors do well in their attempt to make rather complex mathematical concepts palatable to the nontechnical public. They utilize description and graphs rather than mathematical formula. Their books are a good place to start in understanding the ideas of chaos theory.

Much of the actual research in chaos/complexity theory originated in a much more technical format. Casti (Casti, 1989) analyzes methods of mathematical modeling of natural and human systems. Morrison (Morrison, 1991) presents a more technical introduction to non-linear modeling. Glass and Mackey (Glass & Mackey, 1988) and Freeman (Freeman, 1991) present nonlinear theory in application to physiological rhythms. They discuss how chaos dynamics can lead to problems in respiratory, cardiac, neural, and other physiological systems of the human body. They assume an understanding of calculus, but do make efforts to explain in nonmathematical terms. The above-mentioned citations provide some understanding of chaos theory and its application but provide little direction for someone trying to use the concepts for research. Mangel and Clark (Mangel & Clark, 1988) apply the theory to behavioral ecology and provide technical information about the process. Lipstiz and Gildberger (Lipstiz & Goldberg, 1992) use the theory to explain loss of functioning in the elderly. Ruelle (1989) does provide some direction for the researcher who wishes to delve into chaos theory and try to apply it to actual data by providing a method for analyzing time series data for "deterministic nonlinear systems" (i.e., chaos). The mathematics for this are also somewhat complex but may be very useful for those wishing to study social phenomena when time series data is procurable. In another book, Ruelle (1989) relies heavily on mathematics by page four. Tufillaro (Tufillaro, Abbott, and Reilly, 1992) examines the math of nonlinear dynamics and provide the reader with a computer program to help learn some of the concepts. These two texts are a good place to start moving into the mathematics of nonlinear models. Schroeder (Schroeder, 1991) uses some math to describe complexity concepts but uses descriptive writing to help explain it. Drazin (Drazin, 1992), Gulick (Gulick, 1992), Zaslavsky et al. (Zaslavsky, Sagdeev, Usikov, and Chernikov, 1991), Bell (Bell, 1990), and Arrowsmith and Place (Arrowsmith & Place, 1990) plunge into differential equations and complex mathematics in the first few pages of their texts.

Other material is also available. In a 1991 electronic search of the science and engineering abstracts, I located 179 articles on the subject of chaos. A similar search of the same abstracts found 61 articles on nonlinear systems. However, a search conducted on the social science abstracts found only two articles regarding chaos theory. Other articles regarding chaos theory and human systems have been found by tracing citations. This lack of literature does not reflect a lack of interest. A listserver (CHAOSPSYCH) on the INTERNET has posted almost a thousand messages in five months.

In the social science literature, most applications of chaos theory are used as a metaphor for reconceptualizing certain human problems and situations. Michaels (Michaels, 1989) explains chaos theory and applies it to organizational management concepts as a way of explaining why rigid management structures often fail when confronted with nonlinear (Ruelle, 1989) situations. Skinner (Skinner, 1989) takes fractal geometry and uses it as a way of reconceptualizing alcohol addiction as a unidimensional and a multidimensional problem with a great deal of complexity. Parnell and VanderKloot (Parnell & VanderKloot, 1991) ignore most of the concepts of chaos theory and use it as an argument for pressing social workers to use a process-oriented systems approach for helping people. Guess and Sailor (Guess & Sailor, 1993) present excellent material in explaining chaos theory and applying its principles to special education and human behavior. Young (Young, 1991) describes how chaos theory can be applied to social change theory. In another article, Young (Young, 1991) describes its application to symbolic interaction theory. Begun (Begun, 1994) uses the theory to describe "chaotic" families who develop complex boundaries who "are continuously, constantly changing, in unpredictable direction."

Some writers have applied the theory as a metaphor for understanding mental illness and psychotherapy. Schmid (Schmid, 1991) uses the theory as a metaphoric tool for understanding schizophrenia and conceptualizes the mild events that set off a schizophrenia episode as a nonlinear dynamic. Moran (Moran, 1991) applies the "form" of chaos theory to psychoanalysis. Isla (Isla, 1991) reports an experience in exploring computerized fractal patterns similar to what I have described earlier. She conceptualizes it as a process of waiting for the emergence of patterns and applies this to the process of psychotherapy. Lichtenberg and Knox (Lichtenberg & Knox, 1991) did an empirical study of randomness and patterning in group therapy using some aspects of chaos theory as a model of development. Results of the study were negative. Order did not emerge from chaos. Abraham et al. (Abraham, Abraham, and Shaw, 1990) present an excellent visual presentation of application of chaos theory to psychological constructs. One of the better papers is written by Scott Barton (Barton, 1994), who describes chaos theory and its application to the psychology of memory. He points out that much of the application of chaos theory in psychology is problematic because of a imprecise usage of terminology from one discipline to another.

In summarizing the literature, one can see a large difference between the social science use of chaos theory and its use by the physical sciences. The physical sciences tend to use the theory in conjunction with empirical support. They have data to support their models. The social scientists principally use it as a metaphorical tool for explaining some aspect of human behavior without empirical support. Only a few psychologists and economists use data to support their assertions. The few articles in the social work literature follow the trend in the social sciences as I have done in this chapter by using chaos theory as a metaphorical conception without empirical support.

CHAOS AND COMPLEXITY: NEW EXPLANATIONS FOR THE WAY WE ARE

Chaos, complexity, nonlinear-dynamic theory is an entirely new way of conceptualizing the way we think about the world. The theory has obvious value for explaining and reconceptualizing our understanding of human behavior. It also offers compelling reasons for the lack of facility in providing definitive models of human behavior in the social sciences. Chaos theory has a lot to offer to the social sciences. Applications of chaos/complexity theory will become discernible as social science begins to use the theory. All areas where systems theory is applied are likely to find these ideas useful, including family theory, organizational theory, and ecological theory. It is possible to think of cognition as a dynamic feedback system. Perhaps the onset of serious mental disorder could be conceptualized as a bifurcation dynamic moving into chaos. One would expect that it might change our views of people in the same way it has changed the scientific view of the natural world. It offers us a new way of thinking about people.

Part III

SOCIAL WORK TO SOCIAL SCIENCE

Introduction: Social Work Perspectives on the Integration of Social Work and Social Science

Rosemary Sarri

There has been an ebb and flow in the interaction between social work and social science since its formal beginning in the last century, but the last half of the twentieth century has experienced a significant increase in interaction. Most would agree that in this period the social sciences have made significant advances in both theory and research methodology and that there have also been important knowledge developments in social work. Most of the knowledge development and research has taken place in universities and institutes, which has resulted unintentionally in a decline in the interactions between social work practitioners and policy makers in many settings. Moreover, social work educators and practitioners have looked to the social and behavioral sciences for theoretical knowledge and research skill that they could use to advance social practice and policy. As described in chapter 22, the Michigan Joint Doctoral program was begun at the mid-century to foster the integration of social work and social science, and it has demonstrated that both fields have derived benefits from the effort. Unfortunately, while the social sciences appear to have had a great impact on the research done by social workers, social work has had limited, and often nonexistent, influence on the social sciences. The development of systematic practice theory has lagged far behind the application of social science theory, although validated practice theory could contribute new insights to the causes and correlates of social problems and also to the development of empirically tested intervention models.

Social work and social science departments both are nested within the universities that support and constrain them (Friedson, 1986). In turn, universities exist within the larger societal context that influences their development, but society also is influenced by the universities and knowledge that is developed there. One needs only to examine the growth and influence of technology of all types to see clearly the results from contemporary university-society interaction. In contrast, it is increasingly asserted that the university has abandoned its goal of being an instrument of societal change and moral renewal. Instead, disciplines have become oriented to intraprofessional goals that may seldom relate to contemporary social problems. Moreover, the types of field research that are done in the social sciences bear little similarity to the field work of social scientists in the earlier part of the century; for example, that conducted at the University of Chicago. Ernest Boyer (Boyer, 1994) recently noted that urban American is where the nation is now experiencing its most serious strains, while higher education is doing little to work toward solution of the community's problems. The social worker is well-positioned to initiate and test alternative models of intervention and thereby to contribute to knowledge development for both the profession and the social science disciplines.

As a profession, social work has a mandate to work toward the resolution of social problems and the meeting of social needs. The joint doctoral program was established with this as an explicit objective. In pursuit of its mission, social work is concerned primarily with the development of knowledge for purposes of prediction and control rather than explanation.

In recent years, there has been a greater acceptance of funding priorities established by federal, state, and foundation policy makers in much social work research because universities are so dependent upon these funds. Much of the research in the area of human services has emphasized the individual as a causal and target variable. Examples can readily be found in research on poverty and income maintenance, juvenile and criminal justice, substance abuse, mental health, and child welfare. As a result of these emphases, there has been far less research on social structural causes and correlates of social problems and needs. In addition, funders have been reluctant to support developmental or formative research, and there has been little substantial research on institutionalized racism in human service organizations. Research related to intervention modalities has primarily included program evaluation for specific policy and program decision making. Also lacking have been major action research efforts, especially those that involve longitudinal research on major social welfare issues, such as that conducted in the 1960s and 1970s.

It is difficult to estimate the extent to which social science research priorities have influenced social work research, but any review of social work journals indicates that the influence has been substantial. A similar examination of social science journals would find far less evidence of the influence of social work. Thus, it is quite appropriate to ask in what ways social work could contribute to social science and to furthering the integration of social science and social work. One of the most obvious and important influences that social workers could have is in the formulation of challenging questions for research and theory development. Equally important is their access to real-life settings that are often more realistic and appropriate for much research. At present, social science research often continues to be completed in university laboratories or in large-scale telephone surveys that exclude many of the most disadvantaged citizens. Obviously, the validity of such findings for application in social policy and social work practice is limited unless there is further intervention research. Third, social workers can engage in collaborative activities with social scientists and thereby enhance the work of both. Fourth, the results from program evaluation research could be utilized in the development of practice intervention theory and principles.   Lastly, social work is in a position today to develop predictive models with respect to the social welfare policy that is part of the major social transformation in social welfare institutions now underway in this and other societies.   Social workers have rich libraries of case materials and administrative records that can be systematically analyzed as a basis for the development of practice theory.

In Part III, we present chapters that address several of the current issues affecting the integration of social work and social science from the perspective of the former linking itself to social science, along with three chapters that provide an international perspective on issues of integration. Several of these chapters provide provocative approaches for the development of theory and research of particular concern to social work. Gutiérrez's chapter on a theory of empowerment exemplifies such an approach that is grounded in social work practice. She observes that because of major social structural changes there is growing inequality in the United States that requires social workers to develop new approaches to policy and practice. Gutiérrez's framework for empowerment theory includes goals, change processes, and methods. It can be applied at multiple levels of intervention or to link levels of intervention. Her use of case materials helps one to see how she would develop the theory of empowerment practice. Her chapter provides an exemplar of an important new approach to developing social science theory from social work practice.

Mak and Tsang present a conception of education for social work practice in Hong Kong within the context of the welfare state theory that is developing in East and South Asia. They view social work as an interactive process of linking society and the individual. Social workers in Hong Kong are playing significant roles in the development of theories of welfare practice that link social work to social science. Their approach is one of defining the issues and the knowledge needs from the perspective of social well-being, but they also note that solving social problems can contribute to the development of social theory. Their emphasis on the importance of considering the influence of the external environment in their model is useful in today's turbulent social welfare environment.

Ramon's chapter on mental health services and practice in Europe provides an excellent example of the types of issues that must be addressed in practice theory development and research in a particular societal context. She defines social work as an applied social science discipline as well as a profession—a view that differs from definitions usually found in the United States. However, we increasingly note that the social sciences are developing applied sections, so perhaps a similar change can be expected here. Ramon notes that in applying social science theories of mental illness, social workers must often choose between alternatives that are contradictory, lack empirical validation, or do not relate to the practice situation that the worker faces. Thus, a practitioner is often forced to develop practice theory that is more eclectic in its foundations. Ramon further observes that although social workers may take a critical stance toward some aspects of social science knowledge, they seldom articulate this criticism at the conceptual and research levels. She also notes that actually defining and conceptualizing mental distress and mental health poses a substantial challenge for social scientists, one that has not as yet been addressed. Ramon reviews contemporary European mental health systems and, as in the case of Mak and Tsang, we are alerted to the importance of history, culture, and the larger external environment if we are to understand the behavior of these organizations.

In a chapter on increasing the effectiveness of work teams, Vinokur-Kaplan points out that developing the principles in a "real-life" setting forces one to incorporate theory about environmental influences on work teams. She notes that much of the existing theory about work teams is based on research conducted in artificial settings with students as subjects. In her development of an ecological framework, she observes that distinctive features of the human service organization need to be taken into consideration in developing practice theory for work team effectiveness. Her principles for practical application incorporate both knowledge from social science research and from the practice experience and wisdom in "real-life" settings.

Lauffer addresses the critical problems of communication between social practitioners and social scientists. His framework for analysis of communication and subsequent intervention focuses attention on the critical roles of the sender and the receiver, as well as on the intent of the message and on the language of the message itself. He posits that research findings are often variously understood and interpreted by decision makers, who may often dispute the validity of the findings and who are more likely to rely on community consensus and shared understanding. Because the language of researchers' communication often differs substantially from that of practitioners, Lauffer's practice principles can be usefully applied to enhance communication between the two groups so that mutual understanding is one result.

In her feminist critique of social work and social science, Abramovitz asserts that the feminist scholars must incorporate knowledge from the humanities in order to develop theory that is gender sensitive, because both practitioners and scientists have been negligent about gender in the past. Feminists have challenged social science theory of the family, the generalizations about the dysfunctionality of the single mother family, and about gender roles in the community. Abramovitz notes that social policy and practice is influenced by many factors, only some of which come from social science knowledge. She also notes that a feminist theorist studying families of color from a gender perspective must revise contemporary theory about the African American family. Assuming that both racism and sexism are embedded in social science theory, use of social science knowledge paradigms in this area have also shaped the social policy/practice agenda. Thus, there is need to consider: (1) What is knowledge; (2) Who are the researchers; (3) Who controls the knowledge; (4) Who benefits and who loses from the dominant social science paradigms; and (5) Can value-free principles be developed in a gendered, racist, and classist society? She concludes that both social science and social work practice are socially constructed and cannot be abstracted from the political and social milieu. Thus, there is and will be a continuous struggle regarding the development of theory and practice in the area of gender, family, poverty, community, and policy.

Jamrozik discusses the provision and utilization of human services that are linked to quality of life and points out that unexpected factors may influence provision and utilization. Because there is very little research on human resources and social capital in industrial and postindustrial society, one may not think that studying these areas could contribute to our theory of organizational and community behavior. Jamrozik argues that the development of social science and social work practice knowledge must be broad, multidimensional concepts and theories that interpenetrate each other. His study of the residential patterns of social workers in Sydney, Australia, shows that these workers live with other professionals in areas of high income and advanced education. However, because their work is with low-income families and individuals, many have difficulty in understanding and accepting their clients' behavior since they have limited knowledge of the everyday problems of the people that they serve. These biases affect the development of practice principles and the evaluation of outcomes. Such observations, when systematically organized, can be insightful in understanding the behavior of workers in many human service organizations.

Longres addresses the conflicting perspectives in the social science literature about the relationships between social stratification and psychological debilitation. He examines the relationship between debilitation and socioeconomic status, gender and ethnic subordination, and sexual orientation. Only socioeconomic status is consistently correlated with psychological debilitation, so the conclusion that social inequality leads to psychological debilitation is often not supported. People respond in various ways to changing or unequal social status. Although Longres's paper is primarily an example of utilizing social science to develop practice principles, he observes that it is a two-way, not a one-way pattern of influence. A particular theory or scientific generalization is likely to be modified in the process of application. A sensitive researcher can observe this process and subsequently modify the theory after more thorough testing in practice settings with collaborating social workers.

Part III examines the integration of social work and social science from the perspective of the social work profession. Several authors have presented models and approaches whereby fruitful results can be obtained for both practitioners and scientists from collaboration in which social work plays a more active role in research and theory building. Such processes may well increase the ability of the profession to serve its mission more effectively, and also for the university to play a more active role in resolving contemporary social problems and meeting human needs.

13

Macro Practice for the Twenty-first Century: An Empowerment Perspective

Lorraine Gutiérrez

As we move into the twenty-first century, social work methods for dealing with conditions of inequality will become more significant. Over the past decade, income differentials have become more pronounced, and the proportion of the population considered middle class has shrunken (Wallerstein, 1992). Of particular concern is the growth of three sectors of our population that traditionally have possessed little power and few social resources: people of color, older people, and people with disabilities (Johnston, 1987). These trends in the composition and structure of our society challenge social work to create new approaches to policy and practice.

There has been remarkably little discussion within our profession regarding the implications of these demographic trends. We have not adequately explored ways to deal with the increasing need for services or with how we can work with disadvantaged groups to achieve greater equity. By improving the potential of human capital through improved access to quality health care, education, and support services, social service organizations can play a particularly crucial role in creating a society in which diversity contributes to our strength as a nation. Such an investment could reverse trends that suggest that we will soon become a nation of poor children of color and older European Americans, in which neither group will be capable of producing the economic resources necessary for supporting existing social services or other social goods (Ozawa, 1986; Sarri, 1986; Williams, 1990).

This chapter proposes that an empowerment approach to macro practice with organizations and communities could more effectively deal with issues of inequality. This perspective on practice would be focused not on managing diversity, but on creating greater equality in our institutions and society as a whole. Empowerment practice would be focused not on increasing choices within a delimited range of alternatives, but on expanding our choices based on the sharing of power (Garvin, 1985; Gutiérrez, 1990; Pinderhughes, 1989; Rappaport, 1981; Simon, 1990; Solomon, 1976; Swift & Levin, 1987; Wallerstein, 1992).

However, a quick survey of the literature on empowerment reveals considerable differences in the philosophy, goals, and methods being developed and proposed. Within the field are calls for personal responsibility and individual effort (Berger & Neuhaus, 1977) alongside proposals for collective action, participatory management, and grassroots movements (Staples, 1990). This lack of unity within the field suggests that if social service policies and programs are to work toward empowerment, we will need a clarification of the concept. This chapter further clarifies the meaning of empowerment and its relevance to macro practice in social work by integrating it with two sources of information: social science theory and the results from field research involving human service organizations that engage in empowerment practice.[1] An integration of these two sources of knowledge can suggest ways in which empowerment-based macro methods can meet the challenges of the twenty-first century.

THE EMPOWERMENT PERSPECTIVE ON SOCIAL WORK PRACTICE

Empowerment practice in social work originally emerged from efforts to develop more effective and responsive services for two disenfranchised groups, women and people of color. It is based on the assumption that the experience of membership in a group with little social or political power can have personal as well as social costs. Inequity in access to resources prevents individuals, families, and organizations in oppressed communities from gaining the social goods that they require. These direct experiences are compounded by ways in which the actions of larger social institutions create and perpetuate feelings of powerlessness. These feelings can lead to the inadequate functioning of community or family systems, which are then incapable of buffering the negative effects of oppressive institutions (Bricker-Jenkins & Hooyman, 1986; Pinderhughes, 1989; Solomon, 1976). The empowerment perspective proposes that only through changes in the distribution of power can this cycle be reversed.

Some of the confusion in our field comes from the multiple uses of the term "empowerment." Empowerment is described as a goal, as a process, and as a method (See Table 13.1). In addition, although empowerment is defined as integrating both micro-level and macro-level practice, methods for achieving this integration are rarely presented in the research (Simon, 1990; Staples, 1990). If the theory and practice of empowerment are to inform our profession, we will need greater clarity in our definitions. Toward this end, the following discussion takes each dimension of the concept of empowerment separately and describes its application in the field.

Empowerment as a Goal

The empowerment perspective assumes that power is not finite because it can be generated in the process of social interaction (Bricker-Jenkins & Hooyman, 1986; Friere, 1973; Katz, 1984). The social science literature suggests ways in which empowerment practice can contribute to the redistribution of power. It describes power as originating from a number of sources and being expressed in different ways (Barnes, 1988; Gaventa, 1980; Hasenfeld, 1987). Power has been defined primarily as the ability to get what one needs; the ability to influence how others think, feel, act, or believe; and the ability to influence the distribution of resources in a social system such as a family, organization, community, or society (Dodd & Gutiérrez, 1991). Thus, the goal of empowerment involves developing greater power on the personal, interpersonal, or political levels.

Table 13.1
Dimensions of Empowerment

Goal: Gaining personal, interpersonal, and political power
Process of Change: Raising consciousness; increasing efficacy
Method: Strengths-based; educational; democratic

Personal Power involves experiencing oneself as an effective and capable person. One means of increasing personal power is to identify and understand the power one already has. It involves the ability to make choices for one's life and to act upon them. A counselor at an employment program for women describes it like this: "Power, I think has a lot to do with boundaries, and being able to set your boundaries on how much you affect your own life. Empowerment is a state of having power: having the inner tools to move your life in the direction you want to move it . . . [i]n the face of . . . varying outside circumstances."

This dimension of personal power is the one most often identified and described in the social work literature (Parsons, 1991; Pinderhughes, 1989; Simon, 1990). Research on the perceptions of social work practitioners suggests that they most often equate empowerment with autonomy, confidence, and increasing personal choice (Gutiérrez, GlenMaye, and DeLois, 1992). Although the dimension of personal power is important, focusing entirely on this perspective can depoliticize the concept of empowerment and prevent us from looking at the ways in which intergroup relationships can be changed (Simon, 1990).

Interpersonal Power is the ability to influence others through the use of social power. Social power derives from such things as one's social position, role, interpersonal skills, credibility, or attractiveness (Feld, 1987; French & Raven, 1968; Zander, 1979). Some of these bases of power are ascriptive—related to race, gender, or class—but others can be achieved as one develops social skills or attains new social positions. Therefore, identifying skill deficits and learning new skills is a key element of the empowerment process. As described by one community health worker: "We do safe-sex parties, which give folks information on AIDS and how to protect themselves and have fun sexually, and that's a real fun thing, that we show them, give them skills, technical skills, how to make this easier and how to introduce it into their lifestyle." In this example, the process of learning skills associated with safer sexual behavior, including negotiating with partners, is crucial for gaining interpersonal power.

Political power is the ability to influence the allocation of resources in an organization or community through formal or informal means (Gaventa, 1980). Political power is most commonly gained through collective action and collaboration with others. As described by an organizer with an AIDS prevention program, political empowerment involves "going around to the state educating various communities of color about the issues and encouraging them to start coalitions, encouraging them to organize and making their health departments accountable to communities of color." In this example, political power to make government agencies accountable to health care issues involves reaching out and working with other organizations toward the formation of coalitions. These coalitions have been highly successful in the creation of culturally appropriate programs and services to prevent HIV infection in high risk communities.

Empowerment as a Process of Change

Empowerment is an internal process of change that creates the capacity for individuals, families, groups, or communities to gain power. Empowerment theory is based in a conflict perspective that assumes that societies consist of separate groups possessing different levels of power and control over resources. It assumes that one way in which members of less powerful groups are controlled is through ideologies that engender inaccurate beliefs regarding status, opportunities, and resistance. These beliefs encourage individuals to accept the present social structure and prevent them from taking action to improve their lives (Gaventa, 1980).

Developing a critical consciousness is a crucial means of gaining power. Developing a critical consciousness or awareness involves both understanding how the power relationships in society have shaped one's perceptions and experiences and identifying how one can take a role in social change (Gaventa, 1980; Gutierrez, 1990; Kieffer, 1984; Swift & Levin, 1987). Such a consciousness is particularly important in situations of inequality in which individuals have internalized negative beliefs regarding their own identity or potential power. An understanding of how group membership can affect life circumstances is crucial for identifying powerlessness as a source of problems and can lead to a focus on social rather than individual change (Gaventa, 1980; Gutiérrez, 1987; Simon, 1990).

Workers in empowerment-based agencies can readily identify ways in which raising consciousness about group membership and power can contribute to empowerment. One health educator describes it in the following way:

[We] work with churches, already established agencies and organizations, trying to sensitize them to the issues as well to politicize the issues understanding that there is a disease AIDS and how you get it and how you don't get it, but also understanding that there are various issues like racism and sexism and classism that makes this our issue. Engaging our communities to believe that this was a health care issue and so we need to also attach it to other health care atrocities that have already been in our communities and talk about the issue that we don't live as long as we could period— whether AIDS was around or not.

This organizer and others saw discussing the political nature of "personal" issues as one means to engage individuals and communities. As she described it, "If you go into a predominantly African-American audience the whole issue of the genocidal plot is going to come up around AIDS because for that community, being experimented on in a medical situation is reality." Her observations indicate the relative comfort with which some communities discuss the interaction of personal and political issues. For these program participants, these discussions were affirming and engaging.

Social psychological theory can explain how changing consciousness can contribute to empowerment. Several psychological processes that involve changing perceptions of the self in society have been identified as contributing to critical consciousness (Gutiérrez, 1990; Kieffer, 1984; Swift & Levin, 1987). These processes include:

- *Group Identification*, which provides the basis for group consciousness. Elements of group identification include understanding areas of common experience and concern, a preference for one's groups' culture and norms, and the development of feelings of shared fate. Group membership becomes a central aspect of one's self concept (Gurin, Miller, and Gurin, 1980);

- *Group Consciousness*, which involves an understanding of the differential status and power of groups in society. For members of oppressed groups, this leads to feelings of relative deprivation, power discontent, and a tendency to blame the system for problems related to group membership. This understanding is one way of drawing connections between personal problems and social structure (Gurin, Miller, and Gurin, 1980; Klein, 1984); and

- *Self and Collective Efficacy*, which refers to the belief that one is capable of affecting desired changes in one's life (Bandura, 1982; Pecukonis & Wenocur, 1994). In the literature on critical consciousness, it is described as the perception of one's self as a subject of social processes rather than an object—as one who is capable of working to change the social order (Fay, 1987; Friere, 1973; Gutiérrez, 1989).

Empowerment theory suggests that these three components often develop sequentially and that, once developed, they can be mutually reinforcing. Group identification is a necessary but not sufficient condition for group consciousness. Both group identification and group consciousness are necessary, but not sufficient, for the development of collective efficacy. Once an individual has developed a sense of critical consciousness, feedback loops exist that allow the experience of group consciousness to heighten a sense of group identification, or the exercise of collective efficacy to deepen a sense of group consciousness. In these ways, critical consciousness is at once a process and a cognitive state.

How does critical consciousness contribute to empowerment? The tie between efficacy and empowerment is clear: Individuals and groups that believe in their ability to affect change are more likely than others to make efforts to increase their power. The role of the other processes is less direct, but nevertheless crucial: In order for individuals and communities to understand that their problems stem from a lack of power, they must first comprehend the structure of power in society. When powerlessness is identified as a source of problems, then efforts to increase power can take place.

Empowerment as a Method

The empowerment literature also describes empowerment as forms of practice, within different types of social systems, that support the internal change process. For example, a number of articles have described ways in which Paulo Friere's methods of critical education, consciousness-raising methods, and other forms of education have been used in a number of settings (Rose & Black, 1985; Sherman & Wenocur, 1983; Wallerstein, 1992). A second theme in the methods literature has been the democratization of the helping relationship and the use of client expertise in the development and administration of programs (Florin & Wandersman, 1990; Gerschick, Israel, and Checkoway, 1989). A third focus has been on client and community strengths rather than problems (Rappaport, 1981; Zimmerman, in press). These three themes can be articulated as methods for practice.

Viewing practice as a *process of education* emerges from discussions with practitioners in different fields of practice. The educational process is described as dialogical and interactive, with both workers and program participants learning from each other. From the principal of an alternative high school, we hear that:

empowerment comes from knowing and understanding. [T]he more you know and the more you understand, the more you can see your place. And I think we need to see our place. I think a big part of empowerment is to know who I am, and how I fit in the world, and that I have a place, I have something for me to do. It's important for me to be here, and my place in relationship to the world, then to my neighborhood, my community, my country and my world, my responsibilities and how I fit in. That's really important to empowerment. I mean, that's talking philosophically, but I think that philosophical understanding is crucial to education.

The purpose of education in empowerment practice is multidimensional. It includes developing the skills to increase interpersonal and political power, the development of feelings of efficacy, and an increased understanding of the meaning of group membership. A worker with women in jobs programs describes the interaction of these dimensions in this way:

If you have the belief [in yourself] then you're more likely to go after getting that skill, and once you have the skill, the belief is reinforced, and you're believing even more that you can affect your life. Then you go out and do it, and then maybe you feel even more empowered, you know, I have the ability, and skill and the potential. And then that empowers you even more, and then you actually utilize it.

Empowerment-based methods are developed around *democratic process* in the design, development, and implementation of services. Workers, clients, and consumers work together to create, staff, and evaluate programs. Consumers and former consumers are involved in delivering services. Within the empowering organization, power is shared even when there is a hierarchical structure. The input of clients and workers in the organization is solicited at every level. These organizations can be described as consumer-driven.

The director of a mental health program describes how she utilizes the contributions of consumers in this way:

The mandate of [the] county is that the Mental Health programs should be consumer-driven; and so that comes from our basic funding source so all our treatment plans are done in conjunction with the consumer, they have to agree to the treatment plan in order to be treated, and they sign off on the treatment plans, we can't contact anyone without their permission, and they are the ones who give that. [T]hey are also in charge of their meds.

In addition to involving consumers in their treatment, this mental health program involves a group of consumers in an committee that "is on our Advisory Board, the committee is on the clinical team the committee members participate in various aspects of the agency, the decision making. [O]ur mindset will be to be inclusive of them in any kind of program planning." In this organization, as in others, consumers have been instrumental in defining agency rules and procedures, and in providing information on needed programs. Consumer involvement is seen as an important empowering method in itself and as a means for developing the ability to gain and use power in other dimensions.

Another element of democratization is the use of current and past program participants as helpers and workers, where the focus is on peer helping and support. The director of a battered women's shelter illustrates this:

[O]ne of the strongest things about our program is the opportunity of women to get to know other women leaving similar situations. The staff is almost incidental in a way. I think the real healing and growing and strength comes from women sharing their stories with each other and learning from each other and breaking that isolation and feeling connected to other people and stopping the self-blame. I think that's the real strength of our program, that we provide a lot of opportunities for women to share with each other.

Clients can also be involved in teaching skills. A worker at an agency that works with women in the inner city gave the following example of involving a client to help others in this way:

[T]his particular woman was Vietnamese and she had mentioned in her interview that one of the things she'd like to do is help out in the community more. So it was just by chance, right after her interview, a class was starting—and the teacher doesn't speak Vietnamese—so she stayed, and helped in translating, and that was an empowering tool, because she was able to communicate with the teacher and with the Vietnamese people and do this translating.

Individuals from the community can be hired by the program as a means of breaking down traditional client/helper barriers. This can result in the empowerment of individuals and the empowerment of the community to develop leaders who can have the capacity to make changes. A health educator describes how this process felt to her:

I'm from the 12-step program. So as I went to meetings and I saw people that I used to use with and hang out with and do those kinds of things with and saw them, I thought they might have been dead or in jail. When I saw them doing and moving right along, you know, on the other side of the fence, it really gave me a sense of "Oh, yeah, it can be done. You know, I know if they could do it, I know I can do it."

This same worker describes how democratic processes can be used when developing programs within the community: "If we are organizing church communities, we want the church to develop some sort of mechanism to get AIDS information out to their constituency. When the Latino AIDS Coalition gets together the whole idea is for them to do what they are doing in their settings." Creating more democratic organizations that work in partnership with community groups can be a strategy for community empowerment. As these organizations learn to work together, they can then have an impact on the political process.

A third element of empowerment methods *is building on the strengths existing in clients and communities*. The basis of the practice lies in understanding and identifying how individuals, families, groups, and communities are functioning. The focus is on working from strengths and using them to gain more power. A counselor with troubled youth explains it this way:

What I saw them doing is surviving and being fairly capable manipulators, able to use their skills, staying out of the system using their own creative talents. [K]ids would say things like, "I talked my pimp out of beating me up." Well, that's a skill—I mean, it's an ability, and something they can use in another area. Or, if they're good at identifying dangerous drugs and safe drugs—I mean, all those things that are helping them learn from what they already knew or expanding skills into different areas.

The basic assumptions of this method are that program participants have the capacity to make positive changes within themselves and that it is the role of the organization to provide the support and resources necessary to bring about those changes. Empowerment—gaining power—occurs in the course of this social interaction. It is not given, nor can it be taken away.

On the community level, building on strengths means starting where the community is in respect to issues. An organizer for an HIV prevention program for people of color describes the process this way: "The community organizing piece really tried to engage the community in saying, 'You tell us what kinds of ways in which we need to get to the people that you are serving.' You know, for the church, maybe you don't want this kind of presentation for the people that come to your church but what would be good? Where, how can we meet you on your level?" In respect to staffing, building on strengths means looking at workers holistically in respect to what they bring to the organization. One worker explained why she, a former addict, was hired by her organization: "We were hired because we had, you know, this kind of information and this kind of expertise, we also need to use that expertise to get to our target populations and to ask them is this something that you feel is viable." In this way, an organization is strengthened and gains power in the community by basing its work on the abilities of all program participants.

When seen together, these methods—education, participation, and strengths orientation—can be interlocking and mutually reinforcing. Participating in programs within an organization can be educational and can build on strengths. Without seeing participants and communities as competent, organizations cannot work with them as partners. A focus on education can guide the ways in which strengths are developed and participation is structured.

In order for social service programs to carry out empowerment practice, they must develop similar processes within their own administration. Research on organizational empowerment suggests that the ways in which social service organizations are structured can have an effect on individual and community empowerment. The ability of individual workers to share their power with clients and to engage in the range of interventions required for empowerment practice can be dependent on the support they receive for this type of work and on their own feelings of personal power (Gutiérrez, GlenMaye, and DeLois, 1992). Social service organizations that contribute to the disempowerment of workers may undermine their ability to empower clients and communities because many social service workers may become ineffective, hostile towards clients, apathetic, or "burned out" in response to their feelings of powerlessness (Mathis & Richan, 1986; Pinderhughes, 1989; Sherman & Wenocur, 1983). Organizations that empower workers through participatory management, the ability to make independent decisions about their work, communication with and support from administrators, and opportunities for skill development can be more capable of empowering clients (Gerschick, Israel, and Checkoway, 1989; Zimmerman, in press). Such efforts are recognized by the staff of these organizations. As described by one community worker: "[I] think that it is really empowering to get [the] training [that] comes through town, if we find it and it gets circulated and that kind of stuff, then we are encouraged to go. I've learned a lot on the job and feel that I am encouraged to know as much as I possibly can."

CONCLUSION

This exploration of the literature on power and empowerment, illustrated by field observations, provides some insights into how an empowerment-based model for macro practice can contribute to greater equity. By building truly democratic organizations that develop the existing strengths within individuals, families, and communities, the social services can provide a means for generating power within disadvantaged groups. Examples from the field provide evidence of how this work is being conducted in a number of settings.

This integration of social work and social science knowledge with practice-based perspectives can also contribute to theory and practice. For example, empowerment has been discussed within the literature as a philosophy, a psychological process, a goal, and a method of practice. These findings suggest that practitioners are most often thinking of a psychological process of change when they speak of empowerment. One critical element of this change is gaining awareness of the power existing within any individual, family, group, or community. This focus on empowerment as a process was emphasized by practitioners involved in different levels of practice (e.g., individual, group, or community work) and with different populations. It suggests some unity to the concept of empowerment in the field: Although practitioners may work with different groups with different types of goals, empowerment is seen as a method for developing personal and interpersonal power through a process of self awareness. Therefore, changes within the self are considered to be an important element of change on different levels. This challenges theoretical perspectives that have emphasized specific and distinct dimensions and levels of change.

The goal of integrating theory and practice is one of the primary challenges for our scholarship. The integration presented here develops the empowerment concept by demonstrating areas in which theory and practice are in agreement and areas in which there is more conflict or difference. For those areas in which there are reinforcing concepts, ideas, and methods, we can be assured that we may be speaking a common language and working toward common goals. However, for those areas in which conflict and difference are present, we face a particular challenge: How can we use this tension to develop the meaning of empowerment-based practice? If empowerment practice is to fulfill its potential as a means of positive social change, we must find ways to bring together these divergent viewpoints and continue to develop this model of theory and practice.

ACKNOWLEDGMENTS

Funding for the research reported in this chapter was provided by the Graduate School Research Fund and the Social Work Research Fund at the University of Washington.

NOTE

1. For more information regarding the study on empowerment practice, see Gutiérrez, GlenMaye, and DeLois, 1992. Special thanks to Kathryn DeLois and Linnea GlenMaye, who contributed to the collection and analyses of these data.

14

Social Work Education in Context: Hong Kong Polytechnic File

Diana Mak and Tsang Nai-ming

The Department of Applied Social Studies (APSS), Hong Kong Polytechnic, offers a full range of social work training programs in Hong Kong, including the diploma in social work, the bachelor's degree in social work, and the master's degree.[1] Some students take the research route for their M.Phil and Ph.D. awards. In our effort to teach the field of social work, we are often confronted with major issues such as: "What constitutes the knowledge base of social work?" "What is the relationship between social science and social work?" "How can we best facilitate learning for our students?" While many of our views are still being formed, our purpose here is to articulate them as a basis for further development. We welcome readers' reactions and critique.

As social work education cannot be divorced from social work practice, the first section of this chapter will be devoted to our conception of social work practice, with particular reference to Hong Kong. The issues faced by social work educators will be examined in the second section; the third section illustrates some of APSS responses and our aspirations for the future.

CONCEPTION OF SOCIAL WORK

Our background and our exposures shape the way we understand and interpret the world around us; this also has consequences for how we conduct ourselves within our social environments.

Viewed from this perspective, social work is an interactive process whereby the social worker and the client (service user) are brought together in a social context to define the need and to construct the problem they would like to solve (Payne, 1991). This process is based on the relationship established by the participants, who bring with them their knowledge and life experiences. They engage in this process by exchanging views and conceptions of "the problem" faced, the focus of the work, and the resources with which to address it. During the process, social work principles (those that are upheld as "good" and "of value" to life in western societies, such as respect for the individual and client's self-determination) are used as a guide. These principles may also be used to influence and change certain aspects of communal life that are relevant to coping with or alleviating the problem identified. Whan's (Whan, 1986) notion that social work is a "practical-moral involvement" should be stressed here, because in the social work process, participants assess one another's actions and intentions according to some implicit and explicit norms. They justify their actions according to what they term "good," thus affecting each other's way of being. It is in this sense that social work is a moral engagement.

Thus, the construction and evaluation of the social work process is a socially interactive, subjective, and moral one, shaped by the utilization of knowledge and life experiences of the participants in the social context concerned. This does not, however, imply that the social work process cannot be "objectively" articulated.

As the participants in the social work process are closely related to the major institutions of society in both work and life, the process in which they are engaged is also very much a product of the society (Howe, 1979; Payne, 1991). As these actors are also constructive forces in the social processes from which they emerge, the insights they gain during the social work process may help them to become positive forces in contributing to the development of the society and its social processes.

In order to grasp the profession's relationship with its society and social processes realistically, an examination of its social climate is also necessary. In the case of Hong Kong, we will use social welfare, one of the key factors shaping the social work profession, as an entry point.

Although some researchers (George and Wilding, 1985) argue that the institution of social welfare in the western world is the natural outgrowth of ideological transformation, in the case of Hong Kong, it is developed more out of the government and nongovernment sectors' responses to social and natural crises. The Hong Kong government's commitment to social welfare has been conservative, taking a position of "minimum intervention" and leaving things to market solutions. Despite the introduction in the 1970s of long-term plans in social welfare that subsequently guided the social service provisions in the 1980s and 1990's, the implementation of those plans was never guaranteed; moreover, they were always tagged onto economic policies and made subject to economic growth.

While the thriving economy of the 1960s and 1970s fattened the Hong Kong coffer, it did not benefit the poor. During this period, poverty, a squalid living environment, and an extremely skewed distribution of income lay just below the surface of the thriving economy. Inadequate provision of services, poor quality and lax coordination resulted in waves of community action, led mainly by professionally trained social workers. Nevertheless, such community development efforts were short-lived. In the early 1980s, they were quietly removed from the social welfare arena and placed under a policy of administration, the Community Building Program, headed by the Secretary for Home Affairs. In the early 1990's, the government, justifying its move retroactively, stated that community work had, since the last decade, progressed beyond "welfare" and that its inclusion in the Social Welfare White Paper, 1991, could fragment the Community Building Program (Foreword by the Secretary for Health and Welfare, Social Welfare White Paper, March 1991).

Ironically, it was in the same era of the 1980s that the same government, after 140 years of inaction, decided to introduce a democratic element to develop a more representative Hong Kong government. This gave birth to an illusive concept that once again social welfare could return to its macro level. Social workers interested in community work went campaigning for political office. By the early 1990's, there was a frenzied urge to politicize social work. While social welfare acquired a more political stance, the concern of day-to-day social care remained very much on the individual, personal, and micro level, struggling to demonstrate its professional status amid the emerging status of other helping professions.

The 1980s also witnessed the introduction of the neoconservative conception of privatization. Broadly speaking, this idea refers to a general rolling-back of the state apparatus in the production and management of social services. However, in the case of Hong Kong, it is a move that followed a withdrawing government. The process itself focuses more on the introduction of market criteria in the allocation of social service resources than on public policy criteria. This move may be understood on two levels: First, we see a gradual transfer of social service management from government departments to statutory bodies such as the Housing Authority and the new Hospital Authority. While the government is still partially subsidizing these social expenditures, the new corporate bodies are being encouraged to be financially and operationally independent. Access to these services by the poor is further reduced simply because they cannot afford the minimum fees required for service.

Although this trend has not touched the personal social-service sector, the nongovernmental nonprofit-making welfare organizations have started to charge fees for their services—a move not surprisingly much applauded in the Government White Paper, 1991. As the multiple funding of social welfare services will become a reality in the 1990's, social workers of the future will need to be alert to its impact on the quality of service delivered and to the ensuring of comparable service to those who can pay and to those who cannot.

On a second level, a host of market efficiency criteria are now being used to evaluate and audit public expenditures in the social services sphere. A culture of efficiency, effectiveness, and accountability has developed. Consumers' rights are being stressed, and a quality-assurance and performance-oriented approach has begun (Governor's Policy Address, 1992). In order to survive, corporate bodies must justify their existence either by innovative means in optimizing their resources or by resetting their priorities to satisfy their funders. Although this has not yet taken anchor in the narrower social welfare scene, the Director of Social Welfare has announced that "the Social Welfare Department will adopt the concept of consumer service and will publish its performance pledges," hinting, perhaps, that the nongovernmental sector should follow suit (Director's speech at the Plenary Session of the International Conference on Family and Community Care, April 1994).

While the Hong Kong people collectively aspire to a smooth transition back to China's sovereignty in 1997, the cessation of the rounds of talks between the Hong Kong and Chinese authorities on the political scene offers little comfort. The credibility of the Hong Kong government has declined, and confidence in the Chinese government has fallen. Identity problems have resurged. Sociologist

M. K. Lee (Lee, 1992), citing three surveys conducted between 1988 and 1990, attributes this to the fact that vague notions about the future governance of Hong Kong have thwarted the cultivation of attachment to a new political arrangement. With uncertainties ahead and provocative exchanges between the governments, tension remains, and people are emigrating. "The Hong Kong Government estimates that about 62,000 people are leaving the territory every year and this figure has increased from around 20,000 a year in the year before 1987"—with only about 10 percent returning (Skeldon, 1991).

This estimate, if actualized, will produce a loss of about 360,000 people—a number seemingly skewed towards the professionals and the highly skilled. Unfortunately, social work is among the emigrating professions,[2] so much so that emigration became one of the reasons for supporting a three-year expansion in training programs at both the diploma and degree levels in all training institutes from 1989 to 1991. Another impact of this "brain-drain" is that for the sake of expediency, young social workers, inexperienced in their practice, have had to be promoted to posts requiring administrative competence.

Superficially, the people of Hong Kong demonstrate a remarkable ability to cope. They behave with surprising complacency, possibly because they have been conditioned to do so in the face of repeated shocks during the past decade or because the upsetting trauma has been suppressed in exchange for a short-term peaceful existence. Further still, they resign themselves to their fate in order to go on with the hustle and bustle of Hong Kong life. Certainly, the indications of social unrest are not difficult to detect. The brain drain syndrome not only heightens the tension in the society but actually breaks up families. It is not uncommon for many to maintain their jobs in Hong Kong while sending their families overseas to ensure eventual citizenship. Their frequent commuting by air between Hong Kong and the mainland has earned them the popular title of "astronauts." The shift of economic activities northward has required many to divide their work life between China and Hong Kong, and a pattern of establishing a second family across the border is emerging that is affecting marital and family relationships. The number of divorce decrees jumped from 2,060 in 1981 to 6,295 in 1991, while the overall divorce rate increased from 0.09 per thousand in 1972 to 0.97 per thousand in 1992.[3] Single-parent families are on the rise, and the breakup of families seems to be having some impact on children's well-being (Chiu, 1990; Young, 1993; Lam, 1994). The aged population (65 years and over) has grown from about 3.9 percent in 1971 to 9 percent of the total population in 1992, exacerbating the problems that emerge for the elderly and the disabled when breadwinners emigrate overseas and they are left alone or inadequately provided for. Moreover, while the official estimate of the number of mentally ill persons requiring rehabilitation services in 1988 was 21,281, the number rose to 22,331 by 1993.[4] Complex problems such as child abuse, sexual abuse, and domestic violence are surging. The need for social welfare services is increasing.

On the level of direct welfare services supply, some 220 nongovernmental organizations contribute about 80 percent of the services. The Social Welfare Department concentrates on the rest, providing mandatory coverage of statutory services and social security schemes. Budget expenditures and government subventions reflect that some welfare bureaucracies of significant importance have been established.

To summarize, Hong Kong is not only undergoing a rapid transition to a new government but also a more fundamental change; superficially, people go about their daily life apparently unperturbed, but sociological studies reflect their tension and uncertainty about the future and, indeed, even about their own identities. The people of Hong Kong want a smooth transition, but the rows between the authorities give little comfort. Social unrest can be detected, and social problems abound.

Thus, in this context, after the quick responses to the critical issues in the 1960s and 1970s, social welfare is cautiously attempting to meet the need, but always lagging behind demands. It remains basically remedial and conservative, at times interrupted by administrative manipulations. Welfare service delivery is in the hands of two big camps: the Social Welfare Department and the nongovernmental organizations heavily subsidized by the local government as a cheaper executive arm. Quite a number of this latter group have grown into welfare bureaucracies of significant size and importance, employing hundreds of social workers responsible for huge budgets and service units throughout Hong Kong. It is during such social times and amid such social processes that social work in Hong Kong is practiced.

ISSUES FACED BY HONG KONG SOCIAL WORK EDUCATORS

Purpose of Social Work

Concomitant with the welfare planning of the 1970s was a recognition of the role of professionally trained manpower in social welfare. This brought with it an increase in the training programs offered by five out of the seven universities and training institutes funded by the Polytechnic Grants Committee. With the increasing complexity in the problems handled by the social work practitioners, the training institutes began to offer postgraduate training programs leading to the master's and doctorate awards, thus developing a linear model of social work education programs not unlike those found in the United States. Despite the noncommittal social welfare development plans of the mid-1970s to the late-1980s, social welfare manpower expanded. Overall, when compared to our U.K. (Sibeon, 1991) and U.S. counterparts (Sarri, 1988), the Hong Kong social work profession seems to enjoy a better image in the public eye. Nonetheless, its relationship with the Hong Kong society-in-transition and its professional development must be carefully examined with respect to the context previously described.

In this section, we discuss a number of the major issues faced by social work educators. The question of "What is the primary purpose of social work in such a context?" is a crucial issue for the profession. "Social work as cause and social work as function," Porter Lee's two basic conditions of social work established early in 1929 (Howe, 1979), are probably still relevant today. The former sees social workers as fighters for an aim; strongly defending a principle, unearthing new problems, and advocating for their clients, they confront and challenge the social system and work for social reform. The latter views social workers as interpreters of current social standards, reflecting the norms of the society it serves. According to this perspective, social workers work for individual betterment and personal change of behavior. They are a stabilizing force for society. Transferring this to the context of Hong Kong, should the primary purpose of social work be seen "as cause" or "as function"? Should we continue with the social worker's historical mission of social reform and join the urge to run for political office? Or should we educate social workers for individual betterment, emphasizing solely the development of personal social service—a focus accepted as legitimate by both the government and the public?

As the capitalistic system and the conservative remedial model of welfare are likely to stay, Hong Kong social workers have the responsibility to advocate for deprived groups who are disadvantaged by the forces structured within the systems (systems that incidentally include the welfare bureaucracies that were established to help meet clients' needs but that consciously or unconsciously have displaced their original goals). Yet in playing the role of advocate, the social worker needs to be careful neither to be the pawn of the politics at play nor to be deceived by distorted ideologies.

This does not suggest that social workers should relinquish their role as advocates; it simply means that they must be more knowledgeable about the systems and the ideologies they work with, more sensitive to the dynamics of social issues and changing social processes, more astute in their assessment, and more tactful in their intervention. Short-term radical reforms of the systems are unrealistic; moreover, they may even be irresponsible as the social climate of the society is urging a reduction of tension and a smooth transition.

One of the realistic lines to follow is to ground ourselves in the personal social service programs and to become familiar with the individual client's plight, acknowledging that his or her problems are interconnected with the contradictions found in the larger processes in society. Another is to use communities as cases of entry and to understand how the internal and external dynamics interweave to generate personal and common issues for action. All the while, the understanding of the problems and the strategies planned are constructed through analysis and exchanges based on the worker-client relationship, in the light of social work principles. Thus the social worker mediates between the world of the client and that of the broader society, taking social work neither solely as "cause" nor as "function," but rather focusing on the process of searching for an outcome with the client. Social work education needs to encourage students to take on such roles.

Another crucial aspect to heed is the "China factor." Under its modernization process, the existing Chinese welfare system is being challenged, the need to train social workers is beginning to emerge, and a number of higher education institutes have been mandated to launch social work programs. The nation has just started to rearrange its resources better to meet the people's needs. Hong Kong, with a longer history of accommodating its population and with easier access to the West, can conveniently act as a link with and a mediator between China and the West. Social workers must thus possess a more thorough understanding of the two cultures and societies so as to foster an indigenous and authentic movement of social work in both China and Hong Kong. If the ethos depicted in the first section of this chapter continues, this mediating and linking role will not be an uneventful one. While there could be exchanges on service formats, models, skills, and expectations, ideological debates reflecting very different cultural perspectives are also likely to take place. Thus, to prepare for the future and grasp the present, Hong Kong social workers need to be equipped now. Social work curricula must expose students to this area.

Social Science, Social Work, and Beyond

The above discussion brings us to a second perennial problem in social work education: What constitutes the knowledge base of social work? How much social science do we place in the curriculum? Which disciplines? What is their relationship with social work? Underpinning these questions is the more central debate: What is the relationship between theory and practice?

Literature reflects little evidence that social workers use theories explicitly in their practice (Stevenson and Parslow, 1978; Carew, 1979; Waterhouse, 1987). However, Hardiker (Hardiker, 1981), in her research on probation and child care, argued that social workers internalized knowledge with their experience; thus, the conceptual frameworks underlying their practice have not always been explicit.

Other writers (Maas, 1968; Brennan, 1973) opined that this lack of use of a conceptual framework was due to the social sciences, from which the theories, concepts, and ideas were borrowed, and that they were too general and abstract. In addition, they were not derived from the context wherein social workers actually practiced; thus, they were of limited applicability. From a more provocative angle, Sibeon, in *Towards a New Sociology of Social Work* (Sibeon, 1991), asserted that British social work exhibited a "cognitive closure," that it had become "insular" and "increasingly remote not merely from modern social science and social policy discourses but also from the discourses of citizens and those whose needs it is supported to serve."

These arguments are not mutually exclusive; neither are they conclusive. To us, social scientists as "outsiders" are neither necessarily willing nor able to identify the appropriate concepts, models, and theories to be used as organizing and building blocks of knowledge for social work practice; after all, it is not the role of social scientists to prescribe goals for their social work colleagues! As the situation stands, should this role not be the responsibility of social work practitioners and educators? This discussion, though inconclusive, cautions social workers and educators to be sensitive and open to challenges. It also reminds us of our responsibility in developing a knowledge base for our profession.

Some social work educators feel that social science has been unhelpful for practice. Some have claimed that the absence of social science would not lead to second-rate practice; others have suggested that social science be removed from the curriculum (Davies, 1981), while others have defended its inclusion (Evans, 1976; Curnock and Hardiker, 1979; Hardiker, 1981; Payne, 1991). Writers in the latter camp elaborate on the relationship of theory and practice, some of which we have found to be helpful. For instance, Curnock and Hardiker (Curnock & Hardiker, 1979) differentiate between "theory of practice" (theory derived from the social sciences) and "practice theory" (knowledge derived from what social workers do, including common sense, practice wisdom, tacit knowledge). Proceeding from here, English social work educators (e.g. Payne, 1991), and Dutch educators (e.g., Smid and Krieken, 1984) have clarified that there are different types of theories in social work with different purposes; hence, they might relate differently to social work practice.

Payne's (Payne, 1991) analysis of how social work theories relate to one another is a further step in the understanding of social work theories, fulfilling an important link for both social work practitioners and educators. Hardiker's (Hardiker, 1981) teaching exercises, devised to explore the base of social work, serve as a stimulating pedagogic guide to the social work educators.

Before we leave the topic, it is of paramount importance to note the emergence of the concept of "practice theory." While many may want to debate whether implicit knowledge can be termed as "theory," such conceptual thinking opens up a totally new horizon for exploration. It posits not only that theory enlightens practice but also that practice can contribute to theory building. Brennan, early in 1973, pointed out that espoused theories, generalized as they are, needed to be tested in concrete practice; and practice, offering the real-life situations, would help practitioners and theoreticians to gain new insights into theories. Practice could thus expand, redirect, and even generate new theories, offering a bidirectional approach rather than a unidirectional one. Grounding ourselves in practice would be one realistic way to understand social work and to develop its knowledge base in our own society.

So far, we have been summarizing the debate in the western context of the relationship between social science and social work. Being in Hong Kong, however, we have to address this debate in the local scene. As social work can only be understood in the social and cultural context of the participants, the cultural context is of great significance. We have discussed how social work "borrows" heavily from the social science disciplines in terms of knowledge, theories, and concepts, which we refer to as "theory of practice." These theories contribute to the nature of social work and its role in society; they were generated from western societies and hence are the products of these western social and cultural processes. In the short history and rapid rate of social work development in Hong Kong, we have borrowed, almost without question, all these western theories. Practice models have been adopted without querying their ideological and theoretical base and the context in which they were generated; educators teach theories without systematically studying and challenging their legitimacy and whether local circumstances are appropriate for adoption. Therefore, social work practitioners and educators in Hong Kong face a serious problem: the "double-borrowing issue" in social work.

That the issue is of grave concern can be illustrated by one example. "The individual" is a deeply rooted concept in the Anglo-Saxon culture. Judeo-Christian and Greek philosophies have contributed to its importance to western culture. Deriving from it are prime principles such as "respect for the individual" and "client's self-determination." The "individual" is always conceived as a separate entity, enjoying free will and exercising autonomy. This notion takes on quite a different light if viewed in the Chinese context; "the individual," often more appropriately termed "the person," enjoys his or her being in a network of reciprocal relationships. The overtone is much more of connectedness than separateness. Thus, it follows that crucial concepts such as the "self" are interpreted very differently in different contexts.

The above example cites basic concepts crucial to the theory and practice of social work in western culture. Yet we have used them quite casually. In his argument that social work is socially constructed, Payne (Payne, 1991) cautions us about the need to indigenize ("in which important ideas are altered to make them appropriate to local conditions") and to authenticize ("where local ideas are developed in association with imported theories to form a new structure of ideas"). Since it is our responsibility as local social workers to contribute to the understanding of social work in a transitional Hong Kong, the debates in the literature on the theory/practice link and, in particular, on the idea of practice contributing to theory building have become important leads with which to explore this new horizon in indigenizing and or authenticizing social work.

Developing an appropriate knowledge base for social work in Chinese societies is one of the crucial elements in the process of professionalization. The path is an uphill one; the process requires a team of social scientists and social workers to research the bonding between the individual self and the local society. The process needs to realize the bidirectional approach in which theory affects practice and practice affects theory. To build such a team in a volatile Hong Kong situation is not easy. To nurture such an aim requires commitment, effort, and time. Moreover, immersed in a market-oriented culture, Hong Kong social workers have to demonstrate their competency in working with complex situations, under the pressure of a heavy workload, and amid a very uncertain society. With the emergence of other helping professions, the pressure to maintain professional status has grown. This somehow explains the fervor of practitioners and their employers for methods, skills, and various family therapy approaches. Their preference is for "fast food," or narrowly focused models and techniques. Although we are not suggesting here that we are against systematic and empirical knowledge, methods, skills, and techniques, we are nevertheless mindful of a too-focused practice. The dominance of such a philosophy is evidenced by social workers who identify themselves with methods and pride themselves on labels of therapy, while their rationality and humane practice are reduced to an instrumental and technological level and when social work practice and the study of human behavior, are, in the main, represented by and reduced to measurable numbers. In other words, social work has strayed from its purpose when the subjective human helping experience is ignored and the moral and ethical dimension of this human interaction is lost. It is such dominance and the fear of its continued reign that should alert local social work educators to their responsibility to pay special attention to the education and training of social workers.

EDUCATING SOCIAL WORKERS IN TUMULT: THE RESPONSE OF THE DEPARTMENT OF APPLIED SOCIAL STUDIES

Education is for the future. The response of the APSS must be grounded in the present while taking a positive stand towards the future. The APSS conception of the challenge for social work education is as follows: Hong Kong needs committed, educated, and competent social workers who can make meaning of a tumultuous situation, positively positioning themselves amid frustrations. We need workers who are able to cope with uncertainties, ready to work constructively with constraints while being alert to opportunities; we need proactive social workers with vision who are creative yet realistic in their interventions. Future social workers of Hong Kong must be not only competent professionals but also reflective practitioners, humane and compassionate with human sufferings. In order to reach such aims, APSS has developed certain features in its curricula, and they must organize and develop its staff along such direction.

Developing a Committed, Educated, and Competent Workforce

The "2 + 2 + 2 Model." In this model, the triple "twos" stand for the number of years of training that a full-time student has to go through to become a recognized social work professional. In other words, a full-time student, with a minimum entrance requirement of a secondary school graduate, would spend two years attaining an award of the diploma in social sork; he or she would then take a full-time paid job as a social work assistant for a minimum of two years, before he or she would be eligible to apply for the two years' full-time bachelor's degree of social work. Currently a part-time mode is provided for the serving social workers in the profession.

Developing an educated, competent and reflective professional. Social work students need to have a broadened knowledge base, which involves the teaching of related disciplines such as sociology, psychology, economics, and social policy. All of these must be compulsory subjects in the undergraduate program, which will help students to describe and explain personal and social behavior from various perspectives. However, developing a competent professional in a wider educational context within a short time poses challenges to our social scientists; thus, the selection of relevant knowledge from the disciplines needs care. Focusing on themes of study is one strategy. Meanwhile, in order to comprehend the interactive process between the worker and the client, the nature of social work must be examined carefully in its ethical, humanistic, and scientific dimensions. To equip students with adequate practice competence, theories in social work practice are taught with experiential learning methods, in both fieldwork training and in a framework of multilevel intervention at individual, family, and community levels.

The exploration between social science and social work relationship, behind which lies the theory/practice debate, takes place in a number of subjects throughout the curricula. Two examples are as follows:

- A social constructionist approach has been designed in one of the M.A. (Social Work) modules entitled "The Advanced Seminars in Social Work Studies," where students are asked to examine the cultural, historical and linguistic components of their practice in Hong Kong (Tsang, 1994).

- Social scientists and social workers form a team in "co-teaching"—for example, in the subject Integrative Seminar in the final year of the undergraduate level—to address the threefold relationship among "theory," "meta-theory," and "practice" in social work. Social work practice theories are examined in terms of their metatheoretical stance. Students' own fieldwork practices are used to examine their value, assumptions, and theoretical and metatheoretical orientations through class presentations and discussions. Knowledge is not valued just at the espoused theoretical level, but theorizing from one's practice is acknowledged as pertinent, and articulation of tacit knowledge is given a very special status in the process of knowledge building. Knowledge content is important, but the process of the reflective practitioner-in-action is equally significant (Schon, 1983). Concepts and skills are critical, but attitudes are vital. To prepare students for a commitment to a world of work in a tumultuous situation, vision and hope in the future must be cultivated. This is premised on their grounding in reality; thus, one of the aims of our program is educating students to cope with uncertainties. A problem-based approach is adopted in the subject "Introduction to Social Work," and the subject "Self, Culture and Society." Students are engaged in understanding the problem formulation process, thus raising their awareness that in a complex and unpredictable world, it may be more meaningful at times to focus on "situation improvement" rather than stressing "problem solving" all the time. Moreover, the importance of viewing clients' problems holistically and in context is emphasized. Exposing students to the critical hermeneutical approach helps them to understand the clients' predicament that often human suffering is interconnected with the contradictions found in the large processes in society; thus, students become aware of the dynamics of the problems and work realistically towards the betterment of human living.

While one may not be able to shun the managerial tide, social workers need to be trained as competent workers. However, along with making meaning of their own practice, they need to learn to think critically and imaginatively, to be able to face dilemmas and to make independent judgments. "The Art of Reasoning," "Social Ethics," and "Self, Culture and Society," together with other subjects in particular fieldwork, help students to develop along this path.

Preparing for Hong Kong's Political Transition. To lay the groundwork for students to face Hong Kong's return to China, a subject titled "Contemporary Chinese Societies" is compulsory. In addition, an experimental project is underway for student field visits to China to provide students with firsthand information on China's welfare system during modernization. This also offers a forum for students to interact and exchange views with their counterparts— the welfare personnel and service recipients in the China scene.

Pedagogical Concerns. Research has been conducted on learning strategies of the undergraduate students (Tsang, 1992); thus, special attention has been paid to pedagogical strategies. Kolb's Experiential Learning Model (Kolb, 1984), which rests on a contextualistic view of knowledge and the multidimensionality in learning modes, has been used to examine curriculum designs in our programs. Social work practice and methods are delivered in a lecture-laboratory-skill format to provide students with opportunities to relate theory and practice and to receive immediate feedback on their performance. The integrative seminars mentioned above support students in the process of being reflective practitioners. Such pedagogic strategies are demanding on the educator-self; the educator has to shift from a closed to a more open view of knowledge and must shed the expert or teacher-centered role for a more peer-like, student-centered approach.

Developing a Staff Force

A Department of Multiple Disciplines. To nurture the desired features, some fifty-plus social scientists from social work, sociology, psychology, and philosophy are pooled in the Department of Applied Social Studies. They are assigned to work in teams, which are termed "course committees."[5] These course committees, together with student representatives, are responsible for the design, monitoring, and development of programs leading to different awards.

A Triple Role Demand: Practitioner-Educator-Academician. The department recruits its social work staff from local social workers with substantial practice experience in the profession. The Education Development Unit of the Hong Kong Polytechnic provides them with support in becoming educators through orientation, seminars, and workshops. Some colleagues, experimenting with action learning and action research approaches, have begun to engage practitioners as co-researchers and co-learners in the continuous improvement of their practice; meanwhile, this process brings the teaching staff close to practice, where espoused theories are tested and even redirected. We also hope that such partnership between social work educators and practitioners is one realistic way to study the changing social processes of our society in flux; moreover, it may lead us towards the indigenizing and authenticizing of social work knowledge locally and in China. Formally, in staff assignment, it is the department's policy that all lecturers with social work training would normally teach both in the classroom and in the fieldwork setting. This addresses, at least in part, the structural theory-practice split as experienced by our western counterparts; furthermore, it stresses the importance of theory/practice integration. Another way to encourage the bidirectional approach in theory/practice is to encourage teams of teachers to engage in limited direct practice, taking clients referred by welfare organizations with the aim of testing and evaluating the borrowed theories. Such research is presented in research seminars, and findings are shared with the students in class.

In Search of Indigenization and Authenticization of Social Work Knowledge. APSS makes use of some of its M.Phil/Ph.D. student quotas to enroll students from China, researching in areas such as women's role in China, social security, and indigenous model of social work education in China. Colleagues also form themselves in teams and work with our Chinese counterparts in research projects, as well as in the development of social work education in Peking, PRC. Such academic attempts have sharpened issues that reflect possible similarities and differences in theories/practice relationship. This has opened up new fronts for further research. One example is the ongoing study in the constitution of the Chinese self and family during the process of modernization.

Whole Departmental Approach. APSS is mainly composed of two sectors: the academic and the administrative. Readers may note that the department attempts to work in teams. This takes place not only in the academic but also in the administrative sector. The stress is on how the two sectors work together to realize their mission of providing quality education, research, and service. The team spirit developed so far has given us support and strength in the face of the changes we have encountered. The state of art is how to keep a satisfactory balance between the needs of an individual and that of the team or the department, thus allowing adequate space for the person while fulfilling the goals of the collective. We have built our department on trust, and we have faith that we can take up further challenge.

CONCLUSION

The sociopolitical context presents a vulnerable and critical situation for the development of social welfare and social work in Hong Kong. Social work educators need to take this as a positive challenge and to search collectively for ways to address the issues in context. It is not adequate for each individual social work educator to undertake such a mission. It is the department's and the organization's responsibility to facilitate the realization of the mission. Administrators and academics are responsible for the establishment and development of such culture. This is what we term the "whole departmental approach to quality social work education." As individual attempts are vulnerable, collective effort is pertinent in a turbulent time like ours. Thus, it is in this direction that we have begun our search. We realize that we are at the threshold of a new era in Hong Kong, a critical time when uncertainty and tension continue. With what we have presented here, we hope to have demonstrated, as a department, our commitment and contribution to social work education in Hong Kong and her motherland in the years to come.

NOTES

1. APSS has 56 full-time teaching staff and over 1,100 students. The range of programs offered by APSS accords with the career path of the social workers in the profession: the diplomats will be social work assistants; the bachelor's degree graduates, recognized as professional social workers, will take up posts as assistant social work officers in welfare organizations. While promotion does not require further training, it does not prohibit it; in fact, organizations do sponsor experienced social work officers or their equivalent to enroll in our master's program, the aim of which is to train advanced practitioners in direct service or social service administration.

2. The wastage rate in 1992–93 for Assistant Social Work Officers (those with bachelor's degrees, recognized as professionally trained) and above was 6.5 percent; for Social Welfare Assistants (SWA: those with a diploma in social work) was 20.6 percent, while the social work educators exhibited a wastage rate of 23.2 percent.

3. Figures supplied by Judiciary, extracted from "Report on Grounds for Divorce and the Time Restriction on Petitions for Divorce within Three Years of Marriage." The Law Reform Commission of Hong Kong, August 1992.

4. Figures are extracted from the Hong Kong Review of Rehabilitation Program Plans, Hong Kong Government, 1984.

5. In the Hong Kong Polytechnic, a "course" refers to a program of study, embracing a number of subjects or modules, coherently interrelated, leading to a specific award, such as the bachelor's degree in social work (with Honors).

15

The Interface between Social Sciences and Social Work: The Case of European Mental Health Social Work

Shulamit Ramon

Social work is an applied social science discipline. As such, it selectively uses knowledge that originates in other disciplines. An *interface* implies an exchange and a mutuality, enabling both continuity and further differentiation between social work and other social sciences disciplines. I shall be looking at the interface between social work and social science through the specific case of European mental health social work.

Mental distress and health exist in the twilight between reason and unreason, the emotional and the intellectual, the socially unacceptable and the wish to break away from social control, the subjective and the inter-subjective, the individual and society.

What is mental health? What is mental distress? What is mental illness? These are basic questions for which there are no definite scientific answers, within either the social sciences or the natural sciences or within the humanities for that matter. While some of us turn to religion when faced with complex and unclear concepts, most of us turn to popularized versions of science in the attempt to make sense of it, to establish patterns, to predict events and processes.

Given that social work is an applied discipline, we would thus judge it in terms of the above, as well as according to such questions as: Is the discipline helping people in resolving the difficulties they are facing vis-à-vis the suffering that is one of the major hallmarks of mental distress? Is it improving their functioning, and reducing their social isolation? Is the practice of the discipline following the ethical principles that underlie it?

THE CHALLENGE OF MENTAL DISTRESS AND HEALTH TO THE SOCIAL SCIENCES

As well as the fundamental questions as to what is mental distress and what is mental health, many additional questions are raised by the discomforting existence of mental distress, such as:

- Why does one person become mentally distressed while others in the same social situations do not?

- Are there social situations that foster mental distress more than others?

- Is the person opting to be so distressed, or is this beyond their control?

- Is the condition of mental distress influenced by family members, family situations, and life experiences?

- Is the segregation of distressed people useful and desirable for them, their families, their communities, and society at large?

- Is stigmatization a thing of the past, or is it indeed as irreversible as the Deviancy School has argued since the 1960s? (Goffman, 1961; Scheff, 1975).

- What are the implications of suffering from severe mental distress to the self-identity of such a person? To the identity of his/her relatives? To our collective identity? (Breakwell, 1983).

These are some of the questions with which mental distress confronts disciplines such as anthropology, psychology, and sociology.

- Is the financial investment in mental health services justified, in the light of the high level of "unproductivity" of many service users?

- Are the services providing what they are supposed to be offering?

- What is the role of professional and nonprofessional contributions in this field?

- Is care in the community any better, or worse, than hospitalization?

- Is the experience of mental distress and health universal? If not, what are the parameters of the differences, and what do they imply for its causes, interventions, and chances of recovery? (Warner, 1985).

These are some of the questions that mental distress is posing for disciplines such as economics, management, social policy, social work and psychology.

- What is the *social* value of the relatively recently emerging users and relatives organizations? This is a relatively new issue, in need of understanding within organizational theory and the sociology of new social movements and by the application of an historical dimension (Croft & Beresford, 1989; Rogers & Pilgrim, 1991).

- What are the implications of working within the mental health system, including living with policy changes and the emergent focus on users and relatives? Here we would look for contributions from education, psychology (Menzies-Leith, 1970), and social policy (Ramon, 1992).

Let us look now at how the social sciences are meeting the challenges outlined above. On the whole, they provide *insight* into:

- what mental distress/health is;

- what it means to suffer from mental distress;

- the impact of living in close proximity to a sufferer from severe mental distress

- social reactions to mental distress;

- the interaction between the personal and the social reactions;

- the implications of demographic and cultural variables for the probability of suffering from specific categories of mental distress and the probability of being offered specific types of interventions;

- the making of professional cultures and the impact of specific professional cultures on mental health perspectives and service systems (Ramon, 1989; Ramon, 1992);

- the probable career of a service user, based on the interaction between personal and social reactions, as well as on professional reactions and demographic variables;

- understanding the processes of implementing social change through politically agreed-upon policies, including change in mental health services and interventions and the financial cost of such policies;

- the beginning of the understanding of the personal and social costs of policy changes; and

- the beginning of the understanding of the place and value of users and carers organization (Rogers & Pilgrim, 1991; Hatfield, 1987).

Social science knowledge has been useful in increasing our understanding of mental health and distress, thus reshaping its meaning and the meaning of related issues. However, applied social science knowledge is more useful for explaining what happens after a first breakdown than it is for understanding what led to the breakdown. This knowledge, together with the understanding coming out of personal and professional experience, has enabled us to establish some patterns of the process involved. However, all of that still falls short of arriving at specific predictions as to what may happen to a particular individual suffering from mental distress and how it may affect his/her relatives.

Perhaps there is a link between the relative lack of knowledge and agreement concerning the etiological basis of mental distress and the weakness of the contribution of the social sciences both to etiologic understanding and to predictions. Nevertheless, sufficient information exists to enable us to identify groups rather than individuals at risk of suffering from mental distress due to personal and social circumstances/conditions (Caplan, 1959; Holland, 1990).

THE CHALLENGE OF MENTAL DISTRESS AND HEALTH TO SOCIAL WORK

People suffering from variations of mental distress are to be found in all areas of social work and in all client groups. Mental distress challenges social work in the following ways:

- It is a bio-psycho-social phenomenon, while we are lacking conceptual and methodological frameworks which integrate these three dimensions.

- It is frightening yet fascinating.

- It requires working with other professions and with nonprofessionals;

- The client is at times as clear and bright as the worker—or even sharper in his/her understanding than the worker—but unclear and seemingly "elsewhere" on other occasions. Beside the need to understand the significance of such changes, social workers need to know how not to become confused, as well as how to engage such a client and retain a reasonable level of engagement.

- Social workers' mandate demands that they fulfill both care and control functions with people suffering from mental distress. Social workers are reluctant to act in a controlling capacity, though often they seem to be unaware of how controlling their "intuitive" interpretation of the person's reality could be.

- Unlike psychotherapists or psychiatrists, social workers have to intervene at the socioeconomic level, as well as at the psychological level. This duality is difficult to juggle.

- Unlike other members of a mental health team, social workers have to work closely with relatives and with the community—groups that may have interests and views conflicting with those of the index client.

While social sciences knowledge is essential and useful, the fact that there are incompatible approaches within it leaves the social worker who needs to digest and apply this knowledge in the form of a social work strategy in a confused state, all too often resolved by opting for an approach that attracts him or her personally, rather than choosing an approach for its suitability to the client's problem or the client's own preference.

CURRENT EUROPEAN MENTAL HEALTH SYSTEMS CONTEXTS

Europe is a rapidly changing continent, both socially and politically. This is particularly visible in the ex-Communist countries, where parliamentary democracy has been introduced overnight alongside market economies of more than one type. The sense of belonging to Europe is more widespread now than it was even five years ago, not only in the ex-Communist countries but also in the less prosperous Western European countries that have greatly benefited from their European Community membership.

A cursory survey of European attitudes toward mental health illustrates the following divisions: the approach within northern and western Europe is one of viewing mental distress predominantly as an illness to be treated medically as well as psychologically and socially. People suffering from mental distress are perceived as vulnerable and weak, but not as inherently bad. There is a recognition that their difficulties are related to biological, psychological, or social factors (or a combination of all of them) and that, in many cases, people recover fully or partially. There is also a general acceptance that mental distress can happen to each of us. Consequently, sufferers are perceived as having the right to publicly maintained services of high quality, with only a minimal level of segregation when there is a risk either to themselves or to others.

Multidisciplinary professional work carried out in psychiatric outpatient facilities and in community mental health teams typifies this approach, accompanied by day centers and sheltered accommodation. Medication is the most prevalent form of intervention, though counselling, psychotherapy, and sociotherapy are available as well. Services are provided by statutory and not-for-profit organizations, with some outpatient consultations carried out by for-profit individual professionals.

In southern Europe, the approach has moved rapidly in the direction of the first group, especially since they have become members of the European Community (EC). Thus, for example, the EC is providing considerable financial support and professional expertise to the Greek mental health services, following the exposure that the largest hospital in the country has been run as a concentration camp. However, mental distress continues to be perceived mainly as a disease to be treated within medicine. Sufferers are seen as inflicted with the disease because of God's mysterious ways or their own sins. Consequently, hospitals and psychiatrists dominate the scene, with very little other recourse for the majority of the population. This stands in contrast to a viable tradition of community work in each of these countries.

The attitude in Eastern Europe towards mental distress does not differ considerably from that in the second group, insofar as it is dominated by the disease model and hence by the medicalization of mental illness. We are all aware of the use of psychiatric labels and hospitalization as a form of political repression towards dissidents during the Communist regime.

However, in Czechoslovakia, Hungary, Poland, and Slovenia, where people perceive themselves as more western than the Soviet Union was, attempts to align the mental health systems to those of northern Europe are already in motion. These efforts include the development of not-for-profit rehabilitation services, as well as sponsorship by the EC of specific projects and training programs. During 1990–1994, I contributed to one such training program in Ljublijana, the capital of Slovenia. Together with contributors from Austria, France, and Italy, I worked with the Slovenians to construct a training program that includes intensive weekend teaching by people from abroad, which is then supported by tutorials given by Slovenian tutors, followed by a six-month period of practice placement in one of the EC partner-countries. It is interesting and exciting to see how the program has evolved, as well as the much greater readiness for change within the Slovenian mental health system than in the parallel systems of the other four countries: Czechoslovakia, Hungary, Poland, and the Soviet Union. The cultural hegemony of the Anglo-Saxon tradition holds even in this project, despite the tendency of the Slovenians to look towards French and German modes of discourse, which are fundamentally different from Anglo-Saxon pragmatism.

Italy provides an exception to all other European countries in this field, in attempting to change its mental health system radically through a gradual closure of the psychiatric hospitals. By establishing a system of community mental health services during the 1970s and 1980s, Italy attempted to integrate people with severe mental illness through the provision of socially valued opportunities into an ordinary way of life and into an explicit social visibility. This effort is even more exceptional than the development of community services per se (Basaglia, 1968; Holland, 1990).

The only way of making sense of the exceptionality of the Italian case and the reasons for it is through the application of social science knowledge. Such an application illustrates the value of a historical perspective and the psychological impact of the experience of World War II and of being defeated. The war enabled Italian laypeople and professionals to question most closely held beliefs, including those related to mental distress.

Thus focusing on mental distress, the current European contexts present us with formidable opportunities and no less formidable obstacles to a greater understanding and tolerance of mental distress on the one hand and to an improved service system on the other hand.

A number of Western European countries are presently mirroring American policies from the 1960s onward, namely dehospitalization, deinstitutionalization, and care management (Test & Stein, 1980; Bacharach, 1992). While the United States has provided a number of positive examples, it would be only fair to state that it has also tolerated unuseful policies and practices as well. For example, during the twenty years in which many of the American psychiatric hospitals were closed, not even one study focused on the processes and the aftermath of such a closure from the perspectives of the major stakeholders, namely, the clients, the relatives, and the workers. Some European research exists now that is just beginning to address these issues (De Leonardis, Mauri, and Rotelli, 1994; Perring, 1992; Tomlinson, 1991; Ramon, 1992; Zeelen & Weeghel, 1993).

We have learned from service users that they are much more interested in deinstitutionalization (Lawson, 1991; Croft & Beresford, 1989), while professionals are divided in their preferences, the majority of carers being worried as to whether the outcome of the change would entail shifting most of the burden onto them.

The European Users Network is a recent development in this move toward deinstitutionalization. It has representatives from some ten countries, predominantly from northern Europe, but also from southern and Eastern Europe. The network itself is just being formed, but its importance lies in reflecting on the growth of the users movement in Europe throughout the 1980s. The network and user groups throughout Europe focus on the need for nonmedical services in the community. Some of these services are managed directly by service users, where the support takes the form of refuge facilities, finance, accommodation, social activities, and counselling. While not glorifying mental distress, the network attempts to find ways of coping with symptoms more positively rather than viewing them as things to be rid of at any cost (Romme, 1994).

The essential preconditions for a viable users network seem to include:

- a core group of both users and professionals able and ready to contribute to its development;

- endorsement and modest funding by a national or multinational organization (here, support is provided by the European region of the World Mental Health Federation and the Council of Europe, as part of the EC program on reducing social exclusion);

- clear and achievable objectives to start with, which can be agreed by most stakeholders in the field;

- creating early opportunities for an open, but respectable, debate within the users movement, and between them and interested others, such as relatives and professionals; and

- ensuring the autonomy of the network and preventing its control by nonusers, while working together with other organizations.

EUROPEAN MENTAL HEALTH SOCIAL WORK

While mental health social work takes different forms in different countries in Europe, some shared elements exist. These include:

- A clear preference for a psychosocial approach to mental distress and health and for interventions that focus on psychological and/or social dimensions, such as counselling and networking;

- acceptance that good care in the community is preferable to hospitalization and any other form of segregation; and

- the belief that people who suffer from mental distress have full citizen rights, which include the right to be supported by the state when unable to support oneself financially and otherwise

The differences between countries in mental health social work relate to the historical developmental paths of social work, including educational traditions and social prestige. Thus, in northern Europe, social workers offer more counselling and welfare advice than networking and community action, which are more prevalent in southern Europe (Rodrigues, 1991). Social work as an autonomous profession is beginning to develop in a rather haphazard fashion in the ex-communist countries. In no European country are social workers occupying formal leadership positions in multidisciplinary settings.

In northern European countries that have new governments following the New Right, there is a growing attempt to increase the controlling aspect of mental health social work, under the heading of "protection." This is reflected in legislation that provides a more powerful status to mental health social workers vis-à-vis clients and other professions, but only in the context of compulsory measures (Barnes, Fisher, and Bowel, 1990).

At the same time, social workers have initiated all of the important user-led initiatives, in the forms of mutual support groups, policy pressure groups, employment and housing projects, advocacy, and networking. These projects were pioneered despite being perceived by other professions as "suspect" or "risky." In taking on this risk, social workers were motivated not only by their value systems but also by the knowledge coming from the social sciences that isolation and lack of solidarity are a greater risk factor than activating service users as people responsible for their own lives and able to support others and to be supported (Milroy & Hennelly, 1989; Fisher, 1991; Mullender & Ward, 1991). The new initiatives can be typified as a modified revival of community action and groupwork put together.

Likewise, social work lecturers in Budapest are running social centers that provide an opportunity for people with mental health difficulties to share pleasurable activities as well as to air their personal difficulties and look together for solutions (Talyigas & Hegesyi, 1992).

Both of these examples highlight the direct use of social sciences knowledge and the unique contribution of social work knowledge and skills in putting to new use the insight gained from the social sciences. They also reflect that the innovative responses to the new sociopolitical context have come in social work primarily from those who disagree with some, if not all, of fundamental aspects of the dominant political ideology. For example, in the fundamental critique of traditional psychiatry that took place in northern Europe and in Italy in the 1960s and 1970s, social workers were more involved than either psychiatrists or nurses (Ramon, 1985). The greater readiness to adopt a critical position of traditional psychiatry and to move from it to more challenging ways of work that enable and empower service users than before came to social workers through the value base of their profession and through the insight provided by the social sciences.

Mental health social workers (like social workers in general) have been— and continue to be—more involved than other professions in working with refugees, new migrants, and members of ethnic minorities, even when this type of work has been unpopular.

The focus in social work values on people's individual rights to be valued citizens and to be supported in adversity has met in the social sciences knowledge a legitimization and reinforcement of the need to work with the marginalized and the isolated and of the need to work on reconnection to society through socially valued means, both individually and collectively (Hokenstand, Khinduka, and Midgeley, 1992).

We can observe now the convergence of the active minority of social workers in northern Europe with the majority of social workers in southern Europe in recognizing the need to enable collective solidarity and not only to alleviate individual suffering and encourage well-being. Moreover, it is the growing wish of social workers in southern and Eastern Europe to be engaged in more in-depth individual and family work. This is an interesting illustration of new meeting points between sociopolitical developments in Europe, the impact of social science knowledge, and social work values.

Yet so far social work has insufficiently capitalized on its own practice experience and research, which demonstrates the usefulness of psychosocial holistic and preventive work (Corney, 1981; Fisher, 1991). Social work also has not made use of these findings to take a more critical look at itself in terms of the risk of imitating other professions or of depersonalizing and rebureaucratizing their professional activity (Brandon, 1991).

The next phase—that of rewriting some elements of social sciences knowledge to reflect these developments in mental health social work—is yet to take place.

In summary, Europe, European mental health systems, and mental health social work in all of the European contexts are facing unprecedented challenges. The need for mental health social work is expanding in the light of the changes currently taking place in Europe. This is joined by the government-led demand for greater expertise in relatively new areas for European social work, such as care management and enabling the active participation of users and carers in imaginatively planning and implementing care packages. Paradoxically, the unimaginative, bureaucratically led introduction of such useful ways of work may lead to the abandonment of past ways of work that have proved to be supportive and effective, unless social workers are able to defend their position against more managerial and mechanistic ways of working.

In effectively confronting these challenges, social science knowledge is indispensable to mental health social work, both to the understanding of basic social and personal processes and to the use of evaluative research, which is sensitive enough to capture not only outcomes but also processes of work and their intrinsic value (Marris & Rein, 1972; Gould, 1989).

Although social workers in mental health and in other areas of social work have taken a critical stance towards some elements of social science knowledge in their practice, they rarely articulate this stance at the conceptual and research levels. European mental health social work provides the social sciences with a unique case study in which to test and revise its theoretical base, as a subsystem interfacing with a number of other subsystems—all in transition.

16

Integrating Work Team Effectiveness with Social Work Practice: An Ecological Approach

Diane Vinokur-Kaplan

Social work has long appreciated the value of team work; as early as the 1920s, psychiatrists, psychologists, and social workers were team members in mental health clinics (Ducanis & Golin, 1979, 3). Today's social workers, here and abroad, continue to work in teams (Payne, 1982), often in interdisciplinary collaboration with other professionals, staff, volunteers, paraprofessionals, and consumers (Andrews, 1990, 175, 176). They are often members of clinical assessment and treatment teams in hospitals and child protection agencies (Gilgun, 1988; Toseland, Palmer-Ganeles, & Chapman, 1986), while others serve on community outreach teams to the severely mentally ill (Bond et al., 1991). School social workers are mandated to work with other professionals on educational plans for disabled students (Radin, 1992). Administrators participate in intra- and interagency management teams (MacNair, 1980; Schon & Rein, 1993). Thus, teams and their effectiveness provide a rich topic for social work research on service delivery.

Ducanis and Golin (Ducanis & Golin, 1979, 3–5) outlined three factors that encouraged the importance and prevalence of interdisciplinary teams in human services:

- The concept of the "whole client," in which the multiple, related needs of a client were recognized, and an array of needed services were provided in a coordinated, unfragmented approach;

- The needs of the organization to clarify the lines of communication and authority within the agency as greater professional specialization developed (e.g., in child guidance clinics, hospitals, and other agencies); and,

- External mandates, in which such forces as "legislation, government regulations, and requirements of various third party payers . . . [saw] team responsibility in assessment, diagnosis and treatment . . . as one way to improve the quality of care and provide for professional accountability" (p. 5).

In addition, some agencies use teams to provide greater continuity of treatment for long-term patients and mitigate the impact of staff turnover in such "high burnout" fields as community mental health (Bond et al., 1991).

Teams may be seen as expensive staff arrangements, especially given the type of professionals involved; yet the strength of the factors above, and perhaps the current corporate emphasis on using teams, have maintained and sometimes increased their place in human services. Indeed, rather than disbanding teams, some hospitals have invested heavily in improving small group processes to help staff serve clients more effectively and efficiently. In a cost-benefit analysis of the nineteen Quality Improvement Teams active in the total quality management implementation at the University of Michigan Medical Center (1987-1991), "the present value of the benefits was 7.2 times, or 720 percent, the present value of costs" (Gaucher & Coffey. R.J., 1993, 24). Thus, such training may lower overall costs while increasing efficiency, effectiveness, and client satisfaction.

Interestingly, organizational researchers have also recently emphasized the use of work teams to better serve customers (Bettenhausen, 1991; Hackman, 1990; Sundstrom, DeMeuse, & Futrell, 1990; Tannenbaum, 1968). Quality circles, management teams, and other "small groups of interdependent individuals who share responsibility for outcomes for their organizations" (Sundstrom, DeMeuse, and Futrell, 1990) play important roles in transforming management and in enhancing productivity and product quality in today's global economy.

Thus, work teams and their effectiveness provide an interesting example of a long-standing organizational arrangement in social work being revisited with the benefit of recent social science conceptualizations. Human service teams' special attributes also suggest opportunities to broaden the study of teams to settings beyond the worlds of business, industry, and the military, where they are often focused (Tannenbaum, 1968).

Three characteristics of human services settings noted by Hasenfeld (Hasenfeld, 1992) distinguish human service teams and influence definitions of their effectiveness: (1) people are the "raw material" on which they work; (2) the work includes moral judgments and statements about the social worth of clients; and (3) the direct provision of services is most often provided by women, many of whose clients are also women and frequently poor (Hasenfeld, 1992, 4–9). Human services teams also often include other professionals, and they interact with concerned family members as well. Thus, they confront special challenges regarding composition and complexity. Moreover, their long-term human impact and their moral and social concerns may be more salient than those of teams in other settings (such as sports, business, and industry).

Some differences between teams may be clearer when comparing a clinical team deciding to admit, treat, and later to discharge a seriously mentally ill patient into the community to an idealized industrial team seeking to produce a better toothbrush. First, the *opportunities to experiment before implementing change* may differ. The product team can experiment with product prototypes before actually implementing a production change. In contrast, human service teams may have only one, time-limited chance to intervene with a volatile or resistant individual or group (e.g., by admitting the person to the hospital).

Thus, they encounter particular time pressures on decision making. They must also consider the social and judicial sequelae that may rapidly unfold for the individual involved, as well as that person's significant others, such as parents, spouse, or children.

Second, the product team's *quality of interaction with consumers* may be limited to observing a focus group trying out the toothbrush. In contrast, the human service team may have more direct, intense, and ongoing interaction with the clients and significant others.

Third, *the goals of decision-making* may differ. The corporate team's basis for decision making may focus mainly on the generation of profits. In human services, decisions are based on such broadly defined concepts as "a danger to self or others" or "the best interests of the child." While a product team may search for mass appeal in designing their product, human service professionals seek an individualized, customized approach to alleviate an individual's suffering within the context of current practice and law.

Fourth, *measures of success* may differ. While the product team may equate its success with immediate short-term sales figures, a treatment team may monitor a client's long-term progress toward more abstract and morally laden goals, such as "independent living," over a longer period of time.

Fifth, the *field of influence and targeted action* the team is trying to produce in consumers differs. A product team is often trying to influence a single individual's purchase choice. In contrast, a human service team may be working with various aspects of a client's behavior, plus multiple collateral parties as well, incorporating often ambiguous and conflicting data for decision making. For example, the interdisciplinary team of the Central Minnesota Incest Treatment Program (Gilgun, 1988) was comprised of 14 members, including social workers, a clinical psychologist, and three volunteer grandparents. They, in turn, had collateral contacts with teachers, foster parents when the children were in foster care placement, and prison officials when the perpetrators were in prison (see pages 232, 235).

Sixth, the *competitive environment* differs. There are often competing product teams with overlapping stakeholders vying for the consumer's dollar for a similar product. In contrast, in human services, there is often only one publicly designated and accountable team that will handle cases in a particular locale (i.e., psychiatric hospital admissions, child abuse).

Seventh, *the basis for establishment of a team and its membership* may differ. While employees empowered by the private sector may decide to establish a new product team, social workers may suddenly find themselves members of mandated teams, required by law or by new standards of professional practice.

Thus, the human service team must contend with pressurized, publicly scrutinized decision-making and practice that has major impact on the lives of the distressed, their loved ones, and their communities.

SOCIAL WORK AND WORK TEAMS

Despite the prevalence and importance of teams in social work, social workers (and other helping professionals) often do not use teams in a self-conscious manner to benefit clients (Abramson, 1993; Andrews, 1990; Chase, Wright, and Ragade, 1981). For example, in mental health teams, members may over-rely on their psychodynamic interpretation of the patient's actions vis-à-vis the team members to "explain" their own troubled team behavior, rather than examining their own group's unconstructive dynamics (Butterill, O'Hanlon, and Book, 1992). Helping professionals are also often unaware of or untrained in how their team "fits in" to the functioning of their department or the organization as a whole. Thus, while they may work well together on discrete tasks, such team members may be befuddled by "directives from above." Moreover, direct practitioners may have difficulty articulating their need for further organizational clarity of the team's role, and in advocating for needed coaching, consultants, and supportive resources to assist their teams.

However, if social workers were to adopt and adapt recent ecological approaches to team effectiveness (Sundstrom, DeMeuse, & Futrell, 1990; Friedlander, 1987; Hackman, 1987; Hackman, 1990), in their own settings, they may better understand their team's goals and enhance its effectiveness. Illustrations are provided below, using the example of interdisciplinary psychiatric treatment teams, on which social workers frequently serve. They draw from previous empirical research (Bailey, Hesel-DeWest, Thiele, & Ware, 1983; Bond et al., 1991; Rendell, 1988; Toseland, Palmer-Ganeles, & Chapman, 1986), as well as the author's recent study of such teams in public psychiatric hospitals (Vinokur-Kaplan, 1992; Vinokur-Kaplan, 1995a; Vinokur-Kaplan, 1995b; Vinokur-Kaplan & Walker-Burt, 1994).

Work Team Terminology and Definitions

The terms "group" and "team" are used interchangeably (Hackman, 1990, 14), as are "work group" and "work team." The latter specifically emphasize their greater organizational context. In a social work context, a team has been defined as "a number of individual staff members, each of who possesses particular knowledge and skills, who come together to share their expertise with one another for a common purpose" (Toseland, Palmer-Ganeles, & Chapman, 1986, 46). Here, the purpose of a human service organization is to enhance the functioning of clients and their environments and to improve the effectiveness or comprehensiveness of the services that clients receive.

Team Effectiveness

Earlier models of team effectiveness concentrated on whether the group accomplished the task or decision with which it began—a short-term, task-oriented perspective. Recent models (Sundstrom, DeMeuse, & Futrell, 1990; Hackman, 1990; Tannenbaum, Beard, & Salas, 1992) also look at members' "satisfaction, participation, and willingness to continue working together" as a second indicator of team effectiveness (Sundstrom, DeMeuse, & Futrell, 1990, 122). This team viability component reflects the fact that some groups may "win a battle, but lose the war"—complete their task under duress but never wish to work together again. This situation represents an expensive loss of organizational resources and continuing collaboration. Illustratively, Leiter's

Table 16.1
Conceptual Model of Team Effectiveness

Independent Variables	Process Criteria of Effectiveness	Dependent Variables: Outcome Criteria
Initial Group Conditions	**Enabling Group Conditions**	**Team Effectiveness**
1. Group structure: size and composition	1. Sufficient effort is given to accomplish task.	1. **HIGH QUALITY "PRODUCT"—INDIVIDUALIZED TREATMENT PLAN— PRODUCED**
2. Task clarity	2. Adequate knowledge (content and skills) brought to bear on task work.	A. Adequate *quality* in ITP produced
3. Supportive organizational context	3. Task performance strategies are used that are appropriate to work and to the setting in which it is being performed.	1. Clear diagnosis included.
4. Expert coaching & process assistance available		2. Clear and adequate description of patient's psychosocial and medical needs included.
5. Conducive physical environment (setting for meeting)		3. Appropriate steps for active treatment included:
		a. Clear, appropriate goals.
		b. Clear, appropriate objectives & steps.
		4. Overall, quality of ITP meets standards required by hospital.
		B. Adequate *quantity* in ITP produced
		1. Diagnosis included.
		2. Adequate quantity of steps for active treatment included.
		3. ITP meets overall standards of hospital in terms of number of elements to be included.
		C. Timeliness: ITP is completed in the time period as required by the hospital.

2. **TEAM WISHES TO CONTINUE WORKING TOGETHER.**
   There is continued willingness for members of the team to keep
   working in the future.

3. **TEAM CONTRIBUTES TO WELL-BEING & GROWTH**
   OF MEMBERS

   A. Team contributes to the *professional growth* of each member
      (learn new things).

   B. Team contributes to *personal well-being* of each member
      (fulfillment of personal needs).

4. **OVERALL SATISFACTION WITH TEAM AND ITS**
   EFFECTIVENESS.

   A. General satisfaction with the working together with other team
      members.

   B. General satisfaction with the way the team *develops* ITP.

   C. General satisfaction with the way the team *implements* ITP.

Note: ITP = Individualized Treatment Plan.

(Leiter, 1988) study of communication and burnout in a multidisciplinary mental health team found that burnout was higher for workers who communicated extensively with their coworkers regarding work but maintained relatively few informal, supportive relationships with coworkers.

Hackman has also included a third specific dimension of team effectiveness that suggests the long-term, more qualitative value of groups: "the degree to which the group experience contributes to the growth and personal well-being of team members" (Hackman, 1990, 7). For example, in an application of Hackman's model to treatment teams in psychiatric hospitals (Vinokur-Kaplan, 1995b) (see Table 16.1), team members were asked specifically to what extent the team contributed to their professional development and personal well-being. Positive personal rewards may energize professional staff who work together for long periods of time and provide ballast and social support to team members, especially in times of workforce cutbacks, work overload, and budget cuts.

In sum, recent models of team effectiveness have utilized a more long-term and comprehensive approach, possibly realizing that many teams continue to work together on similar or varied tasks over time. These models include the evaluation of the team's performance, plus the relationships between members. They sometimes also specify the individual development of team members involved—an aspect especially consonant with ongoing professional development in human service settings.

FACETS OF AN ECOLOGICAL FRAMEWORK

Coincident with this broader conceptualization of team effectiveness, several organizational theorists have used a broader, ecological framework "to describe [work group] operations within the context of the larger systems in which they are embedded" (Sundstrom & Altman, 1989, 177), contending that "work teams can best be understood in relation to external surroundings and internal processes" (Sundstrom, DeMeuse, & Futrell, 1990, 121). This perspective overcomes the limitations of some past small group research, whose findings were constrained by the temporary or specialized action settings in which groups were studied. For instance, such studies often used undergraduate college students, who have no long-standing, relevant organizational affiliation (Friedlander, 1987; Sundstrom, DeMeuse, & Futrell, 1990). In other cases, training or "T-groups" using nondirective leadership styles were observed by researchers to develop a theory of group development (Wheelan, 1994, 9). Such groups were used to help individuals "understand group dynamics and development through participation in an ongoing group [and learn] about how they as individuals interact in groups" (Wheelan, 1994, 10–11). However, this emphasis on more naturally occurring groups removes them from the more goal-directed organizational environment in which work teams perform.

Thus, this ecological perspective prevents practitioners from looking at teams as totally separate from the organizational environment in which they work. Ancona and Caldwell's (Ancona & Caldwell, 1988) comments on corporate teams are also relevant to social workers:

Work groups in organizations do not exist in a vacuum. Hence their effectiveness may be as much a function of how they deal with problems in their environment as of how well the group members deal with each other. This external perspective assumes that the group must manage relations with outsiders (inside or outside their own organization) because it often depends upon those outsiders for resources or information (Pfeffer & Salancik, 1978; Ancona & Caldwell, 1988, 468–469).

Thus, an ecological approach is sensitive to the realities of the organization's context, structure, constituencies, and norms with which a social worker would be interacting while serving as a team member. Moreover, this perspective dovetails with prior research that applied general systems theory to team decision making. This earlier research emphasized the flow of information and feedback loops into, within, and out of a hospital's psychiatric service, the location of decision nodes, and decision-making echelons as pragmatic tools for improving interdisciplinary team functions (Chase, Wright, & Ragade, 1981). Also, recent input-throughput-output models of team effectiveness have specified the influence of organizational and situational characteristics on team effectiveness (Tannenbaum, Beard, & Salas, 1992). Furthermore, both ecological and systems approaches are "social work–friendly" and widely taught, since they focus on the relationship of a subject to the environment.

Sundstrom et al. (Sundstrom, DeMeuse, & Futrell, 1990) have focused on three main facets of an ecological framework:

Organizational Context. Such organizational aspects as the reward system, organizational culture, mission clarity, physical environment, and training resources were omitted from earlier research. They are now included, since "such factors can augment team effectiveness by providing resources needed for performance and continued viability as a work unit" (Sundstrom, DeMeuse, & Futrell, 1990, 121).

Boundaries. Since work groups operate in an organizational context, they must manage relations or transactions with other individuals or groups in the larger social system in which the group operates (Hackman, 1990, 4–5). Thus, "an ecological view depicts boundaries as both separating and linking work teams within their organizations." (Sundstrom, DeMeuse, & Futrell, 1990, 121). Moreover,

[b]oundaries at least partly define how a group needs to operate within its context to be effective. If the boundary becomes too open or indistinct, the team risks becoming overwhelmed and losing its identity. If its boundary is too exclusive, the team might become isolated and lose touch with suppliers, managers, peers, or customers (Alderfer, 1987; Sundstrom, DeMeuse, & Futrell, 1990, 121).

Thus, inattention to boundary management and resource dependencies by both team members and administrative supporters can diminish the team's long-term effectiveness on behalf of their clients. An ecological perspective would encourage an in-patient treatment team to improve its relationships with admissions and discharge planning teams, while not losing its own identity and expertise.

Ancona and Caldwell (Ancona & Caldwell, 1988) proposed a set of activities that work group members use to manage their relations with outsiders. These roles and activities can help social work team members conceptualize their team's boundaries, their roles within the "bigger picture" of their organization, and the constituencies or "stakeholders" on whom their team's successes are dependent.

Team members concerned with initiating transactions with external groups engage in "scout" and "ambassador" activities; those associated with responding to others undertake "sentry" and "guard" activities; and those concerned with the actual definition of the group and its membership include "immigrants" (those seeking entry to a team), "captives" (those assigned to a team), and "emigrants" (those leaving the team to represent it to outsiders.) For example, in a hospital setting, a chosen in-patient team member can informally scout out— or formally become an ambassador to—the admissions teams. This boundary crossing can help coordinate patient flow and contact with patients' family members. Such positively stated roles and activities can also countervail against others' fears of "intruders" and "turf stealers."

Team Development. This facet refers to the way teams change and develop new ways of operating as they adapt to their context, including such structural aspects as norms and roles (Sundstrom, DeMeuse, & Futrell, 1990, 121). Much of the work on group processes and group development has focused on Tuckman and Jensen's (Tuckman & Jensen, 1977) model of "forming, norming, storming, performing, and adjourning." However, Sundstrom et al. (Sundstrom, DeMeuse, & Futrell, 1990) have cautioned that "considering the variety of relationships between work teams and organizational contexts, it seems unlikely that a single sequence can describe the development of all kinds of teams" (p. 127). Such a warning is certainly relevant to human services teams. Moreover, the forming of the team may be due to changing formal, external mandates and standards for interdisciplinary collaboration, rather than the organization's own initiative.

PRACTICAL APPLICATIONS AND IMPLICATIONS

What use can social workers and other human service professionals make of an ecological approach to work teams?

Teams are "made and not born," and they are parts of larger organizations.

Successful teams require interpersonal skills and environmental support, both of which require socialization and training. Thus, social workers and their teammates must be educated in interpersonal and group skills that facilitate group functioning (such as active listening, social influence, communication, shared leadership, and skills for efficiently running team meetings). However, they must also be cognizant of the organization, or ecology, in which they function, and their dependencies on other parties inside and outside the organization. This requires education on organizational theory and structure, as well as positive conceptions of boundary-spanning and liason roles that social workers can play.

Team effectiveness can die or "go to seed" if not cultivated.

The ecological perspective makes us acknowledge that teams require "care and feeding" not only by members (Mahrer & Gagnon, 1991) but also by the organizations in which they are functioning. Thus, their boundaries, goals, and technical support should be scrutinized. This recommendation to social workers parallels a general suggestion of Hackman: "Those who create and lead work groups might most appropriately focus their efforts on the creation of conditions that support effective team performance rather than attempting to manage group behavior in real time" (Hackman, 1990). It also echoes Katz and Kahn's (Katz & Kahn, 1978) principle of equifinality, since, as Hackman states, "there are many different ways a group can behave and still perform work well, and even more ways for it to be nonproductive" (Saunders & Whiteford, 1989).

Indeed, Gaston (Gaston, 1980) describes such facilitation in a previously demoralized psychiatric hospital. Therein, staff effort was not encouraged through the new director "directing" staff; rather, "he communicated his confidence to employees that they could organize themselves and their resources innovatively to discharge their patient responsibilities competently and thereby earn his continuing approval" (p. 410). Meanwhile, he provided administrative support and information, and learned about organizational barriers interfering with the execution of their treatment plans.

Moreover, a team's formal and informal boundaries should be clarified and analyzed in terms of the organization's goals. For example, imagine a hospital's admissions team that is not allowed time or given encouragement to meet with inpatient treatment teams therein. As a result, a patient's journey of crossing the boundary from admissions to treatment may be needlessly bumpy and possibly derailed, thus compromising the organization's goals of continuity and quality of care for patients.

Furthermore, the organizational support of teams requires adequate time and technology to aid their tasks. For example, in this author's observations of treatment-team members in public psychiatric hospitals during a time of retrenchment (Vinokur-Kaplan, 1992), some complained that, like Rodney Dangerfield, they "get no respect." Their scheduled team meetings were frequently interrupted: other events newly scheduled by the hospital preempted their meetings; team members were frequently called out of team meetings by staff, administration, or patients' families; phone calls to staff were redirected to the team's meeting-room phone, thus disrupting the team's discussion. However, following hospital-sponsored training on team development, team members articulated an action plan. It included simple but important actions such as avoiding interruptions of team meetings by using new answering machines, using the call-forwarding option on the phone in the treatment team meeting room so it would not ring and interrupt their discussions, and having the team coordinator send pointed memos to hospital administrators, informing them that "pulling out" psychiatrists during scheduled team meetings prevented the team from processing an overflow of admissions.

Temporal and professional boundaries also inhibited the ability of paraprofessional and afternoon or night shift direct-care staff from participating in team meetings or at least forwarding input, since they did not know when "their" patients were having their treatment plans reviewed. Such boundaries also need to be reviewed and remedied so that the plan for patients' treatment can be based on more complete information.

All of these illustrations point out the importance of institutional support of teams, which a more ecological perspective would promote. It is not enough for teams to be there "on paper," often because of a legal mandate, an accreditation requirement, or infatuation with the latest management fashion; they also must be there in spirit, integrated fully into the organization's structure and fully cognizant of the agency's mission and their role within it. Without linkage to the organization's culture, resource allocation, and structure, the effectiveness of work groups is compromised.

Teams may need help and coaching, especially in changing environments.

Hackman has emphasized that the availability of "coaching and consultation" can be an important point of leverage for creating conditions that enhance group task performance (Hackman, 1990, 11–14), especially if members have had relatively little experience working together or if they are working in a turbulent environment. Coaches can help team members vis-à-vis Hackman's three process criteria of team effectiveness: (a) expending ample effort, (b) having sufficient knowledge and skill, and (c) participating with task-appropriate performance strategies.

a. *Regarding efforts.* Coaches help teams to maintain their team spirit and active membership in the group. They receive assistance in minimizing coordination and motivation decrements and in building commitment to the group and its task. As an example, following team-building training that encouraged improved communication, one clinical treatment team developed a team song and also arranged to have periodic social dinners together; in this way, they could know one another better and thus possibly work together better.

b. *Regarding knowledge and skill.* Herein coaches give assistance to team members in avoiding inappropriate "weighting" of different individuals' ideas and contributions and in learning how to share their expertise to build the group's repertory of skills (Hackman, 1990, 12). This issue is especially salient in interdisciplinary clinical treatment teams, given the status differences sometimes found between professionals and para-professionals (Gomez, Ruiz, and Langrod, 1980) or between physicians and other professionals (Abramson, 1993, 46–47).

c. *Regarding performance strategies.* Members may need help to avoid flawed implementation of performance plans and to develop creative new ways of proceeding with the work (Hackman, 1990, 12). Group performance was aided in one particular psychiatric treatment team by having the members agree to dictate their respective parts of the treatment plan into a common dictating machine, thereby hastening the physical production of their treatment plan and facilitating its implementation on the patient's behalf.

How can coaches be obtained in times of tight resources? Vinokur-Kaplan and Walker-Burt (Vinokur-Kaplan & Walker-Burt, 1994) have urged psychiatric hospital administrators to seek out or develop in-house trainer/consultants among their own staff to provide needed information and skills to other units in the hospital. Such a strategy is not only possibly cost-effective; it also may provide more challenge to (and possibly enhances the job satisfaction of) dedicated employees. Moreover, treatment or management teams might improve their performance by using in-house videotaping to review team meetings. Also, some facilities provide computerized visual analysis and feedback on their group's process and actions, which are taped and simultaneously coded into SYMLOG by hidden observers (Losada & Markovitch, 1990).

Interdisciplinary teams including social workers may have special needs in order to be most effective.

The high differentiation within interdisciplinary work teams, whose membership is composed often of expert professionals, requires several organizational resources to succeed: The overall culture of the organization must demonstrate appreciation and respect for all disciplines; the administration must allow adequate time and territory for team members to meet and learn about each other's perspectives and how they contribute to the overall plan for the patient's treatment. Moreover, the need for continuing professional fulfillment and development of each team member must be considered, to help assure the continued viability and vitality of the team. Finally, the parent organization must appreciate the complexity of the team's composition, the clients at hand, and the ambiguous information that is sometimes processed by the group, so that adequate time and resources will be allocated to these important decision-making procedures, with prime consideration given to the well-being and fair treatment of the client.

Social work research contributes to team effectiveness research.

Research on team effectiveness and development is difficult and expensive to conduct. In a recent literature review, Tannenbaum et al. (Tannenbaum, Beard, and Salas, 1992) commented, "It is often impossible to conduct true field experiments" (p. 146), and they found only seventeen rigorous empirical studies of team building since 1980 in an extensive bibliographic search—of these, less than half had any connection to nonmilitary public agencies or human services. Thus, any new rigorous field studies of teams in social work will contribute to overall social science knowledge.

Some social work research has already contributed to general knowledge about teams by providing compelling examples and discussing applied practice issues in a wide variety of settings (Garner, 1988; Lecca & McNeil, 1985). Social work research has presented survey results of the stereotyping of disciplines (Folkins, Wieselberg, and Spensley, 1981), the roles played by various professionals on teams, (Toseland, Palmer-Ganeles, and Chapman, 1986), and the inclusion of paraprofessionals (Lichtenberg & Roman, 1990). Models of interprofessional social work education (Billups, 1986), team role training (Lister, 1982), effective group membership (Bertcher, 1987), and effective meetings (Tropman, 1987) have also been described. Such scholarship has contributed to better understanding of the variety and realities of boundaries and team composition and has suggested practical means for team development and organizational support that can influence team effectiveness.

Moreover, the longer, more intensive, and publicly accountable relationship of teams with their clients coincides with the longer-term perspective of team effectiveness now being broadly adopted as part of quality management's attention to the legitimate needs of internal and external customers in various settings (Gaucher & Coffey, 1993). Furthermore, social work's own emphasis on enhancing the relationship between individuals and their environment is now echoed in the fuller attention given to the importance of individual growth and harmonious group relations in overall team effectiveness in any setting. Moreover, the empowerment of employees through team participation, long advocated by some leaders in social work practice (Burghardt, 1982, ch. 9), resonates in many workplaces today (Schon & Rein, 1993, 85–86). In sum, social work's own concerns help keep the definitions of team effectiveness more comprehensively defined, while social work experiences illustrate the complex, and often difficult, organizational conditions under which important decisions are reached by social workers, their colleagues, and their clients to benefit the lives of those whom social workers serve.

17

Of Penguins and Policies: Communications between Policy Researchers and Decision Makers

Armand Lauffer

COMMUNICATING ABOUT PENGUINS AND OTHER CREATURES

Recently, I attended a wedding in a rural community. With one reception following another, it seemed that everyone was determined to make the out-of-town guests feel welcome. Sunday morning, as we were walking off a pre-wedding brunch, a farmer pulled up to our hotel. "Where do I leave 'em?" he asked the door attendant, pointing to the penguins in the back of his pick-up and explaining that even though it was hazy, he'd seen these three short people in tuxedos along the side of the road. "They don't talk much," he went on, "but I reckoned they needed a ride to the wedding."

"Well, you can't leave 'em here," snorted the attendant. "Those're penguins, not guests. Better take 'em up the road to the zoo in Greensville." The farmer had never been to the zoo nor, apparently, had he heard of penguins. "Well, I don't know about that," he replied. "I was on my way to church anyway. I'll ask my preacher."

The next day, as we were preparing to leave for the airport, the same farmer pulled up again. He still had the three penguins in the back, but this time they were wearing sun glasses. "Didn't I tell you to take 'em to the zoo?" the attendant asked. "Yup. My preacher agreed, and I did," explained the driver. "And we had a good time. But, it was so sunny this morning that I'm taking them to the beach and wanted to know if any of the out-of-towners want to come along."

All this is to say that the subject of understanding and making use of information is more complex than we might like it to be, and all the more so when the senders and receivers of a message are likely to ascribe very different meanings to it. In processing new information:

- We tend to see what we are accustomed to seeing;

- We understand the meaning and intent of communicated messages in terms of our experience; and

- Just because a consultant knows how to load and unload baggage or hold a door open, we are not necessarily going to limit our actions to his or her recommendations without checking with those we consider authorities.

The penguin story is funny because of its absurdity. The miscommunication and the misuse of relevant (social science) knowledge in social work practice and social policy are not.

Whether we see ourselves primarily as social researchers or as social workers, allied practitioners, and policy makers, we have all experienced problems of miscommunication or misuse of data. Contrary to much of what is taught in professional schools, practice- or policy-oriented research and decision making have little to do with one another. Even under the best of circumstances, research as a process and data as its outcome are only minimally used in practice or policy making. The reasons for this are not very difficult to understand.

In my analysis, I'll begin by sharing some assumptions about communicating scientific data for community and agency decision making. I'll then explore why researchers and those charged with policy and action have such a hard time bridging the gulf in understanding between them. In conclusion, I'll suggest how the conduct of social research might be structured to increase the likelihood of productively utilizing study results. References on diffusion and utilization can be found at the end of the chapter.

ASSUMPTIONS ABOUT COMMUNICATION AND COMMUNICATORS

Communication is a process whereby:

- a message is transferred via some

- channel(s) by

- a sender to

- a receiver with

- the intention of influencing knowledge, attitude or behavior.

Each of these five variables—the message, the channel(s) of communication, the sender and receiver, and the intention—must be in sync with each other if communication between the practice- and policy-oriented researcher and the practitioner or policy-oriented decision maker is to be effective. Unfortunately, this is rarely the case. A number of problems seem to intrude, creating static or diversion in the communication process.

Problems in Sender-Receiver Perceptions

Perhaps the most serious problem lies in the lack of complementarity of perceptions between the partners involved in the communication process. The more alike the sender and the receiver of a message—that is, the closer they are in terms of shared language, professional and organizational culture, experience, or significant personal characteristics—the more likely they are to understand each other. Moreover, the more respectful the partners are of each other and the more they are able put themselves in the others' shoes, the more likely it is that messages between them will be understood.

Unfortunately, practice- and policy-oriented researchers and decision makers in social service settings are, in significant ways, more dissimilar than alike in many of these characteristics. Nor are they always empathic or respectful towards each other. Social scientists tend to be data and concept oriented. The ideas and information they communicate professionally emanate from a disciplinary perspective.

Social scientists and decision makers, respectively, display typcial characteristics of senders and receivers as follows:

Social Scientists	Decision makers
Data and Concept Oriented	People and Process Oriented
Cosmopolitan	Local
Independent	Institutionally Bound

Although they sometimes work in teams, most social researchers tend to behave as independent actors. Cosmopolitan in their orientations, they look to other social scientists for verification and status and for reference group approval. Decision makers in social service settings are a much more heterogeneous lot.

While many decision makers are volunteers and lay community leaders, others are likely to be social work and allied professionals engaged in management or in such direct practice fields as counseling, fund-raising, community relations, or education. Some are oriented towards sectarian and ethnic concerns or serve populations with special needs and interests. More local than cosmopolitan in their orientations, they tend to be people rather than data oriented.

The one characteristic that almost all decision makers in the social services share in common is their *lack* of independence as actors. Organizationally or institutionally bound, their interpretation and use of data must incorporate the agreements of many parties and accommodate the capacities of the systems in which they operate. In their understanding and use of data, they tend to be concerned with how others are likely to interpret or apply the results of research.

Problems in the Message and its Intention

This lack of independence may help explain why the conclusions of many studies of agency services and of populations for whom services might be provided are ignored or underutilized. The disregard of study results often comes as a shock to social researchers, who assume that because their studies were commissioned by decision makers, the findings—whether reassuring or alarming—will be utilized. But this assumption does not take into account community or organizational dynamics and the differences in the *perceptions* of information and its meanings to both researchers and social work or other decision makers. From the researcher's point of view, decision makers are often resistant to and unappreciative of their findings' significance. From the consumer's point of view, researchers are often limited in their understanding of what their instruments measure.

The following lists indicate how research findings are often understood by these participants:

By Researchers	By Decision Makers
Empirically	Intuitively
As Functional and Developmental	As Dysfunctional and Destabilizing
Relatively Immediately	After Considerable Lag Time

The miscommunication between social researchers and decision makers stems from a number of differences in the ways that each group deals with new information. First, although scientific data sometimes support a researcher's hunches, the findings of research are often counterintuitive; that is, they often demonstrate relationships that contradict "conventional wisdom" or traditional understandings. Arguments that research findings are statistically valid may not always convince decision makers. Whatever the findings suggest, practitioners often "know in their bones" that the data don't tell the whole or "real" story, citing experience and shared understandings. Policy makers, executives, and service providers are rarely accustomed to dealing with data or adept at drawing inferences from it for their decisions. Researchers may be accurate in pointing out that this is because of *receiver* bias, lack of sophistication, or vested interest in the status quo, but decision makers, in turn, may not be far from the truth in pointing to the narrowness in the focus of the research process. In effect, both parties may differ in their interpretations of validity; the one basing conclusions on methodological rigor, the other on community consensus and shared understanding.

Second, new information is often perceived as *dysfunctional* when it challenges organizational missions and the values of participants in the system. Data showing that HIV infection can be reduced by the distribution of condoms in high schools or of sterile needles on city streets may threaten powerful community norms. Evidence of spouse battering and child abuse may remain unrecognized because an agency has no internal client information system to record the extensiveness of the problem. Acceptance of new information from studies or other sources might require reformulation of agency missions, expanding services to new clients, or retooling to assure staff commitment and competence.

However, change is not always perceived as a welcomed opportunity. Many social service agencies and interorganizational structures are likely to aim for relative stability, avoiding rapid changes with which they are unequipped to cope. In public settings, laws and government regulations are used to prohibit certain actions. In voluntary organizations, changes in program and policy often require extensive processing, and process takes time. Because *new information can be destabilizing*, at least in the short term, it may be difficult to absorb—and for this reason is often ignored or rejected. In contrast, social scientists tend to see their information as contributing to development and in that sense, they see it as *stabilizing* in the long term.

Third, there is often a *time lag* between first efforts at the dissemination of information and its reception, acceptance, and utilization. Both researchers and their sponsors often assume that there is a direct line between information and action. This is rarely the case. Instead, the process is more likely to operate as a sequence of separate stages, beginning with (1) first awareness and interest moving through (2) assessment of importance and utility to (3) decision to use or reject and, if the decision is to use, through (4) trial usage and confirmation of utility and finally to (5) partial or total adoption. If researchers and decision makers wish to communicate effectively, they must be realistic about what can be expected at each stage.

In fact, some observers suggest that different communication channels may be appropriate at different stages. Channels of communication can be formal or informal, media-based (written reports, news coverage) or interpersonal, and distant or proximate. Establishing these channels and keeping them open may require attention to ways of bridging the gap between researchers and decision makers.

Problems in the Use of Appropriate Communication Channels

Researchers often use formal means to communicate with each other: project reports, scholarly papers, and the like. To communicate with social service providers and lay decision makers, these reports are generally rewritten in relatively nontechnical language, with graphs or charts designed to be easily understood. Although questions may arise over how much information to include and for whom, time and budgetary constraints generally limit the range of options. For this reason, a single document must often do the whole job of communicating both findings and recommendations. Unfortunately, these reports, in and of themselves, are not likely to be *persuasive* to decision makers. Fortunately, others may find them interesting.

For example, the press (including agency house organs) is likely to report on the highlights of studies it deems somehow relevant. Clergy may speak from the pulpit of findings they consider important to their constituents. Agency executives may interpret them in summary reports to their staff or boards. These persons become the intermediaries between the researchers and the decision makers and are sometimes best able to create first awareness and interest. They are able to do this because they reduce the formality of the presentation and make it more proximate and accessible. But this is only part of the whole job of persuading individuals, groups, or organizations to act.

At the community and agency levels, interpersonal *persuasion* is necessary at each of the subsequent stages: assessment of utility, decision to utilize information, trial usage and confirmation, and partial or total adoption. Persuasion is oriented towards helping those charged with decision making and implementation to become more conversant with the findings, more comfortable with their implications, and more accepting of the need to implement changes. Persuasion occurs informally between friends and colleagues through a variety of channels. The more formal include staff meetings and supervisory sessions, board and committee deliberations, or specially designated task forces and action coalitions that include lay and professional personnel.

Decisions about whether and how to use information also occur via these same formal and informal channels. Like acceptance of the message, decisions to take policy and programmatic action also are influenced by the extent to which changes are perceived of as functional or dysfunctional, as well as by the system's capacity to modify itself without threat to its stability. Some decisions are made very slowly, in a political context that requires gradual movement towards consensus on what is both desirable and feasible. This can be frustrating both to researchers, who may have clear notions of the policy options that ought to be considered, and to policy makers, whose decisions must be legitimated by the consensus of other influentials. Consensus can be especially fragile or hard to achieve when programs must be acceptable to those who benefit and pay for them and to those charged with their implementation.

BRIDGING THE GAP: LINKING RESEARCH AND ACTION

Social scientists and researchers may be less than committed to or comfortable with the interpersonal process that is so central to much organizational and community decision making and to which decision makers may be committed. Thus, it is unlikely that researchers and decision makers who are unaccustomed to using research findings will have routine ways of communicating with each other. This is unfortunate. Data and their policy implications have a better chance of "taking" if procedures are established that routinely involve (1) researchers with administrators, professional staff, and lay leaders in problem definition and in the exploration of the policy implications of findings before studies are conducted; and (2) operational personnel with researchers in study design and data analysis, as well as in an active process of diffusion designed well in advance of final reports.

Such procedures increase the likelihood that new information will be digested and reflected upon by key actors in a timely fashion. Prior to attempting full scale implementation, they might also permit *trialization*, the testing of policy decisions and program interventions on a trial basis in some parts of the system, or *partialization*, the testing of a single element of a larger innovation in many parts. Multiple forums might also be established in which researchers, decision makers, and members of the consumer public can exchange their understandings of the implications of action.

Since the preceding conditions rarely apply, partial correctives may be needed. These include the use of a variety of interactive assessment tools to help community leaders and agency staff assess the implications of study findings. Among others, such tools include the nominal group technique, Delphi, simulation exercises, force-field analysis, values clarification, and futuring techniques. However useful these might be, it would be more effective if those who must produce and utilize new information could be involved with each other before rather than after the fact. More often, however, sponsors and potential users are rarely ready to invest in the communication process early on, preferring to wait until the data are in and then to decided when and how to act. This is hardly satisfactory.

Those conducting policy-oriented research might do well to reconsider contracts or grants that have planted within them the seeds of failure. Community and agency-based decision makers would do well to consider the action implications of new information before they spend money on research that will yield potentially useful but unused findings. Fortunately, there are many ways of bridging communication gaps between the two groups and of designing coordinated research and action strategies.

The title of this chapter includes the words, "Penguins" and "Policies." Both start with the letter "P." In the preceding analysis, I have used five additional terms that begin with the same letter: (1) perception; (2) persuasion; (3) partialization; (4) procedures; and (5) partners. Each of these terms implies guidelines for improving effective communication between policy researchers and decision makers.

The Five Ps of Effective Collaboration Between Researchers and Decision Makers

Differences in orientation between social researchers and agency decision makers result in alternative *perceptions* of task, data, and implications. Effective communication requires an acceptance of these differences, which, in turn, may require that both parties be realistic in their expectations of each other. These expectations are similar to those that characterize courtship and just as often lead to relationships that go awry.

Those courting each other may have little initial appreciation for where the other is coming from and aspires to go. Each party may have its own set of expectations and may be unaware of the requirements that a satisfactory relationship may imply. Fortunately, researchers and decision makers have a mechanism to bridge the communication gap that is not as readily available to courting couples. This mechanism lies in focus groups, in which the potential applications of research are discussed openly and honestly by researchers and decision makers at early stages of their relationship and then reexamined at later stages.

Persuasion refers to a process whereby the beliefs or actions of others are influenced. Researchers sometimes assume that data and ideas are by themselves persuasive or that it is not their responsibility to use means other than formal presentation to influence behavior. But decision makers operate in a much more interpersonal and political environment, where decisions are influenced by differing perceptions of what may be desirable or feasible and around which there may not be agreement. To be persuasive, researchers must find gap-bridging means of engaging in this transactive environment, either directly or via proxies, and over the period of time it requires for the diffusion process to unfold. That process can be facilitated through *partialization* and *trialization*.

Although these two concepts are drawn from research on the utilization of information and the transfer of innovations, they are often ignored by social researchers. Those who have studied the utilization and transfer processes understand that information and new practices are more likely to take hold if they are introduced in stages. Two approaches are possible. In the first, part of an innovation is introduced throughout the system. Additional components are then introduced in a staged process over time. For example, if evaluation of an agency's programs shows that its success is limited or that its intervention approaches are no longer relevant to current client needs, it might try part of a new intervention approach in many units at the same time.

Take as an example a family service agency interested in moving from a traditional counseling approach to family education and development as a consequence of study results that show families in need of a variety of basic survival skills. To help clinicians make the transition to family-life education, the researchers and decision makers might design a process in which all caseworkers are trained to use educational techniques aimed at helping families to cope more effectively with one aspect of family functioning, say, the management of their financial situations. Once workers are comfortable with this relatively minor redirection, additional new approaches to family building might be introduced over time. These might include such concerns as child care, dispute resolution, or the division of labor.

In the second approach, the total innovation might be installed in only one part of the system and, after it "takes," might then be extended to other units. For example, a traditional family service agency may be interested in restructuring services along the lines of the "homebuilder" model. A "young families" or "senior citizens" department might be set up to engage in more educational and modeling behaviors, where caseworkers teach family members to cope with both crisis and daily survival challenges. If the work of that unit proved both successful and attractive, the homebuilder approach would then be transferred to other departments.

At issue, also, are the *procedures* that researchers and decision makers use to increase the likelihood that research will result in utilization and transfer. To be effective, these procedures would include more than those involved in the conduct of research and the reporting of findings. They would include procedures for the involvement of practitioners and policy makers in research design and in the analysis of findings and their implications. Other procedures might be designed to involve researchers in program design, monitoring, and evaluation. The design of procedures used to create and manage various bridging mechanisms might require no less attention than those used for the conduct of research.

The procedures involved in "action research" are instructive. They require a special kind of *partnership* between researchers and those who commission their work. To be effective, the roles of each partner—the researcher, or the practitioner, and policy maker—remain distinct, but their activities are not separate. The goal of the partnership is the integration of both research and decision making, leading to unified action. It achieves this goal by building experimentation and innovation into the research design. It does so by introducing planned change within an organizational context and then by observing the results of this change on the organization and on key elements of its environment.

In this way, the researcher or research team becomes a more equal partner with those more traditionally involved in decision making about programs and policies. The partnership process engages policy makers and practitioners in asking the key research questions and diagnoses at the same time that researchers are asking operations-oriented questions. An effective collaboration between social researchers and decision makers requires more than the exchange of information. It requires some shared understandings of how the information is to be collected, disseminated, and used.

If taking penguins to the beach seems like a good idea to the persons who have assumed responsibility for them, the admonitions of an outside consultant may have little impact on their decisions.

18

Rediscovering the Lives of Women: A Feminist Critique of the Social Science–Social Work Connection

Mimi Abramovitz

Feminism has sparked an intellectual revolution in the academy and wider society. Among other things, it has revealed that the study of gender, like the study of race and class, uncovers previously ignored information, introduces new understandings of social interactions, and exposes how the construction of knowledge itself supports the status quo (Held, 1985). The feminist revolution has changed the way we must think about almost everything, including the complex relationship among social science, social work, and social policy. As both a theoretical paradigm and a political movement, feminism has exposed the sexist, racist, and classist assumptions infused into all three of these domains, as well as the reluctance of each to pay attention to the mounting feminist correctives and the need for change.

The failure of mainstream social science to take gender into account has rendered it less useful than it should be to social work, where most of the clients and practitioners are female, and often women of color. Indeed, the social science knowledge base developed in the postwar years must be reviewed through the multifaceted lens of gender, race, and class. Because the foundation of social work education is grounded in the powerful theories of social science, it too is open to question. However, drawing on the feminist critique can contribute to a reformulation of ideas in social science, social work, and social policy.

This exploration of the social science/social work/social policy connection highlights several aspects of the feminist critique of social science. I begin by looking at the question of who does the research, as well as the historical tie between sexism, female social scientists, and the origins of social work. After pointing to the gender biases found in seemingly objective social science methodology, I move on to discuss the feminist critique of the theories of the white and the African-American family that still dominate social work and social policy. The conclusion suggests that social work can combine its knowledge of people and society with the growing body of feminist theories to replace a scholarship that marginalizes women and other subordinated groups with one that serves the interests of all.

WOMEN IN THE ORIGINS OF SOCIAL SCIENCE, SOCIAL WORK, AND THE WELFARE STATE

The feminist critique of social science begins with the assumption that who does the research makes a difference. It argues that women's lack of access to research opportunities has shaped the social science/social work/social policy connection from its origins at the turn of the century (Chambers, 1986). Known primarily as social reformers, many of the early female social workers were, in fact, accomplished social scientists; however, sexism in academia has obscured this history. For example, in the early 1900s, in the attempt to legitimize itself as "scientific," the University of Chicago's young sociology department downgraded its tradition of applied research, which focused on solving social problems, in favor of "pure" research (Bernard, 1987; Muncy, 1991; Tyson, 1992). This pure versus applied division assumed gender connotations, since the marginalized scholars were women with Ph.D.s. Despite this heavy toll, academic sexism benefited social work. Along with many other excluded scholars, Jane Addams, Lillian Wald, Grace and Edith Abbott, and Sophonisba Breckinridge left academia and went on to head the University of Chicago School of Social Service Administration, the Social Service Review, and the Children's Bureau and otherwise to become social policy leaders (Bernard, 1987; Muncy, 1991).

The social work profession has never freed itself of sexism. Since 1893, it has tried repeatedly to improve its status by recruiting more men (Brown, 1938). The devaluation of women's intellectual contribution to social work probably underpinned Flexner's unwillingness, in 1915, to sanction it as a profession (Tyson, 1995). The field of social work waited until 1980 to hold its first conference on women's issues, long after the women's movement began. Women may outnumber men in social work; however, the female-populated profession has never been female-dominated.

The origins of social work were also marred by racism. Social work is only now beginning to claim its African-American forebears, including Lugging Hope, who founded the Atlanta Neighborhood Union; Mary Mcleod Bethune, a top official in Roosevelt's New Deal Administration; and Fredericka Douglas-Sprague Perry (Lerner, 1974; Peebles-Wilkins, 1989). These and other black women worked with and wrote about the poor and disenfranchised. But the inability of white women reformers to include lynching, segregation, and other racial injustices on their agenda precluded joint efforts. For many years, the color bar separated the profession's black and white leaders and generated racially segregated social welfare research and policy (Gilkes, 1981; Scott, 1990).

Despite many gains, women still must struggle for their rightful place in the field. This struggle is fueled, in part, by the profession's rather uncritical acceptance of the patriarchal premises of social science research. Neither social science, social work, nor social policy has escaped the ideological or material impact of institutional sexism, racism, or classism. Unlike prejudice and discrimination, the "isms" can accrue to an establishment's practices and policies—including social science methodology and theory—regardless of intention or even awareness of such outcomes.

Social Science Methodology: The Influence of Sexism

A second feminist critique of social science targets the assumptions underpinning "the scientific method" (Collins, 1990; Harding, 1987; Keller, 1982; Perlich, 1989; Reinharz, 1992). For centuries, scholars have debated the possibility of value-free research. Contemporary feminists argue that social science methodologies, like social science theories, are deeply androcentric and culture-bound. Unable to exist independent of its ideological and material contexts, social science cannot be value free. Feminists point out that the ongoing struggle to make positivist research objective rarely targets the biases grounded in the method's patriarchal assumptions.

From the feminist perspective, the seemingly neutral research process—from the selection of topics to the interpretation of findings—has been shaped by patriarchal thinking and a male dominated research establishment (Acker, 1978; Keller, 1992; O'Leary, 1981; Westcott, 1979). From the beginning, this establishment placed Man at the center of the human system and studied people and events from its own standpoint and in accordance with what patriarchal society defined as important to know (Harding, 1987). They studied wars, markets, governments, established organizations, famous leaders, and other spheres of life that routinely excluded women. Little or no interest was shown in families, social clubs, community groups, and other "spaces" traditionally inhabited by women (Fuller, 1978). By dismissing women as citizens outside the home, by excluding housework from the studies of work, and by ignoring women in studies of social stratification and political activism, social science left women role-bound or invisible. The result has been an erroneous picture of women's lives and a seriously distorted understanding of the wider society. Furthermore, if social science research stereotyped or ignored white women, it often degraded or simply forgot women of color.

Sampling procedures and instrument design have also produced sexist data. Researchers frequently used samples composed of young white male college students and generalized their findings to other groups as if no differences existed. They also interpreted women's lives by simply reversing what was found to be true of men (Fuller, 1978), or they studied motivation, aggression, and achievement with male-oriented measures (Harding, 1987). Given the limited applicability of social science to women and other excluded groups, it may be necessary to reread it as the study of men or to redo it in more inclusive ways.

Feminists agree that as long as social science remains gender-blind and blinded by ideology of gender roles, it risks producing flawed research and defending a gendered and unequal status quo (Harding, 1987; Minnich, 1990). However, differences emerge as to what constitutes the best corrective. The feminist empiricists hope to "improve" science by ridding it of sexist, racist, and classist biases and by otherwise making it conform to feminist principles (Harding, 1987). Other feminists want to "change" science more profoundly by breaking out of the positivist paradigm, although they propose more than one exit (Reinharz, 1992). A few find feminism and science irreconcilable on the ground that feminism embodies a political agenda, while science, by definition, does not (Keller, 1982; Perlich, 1989).

Feminist pressures have increased the attention paid to women's issues in the academy. Nevertheless, women remain marginalized as "the second sex" (de Beauvoir, 1953). The study of gender remains highly ghettoized within women's studies departments, courses on women, chapters in books, and units in syllabi. Gender is only rarely treated as an important analytic variable. In many cases, only women have a gender, only blacks have a race, only lesbians and gays have a sexual orientation, and only poor and working people have a class. The failure to use gender as a theoretical construct has left social science's patriarchal frameworks solidly in place (Smith & Noble-Spruell, 1986). This is especially true in social science theories of the family, which I discuss below.

Feminism and Theories of the Family

The third dimension of the feminist critique focuses on the social science theory that includes the grand paradigms of Freud, Parsons, and Marx. Feminists have paid special attention to the Freudian, Parsonian, and Marxian portraits of women and the family because they have dominated social science, social work, and social policy since World War II. While Marxism came under attack during the Cold War years, Freudian and Parsonian theories of family life have flourished, becoming deeply embedded in social science, social work, and social policy, as well as in wider public opinion. Freudian theory portrays women in relation to men rather than as autonomous beings. It defines gender roles as biologically based, views female maturity as conditional upon marriage and motherhood, and locates the home as women's place (Chavetz, 1978; Hyde & Rosenberg, 1980). Drawing on Bales and Slater's (Bales & Slater, 1955) analysis of "instrumental" and "expressive" roles in human groups, Parsons' (Parsons, 1955) theory of the family defines the male-breadwinner/female-homemaker gender division of labor as "normal" and necessary for family stability, the family as a harmonious institution with unitary interests, and other family patterns as "pathological." Despite its loss of functions, Parsons concluded that the smaller, more intimate, and specialized postwar family was uniquely suited to socialize children and to sustain family members emotionally. Based on love, consensus, and strict gender roles, the two-parent family was the linchpin of the social order.

Feminist scholars have critiqued the social science theory of the family for its idealized version of women and family life, its uncritical acceptance of gendered hierarchies, its lack of attention to the social construction of gender, and its defense of the status quo. Feminism has exposed the grounding of the theories in social thought that defines race, class, and gender as biologically determined rather than socially assigned; in legal doctrine that defines women as the property of men, and families as the bulwark of the social order; and in political theory that separates the public and private spheres.

In contrast to "traditional" social theorists, feminists emphasize the social construction of gender and the family and place the traditional paradigms in historical context. For example, they hold that the modern version of gender roles, rather than being biologically determined, first appeared in the early 1800s when the industrial revolution separated household and market production. This transformation produced new social norms that assigned men to the public sphere and women to the private, equating successful manhood with waged labor, family support, and patriarchal control and proper womanhood with marriage, motherhood, and subordination to men. The social construction of gender that evolved over time was enforced consistently through sex-role socialization, sex discrimination, and penalties for nonconformity. The ideology of gender roles hid the social bases of the gender division of labor, as well as its systems of power that allowed for male domination and female subordination.

Feminism has also challenged social science theories of the family as monolithic, unchanging, and unrealistically harmonious. From discussing "the family," feminists moved to "families" to recognize that family structures vary by time, region, class, race, and culture (Collier, Rosaldo, and Yanagisako, 1982; Coontz, 1988; Mintz & Kellog, 1988; Thorne, 1982). The idealized picture of the family as a stable and harmonious unit gave way to the notion of the family as an arena of struggle evidenced by a number of characteristics: the "problem that has no name," identified by Betty Friedan in 1963; high rates of divorce and separation; disputes over the distribution of family resources, rights, and responsibilities (Hartmann, 1981; Mintz & Kellog, 1988); the potential clash of interests between husband and wife, parents and children (Skold, 1988); and finally, male violence and sexual abuse (Schachter, 1982). While they provide love and security for some women, families, for others, may be the site of struggle, violence, and oppression.

Feminists argue strongly against any natural or obligatory vision of women's roles, sexuality, or family structures and argue instead for variation and diversity (Thorne, 1982). Coontz (Coontz, 1988) actually documents the evolution of four different family ideals in the United States from 1600 to 1900, as well as the race and class variation within each period. To feminists, pathologizing alternative family forms—especially single motherhood and gay parents—operates as a mechanism of social control. It stigmatizes differences as deviant, punishes unsanctioned sexuality, and warns women of the power held by authorities and of the need to stay in line. However, while feminists have exposed the limitations of the post-war theory of the (white) family, they have paid virtually no attention to the coexisting but deeply racist theory of the African American family, which I discuss below.

THE PRACTICE AND POLICY CONNECTION

The feminist critique of "the family" first appeared in the early 1970s, but social policy lagged far behind. The theories of Freud and Parsons shaped the nation's understanding—or misunderstanding—of women and the family for many years. Until they were challenged in the late 1970s, the marriage and family texts used to train most social work and other professions were dominated by sexist depictions of women's roles and family life (Chavetz, 1978; Zaretsky, 1982). Reflecting their education, most practitioners viewed women's home role as "natural" and as a necessary backup to the male breadwinner. Likewise, marriage and two-parent households were considered the norm. Together with media pundits, practitioners of many stripes encouraged women to abandon work for family life or, if work was a must, to take jobs for pin money. To do otherwise would undermine the possibility of the harmonious nuclear family, threaten the natural leadership capacities of their husbands, and result in maladjusted children (Chavetz, 1978; Hyde & Rosenberg, 1980).

The standard male-breadwinner/female-homemaker family was locked into place by social scientists and mental health practitioners who maintained that young women suppressed their achievement urges in favor of the wife-mother role, that wives experienced a vicarious achievement through their husband's jobs, and that career women suffered unresolved penis envy or unsatisfied sexual urges (Chavetz, 1978; Hyde & Rosenberg, 1980). At the same time, social observers pathologized nonmarriage, single parenthood, homosexuality, and sex outside of marriage (Mintz & Kellog, 1988). Based on this normal versus pathological dichotomy, practitioners and policy makers defined independent women and nurturing men as examples of troublesome role reversals and blamed working mothers for marital tensions rising divorce rates, and childhood problems ranging from bedwetting to schizophrenia (Mintz & Kellog, 1988). Single mothers of both races became symbols of race and gender insubordination in a society trying desperately to preserve the pre–World War II status quo. Young white single mothers were tagged as "neurotics" to be cured (Boris, 1992). Their black counterparts were demonized as oversexed and lacking a superego and were held responsible for both rising welfare costs and the population explosion (Solinger, 1990). If the white mother only family was considered "broken," the black mother-only family was labelled "disintegrated" and "unstable" (Fineman, 1991).

The shared preference of Freud and Parsons for the nuclear family and women in the home contributed to an ideological defense of the gendered status quo just when it was threatened by postwar conditions. Women's changing roles in the home, increased paid work by wives, greater education of women, the growth of mother-only families, high rates of divorce and illegal abortion, and the transfer of more and more family functions to professionals and the state led many experts to declare the demise of the "traditional" family (Mintz & Kellog, 1988). The popularization of Freudian views on women and Parsons' new theory of the family helped to soothe public anxieties by rationalizing the centrality of the two-parent, heterosexual family, the correctness of the gender division of labor, and the need for women's subordination to men. The portrait of the two-parent family as the model of harmony and "togetherness" became a national ideal. No mention was made of male domination, incest, wife battering, or women's nondomestic interests.

The Freudian and Parsonian family model is deeply embedded in social welfare policy where it reinforces the two-parent family unit, full-time homemaking, and women's economic dependence on men. Since their enactment as part of the 1935 Social Security Act, the nation's income maintenance programs have favored married and previously married women over single women, unwed mothers, and abandoned wives; treated full-time homemakers better than working wives; and penalized employed women (except poor single mothers who are required to work). Paralleling the normal/pathological dichotomy endorsed by social science, social policies still categorize women as "worthy" and "unworthy" of aid and families as "fit" and "unfit" based on women's compliance with prescribed wife and mother roles (Abramovitz, 1988). The "worthy" and "fit" are rewarded with benefits and services (however minimal), while the "unworthy" and "unfit" face punitive programs or denial of aid. To uphold the "traditional" family, the most severe punishment is reserved for the single mothers who qualify for Aid to Families with Dependent Children (AFDC). The mean spirited and punitive welfare reforms proposed in the early 1990s have placed lifetime limits on welfare use and denied aid to children born on welfare and otherwise continued the historic practice of punishing women and families viewed as out of role.

The use of social policy to uphold traditional families is breaking down somewhat as some private and public employers begin to insure domestic partners, to offer family and medical leave, and otherwise to recognize the changing times. But the persistence of the gender division of labor reinstated by postwar social science theories means that even when women work, they still have virtually exclusive responsibility for the home. Despite the near disappearance of the male breadwinner/full-time homemaker family unit, the ideal still governs social policy, backed now by a new set of social scientists, some of whom have an openly conservative political agenda (Mead, 1992; Moynihan, 1986; Murray, 1984). While many social scientists support feminist goals, social science research is also being used today to justify the assault on reproductive rights, the harsh campaign for welfare reform, and the backlash against feminist and gay rights.

The African American Family

The social science/social policy connection has been shaped by racism as well as sexism, by a white as well as a male supremacy. But feminists were slow to recognize that the postwar theory of the happy and stable middle class family that they critiqued coexisted with a theory of the African-American family as matriarchal, pathological, and forever destabilized by the experience of slavery. The theory of the "unstable" black family that permeated social science, social policy, and social work since the turn of the century was fueled by racist misinterpretation of African American families who were more likely than white families to be headed by a woman and to include fictive kin and extended family members.

The model of the backward and culturally deviant African American family dates back to the early 1900s, when post–Civil War scholars argued that black families were racially inferior, disorganized, and unassimilated into white society (Odum, 1910). Between World War I and World War II, these unscientific racial explanations of family structures were gradually replaced by debates over the impact of slavery, migration, discrimination, and African culture on black family patterns. Although fewer of these later scholars linked problems in the African American community to racial inferiority, many remained preoccupied with the overrepresentation of black female-headed households (Franklin, in press). E. Franklin Frazier (Frazier, 1939), a well-known black sociologist of the period, concluded that two-parent families appeared among the blacks who were free, skilled, and propertied; however, because of slavery, rural traditions, and a lack of structure and authority among blacks after the Civil War, female-headed households had become more typical by the 1920s and 1930s.

The prevailing theories of the black family stood essentially unchallenged for forty years, despite the fact that they suffered from limited research technology and a racially biased oral and printed record. Such theories were not reconsidered until Moynihan's 1965 *Report on the Negro Family* sparked a storm of protest and a spate of new studies on the black family. While Frazier had seen the rise of black female-headed families as an outcome of racial oppression and poverty, Moynihan essentially blamed poverty—as well as other problems faced by the African American community—on mother-only black families. Moynihan held that blacks suffered because black women domineered their men, kept their families mired in poverty, and transmitted a "tangle of pathology" across generations.

This view of the African American family was widely contested during the 1970s by scholars who argued that as late as 1950, only 17.2 percent of black families were headed by women and that differences between black and white families were an expression of African legacies, American conditions, the means to economic survival in a society riddled with racism, and varying ideas of proper family forms (Billingsly, 1968; Gutman, 1976; Gutman, 1983; Hill, 1971; Ladner, 1971; Stack, 1974). Some scholars believed that the Moynihan Report, which was released just as the civil rights movement was gaining strength, was used politically to blame black families rather than racism for the mounting protest (Gresham, 1989; Solinger, 1992).

The idea of the "dysfunctional" mother-only black family moved to the backburner until the 1980s, when it resurfaced as the centerpiece of research on the so-called underclass. Social scientists describe the underclass as a socially isolated group of poor people living in disorganized neighborhoods that are characterized not only by high rates of crime, hustling, drug abuse, school dropouts, and joblessness but also by out-of-wedlock births, female-headed households, teen-age pregnancy, and welfare use (Mead, 1992; Moynihan, 1986; Murray, 1984; Rickets & Sawhill, 1988; Wilson, 1986). This victim-blaming construction was fueled not only by the continued growth of mother-only families and the expanding welfare state but also by the conservative political climate and politicians seeking to establish their "toughness." Such thinking was backed by scholars who argued that the poor—especially poor black families headed by a women—developed and transmitted an unproductive culture of poverty across generations.

Social Science, Social Policy and the African American Family

Racism and sexism have always shaped American social policy, and they were both integral to the political realignment that created the New Deal and the modern welfare state (Brown, 1993; Gordon, 1990). Most of the New Deal programs, including the Social Security Act, excluded farm and domestic occupations that were filled primarily with African American women and men and otherwise discriminated against blacks (Abramovitz, 1988; Quadagno, 1994). Harsh AFDC polices became harsher after 1939, when more blacks entered the program. In the 1940s, some welfare departments denied aid to poor black women in order to keep employers supplied with domestics and field hands; others established special investigating units to ferret out unwed mothers. By the 1950s, as racial discrimination and postwar economic changes left more and more black women poor and husbandless, welfare departments increasingly equated unwed motherhood with unfit parenthood, intensified the use of moralistic behavior standards rather than financial need in determining eligibility for aid, and used "suitable home" policies to throw thousands of black women off welfare and their children into foster care.

Although these practices were discredited in the late 1960s, punitive social policies reappeared in the 1980s under the guise of welfare "reform." Aided and abetted by the social science image of a behaviorally defined and feminized "underclass," policy makers cut social programs used by many poor women—black and white—and passed the 1988 Family Support Act, which transformed AFDC from a program that aided single mothers at home into a mandatory work program. President Clinton's 1994 welfare reform bill placed a two-year lifetime limit on AFDC and permitted the states to deny aid to children born on welfare. These proposals proliferate despite the failure of numerous research studies to establish that welfare is the prime factor in the decisions of poor women to work, marry, or have children (Moffitt, 1991; Wilson & Neckerman, 1986).

Women-of-Color Feminist Critique

Feminists of color argue that theories of the black family require serious revision if they are to explain and adequately serve the needs of women of color (Collins, 1990; Dill, 1979; Higginbothan, 1982; hooks, 1981; Jackson, 1972; King, 1988; Omolade, 1987; Zinn, 1990a; Zinn, 1990b). In their view, while black researchers since Frazier have defended the black family against racist interpretations, few of these predominantly male scholars have challenged the underlying patriarchal premises of research that safeguarded the black family by denigrating the mother-only household. The defenders of the black family rarely protested the definition of mother-only families as disorganized and dysfunctional, or Moynihan's revival of the black woman as Sapphire—the stereotype of a domineering matriarch who emasculates black men and weakens the family.

Black feminists argue that idealized versions of women's roles, which were institutionalized during the industrial revolution when slavery was still in force, glorified white womanhood while ignoring the domestic roles of women of color and sanctioning tearing black families apart (Nakamo-Glenn, 1985). For years, African-American women were caricatured as Mammy, the loyal slave or servant; Sapphire, the overly domineering matriarch; or Jezebel, the sexually loose woman (Collins, 1990; Dill, 1979; Scott, 1982; White, 1985). To some black feminist scholars, the degradation of black women by the Moynihan Report was a divisive appeal to male supremacy. The dangerous black women it depicted generated a backlash of new male aggressiveness against African American women, divided the black community during the rise of the black liberation struggle, and split women along race lines just as feminists began to critique American patriarchy (Gilkes, 1981; Gresham, 1989). It also supported repressive social policies based on the theory of the underclass.

Many feminists, both black and white, object to the theory of the underclass as a behavior driven explanation of poverty. Originally targeting black men, the underclass theory has been feminized as well as racialized. Relying on patriarchal expectations that women should marry and should not have children outside of marriage, researchers of the underclass use welfare recipients and female-headed households as proxies for female deviancy and family disorganization; equate them with criminals, drug dealers, and other antisocial types; and recommend cutting social program viewed as undermining the work and family ethics. Two beliefs are clear within most descriptions of the underclass: first, the idea that crime, drug use, school dropouts, and use of AFDC are among the "tangle of pathologies" transmitted across generations by women heading families without men at the helm; and second, that single mothers are lazy, promiscuous breeders of the underclass, who have children to increase their welfare grant and then keep their families forever mired on welfare and in poverty.

This thinking continues the historical pattern of denigrating poor women and families of color who fail to live up to the white, idealized version of womanhood and home. It contains a racist and misogynist distrust of the poor woman of color's capacity to parent. Moreover, it ignores data showing that female-headed households correlate inversely with income in all racial groups, that the growth of single-parent families is occurring across race lines, and that despite lower U.S. welfare benefits, U.S. teen pregnancy rates—including those of white teens alone—lead all other Western nations (Hacker, 1992).

Feminists of color are deeply critical of mainstream social science. However, they also take issue with the white feminist critique of the patriarchal family, arguing that it has been generalized to women of color as if no differences existed. They suggest instead that while male patriarchy oppresses both white and African American women, in a racist society, African Americans must take the entire community—including men—into account (Collins, 1990; Davis, 1983; Franklin, 1992; Nakamo-Glenn, 1985). Without denying domestic violence or the sexist constraints of women's traditional role, they question the applicability of the white feminist analysis of the family as a site of female oppression. While families of color may oppress women of color, they are first and foremost a source of identity, protection, resistance, and support. The pressure for gender role equity so central to white feminists is muted for black feminists by the fact that in lower-income black homes, survival requires the economic interdependence of women and men.

Feminists of color also suggest that a focus on the nuclear family, the separation of public and private spheres, and gender equality fails to recognize that historically, many poor women—including poor women of color—crossed the public/private divide by working as both mothers and providers. Because of racial discrimination and/or poverty, working was a necessity for these women, who could not assume the gender roles prescribed by white society. Feminists of color also point to the serious conflicts of interest that separate white women and women of color. For example, during economic downturns, employers historically have bumped black women from jobs in order to give them to white women. Moreover, women of color who work in white homes free white women for work, child rearing, or leisure, but have little time for their own interests or families (Brewer, 1988; Collins, 1986; Collins, 1990; Davis, 1983; Nakamo-Glenn, 1985; King, 1988; Zinn, 1990a; Zinn, 1990b). White feminist scholars have begun to take heed. They are working, often with women of color, to create a multifaceted lens that focuses on the similarities and differences that accompany gender, race, and class (Anderson and Collins, 1992; Dubois and Ruiz, 1990; Jaggar and Rotherberg, 1993; Rothenberg, 1992).

CONCLUSION

This feminist critique of the social science/social work connection has uncovered ways in which the sexism (racism, classism) embedded in social science research has shaped the social work/social policy agenda since World War II. The research of our profession has become increasingly sophisticated in recent years and can interact more equally with other social scientists than in the past. However, to change the nature of the exchange, we must subject science to the same kind of scrutiny that science demands in all other areas.

The feminist critique has become part of this scrutiny. It ask us to consider the questions of what is knowledge, who controls knowledge, and what is the role of social science in maintaining the status quo? Feminism wants to know if social science can address the needs of anyone other than those already empowered by it and whom science is meant to serve. To this end, it asks a host of epistemological questions that also have a political spin: Who are the researchers? Can value-free research exist in a gender-, race-, and class-biased society? Can the distortions in traditional analyses be corrected? By what methodologies? What are the relative merits of objectivity and subjectivity? Whose voices get heard and whose experiences get documented by the research enterprise? Who benefits and who loses from dominant social science theories? Can we have a feminist research? Can (Kieser, 1994) social science establish the existence of oppression? Are we seeking objective truths or social change? These questions remind us that social science, along with its social work/social policy connections, is socially constructed; that the intellectual cannot be abstracted from the social and the political; and that social work, like the rest of academia, has become an arena of struggle. Once we realize the political contours of social science, we have to determine which side we are on and what role our research can play in creating a more humane society for all.

19

Human Resources in the Industrialized Societies: The Need for New Social Concepts and Perspectives

Adam Jamrozik

The expression "human resources" is frequently used in the language of politics, social science, and economics. However, frequency of usage does not necessarily convey clarity of meaning, and the term is used in a range of contexts and given a variety of meanings and connotations. Conventionally, the term has been used in relation to economic production, but in the real world human resources are utilized in a diversity of areas for different purposes and, correspondingly, are differently valued. In many instances they are also misused, ignored, or wasted.

This chapter examines some of the issues concerning human resources, the diversity of their utilization in contemporary industrialized societies, and their potential contribution to human well-being and quality of life in the societies of the future. Consideration is then given to the questions posed by these issues for the social sciences, for social work, and for other professions engaged in providing services in various areas of social and community need.

The data and arguments presented in this chapter are based on studies in social policy, social welfare, and human resources, which have been conducted for some years at the Social Policy Research Center, University of New South Wales, Sydney, Australia, and reported on elsewhere (Jamrozik, 1991a; Jamrozik & Boland, 1991). The statistics quoted in the chapter refer to Australian society, but they undoubtedly have relevance to other societies as well.

HUMAN RESOURCES IN THE INDUSTRIALIZED SOCIETIES

The nature of human resources and their value are often defined in rather narrow economic terms as productive capacities or abilities, mental or physical. However, ideas, knowledge, skills, and abilities are not easily translatable into precise economic indices. Their value is determined by particular circumstances of time, economic conditions, and the relative scarcity or abundance of the resource as well as by the cultural and normative values of a given society or of its dominant power structure.

The importance of human resources has often been taken for granted. Now, in the industrialized societies—or what some people call "postindustrial" societies—human resources have acquired a new and increased significance, especially in qualitative terms, that is, in terms of knowledge and skills. At the same time, in many countries and in Australia especially, the value of human resources—particularly their potential value as human resources and not simply as factors of production—has received relatively little systematic attention in the social sciences. In the public arena, the often heard rhetoric of "our people (or "our children") are our most precious resource" is rarely reflected in practice, where human beings are more often regarded as "factors of production" than as human resources. Such perceptions reduce the knowledge, skills, physical and mental abilities, and potential of human beings to one dimension of economic utility comparable to other factors of production such as machines or material capital. As a result, much of the existing or potential human resources are ignored and effectively wasted, with detrimental consequences for many societies' economic, cultural, and social development.

In economic research, the conventional approach in studies of human resources is to focus on the formal organizations in which human resources are employed in various productive activities. In such contexts, human resources are differentially valued and rewarded according to people's position in the organizational hierarchy and their perceived value to the firm. However, focusing solely on formal organizations leaves out of the analysis a large field of social and economic activities in the "informal" areas of society, such as the family, friendship networks, and a wide and diverse range of informal organizations. Activities in these "informal" structures do not enter into the conventional calculation of the Gross Domestic Product (GDP), although their value in economic and social terms may be considerable.

The notion of "human resources" needs to be considered as a broad, multidimensional concept that encompasses social, economic, and cultural dimensions and values. The concept that includes such diversity of areas in which human resources are productively used is illustrated by the typology presented in Table 19.1. The typology shows that economic analyses of human resources tend to be confined to the relatively few areas of activities that take place in the "formal" commercial and government settings. The "less formal" areas receive little systematic attention, and the economic value of the activities that take place in them does not enter into the GDP calculation. For example, commenting on the domestic economy, Duncan Ironmonger (Ironmonger, 1989, ix) notes that "households produce many billions of dollars worth of economic output," but that "the work they do and the very large volume of economic production that results from this work are constantly ignored in national statistics."

Ironmonger's observation is valid, although it is arguable whether the value of human productive activities in the informal settings such as the family or the voluntary community organization should be reduced to their economic value equivalents in the formal labor market. Translating the value of household or voluntary community activities into market-equivalents needs to be qualified, for using market criteria to ascertain the economic value of such activities reduces their multidimensional, qualitative, and normative elements to the one-dimensional value used in market calculations (Jamrozik, 1989; Jamrozik, 1992). In addition to being theoretically flawed, such translations also devalue human efforts by reducing the value of human resources to "factors of production." How does one evaluate the quality of love, compassion, or altruism, for example, by market criteria?

Table 19.1
A Typology of the Use of Human Resources in Industrial Societies

	Informal Division	**Formal Division**
Primary Groups	Domestic economy Family Friends Relatives Self-help groups	Family business (e.g., "the corner shop") Cooperative skills exchange
Commercial Organization	"Black" labor market Drug trafficking "Black" economy generally	Private sector labor market Private corporations Public coroporations
Noncommercial Organization	Local welfare organizations Cultural, educational, recreational activities Pressure groups (informal)	Pressure groups (formal) Formal welfare organizations (e.g., RSL, Rotary) Research "think tanks" Educational, research, health organizations, etc.
Government Organization	Lobby activities Informal advisory bodies and individuals	Commonwealth departments State departments Local departments Statutory bodies

Source: Jamrozik, A., and C. Boland, (1991), *Human Resources in Community Services*.

The value attached to human resources employed in the various sectors of the labor market is not uniform. In such industries as community services, the activities, the settings in which the activities are performed, the population that is "acted upon" or "managed," and the aims as well as the outcomes of the activities and the outcomes of the activities are imbued with individually as well as organizationally normative values (Boland, 1989; Jamrozik, 1991a). These "dynamic features" in the use of human resources become increasingly important as the normative values of the "quality of life" concepts compete against the economically rational values of the "standard of living" indicators such as GDP measurements. With the diminishing need for human resources in material production, the decisions about where to engage people in productive activities, what they are to do, and for what purpose and desired outcomes become increasingly a matter of normative and political choices rather than of economic necessities. This also means that current perceptions and definitions of human resources must be thoroughly reassessed so that these resources can be looked upon in a broad social perspective that would facilitate the recognition and appreciation of their multidimensional nature and their potential.

Unemployment: An Endemic Condition of Wasted Resources

One of the biggest problems facing the industrialized countries is the high rate of unemployment that has now become a "structural feature" and the main source of social division and conflict in these societies. It becomes increasingly evident that the market as it now operates is not capable of providing employment for all people who seek it, thus shedding an increasing human residue onto the public income maintenance provisions.

Nor is there any indication that full employment to the extent known in the 1950s and 1960s will return in the foreseeable future. Full employment of that kind will not be possible, if only because the productive capacity of the industrialized countries will continue outstripping the capacity of consumption, as Theobald was predicting some years ago when full employment was still prevalent (Theobald, 1965). Efforts to maintain employment through high rates of consumption have been an integral part of western economies for a long time. These efforts have ranged from built-in obsolescence, ever-increasing advertising, and pressures to buy the latest product, to the creation of new credit facilities. Whatever positive effects these efforts have achieved, such as providing a stimulus for scientific discoveries, technological innovation, and higher standards of living, they have also led to the accelerated use and exhaustion of earth resources, many of them nonrenewable. Despite these efforts, high rates of unemployment have now persisted for two decades, and there is no indication of any significant reduction in these rates.

Is unemployment, then, a more-or-less permanent endemic condition in the industrialized countries, a price that has to be paid for technological innovation, efficiency, and relative affluence for the majority of the population? Is it the case that some people have to suffer so that the majority can enjoy a good life? This is an issue that calls for high priority in consideration not only by political decision makers but also by the social sciences; it is certainly an important issue for consideration by the social work profession.

UTILIZATION OF HUMAN RESOURCES IN AUSTRALIA

Like many countries in the world today, Australia has for some time now been experiencing something of a crisis. The crisis has been perceived and interpreted mainly in economic terms, but it has been a multidimensional crisis, as it entails problems of economic performance, changing social structure, and corresponding new forms of inequality, as well as tensions related to the multicultural composition of the population and the country's place in the world economy, geography, and culture.

Some explanations of this condition of crisis can be found in the worldwide changing scenario in politics and economy. However, explanations can also be found in the country itself: in its history and in its more recent social, political, and economic developments. To a certain extent, Australia has not yet adequately dealt with its "colonial inheritance," which still weighs heavily on its people's mode of thinking—on their attitudes toward other countries and toward the new settlers in the country itself. This inheritance is still evident in the country's core social institutions, such as the education system, organized religions, professions, and political institutions. To this day, Australia has not yet fully reconciled itself to its isolated geographic position; only now the federal government is taking some positive steps in that direction, against considerable resistance from conservative quarters.

Australia has considerable natural material wealth, but much of it—such as its mineral resources of coal, iron ore, other metals, and oil—is exhaustible and non-renewable. One of the causes of current economic difficulties was the economic policy adopted by the Australian government in the 1970s after the oil crisis and consequent worldwide energy crisis. The policy was based on the belief that the energy crisis placed Australia in a favorable position for becoming the energy supplier to the industrialized countries. Priority was therefore given to investment in extractive industries rather than the manufacturing industries that were already showing signs of decline in the mid-1960s. The energy crisis did not last long, and while the industrialized countries elsewhere used that period to concentrate efforts towards change to high technology industries and new methods of production, Australia was left behind and has not been able to recover since. Some progress in industry restructuring is being achieved now, but the process entails considerable human cost, with unemployment now hovering around 10 percent of the labor force.

The most neglected resources in Australia have been human resources. Traditionally, exploitation of material resources has received much attention, but the development of human resources has been neglected. Frequently this has led to shortages of human skills and expertise. Employers might have been emphasizing the importance of management in the private sector of industry, but there has always been a fear of "overeducated" workers as potentially disgruntled and dissatisfied with monotonous factory tasks and therefore potentially troublesome. Even now, in the extensive measures taken by the government to restructure the entire post-school education system, emphasis is on vocationalism and training rather than on a broad educational base that would enable people to adapt their basic skills and knowledge to the changing occupational structure of the labor market.

Human Resources in the Formal Labor Market

Like the trends in other industrialized societies, the use of human resources in the formal Australian labor market has shifted from material production to other areas of employment—the most prominent shift being to industries engaged in the management of material and social production. These "management industries" include three sectors defined by the Australian Bureau of Statistics (ABS) as finance, property, and business services; public administration; and community services, which include health, education, welfare and religious organizations, as well as other community services such as police, sanitation, and corrections. The extent of this shift over the past 25 years (1966–1991) is shown in Table 19.2.

The shift of human resources from material production to management activities has been three-dimensional, entailing the quantity, the quality, and the gender of the labor force. As shown in Table 19.2, the number of persons employed in all industries increased over the 25 years by 59.0 percent, but employment in the five sectors of industry engaged in material production remained static. In manufacturing industries, it decreased by 10.2 percent. By contrast, employment in the management industries increased over that period by 187.5 percent, or over three times greater than the rate of increase in the total employment.

Second, of the 2845 thousand increase in the number of employed persons over that period, 1767 thousand (62.1%) were women, and 1087 thousand of this increase (38.2%) went into the management industries (these details are not shown in Table 19.1). Furthermore, the majority of the increase in women's employment (69.5%) was accounted for by married women, and the majority of these (64.0%) found employment in the management industries. On the qualitative dimension, the significance of the shift of human resources to these industries can be ascertained from Table 19.3, where it is shown that in 1991 (Australian Bureau of Statistics, 1991b), employment in the management industries accounted for one-third of all employed persons, but accounted for 70.0 percent of all employed persons with tertiary degree qualifications.

The most significant *social* consequence of these shifts in the labor market has been in the socioeconomic structure of the Australian family. The people who benefited from the new employment opportunities were mainly those who entered the labor force for the first time, not those who had lost jobs in the shrinking sectors of industries engaged in material production. Chronic unemployment became a feature among people with skills in manual trades and in related occupations. Second, the entry of women into the professional and related nonmanual jobs in the expanding management industries gave rise to the two-income, high-income, middle-class family and to a corresponding increase of inequality in the distribution of family incomes. Certainly, the positive side of these shifts has been the development of the potential of hitherto unused female human resources in some population strata, but at the cost of discarding human resources in other sections of the population.

Human Resources in Community Services

Of the three sectors included in the management industries category, the sector of community services was the largest employer in 1991, both in the quantity and the quality of the labor force, accounting for 17.6 percent of all employed persons and for 40.1 percent of all employed degree holders. This

Table 19.2
Changes in Employment, Australia, 1966–91 (N in thousands)

	1966		1991		Change 1966–1991		
	N	%	N	%	N	%	Ratio[1]
All Industries	**4823.9**	**100.0**	**7669.2**	**100.0**	**2845.3**	**59.0**	**0.00**
Men	3365.6	69.8	4443.7	57.9	1078.1	32.0	0.54
Women	1458.2	30.2	3225.5	42.1	1767.3	121.2	2.05
Married women	761.2	15.3	1990.0	25.9	1228.8	161.4	2.74
Material Production	**2222.6**	**46.1**	**2223.6**	**29.0**	**1.0**	**0.0**	**0.00**
Agriculture and related	429.6	8.9	407.1	5.3	-22.5	-5.2	–
Mining	58.0	1.2	95.5	1.2	37.5	67.7	1.10
Manufacturing	1232.5	25.5	1107.1	14.4	-125.4	-10.2	–
Electricity, gas, water	96.5	2.0	103.7	1.4	7.2	7.5	0.13
Construction	406.0	8.4	510.2	6.7	104.2	25.7	0.44
Distribution Services	**1368.9**	**28.4**	**2122.2**	**27.7**	**753.3**	**55.0**	**0.93**
Wholesale and retail trade	993.5	20.6	1590.5	20.7	597.0	60.1	1.02
Transport and storage	270.0	5.6	399.2	5.2	129.2	47.9	0.81
Communications	105.4	2.2	132.5	1.7	27.1	25.7	0.44
Management Industries	**945.4**	**19.6**	**2718.2**	**35.4**	**1772.8**	**187.5**	**3.18**
Finance, property, business services	294.4	6.1	893.9	11.7	599.5	203.6	3.45
Public administration	165.0	3.4	359.3	4.7	194.3	117.8	2.00
Community services	486.0	10.1	1465.0	19.1	979.0	201.4	3.41
Recreation, Personal Services	**287.0**	**5.9**	**605.2**	**7.9**	**318.2**	**110.9**	**1.88**

Sources: Australian Bureau of Statistics (1987), *The Labor Force, Australia; Historical Summary 1966-1984*, Cat. No. 6204.0; Australian Bureau of Statistics (1991); *The Labor Force, Australia, August 1991*, Cat. No. 6203.0.
[1] Ratio to the total increase in the labor force.

Table 19.3
Employed Persons 15 to 69 Years: Educational Attainment and Industry Group, Australia, February 1991 (N in thousands)

Industry group	All employed (a)	All post-school (b)	With degree	Trade qualifications	Certificate or Diploma	Without post-school qualifications (c)
All industries						
N	7651.8	3752.2	875.0	1242.2	1604.1	3758.9
%	100.0	49.0	11.4	16.2	21.0	49.1
Material production						
N	2328.3	1100.4	122.1	640.9	328.2	1214.6
% in group	100.0	47.3	5.2	27.5	14.1	52.2
% of all employed	30.4	29.3	14.0	51.6	20.5	32.3
Distribution Services						
N	2153.8	811.7	103.5	355.4	343.9	1242.8
% in group	100.0	37.7	4.8	16.5	16.0	57.7
% of all employed	28.1	21.6	11.8	28.6	21.4	33.1
Management Industries						
N	2593.3	1608.4	612.8	157.6	827.6	976.8
% in group	100.0	62.0	23.6	6.1	31.9	37.7
% of all employed	33.9	42.9	70.0	12.7	51.6	26.0
Recreation, Personal Services						
N	576.5	231.8	36.7	88.2	104.4	324.7
% in group	100.0	40.2	6.4	15.3	18.1	56.3
% of all employed	7.5	6.2	4.2	7.1	6.5	8.6

Source: Australian Bureau of Statistics (1991) *Labor Force Status and Educational Attainment, Australia, February 1991,* Cat. No. 6235.0

a. Includes persons still at school. b. Includes persons with other (unstated) qualifications. c. Includes persons who never attended school and those whose attendance at a secondary school could not be determined.

Material Production: agriculture & other primary; mining; manufacturing; electricity, gas, water, construction. **Distribution Services:** wholesale & retail trade; transport and storage; communication. **Management Industries:** finance, property, business services; public administration and defense; community services. **Recreation, Personal Services:** Entertainment, restaurants, hotels, personal services, domestic services, etc.

sector has also become the largest employer of women. As of August 1991, close to two-thirds (65.2%) of persons employed in community services were women, who constitute a majority in most of this industry's occupations (Table 19.4). In the remaining industries, women account for only 36.6 percent of all employed persons, and they account for the majority of employees in only two occupational groups: clerical, and sales and personal services.

Should these developments be a cause of concern? If there is a cause for concern, it is not in the growth of employment in community services per se, but in some aspects of the outcome of that growth. Of necessity, given the limited scope of this chapter, only a few of these aspects will be mentioned here. First, while there has been a considerable increase in the numbers of people entering tertiary education, the disparity in access to education between socioeconomic groups remains high, beginning with qualitative differences at the level of primary and secondary education and culminating in differences in access to tertiary education (Jamrozik, 1991a). Second, as noted earlier, the growth of employment in community services, together with the opportunities for women in professional employment in these services, has given rise to two-income families among the professional occupations. This has resulted in rising inequalities in family incomes, as there has been no comparable growth in two-income families among the lower, manual, unskilled occupations. The professional providers of community services are also among the main consumers of these services—especially of the services that facilitate social functioning of the recipients and their families, such as good schools, tertiary education, preventive community health services, paid maternity leave, and child care.

The differences in incomes and corresponding lifestyles have also led to increasing socioeconomic differences in the spatial distribution of the population in the large cities. For example, a recent study of these issues in Sydney—the largest city in Australia and a city approaching four million inhabitants—shows a high degree of concentration of certain population characteristics (e.g., tertiary education, income, male and female professional employment, employment in community services) indicating spatial distribution of cumulative advantage or disadvantage (Jamrozik & Boland, 1991). The spatial distribution of families in the higher income groups was found to be almost identical with the distribution of the "helping professions," indicating a high level of positive correlation between professional occupations and high family incomes.

Prominent among the high concentration of the population engaged in professional occupations in the affluent areas were those involved in the social professions, such as social workers and related occupations. By comparison, the frequency of these professions in the low socio-economic status areas was extremely low. Professional service providers in the fields of health, education, and welfare thus tend to be socially as well as spatially separated from the recipients of these services; they live in two different social worlds. This means that the providers of social welfare services have a limited direct knowledge and understanding of the everyday problems experienced by the people whom they are meant to serve.

Table 19.4

Occupational and Gender Composition of Employment: All Industries and Community Services, August 1991 (N in thousands)

Industry/Occupation	(1) All Employed		(2) Men		(3) Women		
	N	%	N	%	N	%	Ratio[1]
Industries excluding community services, all employed	6204.2	100.0	3933.3	100.0	2270.9	100.0	36.6
Management and professions	**1495.4**	**24.1**	**1139.2**	**29.0**	**356.1**	**15.7**	**23.8**
Managers and administrators	807.4	13.0	607.9	15.5	199.4	8.8	24.7
Professionals	497.1	8.0	370.3	9.4	126.8	5.6	25.5
Paraprofessionals	190.9	3.1	161.0	4.1	29.9	1.3	15.7
Clerks, sales, personal services	**2130.2**	**34.3**	**683.8**	**17.4**	**1446.4**	**63.7**	**67.9**
Clerks	1092.4	17.6	280.2	7.1	8112.2	35.8	74.3
Salespersons, personal services	1037.8	16.7	403.6	10.3	634.2	27.9	61.1
Trades, plant operators, drivers	**1641.1**	**26.5**	**1448.1**	**36.8**	**193.0**	**8.5**	**11.8**
Tradespersons	1100.8	17.7	996.8	25.3	104.0	4.6	9.4
Plant/machine operators, drivers	540.3	8.7	451.3	11.5	89.0	3.9	16.5
Laborers and related	**937.6**	**15.1**	**662.3**	**16.8**	**275.3**	**12.1**	**29.4**

Community services, all employed	1465.0	100.0	510.4	100.0	954.6	100.0	65.2
Management and professions	**865.9**	**59.1**	**363.0**	**71.1**	**502.9**	**52.7**	**58.1**
Managers and administrators	41.7	2.8	25.6	5.0	16.1	1.7	38.6
Professionals	536.9	36.6	238.5	46.7	298.4	31.3	55.6
Paraprofessionals	287.3	19.6	98.9	19.4	188.4	19.7	65.6
Clerks, sales, personal services	**355.6**	**24.3**	**35.9**	**7.0**	**319.7**	**33.5**	**89.9**
Clerks	237.9	16.2	26.1	5.1	211.8	22.2	89.0
Salespersons, personal services	117.7	8.0	9.8	1.9	107.9	11.9	91.7
Trades, plant operators, drivers	**69.7**	**4.8**	**54.0**	**10.6**	**15.8**	**1.7**	**22.7**
Tradespersons	44.7	3.1	31.9	6.3	12.9	1.4	28.9
Plant/machine operators, drivers	25.0	1.7	22.1	4.3	2.9	0.3	11.6
Laborers and related	**173.7**	**11.9**	**57.5**	**11.3**	**116.2**	**12.2**	**66.9**

Source: Australian Bureau of Statistics (1991) *The Labor Force, Australia, August 1991*, Cat. No. 6203.0

In considering the value of human resources in the social perspective mentioned earlier, their use in the provision of community services is of utmost importance. Health, education, child care, and related services constitute the core of social policy in an industrialized society, as it is these services that facilitate people's functioning in social and economic life. Not only is an adequate, effective, and equitable provision of these services essential to the functioning of the market economy, but it can also reduce the need for income support payments by enhancing people's social functioning. As Marshall argues, "Welfare fulfills itself above all in those services which are its own in every sense—health, education and 'personal social services' and, with increasing emphasis, community services for the preservation and development of the physical, social and cultural environment. It is by strengthening these that the civilizing powers of welfare can be most effectively increased" (Marshall, 1981, 135).

Unfortunately, the provision of services that enhance the social functioning of the recipients has been one of the problematic areas of social policy. For while these services are of great value to the recipients and represent an important investment in human resources, they have also become another source of inequality in society. Far from acting as a countervailing force to the inequalities generated in the market, the differential access to them has in many ways reinforced these inequalities. As these services are likely to be increasingly important in the future, the quality of life in Australia will depend to a large extent on the performance of these services in terms of equitable access and outcome.

Immigrants and Ethnic Minorities

Another important area related to the use of human resources in Australia has been the immigration program and the growing multicultural characteristics of its population. To overcome the shortage of human resources in the labor market, Australia has been promoting immigration, and since 1947 a substantial proportion of the labor force has been provided by immigrants (Jamrozik, 1991b). Throughout much of this period, emphasis was manifestly given to the economic aspects of immigration, with priority of admission allocated to persons with occupational qualifications and experience. Yet to this day, immigrants—cspccially those from non-English speaking countries—have considerable difficulties in having their educational and occupational qualifications accepted by educational institutions, by trades, and especially by professional bodies. For this reason, many of them, irrespective of their occupational qualifications and experience, are still found in the lowest ranks of the occupational hierarchy performing manual, low-paid tasks (Jamrozik, 1991a). Some progress might have been achieved in overcoming these difficulties in recent years, but the problem seems to be repeated with each new wave of immigrants. How much waste of human resources and what potential loss of knowledge and skills has been incurred through the host society's resistant attitudes to newcomers is difficult to estimate, but loss and waste must have been substantial.

The waste of the imported human resources is not in their economic value alone, but also in their potential contribution to social and cultural aspects of the Australian society. The perception that the value of these human resources is confined mainly to their immediate economic value as a *supplementary labor force* has meant that much of the imported knowledge and skill has not been utilized. As shown in the conceptual framework presented in Table 19.5, widening the perception can reveal not only the possibilities of realizing the economic potential of the imported knowledge and skill but also the possibility of integrating that potential into the local culture and thus further increasing its economic value. It is in the cultural integration of Australian society that, after all these years of mass immigration, little progress has been achieved. Notwithstanding the proclaimed policy of multiculturalism since the mid-1970s, Australian core social institutions have remained largely impervious to cultural influences from non-English-speaking countries and have remained remarkably monocultural.

In looking at the Australian experiences in economic performance, in the education system, in the development and provision of community services generally, and in the attitudes towards the new settlers, it is not difficult to conclude that the potential for fully utilizing the country's human resources—those locally present, those imported through immigration program, and those that can be developed—has yet to be realized in both policy and practice. To realize this potential, the perspective on the value of human resources will need to shift from the narrow concepts of economic utility to a wider social perspective encompassing social, economic, and cultural dimensions. This will be the task for the social scientists and for the professions grounded in the social sciences such as social work.

The trends in Australia have been somewhat similar to those observed in the other industrialized countries but with one important distinction: In relative terms, Australia has been losing ground in economic and social development ever since the early years of this century, and in terms of its standard of living it is now somewhere in the bottom half of the OECD countries. This decline became quite evident in the early 1980s, indicated by the loss of value in the Australian currency and in the growing foreign debt. This does not mean that the country is poor, but it does mean that the country is no longer in the "first league."

The restructuring of the economy that is now taking place in Australia may possibly succeed, provided the government has enough political will and the ability to explain the nature of the problem to the electorate. At present, close to one million persons are recorded as unemployed—10 percent of the labor force. This average conceals extremes, and in some areas of the country unemployment hovers around 20 percent. An increasing percentage of the unemployed persons consists of the long-term unemployed—some for over two or three years. This "lost" population represents a great waste of human resources and also bears the cost of industry restructuring. Thus, a question of considerable importance concerning the future social policy and attitudes towards human resources is whether and at what stage of economic recovery the currently experienced trends towards greater inequalities can be arrested or reversed.

Table 19.5
Contribution of Knowledge and Skills by Immigrants: A Conceptual Framework

	Levels of Skills Integration			
	(i) Retained by the immigrant	(ii) Transferred to other person(s)	(iii) Incorporated into production process	(iv) Integrated into local culture
L E V E L S	1. **Supplementary**: Skills are imported to fill in the gaps/overcome shortages of particular skills in the resident labor force.			
O F	2. **Complementary**: Skills are imported to enlarge the range of skills within the existing structure of trades and/or professions.			
S K I L L S	3. **Qualitative**: Skills are imported to raise the levels of existing skills, to apply new technologies and methods of preparation.			
S O U G H T	4. **New Skills**: Skills not present in the resident labor force are imported to start new industries and open new area of industrial activity.			

Source: Jamrozik, A., Urquhart, R. and Wearing, M. (1990), *Immigrants' Contribution to Skills Development and Occupational Structure*, Melbourne, Bureau of Immigration Research

CONCLUSIONS

The need for new concepts and perspectives on human resources is an issue of great urgency. So far, much has been written about the future of work, with a variety of predictions and proposed solutions to the perceived "scarcity of work" and the consequent unemployment. There is a strong body of belief that work as it is now understood—that is, regular paid employment—will continue to be increasingly scarce and that the whole concept of work will have to change (Gorz, 1980; Jones, 1982). A number of solutions have been suggested and some have been adopted, including rationing of work through a shorter work week or year, work sharing, or a shorter working life. On the other hand, the dominant belief in the industrialized countries is that the solution is to be found in more productive work, in greater competitiveness on the world market, in lower wages, and in more consumption of goods and services. All these, it is claimed, will create more demand for labor.

Paid employment is, for most people, still the main source of income. Income provides not only the basic necessities of life such as food and shelter, but also personal satisfaction, social status, freedom, and autonomy and control over nonwork time and leisure pursuits (Jamrozik, 1986). Those excluded from paid employment are also excluded from participation in other aspects of social life and are reduced to a new form of subsistence living and to the status of "noncitizens."

The wasted human resources of the "surplus population" present one of the most serious problems now faced by industrialized societies. There is a growing body of belief, not necessarily translated into action, that the problems now experienced in those countries will not be solved by economic measures alone (OECD, 1981). The opinions on possible options differ widely, but it is now more apparent than ever before that either the presence of wasted human resources through unemployment will have to be accepted as a permanent state of affairs or new, as yet unexplored options may need to be considered. The arguments presented in this chapter suggest that such options will have to include a radical reconceptualization of the value of human resources. Any such reconceptualization cannot be, and will not be, successfully carried out within the context of the formal labor market alone, and certainly not within the context of its present structure. The perspective on human resources will have to be widened considerably so as to include the entire economic as well as social organization. This will be one of the most important tasks for the social sciences—and for social work—to face in the years to come.

The recent trends in the world economy and the current "crisis" experienced in many countries, rich and poor, clearly indicates that the perception of issues, the guiding theories, and the corresponding methods of intervention and management are seriously flawed. There has been also a considerable element of hypocrisy in politics, especially in governments of the affluent countries, in the allocation of their resources both internally and externally. For example, the end of the Cold War has created a great opportunity for releasing human and material resources from the production of weapons to economically and socially useful production and to the restoration of the already destroyed or severely damaged environment. Unfortunately, such a shift has not taken place.

Challenges for the Social Sciences

The currently prevailing attitudes towards the value of human resources will lead unavoidably to growing inequalities, human tragedies, and increasing social conflicts. In order to reverse these trends, the direction of the social sciences will also need to change. Social scientists will need to fundamentally reappraise the value assumptions of their theories and the value base of their endeavors. This reappraisal will need to entail a critical assessment of the entire social science paradigm: theories, issues selected for the research agenda, methods of data collection and analysis, and methods of dissemination of research findings.

Social scientists must also resist becoming the servants of power. To be true to their vocation, they must not allow their research to be used as validation of politics of inequality or politics of oppression. Their perception of local and national issues also must be viewed increasingly in the global perspective. With the globalization of certain areas of economic production, capital is frequently shifted from one country to another, with benefits for some and corresponding losses for others. Similarly, seeking solutions to some social problems in one country may lead to detrimental consequences in another.

Challenges for Social Work

Concern with human resources has always been at the heart of the social work endeavor, but this concern has included a high degree of ambivalence. Throughout its history, social work has oscillated between methods of intervention that depend on social explanations of social conditions and human problems, on the one hand; and individualistic theories, explanations, and corresponding "remedial" methods of intervention, on the other. While these two orientations are not necessarily mutually exclusive, the former entails attitudes and methods seeking societal change in the allocation of resources, while the latter leads to the methods seeking preservation of the stability of the social order and its inequalities.

This oscillation within the social work profession has been a perennial issue that has not yet been resolved by social workers. The issue is likely to remain on the agenda for debate on the role of social work for years to come because it seems to be inherent in the profession itself. It must be acknowledged that, to a varied extent, this issue is present in all professions, especially in the social professions such as medicine, law, and education. However, the issue is sharper in social work because of the strong humanitarian value base to which social workers subscribe.

It must also be acknowledged that efforts to develop a social orientation have meant considerable difficulties for social workers in obtaining social approval and the legitimacy of a fully fledged profession. In contrast, a desire to be a "helpful" profession, providing remedial services and receiving societal approval, has always had a seductive attraction for social workers. The individualistic remedial orientation has become prominent over the past two decades or so (at least in Australia) and has fit well into the economic and social policies of governments.

In the coming century, if the present trends in world politics and economy continue in the same direction as they have now, the pressures on social workers to play the "remedial" role will increase. As social inequalities in most countries continue or even increase, social workers will be expected to contain the resentment of the "surplus population" (or the "underclass," as this population is now frequently called) and act as instruments of social control by their methods of "helpful intervention"—thus lessening the need for more overt methods of control and coercion.

This is the challenge social workers will have to face, and the challenge will be greater than in the past because the issues will be sharper, more distinctly global, and more threatening to the established political and economic powers.

To meet the challenge, social workers will need to reassess their role in the social sciences both as the users of the knowledge generated in these sciences and, even more, as the contributors to the knowledge in these sciences. Social workers' contributions to the social sciences have considerable potential to enhance the scientific base of these sciences and to reestablish their value base, which will then enable the social sciences to contribute to the societies' well-being. This was the role the Founding Fathers and Mothers of social sciences and social work envisaged for these disciplines, and this is the role to which we should aim to return.

20

Social Stratification and Psychological Debilitation: A Review with Practice Implications

John F. Longres

This chapter focuses on the relationship between social stratification and psychological debilitation. The term *stratification* is used here to refer to economic inequality, racial and ethnic stratification, gender stratification, and stratification based on sexual orientation. Although stratification based on age and physical abilities must also be considered, these factors will not be addressed in this chapter. The term *psychological debilitation* is used inclusively to refer to any private trouble experienced by individuals, ranging from severe mental illness to distress and problems of self-esteem. The author tests the hypothesis that people who are on the lower rungs of a stratification system will be at greater risk for psychological debilitation.

The paper is an example of a methodology of integration and follows in the tradition developed here at the University of Michigan by Eugene Litwak and Jack Rothman (Rothman, 1974). It uses a systematic review of the research to determine the state of knowledge in a particular area for the purpose of deriving generalizations for practice. The methods are analogous to those used in meta-analytic procedures (Rosenthal, 1984; Cooper, 1989). Empirical studies bearing on the hypothesis were located using library searches and searches of various abstracting services including social work abstracts, psychological abstracts, and the social science index. These were searched using key words derived from both of the principal variables. Published studies were also obtained informally from colleagues and students. No unpublished material was used. Although quantitative analysis is desirable, it was not used because of (a) difficulties in finding comparable conceptual measures of both stratification and debilitation, (b) the scarcity of studies reporting data for computing effect-size statistics, and c) problems of weighting studies in terms of their methodological rigor. The study therefore approaches the hypothesis in a qualitative and exploratory manner. By looking at the research bearing on the relationship between stratification and psychological debilitation, the review presented here aims to convert research findings into practice implications.

An understanding of the psychological effects of inequality is relevant to all fields of direct practice. It is primarily useful to those working in mental health services—where psychological well-being is the chief object of intervention—but it is also useful to those working in other fields, such as juvenile justice and child welfare. Mental health functioning underlines most discussions of social work process (Wakefield, 1988), since all practitioners must tune into the psychology of their clients and constituents if they are to accurately empathize, assess, and deliver appropriate services. This in no way is intended to suggest that psychological functioning is the only concern of social workers, but rather that it is an element relevant to all forms of practice.

By focusing on the psychological effects of stratification, I wish to contribute to progressive models of social work practice that share a common focus on systems of structured inequality, or inequality rooted in the organization of society rather than in situational and personal attributes. By progressive I refer in particular to radical, feminist, and ethnic empowering models of practice. Radical social work, for instance, emphasizes inequality based on relationships around the means of production. Feminist social work emphasizes inequality based on reproductive and family relations. Ethnic-sensitive practice emphasizes inequality based partly on reproduction—control over the American phenotype, and on partly culture—control over the language, religion, and other traditions of American society.

This chapter will describe the conflicting points of view regarding the relationship between stratification and psychological debilitation. It will then go on to independently examine the relationship between each of the four status considerations and psychological debilitation. The paper will end with a discussion on the implications for social work practice.

INEQUALITY AND PSYCHOLOGICAL WELL-BEING

It is often argued that individuals from subordinated groups will internalize the stigma associated with their low status. Internalized stigma has been variously described as spoiled identities (Goffman, 1965), identification with the aggressor (Lichtenberg & Roman, 1990), learned helplessness (Spendlove, Gavelek, and MacMurray, 1981), surplus powerlessness (Lerner, 1986), hidden injuries (Sennett & Cobb, 1972), fear of freedom (Fromm, 1941), traits due to victimization (Allport, 1954), and inferiorization (Adam, 1978b). Regardless of terminology, subordinated people are said to be trapped within hostile environments, exposed to individual and institutionalized forms of discrimination that wreak havoc on their psyches and leave them debilitated. I refer to this, therefore, as the psychological debilitation hypothesis.

A good hypothesis is one that is not obvious; it is a statement that one has reason to believe is true but for which adequate evidence may be lacking. In this regard, the debilitation hypothesis is a good one. Although it is reasonable to assume, as many have, that debilitation will take place under the onslaught of pervasive external hostility, there are intuitive reasons for doubting the hypothesis. For instance, one might equally hypothesize that subordination will provoke resistance and the tendency to reject and overcome stigmatization. Much of the literature that flows from Marxian class analysis, feminist analysis, and analysis of ethnic and racial consciousness in fact does run contrary to the debilitation hypothesis. Such analyses hypothesize that subordination encourages a sense of community and generates a counter-ideology that helps the individual ward off any negative psychological effects of subordination.

The debilitation hypothesis is also not obvious because—being primarily focused on people in positions of subordination—it does not give us a very clear prediction of the psychological effects of superordination. Since the opposite of debilitation is habilitation, one might hypothesize that people in superordinate positions will be made psychologically stronger by their exalted status. Indeed, that is the major implication of the debilitation hypothesis; if subordinates are psychologically weakened, then superordinates are psychologically strengthened. Yet there are reasons for suggesting that such may not be the case. Feminists, for instance, point to the debilitating effects of the male gender role; men, they argue, are less expressive than women and less able to show warmth, tenderness, and empathy in interpersonal relations. Barbara Ehrenreich (Ehrenreich, 1990) hints at debilitation when she argues that a "fear of falling" pervades the psyche of members of the professional middle classes (Ehrenreich, 1990). Lichtenberg and Roman argue that "projection upon a primed vulnerable other" is a common trait of people in dominant positions (Lichtenberg & Roman, 1990). The debilitation hypothesis therefore cannot be taken for granted and must be subjected to empirical investigation.

LOWER SOCIO-ECONOMIC STATUS AND PSYCHOLOGICAL WELL-BEING

The clearest support for the debilitation hypothesis is to be found in the research on socioeconomic status. As Kessler and Cleary write, "The comparatively higher rates of distress in the lowest social strata is one of the most consistently documented findings in the literature on psychiatric epidemiology" (Kessler & Cleary, 1980). This is especially the case with severe forms of mental illness (Dohrenwend et al., 1980; Link, Dohrenwend, and Skodol, 1986; McLeod, 1990), but it is also the case with respect to milder forms of psychological distress (McLeod, 1990; Hornung, 1977; Pearlin & Johnson, 1977; Mirowsky & Ross, 1983). By extension, the research supports the notion that higher socioeconomic status is associated with psychological health.

Although there is a clear association between stratification and debilitation, there is no clear evidence as to which causes which. The debate centers on two apparently competing positions. The "social causation" position—in keeping with the way I have formulated the debilitation hypothesis—holds that lower socioeconomic status sets the stage for mental problems; various life circumstances associated with class subordination predispose to psychological debilitation. The "social selection" position challenges this argument. Drawn boldly, it argues that psychological debilitation comes first: that—in keeping with a functionalist analysis of social class (Davis & Moore, 1945)—debilitation causes socioeconomic inequality. In other words, psychologically debilitated people—because either of genetic or learned deficiencies—end up in the lower classes.

The bulk of the evidence seems to point in favor of the social selection position. This appears especially true with regard to schizophrenia, which is increasingly accepted as a genetically linked disability, but also with regard to milder forms of debilitation (Specht, 1986; Langner & Michael, 1963; Brown, Brhol-Chain, and Harris, 1979; Brown & Harris, 1978; Kessler, 1979).

Although attempts to support a purely social causation model have failed, not all the evidence refutes the social causation position either. David Cohen believes that the evidence about the biological basis of schizophrenia is not as strong as many would have us believe (Cohen, 1989; Dohrenwend, 1970). Dohrenwend and his associates also contend that noise, heat, humidity, fumes, and other physical hazards associated with working class occupations may prove especially stressful for young workers (Link, Dohrenwend, and Skodol, 1986). Link finds evidence that negative labeling—defined as psychiatric treatment— exacerbates psychological troubles and facilitates downward mobility. Dohrenwend and his associates also contend that the relative importance of social selection may vary according to the type of illness or distress being examined. Using a representative Israeli sample, they found evidence that although schizophrenia may be rooted in ethnic group and therefore in family genetics, severe depression, antisocial personality, and substance use disorders are more likely to be rooted in social causes (Dohrenwend et al., 1992).

Contemporary researchers therefore appear to be piecing together a model that recognizes the importance of social selection without completely discarding social causative processes. They are aiming to show that social causation either additively or interactively increases the risk of debilitation.

We may conclude therefore that lower socioeconomic people are at greater risk for severe and minor psychological debilitation. Although social causation cannot solely account for debilitation, social causation may be implicated in certain forms of debilitation, it may increase the likelihood of genetic or congenital predisposition, or it may act to increase the vulnerability of lower class people through childhood socialization, environmental hazards, the relative absence of social resources, and/or because of negative labeling.

ETHNIC SUBORDINATION AND PSYCHOLOGICAL WELL-BEING

Research on the psychological effects of racial and ethnic subordination has a long tradition. Throughout much of this tradition, studies have supported the hypothesis of psychological debilitation. Perhaps the most frequently cited have been the studies of Kenneth and Mamie Clark, completed over 30 years ago. Clark and Clark found that a significant minority of black children preferred white dolls to black dolls or identified themselves as white when given line drawings of white children and black children (Clark & Clark, 1939; Clark & Clark, 1958). They interpreted these findings to mean that black children suffered from diminished self-esteem.

Although Fish and Larr reported that between 1960 and 1972 black children were less likely to misidentify themselves in line drawings (Fish & Larr, 1972), some recent replications suggest that the phenomenon may still be evident. Beuf (Beuf, 1977) found that American Indian children showed a preference for white dolls over Indian dolls. At the 1987 meeting of the American Psychological

Association, Darlene Powell-Hopson and Sharon McNichol, reporting on their independent replications of the Clark study, also found that black children in the United States and Trinidad preferred to play with white dolls rather than black dolls (Goleman, 1987).

Studies of subjective well-being—feelings of happiness and satisfaction with life as well as with family and friends—also have pointed to psychological debilitation among African Americans. A series of studies by Campbell and his associates have consistently reported lower levels of happiness and satisfaction among African Americans (Campbell, Converse, and Rodgers, 1976; Campbell, 1981). More recently, Thomas and Hughes showed that differences between whites and blacks on general life satisfaction, personal and marital happiness, trust in others, and anomia remained generally constant between 1972 and 1985 (Thomas & Hughes, 1986).

Some studies on locus of control also suggest that African Americans have a greater likelihood of believing that their success in school, as well as in life, is more generally controlled by external forces: powerful others, luck, or circumstances beyond their control. In a review of 31 studies comparing whites and blacks on locus of control, Sandra Graham (Graham, 1989) reports that 12 studies showed that blacks were significantly more likely than whites to believe that their lives were controlled by powerful outside forces. In the remaining 19 studies, she either found no significant differences or obtained mixed findings. In no study, however, were whites significantly more likely than blacks to believe that outside forces determined their successes or failures.

Findings such as these point to the conclusion that racial and ethnic subordination has negative effects on psychological well-being. Yet such a conclusion may be unwarranted, given the existence of considerable contradictory findings. Since the 1970s, for instance, most studies using pencil-and-paper tests fail to report lower levels of esteem among racial and ethnic minorities (Simmons, 1978; Foster & Perry, 1982; Fish & Larr, 1972; Baughman, 1971; Brigham, 1974; Heiss & Owens, 1972; Lerner & Buehrig, 1975; Rosenberg & Simmons, 1972). These studies contend that when socioeconomic status is controlled, the global self-esteem of blacks is at least as high as that of whites. This is true when average scores are compared as well as when dispersion around the mean is compared (Taylor & Walsh, 1979).

Sandra Graham, while recognizing the number of studies reporting lower levels of internal locus of control among blacks, asserts that methodological problems, coupled with the large number of studies that find mixed or no significant differences, force us away from making any generalizations about psychological well-being (Graham, 1989). For instance, the literature suggests that the lack of an internal sense of control is debilitating much in the same way that a sense of powerlessness is considered debilitating. Yet realizing that one has limited control may in fact be a realistic and accurate appraisal of a minority person's situation.

Studies of mental illness also suggest that ethnic and racial subordination has no effect on well-being. Warheit, Holzer and Avery (Warheit, Holzer, and Avery, 1975) examined the relationship between race and mental health on five scales of psychological disorder. Although they found significant differences favoring whites on all five scales—once age, sex, and, in particular, socioeconomic status were taken into account—racial differences persisted in only two of the five and on one of these significance was quite minimal. Robins et al. (Robins et al., 1984), in presenting findings from the National Institute of Mental Health sponsored Epidemiological Catchment Area project, reported that differences between rates of total disorders between blacks and other groups generally were not significant.

As is evident, the bulk of the empirical literature has focused on comparisons between whites and blacks. Because of this, we know very little about the psychological well-being of other racial and ethnic minorities. Yet the little evidence there is suggests that, as with blacks, there is apparently no clear relationship between subordinate status and psychological debilitation. For instance, with regard to Latinos, Roberts reports that any differences in the prevalence of nonspecific distress among people of Mexican origin can be accounted for largely by differences in socioeconomic and demographic circumstances (Roberts, 1987). He also reports that surveys conducted in Los Angeles have found little difference between Latinos and non-Hispanic whites with regard to clinical depression or total psychiatric impairment (Roberts, 1987).

GENDER SUBORDINATION AND PSYCHOLOGICAL WELL-BEING

A good deal of the research on women also points in the direction of psychological debilitation. Feminist Freudians such as Juliette Mitchell (Mitchell, 1975) contend that unconscious envy of the male status is a likely psychological consequence of gender subordination.

Some empirical work also points to psychological debilitation. An early study by Horner (Horner, 1972) asserted that women "have a motive to avoid success, that is a disposition to become anxious about achieving success because they expect negative consequences (such as social rejection and/or feeling of being unfeminine) as a result of succeeding." More recently, Steil (Steil, 1989) contends that unmarried as well as married women "suffer far greater mental hazards, and present a far worse clinical picture than married men." She points to a review of seventeen studies that found that married women fared better than unmarried women on tests of psychological well-being, although both fared significantly worse than married men.

Kessler and McRae (Kessler & McRae, 1981) agree that while most studies have consistently shown that women report higher levels of emotional distress than men, the differences have been declining as a function of contemporary changes in gender role expectations. They also document a reduction in the relationship between sex and psychophysiological symptoms.

Epidemiological studies of mental disorders present a somewhat different picture, however. In the National Institute of Mental Health sponsored Catchment Area Project, Regier and his associates (Regier et al., 1988) found that women showed slightly higher rates for all disorders combined. However, some important differences were evident when individual disorders were compared. Women had higher rates of affective, anxiety, and somatization disorders, while men had significantly higher rates of substance use and antisocial personality disorders. They concluded that men and women are more or less equally likely to experience mental disorders. The likelihood of a disorder does not vary by gender as much as the type of disorder.

Taking such conclusions a step further, Newmann (Newmann, 1984) challenges the finding that women are more likely to suffer affective disorders than men. Although she does not address the National Institute of Mental Health findings, she asserts that the significant gender differences often reported result from the greater likelihood that women will report relatively mild, clinically trivial, or normal symptoms of distress. Most scales used to measure depression include a sadness dimension. Sadness, she asserts, is not the same as clinical depression. When scores for sadness are eliminated, there is no significant difference in the depression scores of men and women. That is, she claims that the difference in the depression scores of men and women is largely in their willingness to express sadness, not in the likelihood of expressing other more serious symptoms.

GAY AND LESBIAN SUBORDINATION AND PSYCHOLOGICAL WELL-BEING

Research on lesbians and gays is marred by the apparent inability to draw representative samples. Most sampling either involves clinical samples or volunteers from the "out" lesbian and gay communities. Joseph Harry (Harry, 1990) has recently suggested an interesting way to get around these limits. Much as researchers add questions on gender, race, and socioeconomic status to their research instruments, they could simply add questions on sexual orientation. As far as I know, however, researchers studying the issue of psychological debilitation have not begun to do this.

Contemporary research among lesbians and gays is usually framed within the context of the question: "Does psychopathology bring about homosexuality?" Bieber and his associates (Bieber et al., 1962), who believed that homosexuality was pathological, found that homosexual men reported higher levels of gender confusion and insecurity about their masculinity during childhood and adolescence. By this means, he aimed to demonstrate the pathological origins of homosexuality.

The assumption that homosexual men and women are mentally disordered has been challenged. Beginning with the work of Evelyn Hooker, research continually has reported no significant differences in the psychological well-being of male homosexuals and heterosexuals (Hooker, 1957; Hooker, 1965; Weinberg & Williams, 1975). Contemporary studies of lesbians reach a similar conclusion (Hopkins, 1969; Oberstone & Sukoneck, 1976). Freedman (Freedman, 1971), for instance, found no significant difference in psychological adjustment between homosexual and heterosexual females.

Clinical evidence also indicates that there is no homosexual or heterosexual character type. According to Friedman (Friedman, 1988), homosexual, bisexuals, and heterosexuals exhibit the entire range of character types and structures, albeit possibly in somewhat different relative profiles.

Although most studies were framed to answer the question, "Does psychopathology cause homosexuality?" they can also be used to answer the question: "Do homosexuals suffer psychopathology as a result of prejudice and discrimination?" As they are correlational and only look at the joint occurrence of homosexuality and psychopathology, the results can be interpreted in the light of either question. Thus, studies that show no significant correlation between psychological well being and sexual orientation can be used to argue both that psychopathology does not cause homosexuality as well as that homosexuals are not more likely to suffer psychopathology as a result of subordination.

In a slightly different vein, some theorists assert that while homosexuals are not clinically disturbed, many nevertheless carry around with them stresses related to "internalized homophobia." Homophobia is usually described as an irrational and persistent fear or hatred of homosexuals or homosexual behavior (Gramick, 1983). Internalized homophobia is therefore used to describe the self-deprecating feelings homosexuals may hold about themselves or other homosexuals. Any inability to accept oneself, to come out, to couple, and to live a happy and contented life is often attributed to self-hate on the part of lesbians and gays (Hodges & Hutter, 1979). As fruitful as this concept may prove, to date there has been only one empirical study that bears on this theme. Kitzinger (Kitzinger, 1987), as part of a larger study on identity, found very little evidence of internalized homophobia among her nonrandom sample of lesbian adults. Thus, the degree to which internalized homophobia pervades and, moreover, psychologically debilitates homosexuals, lesbians, gays, or bisexuals is largely unknown.

SUMMARY AND IMPLICATIONS FOR PRACTICE

This review suggests that with the exception of socioeconomic status, there is no consistent evidence that subordinate status leads to psychological debilitation. Furthermore, with regard to social class status, it is not altogether clear the degree to which social factors related to inequality or selection factors related to genetic and individual traits are operating. Although some studies on race, gender, and sexual orientation point to psychological debilitation, many do not—or at least raise doubt as to its inevitability. Although there is evidence that ethnic minorities, women, and homosexuals may show different debilitating symptoms than people in superordinate statuses, there is little evidence that they have more symptoms or that their symptoms are worse. By extension, these findings also suggest that male status, majority status, and heterosexual status create little or no clear mental health advantage for their incumbents.

Although these conclusions are rooted in empirical evidence, they must be accepted with a good deal of caution. Researchers are in agreement that the definitive work on this subject is yet to be done. The number of studies is relatively small—especially when we step away from the realm of socioeconomic status—and their level of sophistication varies. Conceptual and methodological problems abound. Psychological debilitation can be operationalized in many ways and the ways in which it is operationalized may have a great deal to do with the outcome of a study. It must also be stressed that this is a highly politicized area of research, and the scientific method is more easily compromised under such circumstances. Class conflict, to use the Marxian phrase, is easily waged in the research arena. Any number of researchers contend that bias so pervades this area that little research can be accepted at face value (Adam, 1978b).

Nevertheless, the findings suggest that social inequality does not lead inevitably to psychological debilitation. They suggest that there is no one clear way by which people respond to their social status circumstances. Some among the subordinate will indeed become psychologically debilitated, but others will not. In like fashion, some among the superordinate will become strengthened, while others will not. Subordinate and superordinate statuses both appear to generate stress. For subordinates, the stress is associated with the desire to resist and improve their condition against a backdrop of limited opportunities. For superordinates, the stress is associated with the desire to maintain advantage and hold on to resources against a backdrop of challenging subordinates. The effect is that both subordinate and superordinate may be equally vulnerable to debilitation and equally capable of finding the resilience to maintain psychological balance.

These findings should not be taken to mean that social inequality is of no consequence in understanding the life chances of subordinate people. The effects of social stratification are seen daily in the material and political well-being of people. Segregation, prejudice, discrimination, stereotyping, inadequate housing, debt, and the ability to participate freely in community life all reflect inequality. The results uncovered here in no way diminish the suffering endured by the subordinated. They simply indicate that the suffering does not appear to lead to psychological debilitation.

It is clear that more research is needed to resolve the issues raised here. Yet social workers like myself, who want to convert research findings into practice generalizations, cannot afford the luxury of waiting for more research. The need to develop policy, programs, and interventions forces social workers to take the next step: What are the best practice generalizations that can be made given the present state of knowledge? The state of knowledge is not ideal but the following recommendations reflect what can be presently discerned.

First, it may be presumed that people of lower socioeconomic background will likely present greater mental health problems than people of higher socioeconomic background. The reasons for this are not altogether clear. It may be that class status is more central to psychological well-being than other statuses. Or it may be that historical conditions are operating today that protect people in other statuses while leaving lower-class people unprotected from psychological debilitation. Regardless of the reason, in working with people from lower socioeconomic status, progressive social workers cannot expect to solve their problems by simply working within an environmental or social causation framework. They will also have to be give attention to overcoming personal limitations; in other words, to helping individuals take better advantage of any opportunities made available to them.

Second, with regard to other subordinated groups, mental health services should not be promoted on the basis of any presumed greater need. Women, racial and ethnic minorities, and lesbians and gays do not appear to be at any greater risk for mental health problems than men, white European Americans and heterosexuals. They may need mental health services as individuals and/or because of their economic status but not because they are members of a group that is at higher risk of psychological debilitation.

Given this consideration, the findings bear on the growth of mental health services in the United States today. Kenneth Kenniston (Kenniston, 1968) argued that the community mental health movement put out the flames of the race rebellions of the 1960s by converting economic and political problems into mental health problems. The findings here suggest that racial and ethnic minorities, women, and lesbians and gays are, in general, more in need of economic, political, and social services than of mental health services.

Similarly, social workers outside the field of mental health should not anticipate that women, racial and ethnic minorities, and gays and lesbians will present particular challenges to effective service delivery because of any presumed psychological problems. Again, such problems may exist, but they should not be expected on the basis of group status alone.

Finally, the findings in no way mean that structural inequality is an irrelevant consideration for understanding psychological well-being. Rather, they mean that inequality itself is the problem—not subordination, not superordination, but the whole relationship of subordinate to superordinate.

Social inequality may be thought of as a stressor, a condition in the larger social environment that threatens the well-being of subordinate and superordinate alike. Like many perspectives—cognitive dissonance, balance theory, exchange and equity, anomie, role and reference group theory—a social psychology of inequality may turn out to be an indeterminate theory. How people will respond to the stress of inequality cannot be predicted simply from knowing their position in a status hierarchy. It will depend rather on a number of intervening bio-psycho-social factors including health and fitness, coping and adaptation abilities, and the existence of supportive peers, family, and community. At this point in history it appears that although people in lower socioeconomic positions are likely to become debilitated, those in other subordinated positions may not.

Our task as progressive social workers, then, is to assess the link between social stratification and psychological functioning and, in the event of finding a link, to intervene in ways that will improve psychological functioning. In so doing, social workers are likely to find themselves working not in behalf of subordinate people alone, but in behalf of helping subordinate and superordinate alike to eliminate the stress provoked by inequality and to produce a more equitable society.

Part IV

THEMES AND PERSPECTIVES

21

Themes and Perspectives on Integration and Related Models

Edwin J. Thomas

The papers and presentations given at the Integration Conference reflected great variety of content and diversity of perspective. I will make no effort to summarize the many interesting and informative individual presentations or to evaluate the merits of particular papers. Rather, my intent is to underscore and draw together some of the themes, perspectives, and approaches contained in the presentations and, in so doing, to place the contributions in a larger context. Papers for a selected number of the presentations appear as articles in this book. In addition to discussing and analyzing selected conference themes and perspectives in terms of how they reflect various aspects of integration, I will devote my remarks to the models of integration of social science (SS) and social work and welfare (SW/W) related to the conference presentations, to some of the more general implications, and to consideration of areas for further work.

SELECTED THEMES AND PERSPECTIVES

It became clear early on that it would be a challenge to identify and group the diversity of themes and to relate them to the integration of SW/W and SS in a meaningful fashion. However, when viewed more broadly, some of the seemingly unrelated topics began to fall in place. Some of the presentations were addressed largely to SS, to SW/W, or to aspects of the social context (e.g., social, cultural, economic, and political conditions, including values and ideology). Other presentations discussed topics which involved the relationships between SS, SW/W, and/or the social context. The various topics and their relationships suggested a framework for depicting and analyzing problems of integration, which is presented in Figure 21.1.

In this framework, the principal components that may be objects of analysis are SS (A in Figure 21.1), SW/W (B), or the social context (C), along with the relationships between these components (linkages 1–6). Because the three components and connecting linkages form something of a triangle, they may be thought of as the *integration triangle*. Although all parts and relationships in the triangle are relevant to SS and SW/W, as broadly conceived, some are more central to the SS-SW/W connection itself. Thus, if one's interest is mainly in the interface of SS and SW/W, linkage 1, from SS to SW/W, and linkage 2, from SW/W to SS, can be viewed as primary. These are complementary linkages that represent the events, influences, and information that directly serve to connect and bring SS and SW/W together. In the case of linkage 1, three types of potential contribution of SS to SW/W are represented in Figure 21.1—the substantive (e.g., a sociological theory), the methodological (e.g., a psychological instrument to assess spouse abuse), and the organizational (e.g., a morale-enhancing organizational structure). The addition of the social context broadens the scope of analysis considerably, now bringing in the possible influences of the social context on SS (linkage 3) and on SW/W (linkage 4).[1] Although generally at least one step removed from the SS-SW/W interface itself, these relationships nonetheless may have important implications for the SS-SW/W connection. The breadth of analysis is further extended by introducing the possible impact of SS and SW/W on the social context (linkages 5 and 6, respectively).[2] These latter influences, of course, generally would be related only remotely to integration unless they could be shown to affect some aspect of the social context in such a way as to have an impact on SS, SW/W, or their relationship.

The triangle framework provides a basis for discussing and organizing conference content and themes. Selected themes and perspectives reflected in the conference presentations are discussed below as they relate to each of the three components (social context, SS, and SW/W) and to the relationships between them. Any given presentation could illustrate one or more themes or perspectives.

Social Context

In their descriptions of conditions in different countries, the international presenters (Jamrozik, Mak and Nai-ming, and Ramon, chapters 6 and 19, 14, and 15 in this book, respectively; Malaka, 1992; Zimakova, 1992) made amply clear the impact of nation states, as geopolitical entities, on aspects of the social context within which SW/W and SS are carried out. Many of these presenters highlighted the importance of values and ideology found in their home nations. Other presentations addressed equity issues such as information as a scarce resource (Katz, 1992), human resources as a valuable commodity (Jamrozik, chapter 19), and feminist concerns (Abramovitz, chapter 18; Alvarez et al., 1992; Mildred, 1992). In his analysis of models of the relationship between knowledge in society and social betterment, Price (Chapter 3) summarized conceptions of society as a machine, an arena of conflict, and a system of cultural symbols, concluding with some implications for integration problems. As I will illustrate further, most of these presentations reflected major changes taking place in conditions of the social context and in aspects of the SS and SW/W relationship.

Figure 21.1
The Integration Triangle for Analyzing Problems Relating to the Integration of Social Work/Welfare and Social Science

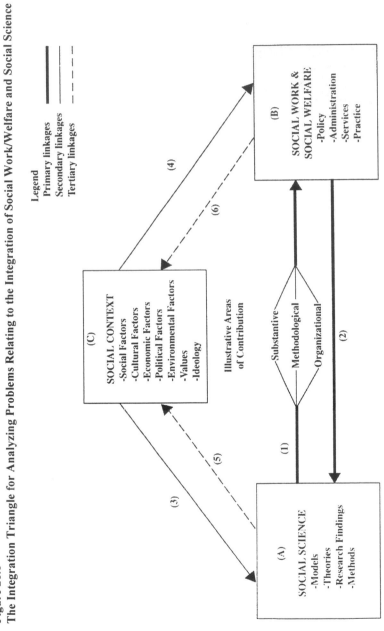

Social Context and Social Science

Some of the presentations also underlined the impact of social context and nation states on SS (linkage 3 in Figure 21.1). Several touched on the biasing effect of the university reward system and environment on the conduct of SS research (Jamrozik, chapter 6; Dolgon, Dresser, and Kline, 1992). With focus on its impact on social inequality, Jamrozik analyzed the effect of government funding in Australia on the research agenda, on the utilization and dissemination of research findings, and on the way research is viewed. In her feminist interpretation of the effects of divorce on children, Mildred (1992) examined how the patriarchal nuclear family can affect the ways in which problems of divorce and its correlates are perceived, defined, conceptualized, and studied.

In contrast to the above, little was mentioned on the reverse impact—namely, that of SS on the social context (linkage 5 in Figure 21.1). An exception was Jamrozik's emphasis on the power of SS research findings to influence the viewpoints of government representatives and officials and the public at large, influences which he said can help shape policy on such matters as social inequality (chapter 19).

Social Context and Social Work/Social Welfare

The influence of nation states on SW/W was also amply illustrated in the presentations (linkage 4 in Figure 21.1). Ramon (chapter 15) underscored differences in SW/W with the mentally ill as practiced in northern, southern, and Eastern Europe. Zimakova (1992) discussed the effects in Russia of changes of the ruling party and the economy on social welfare (SW/W was a field that did not exist as we know it in the former Soviet Union), on poverty, and on the nature of other social problems. Mak and Nai-ming (chapter 14) indicated that SW/W in Hong Kong is moving increasingly toward privatization, reflecting western free-market influences. However, in anticipation of Hong Kong's imminent reunion with the Communist mainland, Mak and Nai-ming suggested that it is also drawing more on Marxist theory—an irony that itself should certainly qualify as a Marxist social contradiction. In her examination of South African SW/W, Malaka (1992) illustrated how one may attempt to realize first-world SW/W principles in the third world through local adaptation and cultural sensitivity. Jamrozik (chapter 19) indicated how the use (and misuse) of human resources in Australia should be viewed as an emerging problem area. The effects of postmodern conditions on the nature of community practice in the United States were detailed in the paper by Fisher and Kling (chapter 8). Dolgon et al. (1992) outlined how the plight of the homeless and housing policies relating to them in Ann Arbor, Michigan, may be adversely affected by contemporary federal, state, university, and local policies. The human problems to be addressed and the potential human service solutions were thus seen as highly dependent on the contextual factors operating in the nation state and its constituent communities.

The reverse impact, now of SW/W on the social context (linkage 6 of Figure 21.1), was far removed from most of the presentations. However, Jamrozik (chapter 6) underscored what he termed a retreat from social explanations in

Australian SW/W and the absence of related SW/W research, which, he said, unwittingly and indirectly served to help sustain inequality in that country.

Social Science

The conference represented the contributions of most of the social sciences—particularly psychology and sociology, but also social psychology, economics, political economy, and anthropology. The dominant model of social inquiry was the scientific method as developed in SS for the particular methodological and substantive issues at hand. However, several presentations critically evaluated the adequacy of applying the SS methods. For example, in his analysis of 72 dissertation papers presented at the Ohio State University Conference on Dissertation Research, Boettcher (chapter 5) judged that 28 of the dissertations employed no theory and, altogether, did not reflect a step-by-step, cumulative building of knowledge. Gambrill's analysis (chapter 2) highlighted the nature of science, its continuing relevance to SW/W, the requirements of scientific method that can easily be slighted, the self-correcting role of scientific inquiry, and the importance of critical and clear thinking in carrying out integration.

Bernstein, Goodman, and Epstein (chapter 11) made reference also to grounded theory and research and Mak and Nai-ming (chapter 14) referred to critical social theory. Feminist theory emerged in the conference as a prominent approach to selected social and scientific questions. Abramovitz (chapter 18), for example, traced social influences on the family and indicated how the model of the patriarchal family may foster gender bias in SS theory, methods, and findings.

The research methods employed in the studies presented were largely those of social science. These methods included conventional field studies and surveys, multivariate modeling, and the apparent rediscovery of qualitative inquiry, participant observation, and inductive methods of developing theory. Particular perspectives on the interpretation and reinterpretation of findings were found in the form of deconstructionist and constructionist analyses (Abramovitz, chapter 18; Dolgon, Dresser, and Kline, 1992; Franklin, 1992; Mildred, 1992). Mace (chapter 12) presented some of the concepts of chaos/complexity theory along with speculations about their possible implications for SW/W.

Social Work and Social Welfare

Diverse perspectives on practice were evident in the conference presentations. In addition to some of the more familiar models of SW/W practice and action were those that placed emphasis on the reflective practitioner (Bernstein et al., chapter 11), the ethnographic/practitioner (Laird, 1992), action research (Lauffer, chapter 17; Weingarten, 1992), use of a management information system in management decision-making (Sheinfeld Gorin and Viswanathan, chapter 9), individual and political empowerment (Gutiérrez, chapter 13), feminist therapy (Alvarez et al., 1992), and the relevance of using local and indigenous knowledge, including what Hartman called subjugated knowledge (Hartman, 1992). Each of these perspectives implied or asserted an emphasis on the ways in which SS and practice/action could be linked. Further details of these perspectives are elaborated below in connection with a discussion of models of integration.

Areas of Relationship/Contribution Between Social Science and Social Work/Welfare

A few of the papers pointed to general problems of integration between SS and SW/W. For example, Gambrill (chapter 2) stressed the importance of the scientific perspective and of thinking strategies that may be employed in practice as critical needs relating to integration. She noted challenges and obstacles to integration that include poor and nonscientific thinking, hasty integration, and the role of conflicting goals and values.

In recognition of the many contrasts between a scientific discipline and a practice profession, Flynn reminded us of differences between economics as an discipline and social work as a profession (Flynn, 1992). Along similar lines, Laws and Rein (chapter 4) indicated that because of the differences between scientific and therapeutic thinking, action and doing can be "crowded out" in favor of analysis; knowledge and practice can become disjointed; and antagonism between SW/W and SS can thereby be engendered. Differences such as these point to some of the problems for which models and methods of integration are required and, indeed, are some of the reasons this conference was convened in the first place.

In contrast to the more general presentations, most papers on SS-SW/W relationships illustrated a particular substantive, methodological, or organizational contribution connecting SS to SW/W (linkage 1 in Figure 21.1). In regard to substantive contributions, Brower and Nurius (chapter 7) drew on theory from cognitive psychology and self theory in their practice conception. In addition to findings from social psychology, Longres (chapter 20) reviewed the literature on gender, socioeconomic status, and racial factors as they relate to possible psychological debilitation; Gutiérrez (chapter 13) covered selected psychological and social psychological factors as they pertain to empowerment; Lambert (chapter 10) presented her survey research findings bearing on the effects of family policies on worker appreciation; and Laird drew on anthropological concepts in her analysis of gay and lesbian families (Laird, 1992).

In regard to possible methodological contributions, the use of SS research methods to gather, assess, and evaluate data for purposes of enhancing practice was illustrated in the presentations that focused on grounded practice (Bernstein et al., chapter 11), action research (Lauffer, chapter 17; Weingarten, 1992), and gathering ethnographic data (Laird, 1992).

Turning now to organizational avenues of integration, Laws and Rein (chapter 4) advocated forums by which theorists, practitioners, and policy makers would get together to try to reduce the distance between practice, theory, and policy. Mak and Nai-ming (chapter 14) indicated that in Hong Kong, social scientists (or philosophers) and social workers co-taught social work courses. An educational model for integrating social work and social science is, of

Table 21.1
Models of Integration of Social Science and Social Work/Welfare

Model	Objectives	Illustrative Methods	Outcomes
Research Utilization	To analyze research utilization processes with an eye toward improving the understanding and methods of utilization in SW/W and related fields	Identify the processes, tactics, and strategies involved in research utilization to determine practices and patterns and to formulate utilization guidelines	Methods and guidelines to select, review, appraise, synthesize, generalize, operationalize, and transform for application and use SS and SW/W research findings relevant to SW/W
Social Research	To conduct social research on SS research issues relevant to SW/W and/or to conduct social research on SW/W problems	Formulate the research problem, select the sample, research site, method, technique, data gathering and analysis methods, and analyze and interpret findings.	SS research findings having application to SW/W and/or SW/W research findings relevant to SW/W
Action Research	To conduct practice/action and research	Gather research data relevant to practice/action, analyze the data, and utilize findings to prepare and implement intervention	Practice change and/or action outcome related research findings
Developmental Research	To design and develop new human service interventions	Conduct human service problem analysis, review state of the art, and design, pilot test, develop, evaluate, and disseminate the intervention	New human service interventions, practice and/or policy.
Sociopolitical Change	To achieve sociopolitical change consistent with a major change goal, such as achieving greater social justice, and to conduct scholarly and/or empirical research, as appropriate	Formulate the value/ideological position, identify issues of existing knowledge, research and/or practice/policy, reconceptualize (or deconstruct) issues, conduct inquiry or apply SS, construct alternative interpretations and evolve practice/policy doctrines and practice methods consistent with the change goal	Practice, action, policy, and/or sociopolitical change and/or research consistent with the change goal

Cont. Table

Empirical Practice	To assess and intervene with practice problems, and, where appropriate, also to conduct related practice research	Use appropriate SS research methods to assess, monitor, and evaluate practice outcomes, including single-case experimental designs, and apply relevant SS theory and research findings in practice	Practice outcomes and, when also targeted, related research findings
Ecological Analysis	To further the ecological understanding of SS, SW/Wand their ecological dynamics with the social and physical environment	Describe, analyze, and explain the ecological units, processes, and interdependencies relating to SS, SW/W, and their relationship, drawing on relevant SS, physical science, and related knowledge and to make related, practical applications	Theory and research findings relevant to understanding the ecological factor relating to SS, SW/W, and their relationship, and/or related practical applications
Education	To provide education and/or training in SS and/or SW/W that provides for the integration of SS and SW/W	Study SS having applications to SW/W and/or SW/W in which there are contributions from SS, conduct SS research on SW/W practice using SS contributions, and/or participate in other integration experiences (e.g., practicums, seminars, projects)	Products, such as research findings, practice/policy outcomes or course syllabi, training programs, and/or curricula; and knowledge and skills utilizing SS and SW/W, conducting research having SW/W applications carrying out practice informed by SS contributions and/or providing education/training that drawn on the integration of SS and SW/W

course, the University of Michigan Doctoral Program in Social Work and Science. Along with selected contextual factors, Vinter and Sarri (chapter 22) described aspects of the past and present status of the Michigan model of integrating social work and social science.

While the main emphases of the above examples involved the contribution of SS to SW/W, there were a few presentations that touched on the opposite direction of influence, namely, the contributions of SW/W to SS (linkage 2 in Figure 21.1). As one means of making good theory, Laws and Rein (chapter 4) advocated starting with practice to see how it could challenge theory. Ramon (chapter 15) recommended a social-systems perspective when examining individual and family problems. Abramovitz (chapter 18) saw feminist theory as one means of equalizing the relationship between SW/W and SS and as a way to challenge existing SS theory. In their presentation of the integration of feminist theory with practice as it relates to a graduate certificate program, Alvarez and her associates (1992) advocated bringing feminist theory and practice together with equal status. In this view, a principle of feminist practice is to use the process of praxis, which was described as entailing a dynamic interplay of community-based action, reflection, and then theory construction. Hartman (1992) appealed to social workers to make greater use of local and indigenous knowledge, with the implication that such knowledge would enhance SW/W practice and complement SS.

MODELS OF INTEGRATION

Just as the presentations embraced a broad range of topics and themes, so did many of the offerings reflect different models of integration. However, although many of the papers could be viewed as being illustrative of a model, there were few that actually articulated the general characteristics of a model or were explicitly connected to a model. Hence, the different models of connecting SS and SW/W generally had to be inferred from particular papers. In this analysis, a model of the integration of SS and SW/W consists of a systematic and distinctive approach to linking contributions of SS to SW/W or of SW/W to SS, or both. In terms of the integration triangle of Figure 21.1, most of the models to be described illustrate an approach to connecting SS to SW/W (linkage 1) or of SW/W to SS (linkage 2), or both. My review of the conference offerings indicated that there were one or more presentations that illustrated or suggested one or another of eight integration models, as outlined in Table 21.1. As will be seen, some of these models are well established whereas others are more provisional and tentative. While the models embrace the more general frameworks suggested by the conference presentations and cover considerable variation of approach, there may be others that merit conceptualization.

As formulated in the table, each model has distinctive objectives, characteristic methods, and outcomes. While space does not permit elaboration here, most of the approaches have a history and identifying literature, although not necessarily in the context of the integration of SW/W and SS. The formulation of integration models thus provides another way of ordering conference contributions in terms of their broader context.

The Research Utilization Process Model

The *research utilization model* emphasizes the processes, tactics, and strategies involved in such activities as selecting, appraising, generalizing, operationalizing, and transforming SS contributions for application and use, drawing mainly on the substantive theoretical and empirical research findings from one or another of the social sciences. Where related to this model, most presentations were based on the application of substantive SS findings to given substantive SS findings to given SW/W problems (Brower & Nurius, Gutiérrez, Longres, chapters 7, 13, 20, respectively; Laird, 1992). The biasing effects of a patriarchal society on SS utilization provided a different perspective on the utilization process (Abramovitz, chapter 18; Mildred, 1992). Deconstructionist and constructionist approaches would appear to be relevant here. Related more generally to knowledge utilization approaches, the methodology of research utilization has been given a great deal of attention and is one of the dominant models of integration (for example, see Gouldner, 1957; Reid & Fortune, 1982; Rubin & Rosenblatt, 1979; Grasso & Epstein, 1992; Glaser, Abelson, and Garrison, 1983; Havelock, 1973; Kirk, 1990; Rothman, 1974; Thomas, 1964; Thomas, 1967; Tripodi, 1974; Tripodi, 1983; Tripodi & Epstein, 1980; Tripodi, Fellin, and Meyer, 1969).

Research-related Models

Social research is a model of integration, inasmuch as the research draws mainly or exclusively on the research methodology of SS, as broadly viewed. Use of SS research methods is identified in Figure 21.1 as a methodological contribution of SS to SW/W. Although not always thought of as a type of integration—perhaps because it is so familiar—social research nevertheless is one of the earliest and perhaps most widely employed means of linking SS and SW/W. As may be seen in the description of objectives for this model given in the table, it may take one of two forms. In the first, the social research methodology is employed in SS to conduct social research on SS issues relevant to SW/W whereas, in the other, social research methodology is used in SW/W to conduct inquiry into SW/W problems. While the objectives and possible outcomes differ, the social research methodology is common to both forms and differs only in how it is applied to the problems investigated.[3] Examples include the reports by Bernstein et al. (chapter 11), based on qualitative inquiry and participant observation, by Lambert (chapter 10), drawn from survey questionnaire data, and by Powell et al. (1992) and Robinson (Robinson, 1992), based on field studies.

Whereas most SS research is planned and carried out independently from the practical domain to which it may apply, *action research* is conducted in close connection with the action it is intended to help guide. This approach to the research-practice/action interface is also well established and recognized in the literature (Argyris, 1970; Corey, 1954; French & Bell, 1973; Lewin, 1946). Conference illustrations of the action research model are Lauffer's paper on action research and planned change, the study of Powell et al. (1992), and the projects on participatory action research described by Weingarten (1992) and Dolgon et al. (1992). These presentations also included some descriptions of aspects of the action research methodology as they applied it to the problem areas they discussed.

As distinguished from SS research, the *developmental research* model is directed toward the objective of designing and developing new human service interventions and employs a distinctive methodology for that purpose (for example, see Mullen, 1981; Mullen, 1994; Paine, Bellamy, and Wilcox, 1984; Reid, 1979; Reid, 1994; Rothman, 1980; Rothman & Thomas, 1994; Thomas, 1978; Thomas, 1984; Thomas, 1990; Whittaker & Pecora, 1981). Among the phases of developmental research are those of intervention problem analysis, design, development, evaluation, and dissemination. Conference examples pertain largely to aspects of interventive design. For example, Gutiérrez's endeavor (chapter 13) to formulate an empowerment approach to practice was based not only on relevant findings from psychology and social psychology, but also on that author's qualitative inquiry and her review of current practice relating to empowerment. With these contributions and others, Gutiérrez proposed an intervention framework for empowerment that had particular change goals, processes, and constituent practice methods. Vinokur Kaplan (chapter 16) drew on current research and practice relating to the team effectiveness method, with emphasis on how this approach to teams could be incorporated into SW/W education and practice. In this transfer to SW/W of team-effectiveness methodology, design and development are necessarily involved in making proper applications.

Practice/Change-related Models

While the other models here certainly have social and political implications, none is necessarily addressed largely and expressly to achieving sociopolitical change. Examples of sociopolitical objectives in the *sociopolitical change* model would be to change inequalities due to such factors as gender, race, ethnicity, sexual orientation, class, culture, disability status, religion, or the distribution of income and other valued resources. Illustrative presentations are those relating to feminist approaches (Abramovitz, chapter 18; Alvarez et al., 1992; Mildred, 1992), and Franklin's deconstruction of problems often attributed to African Americans (Franklin, 1992).

An additional identifying feature of this model is a strong and central value and ideological position (e.g., the doctrines of feminism or neo-Marxism), which is also likely not to be dominant or mainstream (e.g., the feminist positions put forth in the presentations by Abramovitz, chapter 18 this book. See also Alvarez et al., 1992 and the offering on the politics of empowerment for the homeless presented by Dolgon et al., 1992). Another characteristic of this approach would appear to be the explicit reconceptualization of knowledge, where appropriate, including some contributions of SS. For example, Abramovitz and Mildred identified selected gender and patriarchal biases in existing SS knowledge and SW/W practices; and, like Franklin and Dolgon et al., they deconstructed the knowledge and/or practices they thought were objectionable. These presenters then constructed alternative interpretations of the problems that were more consistent with their value and ideological positions.

Action research is also a practice/change model inasmuch as it has social action as an objective (see Table 21.1 and the discussion above on action research as a research model).

Empirical practice is another practice/change model. It is a major contemporary approach to practice in which the practice methods include conducting practice empirically and evaluating it as an integral part of the practice (Barlow, Hayes, and Nelson, 1984; Berlin & Marsh, 1993; Bloom, 1975; Bloom, Fischer, and Orme, 1994; Blythe & Tripodi, 1989; Briar, 1979; Corcoran & Fischer, 1987; Fischer & Hudson, 1983; Gingerich, 1990; Hersen & Barlow, 1976; Hudson, 1982; Jayaratne & Levy, 1979; Mutschler, 1979; Reid, 1994; Schinke, 1983; Thomas, 1975; Tripodi & Epstein, 1980; Wodarski, 1981).[4] To help understand and intervene with practice problems, selected SS research methods, such as those of applied behavior analysis, are used in assessment prior to intervention; appropriate SS and research findings are applied in practice; and practice outcomes are evaluated following intervention, often using single-case experimental designs. There were no presentations that clearly exemplified this model. However, in her paper on integration, Gambrill's approach to practice followed from an empirical stance and was otherwise consistent with this model.

The Ecological Model

Although an ecological perspective in one or another of its expressions has gained considerable currency in SW/W, to my knowledge there has been no recognized application to date of this perspective to problems of the integration of SW/W and SS.[5] With focus on furthering their ecological understanding, an *ecological* model of integration may be provisionally defined as one in which SS, SW/W, and particularly their relationship are analyzed and studied in the larger context of the surrounding influences on the SS discipline, the profession and institution of SW/W, and those of the social and environmental context more generally. Unlike the other models, an ecological model should be particularly applicable to the description, analysis, and explanation of ecological units, processes, and relationships involving SS and SW/W. The other models, in contrast, are largely systematic methodologies for carrying out such activities as research, research utilization, practice/action, and education, which serve to link SS with SW/W.

Considered now from an ecological perspective, the integration triangle in Figure 21.1 may be seen as a general representation of aspects of possible ecological entities (i.e., SS, SW/W, and the social context) and constituent avenues of influence and relationship (i.e., linkages 1-6), again with linkages 1 and 2 being central. As the reader is aware, the figure has been used here as an analytic framework for helping to order and analyze conference themes and topical areas, not as an explanatory framework from an ecological perspective. Even so, the integration triangle should be sufficient at this point to illustrate the general outlines of an ecological model for the integration area.

Although there was also no conference paper that clearly exemplified an ecological model of integration, several papers addressed integration problems in a broader, more ecological context (Abramovitz, Jamrozik, and Price, chapters 18, 6 and 19, respectively). For example, Abramovitz, as indicated, touched on how social context factors influenced the patriarchal family and the role of women in society and how these conditions, in turn, influenced SW/W policy, SS theory and research, and the SS-SW/W relationship. Many of the presentations examined more limited topics, ranging from aspects of the social context vis-à-vis SS or SW/W, to single aspects of the social context (e.g., conditions in a given nation state), SW/W, or SS, to features of the SS-SW/W relationship itself.

The Educational Model

The *educational* model provides for the integration of SS and SW/W through education, in which training is given in SS relevant to SW/W, or in SW/W in which SS contributions have been included, or in both. At least since the 1960s, there has been increasing use of SS in SW/W, with pairing of the two much less common in SS. Education, of course, includes such familiar activities as classroom instruction, practicums in research and/or practice, demonstrations, reading assignments, papers, and projects. As Table 21.1 indicates, however, integration through education requires particular training methods and substantive and/or methodological linkages between SS and SW/W in order for the educational experiences to provide the training likely to make possible the attainment of the integrated knowledge, skills, and other outcomes noted in the table. Although there are many ways to endeavor to achieve integration through education, the Doctoral Program in Social Work and Social Science of the University of Michigan stands as an example of a program designed expressly to provide doctoral training in the integration of SW/W and SS (see chapter 22).

The models described above clearly differ considerably. Each has its distinctive objectives, characteristic methods, and intended outcomes, and thus each could be relevant depending upon the integration issue and one's goals. Although any of the models could well be the exclusive focus of work, aspects of most of the models, in principal, could be used with aspects of others. For example, the research utilization process could well be an essential component in employing any of the other models, and social research could be used along with most of the other models. The developmental research and sociopolitical change models do not necessarily preclude the use of aspects of any of the other models. When viewed in the context of education for integration, models suggest potential approaches and areas around which the integration component of an educational program could be structured.

SUMMARY, IMPLICATIONS, AND CONCLUSIONS

The striking diversity of themes and perspectives covered in the conference presentations raised several challenging questions for me that were not otherwise addressed in any of the conference papers or, for that matter, in most other writings on integration. These questions were (a) what is the subject matter of the integration of SS and SW/W; (b) what, if anything, is the relationship of the many diverse topics to some of the major areas of prior work on integration; and (c), given some tentative answers to the above questions, what are the implications for further work? These questions, of course, are ambitious, but they are important enough to merit trying to come up with some responses for them, however provisional the answers must be at this point. The approach followed in this paper was to endeavor to place the conference contributions in a larger context, including that of the integration subject matter.

To draw together the many varied themes, perspectives, and approaches contained in the presentations, a framework for analyzing and ordering the topics of the presentations was formulated. The principal components of this integration triangle that could be objects of analysis in this framework were SS, SW/W, and the social context, along with the six relationships between these components, as shown earlier in Figure 21.1. These components plus their linking relationships can be seen as one approach to identifying the general topical domain of integration. Each aspect of this domain may be a focus of analysis bearing some relationship to integration now broadly conceived as a specialized, multidisciplinary field of knowledge and research. Although all parts are considered to be important, some aspects in the integration domain are viewed as more central than others. Thus, the complementary linkages of SW/W to SS and, particularly, of SS to SW/W were seen as primary to, if not the defining conditions for, integration. In contrast, however important otherwise, the components themselves and the linkages from the social context to SS and SW/W and, particularly, of SS and SW/W to the social context were considered to be potentially less central, depending upon whether and how their topics were related to the SS-SW/W relationship itself.

The results of ordering conference topics in terms of the integration triangle are necessarily dependent on the characteristics of the particular papers selected for this conference and their topical designations. Within these limits, however, some distinctive emphases emerged. The disciplines, scientific perspectives, findings, and research methods of SS were well represented but, interestingly, with some other types of knowledge touched on as well (e.g., feminist theory, subjugated knowledge, chaos/complexity theory, constructionist analyses). Only a few of the familiar approaches of SW/W practice and action were represented, again along with some less conventional perspectives (e.g., the reflective practitioner, feminist therapy.) Many of the presentations pertained to the SS-SW/W relationship itself including, especially, the substantive, methodological, and organizational contributions of SS to SW/W. However, very few presentations made reference to the possible contributions of SW/W to SS. There was strong emphasis of the social context (e.g., the characteristics of nation states and ideology and values) and their influence on SS and SW/W.[6] In contrast, the influence of SS and SW/W on the social context was not found in the large majority of presentations.

In addition to their topical connections to integration, the papers were seen as being illustrative of one or another model of integration. Each model consists of a systematic and distinctive approach to linking contributions of SS to SW/W or of SW/W to SS, or both. The eight models, as outlined in Table 21.1, were research utilization, a model of the research utilization process; the research-related models of social research, action research, and developmental research; the practice/change related models of sociopolitical change and empirical practice; and the models of ecological analysis and education. As the particular means of achieving integration, all the models (except that of ecological analysis) are in effect the methodologies that have evolved for carrying out the integration activities of research, research utilization, or practice/change of one type or other or for providing education in SS and SW/W.

When cast as models, it was easier to see the relationship of the conference presentations to prior work in the integration area. Identification of integration models was particularly appropriate in light of the fact that very few conference papers actually articulated the general characteristics of a model or connected their topics in any substantial way to prior work on integration. Models in which there are relatively well-established areas of prior research are social research and action research and, to a lesser extent, research utilization, developmental research, and education. One of the best developed contemporary areas of integration involves the model of empirical practice, which was not represented in the presentations. In contrast, there were two models represented in which there has been relatively little prior work involving integration, these being sociopolitical change and ecological analysis.

In conclusion, the analyses here of the conference presentations provide a basis for formulating a general conception of the integration of SW/W and SS. In this conception, integration may be seen as having three related facets. In the first, although still not well developed, integration is a specialized, multidisciplinary field of knowledge and research. Its subject matter, as captured, for example, by the integration triangle, consists of the three principle components of SS, SW/W, and the social context, along with the six linking relationships between the components. Of primary importance in this triangle is the relationship of SS and SW/W.

The second facet is the integration methodology of linking SS and SW/W as reflected in the integration models relating to research, research utilization, practice/change, and education. These are the practical and systematic means by which SS and SW/W are linked and which serve in effect as the methods to guide and realize integration efforts.

The third facet is the integration activities themselves that are carried out by the individuals and others in such areas as research, research utilization, practice/change, and education. The integration activities may range widely in terms of the extent to which they actually serve to link SW/W and SS. Although closely related in principle, these three facets are arenas of integration that may or may not be in synchrony, especially at this early stage.

DIRECTIONS FOR FURTHER WORK

Although SS is increasingly accepted and used in many applied fields and in society at large, much remains to be done to realize the full potentialities of mutual enrichment in the SS and SW/W relationship. If integration is regarded as a desirable and essential practice activity in SW/W and SS, while otherwise still retaining the independence and integrity of each, then work should be oriented toward extending and enhancing the integration of SS and SW/W in such applicable areas as research, research utilization, practice/change, and education.

Considered as a methodology to achieve integration, further effort is needed to explicate and document the methodological details for the areas of integration associated with the models and to conduct and evaluate projects to extend and strengthen the models of integration. There are many unresolved integration problems for which new or different linking methodologies should be evolved. One of these is the continuing difficulty in achieving sufficient utilization of relevant research, a shortcoming for many years now that has engendered much puzzlement, regret, and lamentation in SW/W and many other applied endeavors.

With a view to creating a specialized, multidisciplinary field of knowledge and research, some beginnings have been made, particularly in earlier writings on research and knowledge utilization, in articles in this book, and in the prior work done on some of the integration models. However, there are many needed areas of further work. Among these are the following:

- To pull together and consolidate prior contributions to the integration of SW/W and SS through a systematic review of past and current integration approaches and methods, thus providing a stronger knowledge base for cumulative development of this area;

- To examine possibilities and issues relating to the possible integration of biological and social science perspectives at the different levels of system analysis and intervention;

- To look into the relationship of SS and SW/W to other types of knowledge (e.g., ethics, personal experience, values, religious faith) and the implications for the integration of SS with SW/W;

- To present major, novel advances in the substantive perspectives and research methodologies of the diverse social sciences, with focus on their implications for the SS-SW/W connection;

- To examine the contributions of such areas as computer and information science, meta-analysis, and multilevel analysis in light of their implications for addressing problems of integration; and

- To conduct research on the initiation, utilization, application, and maintenance of integration practices as employed by practitioners, researchers, social scientists, and other end-users to determine how the results of integration are employed and the conditions that facilitate and maintain given forms of integrating SS and SW/W.

ACKNOWLEDGMENTS

This chapter is based on my closing remarks delivered at the First Annual Conference on the Integration of Social Work and Social Science held at the University of Michigan, October 29–November 1, 1992.

NOTES

1. It is recognized that the influences of the social context can be pervasive in the social environment of SS and SW/W. However, they would be represented differently if

Figure 21.1 were intended to depict aspects of an explanatory or causal model rather than an analytic framework. The objects of analysis here are topical areas, each of which is represented with a rectangle or with a line between rectangles to indicate linkage between topics.

2. Although it goes beyond the purview of this chapter, the framework also may aid in analyzing more complex configurations of linkages (e.g., chains, loop backs, multiple connections).

3. Although differing in their objects of analysis, the methods, techniques and other aspects of the research methodology of SW/W are essentially indistinguishable from selected research methods and techniques of the different disciplines of SS, as examination of any SW/W research text or study will indicate (Grinnell, 1985). Hence, the generic use here of the term social research.

4. There are also organizational and administrative counterparts of an empirical practice (Patti, Poertner, and Rapp, 1987).

5. However, pieces of this ecological domain have been studied for some time, but under different guises. For example, there have been prior SS examinations of context factors bearing on SW/W (Wilensky & Lebeaux, 1958) and on the relationship of SW/W and SS (Meyer, Litwak, Thomas, and Vinter, 1967) as well as sociological, political and economic analyses that have addressed substantive issues corresponding to what is viewed here as one or another of the linkages depicted in Figure 21.1.

6. The addition of an international dimension to the conference no doubt also contributed to the heavy emphasis on social-context factors.

Part V

A HISTORY OF EDUCATIONAL INTEGRATION IN ONE PROGRAM

22

Doctoral Education in Social Work and Social Science at Michigan

Robert D. Vinter and Rosemary Sarri

Approximately thirty-five years ago, the first students were admitted to the Joint Doctoral Program in Social Work and Social Science at the University of Michigan. The joint program was launched at a time when professional social work nearly everywhere was seeking both a more assured place within the modern university and a rapprochement with the social sciences. We heeded related efforts as they unfolded on other campuses. But we felt that ours was a broader mission: to serve as a crucible in advancing a "more perfect integration" between social work and the social sciences that would transcend our university and contribute to the well-being of society.

The program continues to be the only truly joint social work and social science advanced degree program, and its unique features continue to attract attention from colleagues at other universities. The distinguishing features of the program and its distinctive accomplishments, therefore, have a more general import for understanding the fundamental problem posed by attempts to foster the integration of social work and social science.

This chapter presents an account of the origins of the program, a review of its primary aims and provisions, an analysis of its developments and achievements over the intervening decades, and a consideration of the program's possible future challenges. It is neither an "official" chronicle of the joint program nor an historical examination of the larger events shaping social work and the social sciences over these decades. While colleagues have graciously offered suggestions and criticisms to prior drafts, we assume full responsibility for focusing on some matters more than others and for our interpretations and assessments.

Components of our framework should be stated at the onset. The first relates to the *contexts* within which we examine the history and evolution of the program. The second component refers to its *significance* for graduate education in social work and social science, and the third involves the *premises* that guided our approach. Figure 22.1 portrays the contexts in which the program is located. The largest is the overarching societal context within which graduate education takes place. The smaller contexts are "social welfare" and "social science" denoting the organizations, constituencies, and cultures that comprise these societal systems. Within these entities are located the "social work profession" and the several "social science disciplines": bodies and associations distinguished by their own traditions and interests and through which individuals pursue their careers.

The Joint Doctoral Program, our focal unit of graduate education, is located within and between these several entities, as are its associated interdisciplinary endeavors. Thus, the kinds of integration and collaboration that the program was designed to foster have been clearly affected over time by various processes and arrangements among these nested contexts.

Figure 22.1
The Joint Doctoral Program in Context

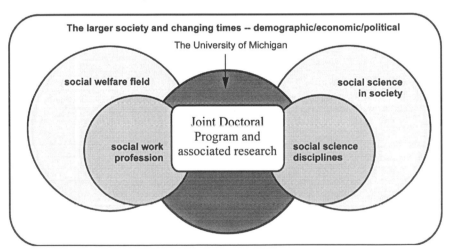

The *significance* of the joint program occurred because it was launched at a time when professional social work was seeking both a more assured place within the modern university and a rapprochement with the social sciences. Its initiation at Michigan was impelled by these aims. The distinguishing features of the program and its accomplishments, therefore, have a more general import for understanding the fundamental problem posed by attempts to foster the integration of social work and social science.

Space does not permit the elaboration of the *premises and values* underlying this effort. Suffice it to say that the values undergirding the program infused the conception, organization, and implementation in its earlier years and were generally shared among those most instrumental in its development.

In the next section we will describe the origins and founding of the Joint Doctoral Program and its stabilization during the years 1951 into 1970. The following section will examine the program's maturation, expansion, and changes during the years 1970–1990. We will document the drastic transformations of the school that attended the program's initiation, and assess the implications of changing external conditions in relation to the conceptions and aims of the program founders. Finally, we suggest some alternatives for future development in the next century.

ORIGINS, FOUNDING, AND EARLY DEVELOPMENT: 1950–1970

Seeking an Academic Home, Professional Status, and a Knowledge Base

By the 1950s, the university had emerged as the societal institution for the advancement of knowledge through scientific research and other forms of scholarship and as the preferred site for training in the major professions. World War II had immensely stimulated science and research, and academics of many kinds had become recognized as sources of critical knowledge.

The role of social work had also strengthened during World War II and practitioners wished to expand into new service areas. In addition, the profession was seeking a more secure anchorage in the university to validate its claims to recognized professional status—following the lead of medicine, law, public health, nursing, and education, which had faced similar validation requirements (Friedson, 1986). Social work schools, once independent or at the margins of academia, were moving toward the central campus and seeking acceptance as full members. Among major universities, however, full membership was likely to be accorded only to professions with a graduate level terminal degree.[1] This, in turn, required vital bases in the established sciences for the teaching of reasonably well-grounded professional practices.

At the time social work claimed knowledge that was a composite of disparate strands drawn from social practice and policy, public administration, and the social sciences. The "science" most directly available to schools included chunks borrowed from other professions (e.g., medicine, typically taught by physicians), and from disciplines such as psychology, child development, and statistics, as well as various psychodynamic theories. Despite the prominence given to these theories, they represented a kind of knowledge only partially applicable to social practice, meagerly validated by empirical research, and generally suspect in academia. Especially important, however, was the profession's reliance on poorly codified practice wisdom or experiential knowledge accumulated through case and community studies and transmitted through teaching by seasoned practitioners.

Further, the profession retained strong ideological emphases, largely based on humanistic philosophy and progressive education, infused with degrees of commitment stemming from the settlement, good government, and social reform movements. During this period, social work continued to espouse special concerns for public social services of many kinds, for the protection of women and children, and for disadvantaged populations (Wilensky & Lebeaux, 1958). Such commitments were somewhat juxtaposed, however, with social work educators' increasing reliance on psychodynamic theories and casework methodology.

A growing number of social work educators and other leaders by this time recognized that the profession's knowledge resources needed strengthening in the sciences to undergird and guide more effective practice, and that it could not gain university entry and status without these essential resources (for example, see Hollis & Taylor, 1952). The disciplines of sociology, psychology, social psychology, economics, and anthropology were viewed as possessing the resources of greatest promise for social work (Geismar, 1984).

Establishment and Transformation of the School of Social Work at Michigan

By 1951, the Regents had decided it was time to establish social work as a separate graduate-professional school equal with the university's other professional schools and to relocate it from Detroit to the central Ann Arbor campus.[2] The Regents also acted to recruit and empower as the first dean someone committed to the public social services and able to energize the school and boost its status and relations within the university.[3]

These expectations were a test: Either the reconstitution and relocation of the school, and the strong mandate given the new dean would result in definite progress toward the high standards set for university professional schools, or the program might well be abandoned.[4] The Regents expected that relations with other schools and departments would be fostered, enrollments would be increased, the curriculum broadened and strengthened, public welfare and other public services would receive priority in the preparation of social workers, and close relations with Michigan state departments and federal agencies would promptly be forged. Finally, tenure-track faculty appointees must hereafter meet higher standards, including advanced degrees—substantial professional experience would no longer be sufficient. Additional university funding was assured, provided that these conditions were met and that the school was also gradually able to garner outside financial support.

Happy Coincidence: A Time, a Place, and the Persons

Recruited as the vigorous new dean, Fedele F. Fauri had a strong reputation in public welfare administration and national policy and a UM law degree rather than an M.S.W.[5] His background and experience demonstrated his broad interests in the social policy problems of the state and nation, beyond those of direct practice. The new dean's stature, interests, and skills admirably matched regental mandates and expectations for the direction and achievements of the new school. Yet significant progress would require several years because Fauri faced daunting challenges for which there were neither models nor guidelines. These challenges confronted social work education as a whole (i.e., developing a solid knowledge base in the social sciences, securely binding the school to the university, and broadening its scope beyond direct services). Unencumbered by tradition or commitment to any theory, Fauri recognized the need to form alliances with the social science disciplines.

Conception of the Joint Program

In 1947, the Russell Sage Foundation, which had long supported social agencies and social research through grants and staff services, hired a new executive, Donald Young. He recognized the common nature of the problems faced by several professions and brought about a radical change in foundation priorities. For the next few decades it would target resources to facilitate the infusion of social science knowledge into professional curricula, including social work.

A few social scientists were faculty members at some social work schools, but most taught specialized subjects and had little influence on the core curricula. The foundation initially placed individual scientists at several schools, but it soon realized that only a sizable and prolonged effort was likely to have a significant effect—and further, that this effort should probably be pursued at a school with little entrenched tradition, preferably somewhere in the Midwest, where state universities had stronger commitments to public policies and services and were less entangled with private social agencies.[6]

Michigan well fit this profile: It was a major state university with a positive stance toward the public sector; it supported very strong social science departments with distinguished and visionary leaders; its culture was hospitable to ventures that spanned academic divisions and to research that addressed societal conditions and problems.

The precariousness of social work's situation at Michigan was typical, but the solution was to be unique. Donald Young quickly perceived the opportunity for a significant investment of funds—provided the scope of effort was greatly expanded beyond the earlier, limited ventures. Young persuaded David G. French, a social worker concerned with strengthening services through research (French, 1952), to remain in Michigan as a foundation fellow to pursue prospects with Dean Fauri.

Their first joint endeavor was the productive 1953–54 interdisciplinary Faculty Seminar on the Research Basis of Social Welfare (FSRB), funded by the foundation. No fewer than 18 leading members of social science departments and schools, including Fauri and others from Social Work, joined in its deliberations (see Table 22.1); David French provided staff service.

The list of faculty members involved in the early joint efforts indicates the scope of participation and the qualities of scholarship they represented. All shared interests in the major problems of the times, in the social policy and programmatic implications of their lines of research, and in actively contributing to the well-being of the society. Some were more action research oriented than others, and some more interested in social betterment and change, but all were engaged leaders of their disciplines. Their participation gave powerful encouragement to the foundation's optimism about the potentials at Michigan. The Faculty Seminar's report to the vice president outlined important areas of mutual interest and cooperative effort across the broad field of social welfare

Table 22.1
Early Faculty Groups Planning and Overseeing the Joint Program

Faculty Seminar on the Research Basis of Social Welfare (1953–1954)

Robert C. Angell, Dept. of Sociology	William Haber, Dept. of Economics
Solomon J. Axelrod, School of Public Health	Amos H. Hawley, Dept. of Sociology
Kenneth Boulding, Dept. of Economics	E. Lowell Kelly, Dept. of Psychology
Eleanor G. Cranefield, School of Social Work	Werner Landecker, Dept. of Psychology
Arthur Dunham, School of Social Work	Ronald Lippitt, Depts. of Sociology, Psychology and Institute for Social Research
Fedele F. Fauri, Dean, School of Social Work	William Morse, School of Education
Ralph C. Fletcher, School of Social Work	Theodore Newcomb, Program in Social Psychology, Sociology and Psych. Departments
David G. French, Russell Sage Foundation	Patricia Rabinovitz, School of Social Work
Clarice Freud, School of Social Work	Josephine Williams, Dept. of Sociology

Coordinating Committee on Social Welfare Research (School of Social Work, 1955–1970)

Amos H. Hawley, Chair, Dept. of Sociology*	Daniel Katz, Dept. of Psychology
Arthur W. Bromage, Dept. of Political Science*	Morris Janowitz, Dept. of Sociology
Solomon W. Axelrod, School of Public Health*	E. Lowell Kelly, Dept. of Psychology
Eleanor G. Cranefield, School of Social Work	John Lederle, Dept. of Political Science and Director, Institute of Public Administration
Fedele F. Fauri, Dean, School of Social Work	Ronald Lippitt, Depts. of Sociology, Psychology and Institute for Social Research*
Robert S. Ford, Horace H. Rackham Graduate School*	James Morgan, Dept. of Economics and Survey Research Center
William Haber, Dept. of Economics*	Dorothy Schroeder, School of Social Work
Roger Heyns, Dept. of Psychology	David G. French, Executive Secretary, School of Social Work

* denotes members of the original Committee; membership rotated.

Supervising Committee, Joint Doctoral Program in Social Work and Social Science

Morris Janowitz, Chair, Dept. of Sociology	Daniel Miller, Dept. of Psychology
Kenneth Boulding, Dept. of Economics	Robert D. Vinter, School of Social Work
Eleanor G. Cranefield, School of Social Work	Henry J. Meyer, School of Social Work and Dept. of Sociology
William Haber, Dept. of Economics	

particularly those involving large populations. It proposed establishing a continuing cross-campus Coordinating Committee on Social Welfare Research (CCSWR) as an evolutionary framework for pursuing interdisciplinary activities (Faculty Seminar on the Research Basis of Social Welfare Practice, 1954).

There was an elegant logic in the strategic intramural alliances being forged by Fauri and French to gain effective collaboration between social work and the social sciences. Exchange and interpenetration were sought between them, but neither as a one-way borrowing to social work nor as processes along parallel but separate tracks. Active participation of leading social scientists was sought from the outset—they must have full membership in a shared mission. The numbers of interested faculty and the avenues for their collaboration were enlarged on a step-by-step basis. The involvement and support of the social science departments was premised on an expectation that their perspectives on and access to social problems and significant populations would be enhanced through the kinds of collaboration planned with the school. The different but reciprocal benefits for both were explicitly recognized, with concrete incentives intended for all. The school would provide support but assume no control over the processes, and social science faculty outnumbered those from social work in each group. The participating disciplines were also assured that credentialed social scientists would be appointed to the school's tenured faculty, as joint and as independent appointments. Underlying the alliance was a premise unique to Michigan: Social science and social welfare should be equal partners based on differing but compatible and mutually reinforcing interests.

Reciprocal Aims and Interests

Let us step back for a moment and summarize the aims and interests of the partners in these collaborative endeavors.

The aims of social work included:

- Facilitating access to the knowledge resources of the disciplines;

- Engaging social scientists in the study of pressing problems in the field of social welfare while instigating research within social welfare and social work; and

- Equipping a cadre of professionals with the knowledge and research skills needed to make contributions through research, through transfer and development of knowledge for social policy and practice and for professional education.

The interests of the social science disciplines included:

- Access to the panorama of populations, organizations, and problems that constitute the social welfare field broadly conceived;

- Collaboration in research and knowledge development focused on problems and issues of mutual concern; and

- Assisting in the transfer, transformation, and utilization of social science methods and knowledge for social policy and practice and for graduate education.

The Innovative Program in Advanced Training and Research

University officials approved the seminar's 1954 report and appointed the inter-unit Coordinating Committee, within the Horace H. Rackham School of Graduate Studies, with further foundation support. Building on the seminar's recommendations, with French as its executive secretary, this committee formulated arrangements by which the interdisciplinary alliance could be continued along two closely connected lines: (1) creation of a Joint Ph.D. Degree Program in Social Work and Social Science, and (2) stimulating research within the school and between it and the disciplines—as detailed in Table 22.2 (Coordinating Committee on Social Welfare Research, 1956). Faculties of the departments and the school affirmed these proposals, albeit with some misgivings. The Rackham School's executive committee gave formal assent for a joint interdepartmental Ph.D. Program under the direction of a supervising committee appointed by the Rackham Dean. Russell Sage also approved the proposals and awarded funding of $250,000 (equivalent to about $1.5 million in current dollars) for five years.

The entire process from the seminar in 1953 to the university and foundation approvals in 1956 spanned just three years. This fast-tracking of such a complex and innovative venture testifies to the soundness of the planning, the commitment of the principals and faculty members, the support of the university and foundation, and the adroit and effective leadership of its initiators.

Implementation of most key elements in the approved plans also proceeded briskly. To serve as head of the program, Henry J. Meyer, a sociologist with ties to the profession, was recruited to a joint appointment in social work and sociology. Simultaneously, the interdepartmental supervising committee was appointed to oversee the Program (see Table 22.1), including its admissions, curricular arrangements for the joint degrees, and the like.[7] This committee assumed its duties and admitted the first seven students in 1957, with the first graduates emerging in 1962. Other social scientists (some with social work credentials) were appointed to the school's faculty, including at least one joint appointment with each cooperating Department. These and other faculty developed the first courses as intended for the School's doctoral-level offerings. Foundation grant monies initially supported these joint positions, but soon the units' own budgets were used in accord with university commitments.

Among the main aims of the Joint Doctoral Program and associated endeavors detailed in Table 22.2, Item 1 was the most critical: mandating a unified social work–social science Ph.D. degree. Before commenting on the degree program itself, other key provisions in the larger plan should be pointed out. Item 4 details how all activities were anchored in the basic structures of the university and assured the social science departments their shared ownership.[8]

A crucial aspect of the overall design is summarized in the Item 5: underwriting the means for continuing the interdisciplinary lines of work was vitally important to the conduct of the program. The program's supervising committee and the larger coordinating committee could offer stimulation and support, but it was imperative that faculty members of the participating units conduct joint seminars, cooperative research and teaching, and other endeavors to advance the shared mission. Finally, we must keep in mind the disciplines' expectations of school assistance in gaining access to the kinds of populations, problems, and policies central to the social welfare field.

Table 22.2
Distinctive Features of the Program in Advanced Training and Research

---

1. A Ph.D. Program leading to a *joint* doctoral degree in social work and in one social science—a single, combined theory and research degree, not a two degree track—with provision for students to obtain the M.S.W. degree if not already possessed;

2. A curriculum providing advanced studies sufficient to meet the basic knowledge and skill requirements of both the profession and the respective discipline (theoretical courses, research methods and supervised training, preliminary exams, and a dissertation relevant to both social work and the discipline), including development of new advanced seminars in social work/social welfare with attention to the integration of such knoweldge;

3. A degree program focused on knowledge development and utilization, to equip persons specifically for the task of bringing together the resources and approaches of social science and social work for research, teaching, and practice (not on traditional professional skills except as embodied in prior M.S.W. studies);

4. A location that firmly embedded the Program and its associated activities within the University's structures: administration with all other Ph.D. programs by the Rackham School of Graduate Studies; continuation of the interdepartmental Coordinating Committee on Social Welfare Research to foster ongoing inter-unit collaborative endeavors; and creation of a Joint Program Supervising Committee with faculty representatives from social work and social science departments to oversee admissions, degree requirements, curriculum, and student progress (and formation of a School Doctoral Faculty group); with professional and support staffing for the Program and for the Coordinating and Supervising Committees;

5. Complementary provisions and resources for stimulating and facilitating research and other knowledge development initiatives focused on problems relevant to the profession and field, and to the disciplines (largely through the Coordinating Committee)—i.e., interdisciplinary faculty seminars, research seed funding, faculty released time, student fellowships and new faculty joint appointments between social work and each of the participating social science departments;

6. A commitment of phased-in University funding to assume full costs fo the Program as Foundation grants were spent down, and the School's assurances of procuring other outside support and recruiting more faculty with social science credentials;

7. Pledges to extend social science knowledge and theory into the M.S.W. professional social work curriculum.

Programs of Joint Ph.D. studies have involved Social Work with the Departments of Sociology, Psychology, the Program in Social Psychology, Political Science, Economics, and, more recently, Anthropology. Excerpted from the Proposal for a Program of Advanced Training and Research in Social Work and Social Science submitted to the Russell Sage Foundation, March, 1956.

Creative use of the early foundation funds supplemented each unit's own allocations to support several initiatives: helping establish a center for organizational studies in the sociology department, conducting a multidisciplinary faculty seminar on correctional programs (with cooperation from the state departments of Corrections and Social Services), and another on social security and income maintenance, as well as startup assistance for interdisciplinary research projects that promptly gained outside funding. Noteworthy among these early ventures was the collaboration involving Wilbur Cohen, James Morgan, and others, leading to the Panel Study of Income Dynamics (which still continues at the Survey Research Center).[9]

Central to all undertakings was, of course, the Joint Degree Program itself (Items 2 and 3 in Table 22.2). In essence, the departments and the school accommodated and meshed their advanced theory and research study requirements to assure a truly joint doctoral degree. The curriculum and character of the study program are presented later in Figure 22.2, Doctoral Curriculum in Social Work and Social Science.

Persuasion and Resistance, External and Internal

New tasks and challenges had to be faced in establishing and sustaining this unusual kind of program. It is helpful to recall some of Coyle's observations from this period about the potentials of the social sciences for professional education. While advocating their contributions, she reported the views of many as follows: It is clear that within the profession there is considerable mistrust and skepticism as to whether the social sciences have anything to offer that might be of practical use to social workers or in social work education. She observed that professionals regarded scientists as holding *differing alien* modes of thought [italics added] (Coyle, 1958).

Fully aware of these apprehensions, faculty involved in the joint program, including Dean Fauri, undertook strenuous efforts to interpret and justify its unique character to a wide range of groups important in the profession and welfare field. The Council on Social Work Education (CSWE) did not accredit advanced curricula; there was concern to maintain the school's legitimization and good standing among peer institutions. Dean Fauri became chair of the CSWE Commission on Accreditation and was later elected president of the council and of the American Public Welfare Association. Another faculty member twice served on the CSWE Curriculum Policy Committee (which formulates the constitutional basis for accreditation standards used in the schools' reviews) to help shape these underlying policies in the direction of a more hospitable stance toward relevant social sciences.[10] Dean Fauri accepted appointment to national and presidential commissions concerned with major social policies and programs, as did Wilbur Cohen.

Participating faculty delivered papers at conferences of professional bodies across the nation and for symposia at other universities, attesting to the fruitful applications of social science for social practice and professional education and documenting some results of the interchanges involving school and department faculty members. Articles and chapters reporting the gains of research on relevant problems were also published in a variety of journals and books, research reports were widely distributed, and books were in progress, as we will summarize below.

Concurrently, great effort was made to assure the financial well-being of the program. The late 1950s and 1960s was fortunately a period of sharp increases in federal (and some states') spending for social programs, for professional education, including social work, and for research on problems relevant to social welfare. Some school faculty members were active on state- and federal-level funding and advisory agencies. Early on, the program and its related activities garnered increasing support from federal, state, and foundation sources for research, demonstration, and training projects, as well as student stipends and dissertation support (cut-backs came in the 1970s). An increasing number of social scientists, doctoral graduates from other social work schools, and allied professionals, were recruited (see Item 6 in Table 22.2), to handle the school's expanding enrollment and its flourishing projects. In view of demonstrated progress, the Sage Foundation awarded a second and terminal grant of about $300,000 for continuing support of the program and for faculty research projects.

Pursuing institutional change through augmentation of functions and resources, as represented by the doctoral program and expansion of M.S.W. studies, was easier than seeking to transform the core M.S.W. Implementation of the 7th aim in Table 22.2, infusion of social science knowledge into the M.S.W. curriculum, was the most difficult to advance. Faculty members with both social work and social science credentials first sought to introduce supplementary content on social organization and processes into the traditional four terms of required courses in Human Growth and Behavior, without success. But because a social group work specialization had been authorized in the late 1950s, the faculty became willing to approve two new Human Behavior in the Social Environment (HBSE) courses that drew directly on knowledge mainly from social psychology and sociology, Group Process, and Social Organization I and II, to be taken by group work and community organization students in addition to all existing requirements.[11]

The synergism provided by the school's first major institutional transformation increasingly impelled more significant curriculum changes. The mandate for a broadened master's–level program extended beyond the new specialization in group work to a revitalized community organization program, followed by administration, soon after by social behavioral practice, policy planning, and research and evaluation. Aided by support from new training grants, almost every principle sector of social welfare had become represented in the curriculum by relevant social services courses, expanded field settings, and additional practice methods courses.

A critical mass of diverse faculty resources and student enrollments was assembled in connection with these newer areas of professional education, which could be accommodated only by a thorough revision of the master's curriculum. Thus, in 1965, it became urgent to begin a lengthy and contentious process of restructuring the M.S.W. curriculum largely around the organization of knowledge bases that were fundamental to those of the doctoral program. This framework explicitly recognized the program's levels of social organization (interpersonal, group and family; organizational; community; and societal), particularly in the HBSE and practice methods areas, thereby providing the necessary foundation for the expanded ranges of practice specializations and fields of service. This new curriculum was finally adopted in 1967 (Meyer, Litwak, Thomas, and Vinter, 1967). Despite the retention of numerous courses reflecting earlier emphases, these changes were still vigorously opposed by a vocal minority of the school's faculty.

With no more than 70–75 full-time students in the mid-1950s, the new school had been among the smaller and less well-known in the university and the nation. But by the end of the 1960s it had become the nation's largest school of social work, with the broadest range of professional studies, the most diverse complement of faculty members, and its unique Joint Doctoral Program.[12] By this time, the newer faculty appointees and the kinds of knowledge they represented had been absorbed within the school's collegium, as had the augmented curriculum and courses, with a high level of integration within the M.S.W. curriculum and between it and the doctoral program.[13]

Some Early Examples of Integration

Examples of early achievements will illustrate how the integration of social work and social science was carried forward during the late 1950s–1970s period—in addition to educating students. Initially these lines of research and scholarship flowed from the early faculty seminar and the interdisciplinary seminars encouraged by the coordinating committee, but others were expeditiously empowered within social work/welfare by the doctoral program and its complementary initiatives and as social science-trained faculty increased at the school. Publications resulting from the early endeavors were particularly important in promptly demonstrating actual achievements generated by the commitment to social work/social science collaboration, and the joint program in particular.[14]

Two of the first research undertakings exemplifying the use of social science tools to address social welfare needs were conducted in cooperation with Michigan departments: One was a controlled experiment using role theory to focus on staff training and reduced workloads for the Department of Social Services; the other, stemming from the early interdepartmental corrections seminar, involved sociology and social work faculty collaborating in field studies of juvenile and adult correctional programs operated by the departments of Social Services and Corrections.[15]

Emerging from the group work specialization needs, Robert Vinter initiated a line of work drawing heavily on social psychology for the formulation and teaching of systematic social group work practice theory. Codification of practice principles was aided by the transfer and application of social science knowledge to this area of practice, followed by explorations and studies within social agencies to formulate what became known as the Michigan Model of group work. Two readers, journal publications, and numerous conference papers ensued from these efforts (Vinter, 1960; Vinter, Sarri, et al., 1967; Glasser, Sarri, and Vinter, 1974).

Another faculty group then collaborated in development of community organization practice methodology, guided by Jack Rothman. Directed by

Eugene Litwak and Henry Meyer, field research began with Sociology's Detroit Area Study, then proceeded to on-site studies of linkages between the Detroit public schools, families, and service agencies. A reader and journal publications also followed (Cox, Tropman, et al., 1970; Litwak & Meyer, 1974).

Studies of correctional programs stimulated two directions of research and teaching, one expanded to studies of diverse organizations that serve people and the other focused on justice system policies and programs. The first gave major impetus to comparative multi-site investigations delineating what soon became known as human service organizations—encompassing social work programs and personnel, among others. These included new antipoverty agencies, public schools, youth service programs, the Job Corps, and executiveship among such organizations. These efforts, extended at Michigan and elsewhere, resulted in journal articles, readers, and the like and—as with other lines of work—contributed to courses at both the masters and doctoral levels (Vinter, 1959; Vinter, 1963; Sarri & Maple, 1972; Hasenfeld, 1972; Hasenfeld & English, 1974).

Stemming from the early comparative studies, the second line of research focused on juvenile and adult correctional policies, programs, and practices—encompassing among others juvenile courts, institutions and programs, halfway houses, and prisons—which also continued through several decades (Vinter, 1959; Vinter, 1963; Sarri, 1967; Sarri, 1971).

The work of Fedele Fauri and Wilbur Cohen proceeded in quite different directions, given their active involvement in public policy formation, service on federal commissions, national welfare bodies, and with the United States Department of DHEW (now DHHS). Because both were directly involved in shaping national policies and legislation, many of their major contributions are embodied in federal and state legislative enactments (from expansion of Social Security, initiation of SSI and SSD, Medicare and Medicaid), rather than published in journals. Both were well versed in relevant statistical, legal, and documentary source materials, and Cohen in particular relied on economists and other social scientists in formulating and justifying his policies (Cohen, 1960a; Cohen, 1960b; Fauri, 1966).

The extramural championing of social work and social science integration and research led school faculty to present papers at conferences, symposia, and seminars to elucidate how these aims could be advanced and to stimulate similar work elsewhere. Some publications resulting from these efforts dealt with the utilization of social science knowledge and methods (Tripodi, Fellin, and Meyer, 1969; Tripodi, Fellin, and Epstein, 1971), and others reported syntheses of research undertakings, both focused on social welfare problems and social work practice (Thomas, McLeod, et al., 1960a; Meyer, Litwak, Thomas, and Vinter, 1967; Thomas, 1967).

This had, indeed, been a period of enriched and amplified integration between the social sciences and social work, as well as a time of productive and rewarding collaboration between the school and the departments.

MATURATION, EXPANSION, CHANGE, AND RENEWAL: 1970–1990

The 1970s was a period of maturation and expansion of/for the Michigan Doctoral Program that paralleled developments nationally. This decade saw almost an explosion of new doctoral programs in social work, although none was a replica of the Michigan model.[16] Sixteen new doctoral programs in social work were begun in the 1970s, almost as many as had existed since the first one was established in 1915. Federal traineeship support, begun in 1947, was extended in the 1960s and 1970s for the majority of all graduate professional programs in social work, although not all fields of practices were equally targeted. Preparation of professionals for the mental health and child welfare fields dominated, more as a result of political and professional influences than from systematic assessment of personnel needs in social welfare (Briar, 1976). Admissions to bachelor and master's degree programs all grew, which produced a greatly increased demand for faculty, to which schools quickly responded by developing doctoral programs.[17] State and federal financial support continued into the early 1970s, although with few new initiatives, and a period of declining federal funding persisted in the latter half of the decade. Overall, the 1970s represented the culmination of programs and initiatives begun in the 1950s.

Most Michigan graduates continued to be employed in schools of social work although some have had distinguished careers in discipline departments. Figueira-McDonough (Figueira-McDonough, 1980) provides some evidence that the nonacademic market also provided a slowly increasing arena for doctoral graduates. Kronick and associates (Kronick, Kamerman, and Glisson, 1989) suggest that some doctoral programs were developed in the expectation that they would enhance the status of the profession whether or not graduates were prepared to advance the knowledge of the profession. Developing a doctoral program in social work is demanding in terms of staff and financial resources, which many schools lack. Because compromises are often made in focus and quality, the result may well be the opposite of what was intended with respect to academic and professional stature.

Efforts of the Council on Social Work Education (CSWE) to control curriculum policy and accreditation standards for doctoral as well as for bachelors' and masters' degrees, was strongly resisted by most doctoral programs, including Michigan. In 1974, the report of the Task Force on Structure and Quality in Social Work Education recommended that the terminal degree for all graduate social work be the doctorate (Ripple, 1974).[18] Doctoral faculty throughout the United States objected, and their response led to the organization of the Group for the Advancement of Doctoral Education (GADE), which continues to play an active collegial role in supporting voluntary change in social work doctoral education. The Michigan program was protected from external professional influences because of its interdisciplinary status as a joint program in social work and social science in the Rackham Graduate School of the University. CSWE's efforts at control ultimately failed when the original recommendation was rejected by the Delegate Assembly in 1976; however, informal efforts at cooptation continued for several years. Although CSWE domination of doctoral programs was strongly resisted, many social work educators were interested in utilizing their development to enhance master's programs. The two most recent Curriculum Policy statements of CSWE provide limited evidence of having been influenced by developments in the social sciences (Council on Social Work Education, 1992). As an informal national body GADE has played an active collegial role in supporting voluntary change in doctoral programs, but it has avoided involvement in more political issues affecting the bachelor and master's degree programs (Holland & Frost, 1987; Rosen & Stretch, 1982).

Nationally, as well as at Michigan, it appears that in the 1970s and 1980s advanced social work programs placed greater emphasis on technology development, on methodology and quantification, and on application of social science knowledge as an end in itself than on training students to address and try to resolve major social problems such as poverty, racism, and sexism. In addition, more emphasis was placed on the individual as the target of change than on social structure and policies. Thus, we saw a pronounced disengagement from social problems and conditions, on the one hand, and a displacement onto more narrow and technical areas of study, on the other. Many private foundations funded research that was complementary to such federal priorities. For example, research to support the *assessment* of social problems such as poverty or mental illness was far better funded than research directed toward *interventions* that would/might resolve these problems (Ohlin, Coates, and Miller, 1978; Miller, 1990). Developments in the social sciences also influenced federal and foundation priorities through the roles played by social scientists on review panels. They often emphasized the use of traditional experimental research models as well as quantitative more than qualitative assessments.

Curriculum Development and Changes

During the 1960s, the curriculum design of the joint program was flexible enough to permit adaptation to policy and knowledge change resulting from major societal events. The first program curriculum modification officially noted in the records occurred in 1968–1969; it appears to have incrementally refined the 1957 basic curriculum. More indirect curricular change was apparent in some of the problems selected by students for research internships, preliminary examinations, and dissertation topics.

Curriculum change in the 1970s appears to have been more significant in the social sciences than in social work. The minutes of the program's supervising committee reflect the increasing departmental interests in assuring that the joint program students met all of the disciplines' curricular requirements. The shift also reflected a growing emphasis on acquiring very sophisticated competence in research methodology and statistics, especially in economics, political science, and sociology.[19] A major strength in the program has been its rigorous training in research methods; all students were required to complete three to four research methods courses in their respective disciplines and also to have some type of research practicum experience. The research courses also provided special opportunities for students in the disciplines and in the program to work together on concrete problems and experiments.

The addition to the school of many new faculty trained in the social sciences in the 1970s and 1980s also provided students with numerous opportunities to collaborate with faculty in a broad range of research areas. Among the areas included were race and ethnic studies, substance abuse, juvenile justice, women's studies, child and family intervention, behavior modification and preschool and K-12 education.

In response to the interests of some students and faculty, the program committee in the 1970s developed and refined a "utilization" internship as an alternative research internship. This was explicitly directed toward developing skills in the utilization of social science knowledge in social work practice. It could involve the engineering of a particular practice intervention, or it might focus on the use of social science knowledge to formulate a new or changed social policy. A small number of students undertook these internships, but the practice was relatively short-lived and essentially ended in the 1980s, perhaps because of the widespread acceptance of more traditional research methodologies. Similarly, development in empirically developed practice theory also lagged throughout these two decades despite pioneering work at Michigan.

The growing numbers of social science trained faculty also provided increased opportunities for using social work research projects to meet dissertation requirements. However, examination of dissertations suggests that the vast majority would be classified as applied or theoretical social science rather than research on practice (per se). A cursory examination of dissertation topics of students in one discipline, sociology, suggests minor differences from those in the joint program, although greater differences are apparent in psychology and political science dissertations where students chose research topics and methodologies more closely linked to social policy and social practice.

Periodically throughout the 1970s doctoral faculty sponsored interdepartmental student-faculty seminars, usually related to specific social policies or problems and research projects. Begun in the 1960s, they provided an important, although indirect, influence on curriculum change; for example, a seminar on innovation and change in K-12 schools, one on the African-American family, and one on mental health and substance abuse.

The essential structure and requirements described in Table 22.3 have remained the same since the program began in 1957, although substantive content has extensively changed. The social science requirements are designed by each of the disciplines and include courses in theory, statistics, and research methods. Some modifications are made in minor and cognate requirements based on a student's social work interests. Social science requirements that have changed several times over the decades typically reflect ongoing changes in the disciplines. The social work requirements originally included 10 credit hours in advanced social work courses—recently increased to 15 hours. Students are expected to be knowledgeable in two levels of intervention in theory, in practice methods, and in two integration seminars. They are required to complete a research or utilization internship and a preliminary examination in social work. The dissertation is jointly chaired by faculty from social work and the student's chosen department. Because the joint program is supervised academically by the graduate school, any additional formal requirements must be met by all Ph.D. students.

It was expected that a degree could be completed in approximately five to six years for a person entering without an M.S.W. and four years for those entering with an M.S.W. However, because of part-time research and teaching, as well as requirements posed by the preliminary examination and dissertation, the median time has been six to seven years (Radin, Benbenisty, and Leon, 1982).

Table 22.3
Doctoral Curriculum in Social Work and Social Science [a]

Social Work	Social Science
Courses: 15 advanced credit hours	Courses: variable by discipline
1. Social Work methods—micro and macro	1. 3-4 theory courses
2. Theory of social practice and policy	2. 3-4 specialization courses
3. Social Policy and Social Service Systems	3. 2-3 statistics courses
4. Research Methods, especially evaluation	4. 2 research methods, may include practicum
Research Internship	
General assessment—Year 3	General assessment—Year 3
Examination related to specialization interests	1-2 Preliminary Exams which may be comprehensive or highly specialized; written and/or oral
Dissertation on a Topic of Student's Choice	
2 social work faculty	2 faculty in student's discipline

[a] This is the advanced curriculum for post–M.S.W. students

A second curriculum change took place between 1974 and 1976 and represented a distinct shift to a curriculum that was designed around five components:

- Foundation courses that dealt with individuals, groups, organizations, and society. These were designed to provide students with social science knowledge at the several levels of intervention, but they differed from regular/typical discipline courses because the focus here was on social welfare and social work issues.

- Social change theory courses were developed for each of the four levels of intervention and were often broader in focus than intervention theory courses.

- Social problem areas were selected by the faculty and students for emphasis; these changed depending upon student interest and faculty resources. Each student was expected to develop special competence in one social problem area.

- Knowledge specifically related to integration of social science knowledge and social work practice in social welfare was promoted through special seminars and individual studies.

- Advanced seminars were offered on specific timely issues to help to integrate foundation, social problem, and change theory knowledge. These often included social science students and faculty from other departments.

With some minor modifications, this curriculum plan/design remained in place until the early 1980s. The review of the Joint Doctoral Program by the Rackham Graduate School in 1982 recommended specific changes in the social work courses of the joint program. Following that, a third major curriculum revision was undertaken in 1983. Because that effort produced the curriculum that still guides the program, we will describe it in greater detail so that the parallels and differences that have evolved over the past 35 years can be identified. The following principles guide the current curriculum:

- The primary emphasis of the program is to apply the methodology, theory, and evidence from the various disciplines to analyze and understand social work and social welfare problems and issues and to develop and test new modes of intervention.

- The social work curriculum should be aimed primarily at knowledge development for both social work and social welfare.

- Students should be exposed to and develop expertise in advancing relevant knowledge for intervention methods and social service systems.

- Relevant ethics and values in policy and practice must be carefully considered. A commitment to groups at risk, including the underserved, poor, and minorities is to receive priority.

- Flexibility should be maintained to adapt to new developments.

- Students should have the opportunity for original specialized study in areas of their choice.

Four areas in the social work curriculum component relate directly to the principal means by which the profession and social welfare achieve their goals: (1) Practice, Intervention, and Policy; (2) Social Service Systems; (3) The Social Context for Practice and Policy; and (4) Research Methods for Policy and Practice. Students are required to elect five courses, with at least one in each area. They are also expected to develop specialized expertise in one social work/social welfare area of their choice. Their choices must also incorporate content pertinent to race/ethnicity and gender issues. Students' course work, preliminary examination, and research internship, and dissertation may all relate to their social work specialization. Completion of a research internship, a practice internship, a practicum on teaching social work methods, and a preliminary examination in social work are all components of the present curriculum, as well as a dissertation that is the joint responsibility of the department and the school.

When compared with the 1957 curriculum, it is immediately obvious that there have been extensive changes, with far more emphasis in later years on specific course completion, additional internship, and preliminary examination requirements. The prior experience and formal training of the student body have not changed substantially, so it should be possible to assess the impact of the curricular changes of the 1980s versus the 1970s, in terms of their effectiveness in producing social work academic and policy leaders. As is clear that the current requirements are aimed far more at preparation for academic roles than for policy or administrative roles, it probably is not surprising that only a small minority of graduates have entered the policy arena, even though that was an important objective of the program's founders.

STUDENT AND GRADUATE CHARACTERISTICS

Students have always been admitted to this program with or without an M.S.W. degree, which can be earned before proceeding with the doctoral studies or integrated with them. The majority of entering students have had at least one advanced degree.

A total of 218 students have been awarded Ph.D.'s in social work and social science, and as Table 22.4 indicates, majors/graduates are equally divided between sociology and psychology (Fromm, 1941), 7.5 percent in social psychology; 6.1 percent in political science; 2.8 percent in economics, and less than 1 percent in anthropology. The latter is the most recently established joint degree, but admissions to anthropology grew rapidly in the late 1980s so these patterns may/will soon change. More than 80 percent of all graduates are employed on faculties in professional schools of social work; about 10 percent are in nonacademic policy/administrative or clinical positions, and another 10 percent in discipline departments.

Applications grew rapidly in the 1970s, then declined during the 1980s and began to increase again in 1990. These shifts were probably due to the changes in financial support, as well as some changes in career interests. Examination of admission and enrollment data reveals somewhat different patterns, but it is difficult to determine the total number of students fully enrolled in the program since its beginning because cumulative records were not kept on all who were admitted. A number terminated when they earned their M.S.W. degrees, having decided to enter social work practice directly. The available information suggests that approximately 55 percent of those who enter actually complete the Ph.D. requirements (Radin, Benbenisty, and Leon, 1982; Radin, 1983; Garvin, 1994).

The numbers of minority students, primarily African-American, grew slowly but steadily increased in the 1970s in response to active recruitment and financial support by the university and the federal government. Although the number of minority students remained below 15 percent throughout the 1970s, growing concern about minority education in social work fostered increased efforts to recruit minority faculty and to provide curriculum content related to African-American studies.[20] Other minority groups continued underrepresented on the faculty and also in the student body. The School of Social Work appears to have been ahead of the social science departments at Michigan in developing graduate level curriculum content related to African-American Studies. The numbers of students of Hispanic, Native American, and Asian backgrounds grew very slowly in the 1970s and 1980s, with little curricular content pertaining to these populations. Only about three to six international students were enrolled each year, but that produced a cohort of about 20 students at any one time. Many of these were fully supported by their respective governments, which expected them to return and become leaders in social work. However, no formal training for such future roles was offered. Moreover, a review of their dissertation topics suggests that nearly all focused their research on problems and issues in the United States. Only in 1990 was a course offered in cross-national comparative analysis of social welfare policies and programs.

The proportion of female students grew steadily during the 1970s and reached a majority that has persisted since 1975. Faculty composition changed much more slowly, with males still a majority in 1990. Likewise, curriculum content on gender remained undeveloped in social work doctoral seminars despite students' substantial pressure for change. Except for the graduate seminars offered by the interdepartmental program in Women's Studies, students interested in gender issues were limited to special studies and dissertation research on these topics.

Table 22.4
Program Graduates by Social Science Majors, 1962–91

Social Science Major	Percentages
Sociology	41.51
Psychology	41.51
Social Psychology	7.55
Political Science	6.13
Economics	2.83
Anthropology	0.47

External events in society such as reductions in federal expenditures for graduate education and for many welfare resulted in greater priorities by agencies to fund psychology rather than sociology or political science. As previous societal concerns about racial, economic, and related issues had waned by this time, the emphasis on clinical practice with individuals reappeared among most schools of social work. At the same time, CSWE accreditation requirements for M.S.W. and B.S.W. programs led many schools to focus more emphasis on practice methods, especially on clinical practice. This trend accelerated in the 1980s. Subsequently, doctoral programs appear to have drifted away from an emphasis on graduates playing leadership roles in social policy and research or social science to an emphasis on teaching clinical methods of practice and complementary human behavior courses.

SIGNIFICANCE OF THE PROGRAM FOR SOCIAL WORK AND SOCIAL SCIENCE GRADUATE EDUCATION

As of 1990, the joint program has thrived and grown extensively. It is recognized nationally and internationally as a leader in the training of social work educators and researchers (Jayaratne, 1979; Thyer & Bentley, 1986). Graduates of the joint program now occupy many important leadership roles in the academic and policy community in the United States and internationally. A large number serve as deans or directors of social work programs; many are distinguished scholars whose research and publications have had significant impact upon social work education or in their discipline; and several occupy important policy positions at the federal and state levels (LeDoux, 1991). It has maintained the original mission and orientation of its founders, while adapting to changed circumstances and needs. Thus, it is appropriate here to assess the significance of this model for interdisciplinary doctoral education and to consider future challenges and opportunities resulting from the global social transformations now underway. First, let us summarize some key elements of the program, how these have evolved and changed over time, and their more general implications for social work education in the United States and internationally.

- The Doctoral program has been very influential in the development of graduate professional education in social work, although opportunity remains for further progress to achieve the goals of the founders.

- Interdisciplinary faculty and faculty-student seminars frequently occurred in the early years of the program; and although they are now less frequent, they continue to play important roles in promoting interdisciplinary activity.

- The active role played by the Interdepartmental Supervising Committee in developing this program has been an exemplar for other departments and schools. It is an essential feature for maintaining the quality and interdisciplinary integrity of the program.

- Active joint appointments with other departments are necessary if social work faculty are not to be isolated from cooperative collegial work with the social sciences. Similarly, the social sciences are dependent on the professions as conduits through which aspects of the human condition are illuminated for study and analysis. Today social work faculty are in a distinctive position to influence development in social and behavioral sciences, at least partly because of the transformation of the welfare state in many societies (Friedson, 1986).

- The literature on social work doctoral programs indicates that no one curriculum model is the best; rather, alternative models exist that reflect the faculty expertise and the philosophy, resources, size, and previous traditions of a school. This chapter, together with prior papers by Radin, Benbenisty, and Leon (Radin, Benbenisty, and Leon, 1982); Hasenfeld and Leon (Hasenfeld & Leon, 1979); and Thomas (Thomas, 1984), represents efforts to assess various aspects of the Michigan program.

- The role of GADE appears to have been focused almost exclusively on fending off pressures from CSWE, on providing a venue for informal faculty discussions, and on studying various aspects of student processing—the latter indicated by much of their literature. Less attention is directed to issues of development of practice theory, to how societal issues or problems are affected by social programs, or even to evaluation of the educational mission. Such measurement would be difficult, but the contribution could be enormous for curriculum development in social work education.

- The application of quantitative methods brought about important knowledge, but it is also necessary to have excellent qualitative research for social policy and practice. In addition, the U.S. university has become a highly professionalized bureaucratic organization, concerned with resource procurement, peer review, publications, tenure, and so forth. It could instead seek to insure that at least the professionals it trains will be committed to the affirmative obligation, "Thou shalt do as much as good as possible." In that way the university might better fulfill the expectation that education is truly a moral enterprise (Barber, 1992; Rosenau, 1992). Recent discussions about the roles of the "public intellectual" reflect a growing concern about social obligations and responsibilities of both the disciplines and the professions.

- Doctoral and faculty research today focuses more attention on technologies for the measurement and assessment of social problems than on the search for social explanation, and even less attention has been directed to research on prevention and intervention, although the latter appear to be needed now more than ever before.

- Donna Franklin (Franklin, 1990) has noted that there is a cyclical pattern of relative emphasis in social work on social action versus. social treatment. The 1990s is already a period of significant social change throughout the world as well as in social, economic, and political conditions in the United States. What role should social work doctoral education play in the social transformations likely to occur? This question is an important challenge for the remainder of the decade.

TRANSFORMATION AND CHALLENGES FOR THE 21ST CENTURY

The keynote speaker at the International Schools of Social Work Conference in Washington in 1992, UN Ambassador Kofi Awoonor of Ghana challenged social work educators and social scientists to address seriously the new world order and the social reality of developing countries. In the past, the interests and activities of U.S. social workers have been confined largely to this country, but this is no longer viable given the interdependence of the planet. Demographers report that only 20 percent of the world's population live in the so-called developed countries; however, professional social work focuses almost all of its efforts on that minority population, which already has many times the resources of the remaining 80 percent. Even within the United States, social welfare resources are allocated primarily to the middle classes, rather than to those in greatest need Many U.S schools of social work now actively assist in the development of social work education and social science in other countries, but most of that effort reflects individual faculty interests rather than systematic efforts by schools or the profession. More active involvement with international social work associations are more than likely to be mutually beneficial if we seek to have curricula and research that meet contemporary global needs.[21]

Both social scientists and social work educators need to reappraise the value assumptions of their theories and the value bases of their endeavors. This will entail critical assessments of social science paradigms, social policies, and social work interventions. This, in turn, necessitates renewed collaboration and interchanges between social scientists, social workers, and policy leaders (Jamrozik, 1992). Both social scientists and social workers need to resist passive acceptance of the priorities assigned by funders. The allocation of resources tends to favor stability rather than change. Pressures to focus on personal responsibility and the safety net are being heard with increasing frequency. But, as Ramon (chapter 15) reminds us, social work exists to challenge the existing social system and has the opportunity to contribute significantly to the social sciences because of the special insights it can and should offer.

There are major challenges to be faced in the latter half of the 1990s and in the twenty-first century by many groups, but social work and social science have particular contributions to make. First, the level and diversity of consumption is equated with quality of life in the developed world, but environmental deterioration demonstrates that this priority can no longer be tolerated. Moreover, if high levels of consumption have been achieved by exploitation of poorer countries, that too is no longer acceptable, as recent discussion of the United Nations have shown (Population Council, 1994). Second, inequality and the pursuit of self-interest have long been rewarded. It is claimed that economic efficiency requires excluding more and more persons from the mainstream economic and social life. We are at a crossroads in both time and place, where modification of priorities can be shifted to achieve greater equality among people within and between states, and among nations, but that will only occur through strong advocacy. Third, ethnic, religious, and racial conflicts today threaten both national and international peace in many parts of the world. The constraints of our contemporary knowledge are not sufficient reasons for failing to tackle these problems. Finally, a serious examination of the role of the university, particularly the role of the professional school, in contemporary society is long overdue, and particularly the role of professional school (Friedson, 1986; Jencks, 1992; Wolfe, 1989; Wilshire, 1988). For more than thirty years these institutions have drifted away from their moral leadership in society, and it is increasingly apparent that such leadership is now urgently needed.

ACKNOWLEDGMENTS

We wish to thank Professors Sheila Feld, Phillip Fellin, Charles Garvin, Yeheskel Hasenfeld, and John Tropman, and Professors Emeriti Norma Radin, Edwin J. Thomas, and Henry Meyer for their thoughtful comments and Dr. David G. French for his sharing of historical materials and memories. We also express our appreciation to Rhea Kish for her critical editorial review. Our account of developments over the decades is almost entirely based on published or archival source materials and present no confidential material about persons or events. Published sources are cited in the text or notes, while other important source materials are found in School of Social Work files or, more often, in the archives of the University's Bentley Library. We are also indebted to Professor Fellin for his succint history of social work at Michigan (Fellin, 1977).

NOTES

1. In 1950 there were only 43 graduate schools of social work offering two-year degrees, almost all within or affiliated with universities (Hollis and Taylor, 1952); in 1948 there were only six doctoral programs in social work, located at Bryn Mawr (the first, established in 1915) and at Chicago, Catholic, Ohio State, Pittsburgh, and St. Louis niversities (Holland & Frost, 1987); by 1957 there were 12 schools offering third-year or other advanced programs (Coyle, 1958), of which a significant proportion were "practice" or clinical study programs.

2. Instruction in social work at Michigan dates back to 1921, when the Regents authorized a Detroit-based program of courses for undergraduates and employed personnel. In 1935 a two-year graduate program leading to the M.S.W. degree was authorized within the new Institute of Public and Social Administration which also

embraced other programs. After 1945 the M.S.W. program was given identity as an Institute of Social Work and strove for a curriculum to "enlarge the technical side of training in the general field of social and public welfare and to relate it to the broader aspects of political and social life (Announcement, 1945)," albeit remaining in its Detroit building. The Institute's executive committee was composed of persons from social science and professional faculties on the Ann Arbor campus, and some of these persons, notably Robert C. Angell, would assist in the School's subsequent transformation.

3. In 1950 the Regents formulated particular mandates for the new school, including the first four: "1. the school's primary orientation must be to State services and public social policies; 2. graduates must be prepared for varied positions across the broad spectrum of public services (Offe, 1987), without concentration in a selected few; 3. the curriculum must achieve a manifest integration of knowledge from social science disciplines, not merely that derived from professional practice; and, 4. primary activities must include research and advancement of knowledge as well as training of personnel for agency employment." Abstracted and quote by Fellin from the Board of Regents, 1950 (Fellin, 1977).

4. A similar approach was taken some years later with public administration, the other major program in the former Institute of Public and Social Administration, when it was reconsituted on the central campus.

5. Dean Fauri was a Michigan native and University of Michigan Law School graduate who had served in several positions with the State Department of Social Services, eventually as its general counsel, then director. After World War II he was called to the Congressional Reference Service in Washington as special counsel to the U.S. Senate Finance Committee, the powerful body that, among other things, expanded the Social Security system. After 20 years with the school as dean and professor of Public Welfare Administration, he became Vice President for State Relations and Planning, the university's chief representative to the state legislature, governor's office, and the like.

6. Personal correspondence with David G. French. Dr. French had previously served as editor of the *Social Work Journal*, which was partially supported by the Foundation.

7. Early in this period the school recruited some faculty with both M.S.W. and social science Ph.D. degrees; they were called "hybrids" and shared the dual orientations of the doctoral students. The first of these were Robert D. Vinter (1959) and Edwin J. Thomas (1956), the latter with a joint appointment in psychology. Social scientists without the M.S.W. who were committed to collaboration between the sciences and the profession and to the aims of the joint program, were soon also successfully recruited.

8. Unlike most university units, the school has never had separate "departments," thus avoiding the likelihood of separated interests and internal hindrances to change. Its subsidiary and changing entities have been called "programs" and the like, and faculty members are expected to be active in more than one program or area of the curriculum. The doctoral faculty group, therefore, has always been one among several. Its duties are identical to those of faculty groups responsible for other areas of the curriculum, although it is accountable to the program's Supervising Committee as well as the school's Governing Faculty. It should be noted that all faculty members were expected to teach in the core master's program, while only those with advanced degrees were eligible to teach doctoral level seminars, although not all did.

9. Wilbur Cohen's joining the school's faculty in this period, following his retirement from a distinguished career in the federal service, supplemented Fedele

Fauri's expertise in the area of public welfare policies and enhanced the school's competence and prestige. Cohen would depart in a few years to serve, first, as assistant secretary of the U.S. Department of Health, Education and Welfare and then as secretary of DHEW (now HHS) under President Lyndon Johnson; he then returned to the university as dean of the School of Education.

10. During this period, for example, the crucial curriculum area previously titled "Development of the Individual" was retitled "Human Behavior and Social Environment" (HBSE), concretely reflecting the expansions of its knowledge bases.

11. The only significant changes up to this time increased the number of credit hours required for the M.S.W. degree from 47 to 56 and reduced the days spent in field instruction from 3 to 2.5 and then to 2 days, to redress the imbalance between class and field studies and to enrich academic content. Reduction of days in field agencies was, as expected, deprecated by some agency representatives, but with little effect. The thesis requirement was also soon abandoned.

12. By 1966 there were 370 full-time students enrolled in the School's M.S.W. program, and 27 full-time doctoral students; by 1967 full-time enrollment was 428, with 52 full-time faculty (Council of Social Work Education, 1967, 1968).

13. During 1958–70 persons with doctorates explicitly appointed to contribute to the integration of social science within the curriculum, to conduct research, and to qualify for teaching in the doctoral program included, in order of appointment: Paul Glasser, Eugene Litwak, William Neenan (joint with Economics), Rosemary Sarri, Jack Rothman, Phillip Fellin, Charles Garvin, Sheldon Rose, Richard Stuart, John Tropman, Yeheskel Hasenfeld, Tony Tripodi, Thomas Anton (joint with Political Science), Richard English, Eileen Gambrill, Irwin Epstein, Sheila Feld, Martin Sundel, David Himle, and Norma Radin.

14. Several of the resultant publications first appeared in the early 1970s because of the typical lag times between completion of manuscripts and their publication in journals; almost all the chapters in readers and compilations we reference were originally published or distributed during the late 1950s and 1960s. Given the remarkable acceleration of productivity during the 1970s and 1980s, space does not permit crediting subsequent materials authored by faculty members.

15. Sociology and social work student dissertations were completed by Oscar Grusky, Bernard Berk, Mayer Zald, Rosemary Sarri, Victor Schneider, and Yeheskel Hasenfeld. See Street, Vinter, and Perrow, 1966.

16. Since the Michigan program began in 1957, many other schools of social work have incorporated varying degrees of social science content into their doctoral curricula, but none has established a joint degree program. The Group for the Advancement of Doctoral Education studies show that there is very little social science theory and methods content in social work doctoral programs. The presence of Michigan doctoral program graduates in leadership positions as deans and directors in a large number of schools has had an impact on increasing social science curriculum in the United States and internationally in recent years.

17. There were 9,335 students in master's degree programs in 1966. By 1980 enrollment had increased to 17,122 full-time and 5,274 part-time students. Bachelor's degree programs grew even more rapidly, from 6,247 in 1970 to 27,051 in 1980 (Council on Social Work Education, 1989).

18. Periodically there are proposals to develop a "practice-oriented" or "clinical" doctorate as the terminal degree for social work. Such recommendations may well reflect a desire for a degree parallel with those of psychologists and psychiatrists.

19. Occasionally students resisted the emphasis on quantification, preferring greater opportunities for theory development and qualitative research in applied social science or in practice. However, unless their work could be empirically verified, they had to be very persistent to have it approved by the departments. The shift toward research methodology for quantitative empirical verification characterized much of social science in the United States from the 1960s to 1980s. In the latter half of the 1980s there was a rebirth of interest in qualitative and action research and also in theory. Examples of the latter include ethnographic and interdisciplinary studies such as that by William Julius Wilson and his colleagues in their study of the underclass in Chicago (Wilson, 1989) and the study of women's social movement organizations by Cheryl Hyde (Hyde, 1991).

20. As recently as 1990 only the Anthropology Department offered a doctoral level course in race and gender theory. However, it is probably that there was content on race and ethnicity in a number of graduate courses, but it was seldom labeled as such.

21. The International Schools of Social Work provides such opportunities. In May 1993, an international conference was held in Kolumna, Russia, sponsored by the Russian Association of Social Pedagogues and Social Workers, and attended by social work educators from Europe, the Middle East, Canada, the United States, Asia, and Africa. They met with educators from the former Soviet Union and Eastern Europe to address together the development of social work. The education and social workers in Russia and the other newly independent states of the former Soviet Union. The activities organized there and in Eastern Europe for the development of social welfare have the potential for significant worldwide contributions to peace and development. NASW is now playing an active role in the development of associations of social workers in Eastern Europe and Russia. In April 1994, the Chinese government endorsed the establishment of the Association for Social Work Education in China. Six major Chinese universities are now providing social work education in close collaboration with social science departments. They too are requesting assistance from countries with well-developed social work education programs. These developments provide challenges for enhancing the integration of social work and social science in the United States, as well as throughout the world.

References

Abbott, A. (1988). *The System of Professions*. Chicago, IL: University of Chicago Press.

Abel, T. (1977). The Operation Called "Verstehen." In F. R. Dallmayr & T. A. McCarthy (Eds.), *Understanding and Social Inquiry*. (pp. 81–92). South Bend: University of Notre Dame.

Abelson, R. P. (1976). Script Processing in Attitude Formation and Decision-Making. In J. S. Carrol & J. W. Payne (Eds.), *Cognition and Social Behavior*. (pp. 333–346). Hillsdale, NJ: Lawrence Erlbaum Associates.

Abelson, R. P. (1981). Psychological Status of the Script Concept. *American Psychologist* 36(7): 715–729.

Abraham, F. D., R. H. Abraham, & C. D. Shaw. (1990). *A Visual Introduction to Dynamical Systems Theory for Psychology*. Santa Cruz, CA: Aerial Press.

Abramovitz, M. (1988). *Regulating the Lives of Women: Social Welfare Policy from Colonial Times to the Present*. Boston, MA: South End Press.

Abramson, J. S. (1993). Orienting Social Work Employees in Interdisciplinary Settings: Shaping Professional and Organizational Perspectives. *Social Work* 38(2): 152–157.

Acker, J. (1978). Issues in the Sociological Study of Women's Work. In A. Armstrong & S. Harkness (Eds.), *Working Women: Theories and Facts in Perspective*. (pp. 134–161). Palo Alto: Mansfield Publishing.

Ackoff, R. L. (1970). *A Concept of Corporate Planning*. NY: Wiley.

Adam, B. D. (1978a). Inferiorization and Self-Esteem. *Social Psychology* 41(1): 47–53.

Adam, B. D. (1978b). *The Survival of Domination: Inferiorization and Everyday Life*. New York: Elsevier.

Adamson, M., & S. Burgos. (1984). *This Mighty Dream: Social Protest Movements in the United States*. Boston: Routledge and Kegan Paul.

Addams, J. (1902). *Democracy and Social Ethics*. New York: Macmillan and Co.

Addams, J. (1910). *Twenty Years at Hull House*. New York: Macmillan and Co.

Agger, B. (1991). Critical Theory, Poststructuralism, Postmodernism: Their Sociological Relevance. *Annual Review of Sociology* 17, 105–131.

Alderfer, C. P. (1987). An Intergroup Perspective on Group Dynamics. In J. W. Lorsch (Ed.), *Handbook of Organizational Behavior*. (pp. 190–222). Englewood Cliffs, NJ:

Prentice-Hall.

Allport, G. W. (1954). *The Nature of Prejudice*. Garden City, NY: Doubleday Anchor.

Alvarez, A., B. Baker, C. J. Butler, I. H. Leonard, J. Meyerson, D. Reed, B. Glover, & S. E. Sutton. Alternative Approaches to Integrating Feminist Theory and Practice: Curricular, Collaborative Workgroup, and Classroom Examples. Paper presented at the *First Annual Conference on the Integration of Social Work and Social Science*. October 29–November 1, 1992. Ann Arbor, MI. School of Social Work, University of Michigan.

Amin, S. (1990). The Social Movements in the Periphery. In S. Amin et al. (Eds.), *Transforming the Revolution: Social Movements and the World-System.* New York: Monthly Review Press.

Ancona, D. G., & D. F. Caldwell. (1988). Beyond Task and Maintenance: Defining External Functions in Groups. *Groups and Organizations* 13(4): 468–494.

Anderson, J. R. (1983). *The Architecture of Cognition*. Cambridge, MA: Harvard University.

Anderson, M., L. Collins, & P. H. Collins. (1992). *Race, Class and Gender: An Anthology*. Belmont, CA: Wadsworth Publishing Company.

Andrews, A. B. (1990). Interdisciplinary and Interorganizational Collaboration. In L. Ginsberg, S. Khinduka, J. A. Hall, F. Ross-Sheriff, & A. Hartman. (Eds.), *Encyclopedia of Social Work* 18th ed., 1990 Supplement (pp. 175–188). Silver Spring: National Association of Social Work Press.

Argote, L. (1982). Input Uncertainty and Organizational Coordination in Hospital Emergency Units. *Administrative Science Quarterly* 27, 420–434.

Argyris, C. (1970). *Intervention Theory and Method*. Reading, MA: Addison-Wesley.

Argyris, C., & D. A. Schon. (1974). *Theory in Practice: Increasing Professional Effectiveness*. San Francisco, CA: Jossey-Bass Publishers.

Argyris, C., & D. A. Schon. (n.d.). Conceptions of Causality in Social Theory and Research: Normal Science and Action Science Compared. Unpublished mimeograph.

Armstrong, J. C. (1980). Unintelligible Management Research and Academic Prestige. *Interfaces* 10, 80–86.

Aronowitz, S. (1981). *The Crisis of Historical Materialism*. New York: Praeger.

Arrowsmith, D. K., & C. M. Place. (1990). *An Introduction to Dynamical Systems*. Cambridge, MA: Cambridge University Press.

Asimov, J. (1989). The Relativity of Wrong. *Skeptical Inquirer* 14, 35–44.

Astley, W. G., & A. H. Van de Ven. (1983). Central Perspectives and Debates in Organization Theory. *Administrative Science Quarterly* 28, 245–273.

Austin, D. (1983). Administrative Practice in Human Services: Future Directions for Curriculum Development. *The Journal of Applied Behavioral Science* 19(2): 141–152.

Austin, D. M. (1991). Decision Making Styles and Leadership Patterns in Nonprofit Human Service Organizations. *Administration in Social Work* 15(3): 1–17.

Australian Bureau of Statistics. (1987). The Labor Force, Australia; Historical Summary 1966–1984. *Catalogue Number 6204.0*. Canberra: Australian Bureau of Statistics.

Australian Bureau of Statistics. (1991a). Labor Force Status and Educational Attainment, Australia, February 1991. *Catalogue Number 6235.0*. Canberra: Australian Bureau of Statistics.

Australian Bureau of Statistics. (1991b). The Labor Force, Australia, August 1991. *Catalogue Number 6203.0*. Canberra: Australian Bureau of Statistics.

Australian Bureau of Statistics. (1992). Household Expenditure Survey, Australia: The Effects of Government Benefits and Taxes on Household Income. *Catalogue No.*

6537.0. Canberra: Australian Bureau of Statistics.

Awoonor, K. (1992). The New World Order, Social Reality in Developing Countries and Global Security. Address to the *26th Congress of the International Association of Schools of Social Work,* Washington, DC.

Bacharach, L. (1992). The Urban Environment and Mental Health. *International Journal of Social Psychiatry* 38(1): 5–15.

Bacharach, S. B., & E. J. Lawler. (1980). *Power and Politics in Organizations.* San Francisco: Jossy-Bass.

Baer, D. M. (1991). Tacting "to a fault." *Journal of Applied Behavior Analysis* 24, 429–432.

Baigrie, B. S., & J. N. Hattiangadi. (1992). On Consensus and Stability in Science. *The British Journal for the Philosophy of Science* 43(4): 335–358.

Bailey, D. (1991). Designing and Sustaining Effective Organizational Teams. R. L. Edwards & J. A. Yankey (Eds.), *Skills for Effective Human Services Management.* (pp. 142–154). Silver Spring, MD: National Association of Social Workers Press.

Bailey, D. Jr., Hesel-DeWest M., J. E. Thiele, & W. Ware. (1983). Measuring Individual Participation on the Interdisciplinary Team. *American Journal of Mental Deficiency* 88(3): 247–254.

Bak, P., & K. Chen. (1991). Self-Organized Critically. *Scientific American* 254(1).

Baker, D., & M. Wilson. (1992). An Evaluation of the Scholarly Productivity of Doctoral Graduates. *Journal of Social Work Education* 28, 204–213.

Bales, R. F., & P. E. Slater. (1955). Role Differentiation in Small Decision-Making Groups. In T. Parsons & R. Bales (Eds.), *Family Socialization and Interaction Process.* (pp. 259–306). New York: Free Press.

Bandura, A. (1977). Self-Efficacy: Toward a Unifying Theory of Behavioral Change. *Psychological Review* 84(2): 191-215.

Bandura, A. (1982). Self-efficacy Mechanism in Human Agency. *American Psychologist* 37, 122–147.

Bandura, A. (1986). *Social Foundation of Thought and Action: A Social Cognitive Theory.* New York: Prentice-Hall.

Banfield, E., & J. Q. Wilson. (1963). *City Politics.* Cambridge, MA: Harvard University Press and the MIT Press.

Banta, H. D. (1984). Enhancing or Rejecting Innovations: Clinical Diffusion of Health Care Technology. In S. Reiser & M. Anbar (Eds.), *The Machine at the Bedside.* Cambridge: Cambridge University Press.

Barber, B. (1992). *The Politics of Education and the Future of America.* New York: Ballantine.

Barley, S. R., & D. B. Knight. (1991). Toward a cultural theory of stress complaints. In B. Staw & L. L. Cummings (Eds.), *Research in Organizational Behavior.* 14 (pp. 1–48). Greenwich, CT: JAI Press.

Barlow, D. H., S. C. Hayes, & R. O. Nelson. (1983). *The Scientist Practitioner: Research and Accountability in Clinical and Educational Settings.* New York: Pergamon Press.

Barlow, D. H., S. C. Hayes, & R. O. Nelson. (1984). *The Scientist Practitioner: Research and Accountability in Clinical and Educational Settings.* New York: Pergamon Press.

Barnes, B. (1988). *The Nature of Power.* Chicago: University of Illinois Press.

Barnes, M., M. Fisher, & M. Bowel. (1990). *Sectioned: Social Work and the 1983 Mental Health Act.* London: Routledge.

Barrow, J. D. (1991). *Theories of Everything: The Quest for the Ultimate Explanation.*

Oxford: Clarendon Press.

Barry, A. (1993). The History of Measurement and the Engineers of Space. *British Journal for the History of Science* 26(December): 459–468.

Barthes, R. (1972). *Mythologies*. New York: Farrar Straus and Giroux.

Bartley, W. W. I. (1990). *Unfathomed Knowledge, Unmeasured Wealth: On Universities and the Wealth of Nations*. LaSalle, IL: Open Court.

Barton, S. (1994). Chaos, Self-Organization, and Psychology. *American Psychologist* 49, 5–14.

Baruch, G., & R. Barnett. (1986). Role Quality, Multiple Role Involvement and Psychological Well-being in Mid-life Women. *Journal of Personality and Social Psychology* 51, 578–585.

Basaglia, F. (1968). *L'istituzione Negata*. Rome: Einuadi.

Bassuk, E. (1984). The Homelessness Problem. *Scientific American* 251(1).

Bateson, G. (1991). *A Sacred Unity: Further Steps to an Ecology of Mind*. Ed. R. E. Donaldson. San Francisco: Harper.

Baudrillard, J. (1975). *The Mirror of Production*. St. Louis: Telos Press.

Baughman, E. E. (1971). *Black Americans: A Psychological Analysis*. New York: Academia.

Bauman, Z. (1988). Sociology and Postmodernity. *Sociological Review* 36, 790–823.

Bavelas, A. (1948). A Mathematical Model for Group Structures. *Applied Anthropology* 7, 16–30.

Bavelas, A. (1950). Communication Patterns in Task-Oriented Groups. *Journal of the Acoustical Society of America* 22, 725–730.

Beach, L. R. (1964). Recognition, Assimilation, and Identification of Object. *Psychological Monographs* 78, 22–37.

Beach, L. R., & T. R. Mitchell. (1987). Image Theory: Principles, Goals, and Plans in Decision Making. *Acta Psychologica* 66(3): 201–220.

Beach, L. R., & T. R. Mitchell. (1990). Image Theory: A Behavioral Theory of Decision Making in Organizations. In B. Saw & L. Cummings (Eds.), *Research in Organizational Behavior*. 12 (pp. 1–41). Greenwich, CT: JAI Press.

Begun, A. Teaching About Families and Urban Poverty: Implications of Chaos Theory. Paper presented at the *Council on Social Work Education Annual Program Meeting*. March, 1994.

Beitman, B. D., M. R. Goldried, & J. C. Norcross. (1989). The Movement toward Integrating the Psychotherapies: An Overview. *American Journal of Psychiatry* 146(2): 138–147.

Bell, D. J. (1990). *Mathematics of Linear and Nonlinear Systems: For Engineers and Applied Scientists*. Oxford: Clarendon Press.

Bennett, L., P. Michie, & S. Kippax. (1991). Quantitative Analysis of Burnout and its Associated Factors in AIDs Nursing. *AIDs Care* 3, 181–192.

Benveniste, G. (1972). *The Politics of Expertise*. Berkeley, CA: Glendessary Press.

Bercher, H. J. (1987). *Group Particapation*. 2nd ed. Newsbury Park, CA: Sage.

Berger, P., & R. Neuhaus. (1977). *To Empower People: The Role of Mediating Structures in Public Policy*. Washington DC: American Enterprise Institute.

Berkeley Planning Associates. (1989). *Employer-Supported Child Care: Measuring and Understanding Its Impacts on the Workplace*. Report prepared for. U.S. Department of Labor, Office of Strategic Planning and Policy Development.

Berl, J., G. Lewis, & R. S. Morrison. (1976). Applying Models of Choice to the Problem of College Selection. In J. Carrol & J. Payne (Eds.), *Cognition and Social Behavior*. (pp. 206–219). Hillsdale, NJ: Lawrence Erlbaum Associates.

Berlin, S. B., & J. C. Marsh. (1993). *Informing Practice Decisions.* New York: Macmillan.

Berlyne, D. E. (1962). Uncertainty and Epistemic Curiosity. *British Journal of Psychology* 53, 27–34.

Berman, M. (1988). *All That is Solid Melts Into Air: The Experience of Modernity.* New York: Penguin Books.

Bernard, J. (1987). Reviewing the Impact of Women's Studies on Sociology. In C. Farnham (Ed.), *The Impact of Feminist Research in the Academy.* (pp. 193–216). Bloomington: Indiana University Press.

Bernstein, S. R. (1989). *Playing the Game of Contracted Services: Administrative, Ethical, and Political Issues for the Nonprofit Agency Manager.* Unpublished doctoral dissertation, City University of New York.

Bernstein, S. R. (1991). *Managing Contracted Services in the Nonprofit Agency: Administrative, Ethical, and Political Issues.* Philadelphia, PA: Temple University Press.

Bernstein, S. R., & I. Epstein. Grounded Theory Meets the Reflective Practitioner: Integrating Qualitative and Quantitative Methods in Administrative Practice. Paper presented at the *Conference on Qualitative Methods in Social Work Practice Research.* August, 1991. Albany, NY.

Bettenhausen, K. L. (1991). Five Years of Group Research: What Have We Learned and What Needs to be Addressed. *Journal of Management* 17(2): 345–381.

Beuf, A. (1977). *Red Children in White America.* Philadelphia: University of Pennsylvania Press.

Biddle, B. J., & E. J. Thomas. (1966). *Role Theory: Concepts and Research.* New York: John Wiley.

Bieber, I. et al. (1962). *Homosexuality: A Psychoanalytic Study of Male Homosexuality.* New York: Basic Books.

Billings, A., & R. Moos. (1982). Work Stress and the Stress-buffering Roles of Work and Family Resources. *Journal of Occupational Behavior* no. 3: 215–232.

Billingsly, A. (1968). *Black Families in White America.* Englewood Cliffs, NJ: Prentice Hall.

Billups, J. O. (1986). A Consortium Experience in Interprofessional Education: Potentials for Advancing Social Development. *Social Development Issues* 10(2): 42–55.

Bishop, J. K. (1983). Adhocracy as an Organizational Structure in a Psychiatric Institution. *Journal of Nursing Administration* 13(1): 20–24.

Black, K. (1951). The Exertion of Influence Through Social Communication. *Journal of Abnormal and Social Psychology* 46(2).

Bloom, M., J. Fischer, & J. Orme. (1994). *Evaluating Practice: Guidelines for the Accountable Professional.* Englewood Cliffs, NJ: Prentice-Hall.

Bloom, M., J. Fischer, & J. Orme. (1995). *Evaluating Practice: Guidelines for the Accountable Professional.* 2nd ed. Englewood Cliffs, NJ: Prentice-Hall.

Bloom, M. (1975). *The Paradox of Helping: Introduction to the Philosophy of Scientific Practice.* New York: John Wiley.

Blythe, B. J., & T. Tripodi. (1989). *Measurement in Direct Practice.* Newbury Park, CA: Sage.

Bohen, H., & A. Viveros-Long. (1981). *Balancing Jobs and Family Life.* Philadelphia, PA: Temple University Press.

Boland, C. (1989). A Comparative Study of Home and Hospital Births: Scientific and Normative Variables. *SWRC Discussion Paper # 12.* Kensington, New South

Wales: University of New South Wales.

Bond, G. R., M. Pensec, L. Dietzen, D. McCafferty, R. Giemza, & H. W. Sipple. (1991). Intensive Case Management for Frequent Users of Psychiatric Hospitals in a Large City: A Comparison of Team and Individual Caseloads. *Psychosocial Rehabilitation Journal* 15(1): 90–98.

Bornstein, R. F. (1990). Publication Politics, Experimenter Bias and the Replication Process in Social Science Research. *Journal of Social Behavior and Personality* 5(4): 71–81.

Boulding, K. (1956). General Systems Theory: The Skeleton of a Science. *Management Science* 2(3): 197–208.

Boyer, E. (1994). Creating the New Amercian College. *The Chronicle of Higher Education*. March 9: 40.

Boyte, H., H. Booth, & S. Max. (1986). *Citizen Action and the New American Populism*. Philadelphia: Temple University Press.

Boyte, H., & F. Riessman. (1986). *The New Populism*. Philadelphia: Temple University Press.

Brams, S. J. (1978). *The Presidential Election Game*. New Haven, CT: Yale University Press.

Brams, S. J. (1985). *Superpower Games: Applying Game Theory to Superpower Conflict*. New Haven, CT: Yale University Press.

Brandon, D. (1991). *Innovation without Change?* London: Macmillan.

Brass, D. J. (1985). Technology and the Structuring of Jobs: Employee Satisfaction, Performance, and Influence. *Organizational Behavior and Human Decision Processes* 35(2): 216–240.

Breakwell, G. (1983). *Coping with Threatened Identities*. London: Methuen.

Brecher, J., & T. Costello. (1990). *Building Bridges: The Emerging Grassroots Coalition of Labor and Community*. New York: Monthly Review Press.

Brecher, J., & T. Costello. (1994). *Global Village or Global Pillage: Economic Reconstruction from the Bottom Up*. Boston: South End Press.

Bremner, R. H. (1960). *American Philanthropy*. Chicago, Illinois: University of Chicago Press.

Brewer, R. (1988). Black Women in Poverty: Some Comments on Female-headed Households. *Signs* 13(2): 331–339.

Brewin, C. W. (1990). Pluralism and Human Knowledge. *Psychological Inquiry* 1(3): 203–204.

Briar, S. (1976). Major Trends and Issues Affecting the Future of Doctoral Education in Social Work and Social Welfare. Paper presented at the *Group for the Advancement of Doctoral Education Conference.*

Briar, S. (1979). Incorporating Research into Education for Clinical Practice in Social Work: Toward a Clinical Science in Social Work. A. Rubin & A. Rosenblatt (Eds.), *Sourcebook on Research Utilization.* Washington, DC: Council on Social Work Education.

Briar, S. (1980). Toward the Integration of Practice and Research. In D. Fanshel (Ed.), *Future of Social Work Research.* (pp. 31–37). Washington, DC: National Association of Social Work.

Briar, S. (1985). Doctoral Research and Social Work Practice. *Proceedings of the National Symposium on Doctoral Research and Social Work Practice.* Columbus: Ohio State University, College of Social Work.

Bricker-Jenkins, M., & N. Hooyman. (1986). *Not for Women Only: Social Work Practice for a Feminist Future.* Silver Spring, MD: National Association of Social Work

Press.

Briggs, J., & D. F. Peat. (1989). *Turbulent Mirror: An Illustrated Guide to Chaos Theory and the Science of Wholeness*. New York: Harper and Row.

Brigham, J. (1974). Views of Black and White Children Concerning the Distribution of Personality Characteristics. *Journal of Personality* 42(1): 145–58.

Brim, O., & S. Wheeler. (1966). *Socialization after Childhood: Two Essays*. New York: J. Wiley.

Bronner, S. E. (1990). *Socialism Unbound*. New York: Routledge.

Brookfield, S. D. (1987). *Developing Critical Thinkers: Challenging Adults to Explore Alternative Ways of Thinking and Acting*. San Francisco, CA: Jossey-Bass.

Brower, A. M. (1988). Can the Ecological Model Guide Social Work Practice? *Social Service Review* 62, 411–429.

Brower, A. M. (1989). Group Development as Constructed Social Reality: A Social-Cognitive Understanding of Group Formation. *Social Work With Groups* 12, 23–41.

Brower, A. M. (1992). The "Second Half" of Student Integration: Life Tasks and the Power of Choice on Student Persistence. *Journal of Higher Education* 63, 441–462.

Brower, A. M., & P. S. Nurius. (1993). *Social Cognition and Individual Change: Current Theory and Counseling Guidelines*. Newbury Park, CA: Sage Publications.

Brown, E. L. (1938). *Social Work as a Profession*. New York: Russell Sage Foundation.

Brown, E. L. (1936). *Social Work as a Profession*. 2nd ed. New York: Russell Sage Foundation.

Brown, E. L. (1942). *Social Work as a Profession*. 4th ed. New York: Russell Sage Foundation.

Brown, G. W., M. N. Brhol-Chain, & T. Harris. (1979). Social Class and Psychiatric Disturbance among Women in an Urban Population. *Sociology* 9, 225–254.

Brown, G. W., & T. Harris. (1978). *Social Origins of Depression: A Study of Psychiatric Disorder in Women*. New York: Free Press.

Brown, J. D., & S. E. Taylor. (1988). Affect and the Processing of Personal Information: Evidence for Mood-Activated Schemata. *Journal of Experimental Social Psychology* 22, 436–452.

Bruno, F. J. (1957). *Trends in Social Work 1874–1956*. New York: Columbia University Press.

Burawoy, M. (1991). The Extended Case Method. In M. Burawoy, A. Burton, A. A. Ferguson, K. J. Fox, J. Gamson, N. Gartrell, L. Hurst, C. Kurzman, L. Salzinger, J. Schiffman, & S. Ui (Eds.), *Ethnography Unbound: Power and Resistance in the Modern Metropolis.* (pp. 271–287). Berkeley: University of California Press.

Bureau of Child Guidance of the Board of Education of the City of New York. (1938). *Five Year Report 1932–1937 of the Bureau of Child Guidance of the Board of Education of the City of New York*. NY: Board of Education of the City of New York.

Burgess, E. W. (1927). The Contribution of Sociology to Family Social Work. *The Family* 8, 191–193.

Burghardt, S. (1982). *The Other Side of Organizing: Resolving the Personal Dilemmas and Political Demands of Daily Practice*. Cambridge, MA: Schenkman.

Burnham, J. C. (1987). *How Superstition Won and Science Lost*. New Brunswick, NJ: Rutgers University Press.

Burst, A., & L. A. Schlesinger. (1987). *The Management Game*. New York: Viking.

Burud, S., P. Aschbacher, & J. McCroskey. (1984). *Employer-Supported Child Care: Investing in Human Resources*. Boston: Auburn House.

Butterill, D., J. O'Hanlon, & H. Book. (1992). When the System Is the Problem, Don't

Blame the Patient: Problems Inherent in the Interdisciplinary Inpatient Team. *Canadian Journal of Psychiatry* 37, 168–172.

Cammann, C., M. Fichman, G. D. J. Jenkins, & J. Klesh. (1983). Assessing the Attitudes and Perceptions of Organizational Members. In S. Seashore (Ed.), *Assessing Organizational Change: A Guide to Methods, Measures, and Practices.* (pp. 71–119). New York: Wiley.

Campbell, A. (1981). *The Sense of Well-Being in America.* New York: McGraw-Hill.

Campbell, A., P. E. Converse, & W. L. Rodgers. (1976). *The Quality of Life in America.* New York: Russell Sage Foundation.

Campbell, D. T., & J. C. Stanley. (1963). *Experimental and Quasi-experimental Designs for Research.* Rand McNally College Publishing Co.

Cantor, N., & J. F. Kihlstrom. (1989). Social Intelligence and Cognitive Assessments of Personality. In R. S. Wyer & T. K. Srull (Eds.), *Advances in Social Cognition, Volume II: Social Intelligence and Cognitive Assessments of Personality.* (pp. 1–59). Hillsdale, NJ: Erlbaum.

Caplan, G. (1959). *Concepts of Mental Health and Consultation.* New York: Children's Bureau Publications.

Carew, R. (1979). The Place of Knowledge in Social Work Activity. *British Journal of Social Work* 8, 349–364.

Carlson, R. E. (1967). Selection Interview Decisions: The Relative Influence of Appearance and Factual Written Information on an Interviewer's Final Rating. *Journal of Applied Psychology* 51, 461–468.

Carlson, R. E., & E. C. Mayfield. (1967). Selection Interview Decisions: The Effect of Type of Information on Inter- and Intra-Interviewer Agreement. *Personnel Psychology* 20, 441–460.

Carniol, B. (1992). Structural Social Work: Maurice Moreau's Challenge to Social Work Practice. *Journal of Progressive Human Services* 3, 1–20.

Carson, A. D., T. Madison, & J. W. Santrock. (1987). Relationships between Possible Selves and Self-Reported Problems of Divorced and Intact Family Adolescents. *Journal of Early Adolescence* 7, 191–204.

Castells, M. (1983). *The City and the Grassroots.* Berkeley: University of California Press.

Casti, J. L. (1989). *Alternate Realities: Mathematical Models of Nature and Man.* New York: John Wiley & Sons.

Casti, J. L. (1990). *Searching for Certainty: What Scientists Can Know about the Future.* New York: W. Morrow.

Catania, A. C. (1991). The Gift of Culture and Eloquence: An Open Letter to Michael J. Mahoney in Reply to His Article "Scientific Psychology and Radical Behaviorism." *Behavior Analyst* 14, 61–72.

Chambers, C. A. (1986). Women in the Creation of the Profession of Social Work. *Social Service Review* 60(1): 1–33.

Charniak, E. (1972). *Towards a Model of Children's Story Comprehension.* Unpublished doctoral dissertation, Massachusetts Institute of Technology, Laboratory for Artificial Intelligence, Cambridge, MA.

Charniak, E. (1988). Motivation Analysis, Adductive Unification, and Nonmonotonic Equality. *Artificial Intelligence* 34, 275–295.

Chase, S., J. H. Wright, & R. Ragade. (1981). Decision Making in an Interdisciplinary Team. *Behavior Scientist* 26, 206–215.

Chavetz, J. S. (1978). *Masculine, Feminine or Human? An Overview of the Sociology of Gender Roles.* Ithaca, NY: F. E. Peacock.

Cheng, J. L. C., & W. McKinley. (1983). Toward an Integration of Organization Research and Practice: A Contingency Study of Bureaucratic Control and Performance in Scientific Settings. *Administrative Science Quarterly* 28(1): 85–100.

Cheung, K. M. (1990). Interdisciplinary Relationships between Social Work and Other Disciplines: A Citation Study. *Social Work Research and Abstracts* 26, 23–29.

Child, J. (1972). Organization Structure, Environment, and Performance - The Role of Strategic Choice. *Sociology* 6, 1–22.

Child, J. (1973). Strategies of Control and Organizational Behavior. *Administrative Science Quarterly* 18, 1–17.

Chiu, L. P. W. (1990). Child Psychiatric Problems Associated with Divorce: A Report of Four Cases. *Hong Kong Journal of Mental Health* 19(2): 42–48.

Christie, J. R. R. (1993). Aurora, Nemesis and Clio. *British Journal for the History of Science* 26(4): 391–405.

Chubin, D. E. (1989). Research Malpractice. In D. E. Chubin & E. W. Chu (Eds.), *Science Off the Pedestal: Social Perspectives on Science and Technology.* Belmont, CA: Wadsworth.

Clark, K. B., & M. P. Clark. (1939). The Development of Racial Identification in Negro Preschool Children. *Journal of Social Psychology* 10, 591–599.

Clark, K. B., & M. P. Clark. (1958). Racial Identification and Preference in Negro Children. In E. P. Maccoby et al. (Eds.), *Readings in Social Psychology.* New York: Holt, Rinehart and Winston.

Cocks, J. (1989). *The Oppositional Imagination.* London: Routledge.

Cohen, D. (1989). Biological Basis of Schizophrenia: The Evidence Reconsidered. *Social Work* 34(3): 255–257.

Cohen, J., & R. Cohen. (1983). *Applied Multiple Regression/Correlation Analysis for the Behavioral Sciences.* 2nd. ed. Hillsdale, New Jersey: Lawrence Erlbaum Associates.

Cohen, J. (1989). Deliberation and Democratic Legitimacy. In P. Petit & A. Hamlin (Eds.), *The Good Polity.* London: Basil Blackwell.

Cohen, L., M. Sargent, & L. Sechrest. (1986). Use of Psychotherapy Research by Professional Psychologists. *American Psychologist* 41, 198–206.

Cohen, W. (1960). *The Impact of Unemployment in the 1958 Recession.* Washington, DC: Government Printing Office for the U.S. Congress Committee on Unemployment.

Cohen, W., & W. Haber. (1960). *Social Security: Programs, Problems, and Policies.* Homewood, IL: R. D. Irwin.

Collier, J., M. C. Rosaldo, & S. Yanagisako. (1982). Is There a Family: New Anthropological Views. In B. Thorne (Ed.), *Rethinking the Family: Some Feminist Questions.* (pp. 25–39). New York: Longman.

Collini, S. (1993). Introduction. For C. P. Snow's *The Two Cultures.* Canto ed. (p. vii–lxxi). Cambridge, MA: Cambridge University Press.

Collins, P. H. (1986). Learning from the Outsider Within: The Sociological Significance of Black Feminist Thought. *Social Problems* 33, 524–532.

Collins, P. H. (1990). *Black Feminist Thought: Knowledge, Consciousness and the Politics of Empowerment.* Boston: Unwin, Hyman.

Colman, A. M. (1987). *Facts, Fallacies and Frauds in Psychology.* London: Hutchinson.

Colomy, P., & M. Kretzmann. (1995). Projects and Institution Building: Judge B. Lindsey and the Juvenile Court Movement. *Social Problems* 42(2 May): 191–215.

Committee on the History of Child Saving Work. (1893). *History of Child Saving in the United States.* National Conference of Charities and Corrections.

Community Service Society of New York. (1949). *Social Work as Human Relations.*

New York: Columbia University Press.

Connor, P. E. (1992). Decision-Making Participation Patterns: The Role of Organizational Context. *Academy of Management Journal* 35(1): 218–231.

Connor, W. R. (1991). Why are We Surprised? *The American Scholar* 60, 175–184.

Conrad, P., & J. W. Conrad. (1992). *Deviance and Medicalization: From Badness to Sickness*. Philadelphia, PA: Temple University Press.

Coontz, S. (1988). *The Social Origins of Private Life: A History of American Families 1600–1900*. London: Verso.

Cooper, H. M. (1989). *Integrating Research: A Guide for Literature Reviews*. 2nd. ed. Newbury Park, CA: Sage Publications.

Cooper, J. M. (1931). *Children's Institutions*. Philadelphia, PA: The Dolphin Press.

Coordinating Committee on Social Welfare Research. (1956). *Proposal for a Program of Advanced Training and Research in Social Work and Social Science*. As submitted to Russell Sage Foundation. Horace H. Rackham School of Graduate Studies Mimeo. Archives of the School of Social Work and Bentley Historical Library.

Corbin, J., & A. L. Strauss. (1990). Grounded Theory Research: Procedures, Canons, and Evaluative Criteria. *Qualitative Sociology* 13, 13–21.

Corcoran, K., & J. Fischer. (1987). *Measures for Clinical Practice: A Sourcebook*. New York: Free Press.

Corcoran, M. (1995). Rags to Rags: Poverty and Mobility in the United States. *Annual Review of Sociology* 21, 289–321.

Corey, S. M. (1954). *Action Research to Improve School Services*. New York: Columbia University Press.

Cormier, W. H., & L. S. Cormier. (1991). *Interviewing Strategies for Helpers*. Pacific Grove, CA: Brooks/Cole Publishing Company.

Corney, R. (1981). Clients' Perspectives in a General Practice Attachment. *British Journal of Social Work* 11(2): 159–170.

Corrigan, P., & L. P. Corrigan. (1978). *Social Work Practice Under Capitalism: A Marxist Approach*. London: Macmillan.

Council on Social Work Education. (1992). *Curriculum Policy Statement for 1983 and 1992*. Washington, DC: CSWE.

Council on Social Work Education. (n.d.). *Statistics on Social Work Education, 1060–1970*. New York: Council on Social Work Education.

Covaleski, M. A., & M. W. Dirsmith. (1988). An Institutional Perspective on the Rise, Social Transformation, and Fall of a University Budget Category. *Administrative Science Quarterly* 33, 562–587.

Cox, F., J. Tropman et al. (1970). *Strategies of Community Organization: A Book of Readings*. Itasca, IL: F. E. Peacock.

Coyle, G. (1954). *The Place of the Social Sciences in the Doctoral Programs of Social Work Students*. New York: Council on Social Work Education.

Coyle, G. (1958). *Social Science in the Professional Education for Social Workers*. New York: Council on Social Work Education.

Crimp, D., & A. Ralston. (1990). *AIDS demo graphics*. Seattle: Bay Press.

Crocker, R. H. (1992). *Social Work and Social Order: The Settlement Movement in Two Industrial Cities, 1889–1930*. Urbana: University of Illinois Press.

Croft, S., & P. Beresford. (1989). User-involvement, Citizenship and Social Policy. *Critical Social Policy* 26, 5–18.

Cunningham, A., & P. Williams. (1993). De-centering the 'Big Picture': The Origins of Modern Science and the Modern Origins of Science. *British Journal for the History of Science* 26, 407–432.

Curnock, K., & P. Hardiker. (1979). *Towards Practice Theory*. London: Routledge and Kegan Paul.

Curriculum Committee Reports to the Governing Faculty. (1966). *Proposals for a New Professional Curriculum*. School of Social Work, University of Michigan, Ann Arbor.

Curriculum Committee Reports to the Governing Faculty. (1968). *The New Professional Curriculum: Progress in Planning and Implementation*. School of Social Work, University of Michigan, Ann Arbor.

D'Aunno, T., R. I. Sutton, & R. H. Price. (1991). Isomorphism and External Support in Conflicting Institutional Environments: A Study of Drug Abuse Treatment Units. *Academy of Management Journal* 34, 636–661.

Daft, R. L. (1989). *Organization Theory and Design*. 3rd ed. St. Paul, MN: West.

Dalton, R., & M. Kuechler. (1990). *Challenging the Political Order: New Social and Political Movements in Western Democracies*. New York: Oxford University Press.

Dangel, R. F., & R. A. Polster (Eds.). (1984). *Parent Training: Foundations of Research and Practice*. New York: Guilford.

Dasgupta, P. (1993). *An Inquiry into Well-being and Destitution*. New York: Oxford University Press.

Davies, S. P. (1950). The Relation of Social Science to Social Welfare. *Social Work Journal* 31(1): 20–26.

Davis, A. Y. (1983). *Women, Race and Class*. New York: Vintage Books.

Davis, K., & W. E. Moore. (1945). Some Principles of Stratification. *American Sociological Review* 10, 242–249.

Davis, M. (1992). *City of Quartz*. New York: Vintage Books.

Dawes, R. M. (1988). *Rational Choice in an Uncertain World*. San Diego, CA: Harcourt Brace Jovanovich.

Dawes, R. M., & B. Corrigan. (1974). Linear Models in Decision Making. *Psychological Bulletin* 81(2): 95–106.

Dawes, R. M., D. Faust, & P. E. Meehl. (1989). Clinical Versus Actuarial Judgment. *Science* 243, 1668–1674.

Dawes, R. (1994). *House of Cards: Psychology and Psychotherapy Built on Myth*. New York: Basic Press.

Day, P. J. (1989). *A New History of Social Welfare*. Englewood Cliffs, New Jersey: Prentice Hall.

de Beauvoir, S. (1953). *The Second Sex*. New York: Knopf.

De Leonardis, O., D. Mauri, & F. Rotelli. (1994). *L'impresa Sociale*. Milan: Anabasi.

Debord, G. (1983). *Society of the Spectacle*. Detroit: Black and Red.

DeJong, G. (1982). An Overview of the FROMP System. In W. Lehnert & M. Ringle (Eds.), *Strategies for Natural Language Processing*. (pp. 312–355). Hillsdale, NJ: Lawrence Erlbaum Associates.

Delgado, G. (1986). *Organizing the Movement: The Roots and Growth of ACORN*. Philadelphia: Temple University Press.

DeMartini, J. R., & L. B. Whitbeck. (1987). Sources of Practice Knowledge. *Journal of Applied Behavioral Science* 23, 219–231.

Dewdney, A. K. (1985). Computer Recreations: A Computer Microscope Zooms in for a Look at the Most Complex Object in Mathematics. *Scientific American* 253(2).

Dewey, J. (1939). *John Dewey's Philosophy*. New York: Modern Library.

Dill, B. T. (1979). The Dialectics of Black Womanhood. *Signs: Journal of Women in Culture and Society* 4, 343–355.

DiMaggio, P. J. (1988). Interest and Agency in Institutional Theory. In L. G. Zucker

(Ed.), *Institutional Patterns and Organizations: Culture and Environment.* (pp. 3–21). Cambridge, MA: Ballinger.

DiMaggio, P. J., & W. W. Powell. (1983). The Iron Cage Revisited: Institutional Isomorphism and Collective Rationality in Organizational Fields. *American Sociological Review* 48, 147–160.

Dodd, P., & L. Gutierrez. (1991). Preparing Students for the Future: A Power Perspective on Community Practice. *Administration in Social Work: Empowerment Issues in Administrative and Community Practice* 14(2): 63–78.

Dohrenwend, B. P., B. S. Dohrenwend, M. S. Gould, B. Link, R. Neugebauer, & R. Wunsch-Hitzig. (1980). *Mental Illness in the United States: Epidemiological Estimates.* New York: Praeger.

Dohrenwend, B. P., I. Levav, P. E. Shrout, S. Schwartz, G. Naveh, B. G. Link, A. E. Skodol, & A. Stueve. (1992). Socioeconomic Status and Psychiatric Disorders: The Causation-Selection Issue. *Science* 255, 946–952.

Dohrenwend, B. P. (1970). Measures of Psychiatric Disorders in Contrasting Class and Ethnic Groups. In E. H. Hare & J. K. Wing (Eds.), *Psychiatric Epidemiology.* (pp. 159–202). London: Oxford University Press.

Dolgon, C., L. Dresser, & M. Kline. The Politics of Empowerment: Homelessness, Development, and Resistance in Ann Arbor. Paper presented at the *First Annual Conference on The Integration of Social Work and Social Science.* October 29–November 1, 1992. Ann Arbor. School of Social Work, University of Michigan.

Donnison, D. (1972). Research for Policy. *Minerva* 10(4): 519–536.

Drazin, P. G. (1992). *Nonlinear Systems.* Cambridge, MA: Cambridge University Press.

Drumta, J. (1991–1992). Power to the People. *World View* 4, 8–13.

Dubois, E. C., & V. L. Ruiz. (1990). *Unequal Sisters: A Multicultural Reader in U.S. Women's History.* New York: Routledge.

Ducanis, A. J., & A. K. Golin. (1979). *The Interdisciplinary Health Care Team: A Handbook.* Germantown, MD: Aspen Systems Corporation.

Dunlap, K. W. (1993). A History of Research in Social Work Education: 1915–1991. *Journal of Social Work Education* 29(3): 293–301.

Durning, A. B. (1989). Action at the Grassroots: Fighting Poverty and Environmental Decline. *Worldwatch Paper* 88, 1–70.

Eastman, W., & J. R. Bailey. (1994). Examining the Origins of Management Theory: Value Divisions in the Positivist Program. *Journal of Applied Behavioral Science* 30(3): 3132–328.

Economic Planning Advisory Council. (1987). Aspects of the Social Wage: A Review of Social Expenditures and Redistribution. *Council Paper No. 27.* Canberra: Economic Planning Advisory Council.

Edelman, M. (1977). *Political Language: Words that Succeed and Policies that Fail.* New York: Academic Press.

Ehrenreich, B. (1989). *Fear of Falling: The Inner Life of the Middle Class.* NY: Pantheon.

Ehrenreich, J. H. (1985). *The Altruistic Imagination: A History of Social Work and Social Policy in the United States.* Ithaca, New York: Cornell University Press.

Eisenhardt, K. M., & L. J. Bourgeois. (1988). Politics of Strategic Decision-making in High Velocity Environments. *Academy of Management Journal* 31(6): 737–770.

Ellul, J. (1964). *The Technological Society.* New York: Vintage Books.

Ellul, J. (1965). *Propaganda: The Formation of Men's Attitudes.* New York: Vintage Books.

Ellwood, C. A. (1919). Social Facts and Scientific Social Work. *Proceedings of the*

National Conference of Social Work, May 15–22, 1918. (pp. 686–692). Chicago: Rogers and Hall.

Elster, J. (Ed.) (1985). *The Multiple Self.* New York: Cambridge University Press.

Embler, W. (1966). *Metaphor and Meaning.* DeLand, FL: Everett/Edwards.

Emmons, R. A. (1986). Personal Striving: An Approach to Personality and Subjective Well-being. *Journal of Personality and Social Psychology* 51, 1058–1068.

Emmons, R. A., & L. A. King. (1989). On the Personalization of Motivation. In R. S. Wyer & T. K. Srull (Eds.), *Advances in Social Cognition, Volume II: Social Intelligence and Cognitive Assessments of Personality.* (pp. 111–122). Hillsdale, NJ: Erlbaum.

Encel, S. (1970). *Equality and Authority: A Study of Class, Status and Power in Australia.* Melbourne, Australia: Cheshire.

England, H. (1986). *Social Work as Art: Making Sense of Good Practice.* London: Allen and Unwin.

Epstein, B. (1990). Rethinking Social Movement Theory. *Socialist Review* 90(1).

Estroff, S. E. (1989). Self, Identity, and Subjective Experiences of Schizophrenia: In Search of the Subject. *Schizophrenia Bulletin* 15(2): 189–196.

Evans, R. (1976). Some Implications of an Integrated Model of Social Work Theory and Practice. *British Journal of Social Work* 6(2).

Eysenck, H. J. (1987). The Growth of a Unified Psychology: Ordeal by Quackery. In A. W. Staats & L. P. Mos (Eds.), *Annals of Theoretical Psychology.* 5 (pp. 91–113). NY: Plenum Press.

Faculty Seminar on the Research Basis of Social Welfare Practice. (1954). *Research in Social Welfare: A Proposed Program for the University of Michigan.* Ann Arbor, MI: University of Michigan.

Falkenhainer, B. A. (1990). Unified Approach to Explanation and Theory Formation. In J. Shrager & P. Langley (Eds.), *Computational Models of Scientific Discovery and Theory Formation.* (pp. 157–196). San Mateo, CA: Morgan Kaufman.

Fauri, F. F. (1966). *Having the Power, We Have the Duty.* Washington, DC: Government Printing Office.

Fay, B. (1987). *Critical Social Science.* Ithaca, NY: Cornell University Press.

Feifel, H. (1959). *The Meaning of Death.* New York: McGraw-Hill.

Feld, A. (1987). Self-Perceptions of Power: Do Social Work and Business Students Differ? *Social Work* 32, 225–230.

Fellin, P. (1977). School of Social Work. In F. Brinkman (Ed.), *The University of Michigan - 1940–75.* Ann Arbor: University of Michigan.

Fellin, P., & R. Vinter. (1969). Curriculum Development for Contemporary Social Work Education. In W. Kindelsberger (Ed.), *Modes of Professional Education.* New Orleans: Tulane University.

Fernandez, J. (1986). *Child Care and Corporate Productivity.* Lexington: D.C. Heath and Co.

Fiedler, F. E., & J. E. Garcia. (1987). *New Approaches to Effective Leadership: Cognitive Resources and Organizational Performance.* New York: Wiley.

Figueira-McDonough, J. (1980). *Doctoral Programs in Social Work: The Market for and Training of Social Work Ph.D.'s in the Seventies.* Unpublished doctoral dissertation, Michigan State University, School of Social Work, East Lansing.

Fineman, M. (1991). Images of Mothers in Poverty Discourses. *Duke Law Journal* 2, 274–295.

Fischer, J., & W. W. Hudson. (1983). Measurement of Client Problems for Improved Practice. A. Rosenblatt & D. Waldfogel (Eds.), *Handbook of Clinical Social Work.*

San Franciso, CA: Jossey-Bass.

Fischer, J. (1981). The Social Work Revolution. *Social Work* 26(3): 199–207.

Fish, J. E., & C. J. Larr. (1972). A Decade of Change in Drawings by Black Children. *American Journal of Psychiatry* 129(4): 421–426.

Fisher, M. (1991). Client Participation in Case Management. *Social Work and Social Sciences Review* .

Fisher, R. (1992). Organizing in the Modern Metropolis. *Journal of Urban History* 18, 222–237.

Fisher, R. (1994). *Let the People Decide: Neighborhood Organizing in America*. Boston, MA: Twayne.

Fisher, R., & J. Kling. (1988). Leading the People: Two Approaches to the Role of Ideology in Community Organizing. *Radical America* 21(1): 31–46.

Fisher, R., & J. Kling. (1991). Popular Mobilization in the 1990s: Prospects for the New Social Movements. *New Politics* 3, 71–84.

Fisher, R., & J. Kling. (1993). *Mobilizing the Community: Local Politics in the Era of the Global City*. Newbury Park, CA: Sage Publications.

Fiske, S. T., & S. E. Taylor. (1991). *Social Cognition*. 2nd ed. New York, NY: McGraw Hill.

Flacks, D. (1990). The Revolution of Citizenship. *Social Policy* 21, 37–50.

Flexner, A. (1915). Is Social Work a Profession. *Proceedings of the National Conference of Charities and Correction at the Forty-Second Annual Session*. May 12–19, 1915. Baltimore, MD. Chicago, IL.

Florin, P., & A. Wandersman. (1990). An Introduction to Citizen Participation, Voluntary Organizations, and Community Development: Insights for Empowerment Through Research. *American Journal of Community Psychology* 18, 41–54.

Flynn, P. (1992). Do Not Say That You Are a Social Worker. Paper presented at the *First Annual Conference on The Integration of Social Work and Social Science*. October 29–November 1, 1992. Ann Arbor. School of Social Work, University of Michigan.

Folkins, C., N. Wieselberg, & J. Spensley. (1981). Discipline Stereotyping and Evaluative Attitudes among Community Mental Health Center Staff. *American Journal of Orthopsychiatry* 51(1): 140–148.

Folks, H. (1902). *The Care of Destitute, Neglected, and Delinquent Children*. New York: Macmillan.

Folks, H. (1904). Problems in the Administration of Municipal Charities. *Annals of the American Academy of Political and Social Science* 23, 268–280.

Foster, M., & L. R. Perry. (1982). Self-valuation among Blacks. *Social Work* 27(1).

Foucault, M. (1973). *The Birth of the Clinic: An Archaeology of Medical Perception*. London: Tavistock Publications, Ltd.

Frank, A. G., & M. Fuentes. (1990). Civil Democracy: Social Movements in Recent World History. In S. Amin et al. (Eds.), *Transforming the Revolution: Social Movements and the World-System*. New York: Monthly Review Press.

Frankfurt, H. M. (1971). Freedom of Will and the Concept of a Person. *Journal of Philosophy* 68, 5–20.

Franklin, D. L. (1986). Mary Richmond and Jane Addams: From Moral Certainty to Rational Inquiry for Policy and Practice. *Social Service Review* 60(4): 483–502.

Franklin, D. L. (1990). The Cycles of Social Work Practice: Social Action vs. Individual Interest. *Journal of Progressive Human Services* 2(1): 59–80.

Franklin, D. L. (1992). Feminization of Poverty and African American Families: Illusions and Realities. *Affilia* 7(2): 142–155.

Franklin, D. L. (1992). Early Child Bearing Patterns Among African Americans: A Socio-Historical Perspective. In M. K. Rosenheim & M. Tests (Eds.), *Early Parenthood and the Transition to Adulthood.* New Brunswick, NJ: Rutgers University Press.

Franklin, D. L. (1992). Afro-American Single Mother Families: Deconstructing a Social Problem. Paper presented at the *First Annual Conference on the Integration of Social Work and Social Science.* October 29–November 1, 1992. Ann Arbor. School of Social Work, University of Michigan.

Fraser, M. W. (1994). Scholarship and Research in Social Work: Emerging Challenges. *Journal of Social Work Education* 30(2): 252–266.

Fraser, M., J. M. Jensen, & R. E. Lewis. (1991). Training for Research Scholarship in Social Work Doctoral Programs. *Social Service Review* 65(4): 597–613.

Fraser, M., Taylor Mary J., R. Jackson, & J. O'Jack. (1991). Social Work and Science: Many Ways of Knowing. *Social Work Research and Abstract* 27(4 December): 5–15.

Frazier, E. F. (1939). *The Negro Family in the United States.* Chicago: University of Chicago Press.

Freedman, M. (1971). *Homosexuality and Psychological Functioning.* Monterey, CA: Brooks/Cole Publishing.

Freeman, W. J. (1991). The Physiology of Perception. *Scientific American* 264(2): 78–85.

French, D. G. (1952). *An Approach to Measuring Results in Social Work.* New York: Columbia University Press.

French, J., & B. Raven. (1968). The Bases of Social Power. In D. Cartwright & A. Zander (Eds.), *Group Dynamics.* 3rd ed. New York: Basic Books.

French, W. L., & C. H. Bell. (1973). *Organization Development.* Englewood Cliffs, NJ: Prentice-Hall.

Friedlander, F. (1987). The Ecology of Work Groups. In J. W. Lorsch (Ed.), *Handbook of Organizational Behavior.* (pp. 301–314). Englewood Cliffs, NJ: Prentice-Hall.

Friedman, D. (1989). The Productivity Effects of Workplace Centers. Paper presented at the *Conference on Child Care Centers at the Workplace.* Chicago.

Friedman, R. C. (1988). *Male Homosexuality: A Contemporary Psychoanalytic Perspective.* New Haven: Yale University Press.

Friedson, E. (1973). Prepaid Group Practice and the New "Demanding Patient". *Milbank Memorial Fund Quarterly* 51, 13–21.

Friedson, E. (1986). *Professional Powers: A Study of the Institutionalization of Formal Knowledge.* Chicago, IL: University of Chicago Press.

Friere, P. (1973). *Education for Critical Consciousness.* New York: Seabury Press.

Fromm, E. (1941). *Escape from Freedom.* New York: Farrar and Rinehart.

Fuller, M. (1978). Sex Role Stereotyping and Social Science. In J. Chetwynd & D. Hartness (Eds.), *The Sex Role System: Psychological and Sociological Perspectives.* (pp. 143–157). Boston: Routledge and Kegan Paul.

Gabbay, J. (1982). Asthma Attacked? Tactics for the Reconstruction of a Disease Concept. In P. Wright & A. Treacher (Eds.), *The Problem of Medical Knowledge.* Edinburgh: Edinburgh University Press.

Gadamer, H. G. (1979). *Truth and Method.* London: Sheed and Ward.

Gagne, R. M. (1985). *The Conditions of Learning.* 4th ed. New York: Rinehart and Winston.

Gagne, R. M. (1987). *Instructional Technology: Foundations.* Hillsdale, NJ: Erlbaum.

Galambos, J. (1986). Knowledge Structures for Common Activities. In J. Galambos, R.

Abelson, & J. Black (Eds.), *Knowledge Structures.* (pp. 21–47). Hillsdale, NJ: Lawrence Erlbaum Associates.

Galbraith, J. (1973). *Designing Complex Organizations.* Reading, PA: Addison-Wesley.

Galinsky, E. (1988). Business Competitive Policies and Family Life: The Promises and Potential Pitfalls of Emerging Trends. Paper presented at the *Women and Labor Conference.* Labor Education Center, Institute of Management and Labor Relations. Rutgers University.

Galinsky, E., D. Friedman, & C. Hernandez. (1991). Corporate Reference Guide to Work-Family Programs. *Families and Work Institute.*

Galinsky, E., D. Hughes, & J. David. (1990). Trends in Corporate Family-Supportive Policies. *Marriage and Family Review* 15, 88–94.

Gambrill, E. D. Distinguishing Between Propaganda and Scholarship. Paper presented at *12th Annual Conference on Critical Thinking.* 1992. Sonoma, CA.

Gambrill, E. D. (1990). *Critical Thinking in Clinical Practice.* San Francisco, CA: Jossey-Bass.

Gambrill, E. D. (1994). Social Work Research: Priorities and Obstacles. *Research on Social Work Practice* 4, 359–388.

Gambrill, E. D., & L. Gibbs. (1995). Making Decisions About Clients: Is What's Good for the Goose Good for the Gander? Unpublished manuscript. School of Social Welfare, University of California at Berkeley.

Gardner, M. (1981). *Science: Good, Bad and Bogus.* Buffalo, NY: Prometheus.

Gardner, R., III, et al. (1994). *Behavior Analysis in Education: Focus on Measurable Superior Instruction.* Pacific Grove, CA: Brooks/Cole Publishing.

Garner, H. G. (1988). *Helping Others through Teamwork.* Washington, DC: Child Welfare League of America.

Garvin, C. (1985). Work with Disadvantaged and Oppressed Groups. In M. Sundel, P. Glasser, R. Sarri, & R. Vinter (Eds.), *Individual Change Through Small Groups.* 2nd ed. (pp. 461–472). New York: Free Press.

Garvin, C. (1994). Report to the Doctoral Committee. Ann Arbor. University of Michigan, School of Social Work.

Gaston, E. H. (1980). Developing a Motivating Organizational Climate for Effective Team Functioning. *Hospital & Community Psychiatry* 31(6): 407–412.

Gaucher, E. J., & Coffey. R.J. (1993). *Total Quality in Health Care: from Theory to Practice.* San Francisco: Jossey-Bass.

Gaventa, J. (1980). *Power and Powerlessness.* Chicago, IL: University of Illinois Press.

Geertz, C. (1983). Ideology as a Cultural System. In C. Geertz (Ed.), *The Interpretation of Culture.* New York: Basic Books.

Geismar, L. L. (1984). Strengthening the Scientific Basis of Social Work. In M. Dinerman & L. L. Geismar (Eds. and co-authors), *A Quarter-Century of Social Work Education.* New York: National Association of Social Workers.

Gerschick, T., B. Israel, & B. Checkoway. (1989). *Means of Empowerment in Individuals, Organizations, and Communities: Report from a Retrieval Conference.* Ann Arbor, MI: Center for Research on Social Organizations.

Gerson, E. M. (1991). Supplementing Grounded Theory. In D. R. Maines (Ed.), *Social Organization and Social Process: Essays in Honor of Anselm Strauss.* (pp. 285–301). New York: Aldine de Gruyter.

Gibbs, L. E. (1991). *Scientific Reasoning for Social Workers: Bridging the Gap Between Research and Practice.* New York: Macmillan.

Giles, T. R. (1993). *Handbook of Affective Psychotherapy.* New York: Plenum Press.

Gilgun, J. F. (1988). Decision Making in Interdisciplinary Treatment Teams. *Child*

Abuse and Neglect 12, 231–239.

Gilgun, J. F. (1992). Hypothesis Generation in Social Work Research. *Journal of Social Service Research* 15, 113–135.

Gilkes, C. T. (1981). From Slavery to Social Welfare: Racism and the Control of Black Women. In A. Swedlow & H. Lessinger (Eds.), *Class, Race and Sex: The Dynamics of Control*. Boston: G. K. Hall.

Gillespie, D. F., & C. Glisson (Eds.). (1992). *Quantitative Methods in Social Work: State of the Art*. New York: Haworth Press.

Gingerich, W. J. (1990). Rethinking Single-Case Evaluation. In L. Videka-Sherman & W. J. Reid (Eds.), *Advances in Clinical Social Work Research*. (pp. 11–24). Silver Spring, MD: National Association of Social Work.

Gitterman, A. (1991). Introduction: Social Work Practice with Vulnerable Populations. In A. Gitterman (Ed.), *Handbook of Social Work Practice with Vulnerable Populations*. (pp. 1–34). New York: Columbia University Press.

Glaser, B. G. (1991). In Honor of Anselm Strauss: Collaboration. In D. R. Maines (Ed.), *Social Organization and Social Process: Essays in Honor of Anselm Strauss*. (pp. 11–16). New York: Aldine de Gruyter.

Glaser, B. G., & A. L. Strauss. (1967). *The Discovery of Grounded Theory: Strategies for Qualitative Research*. New York: Aldine de Gruyter.

Glaser, E. M., H. H. Abelson, & K. N. Garrison. (1983). *Putting Knowledge to Use*. San Francisco, CA: Jossey-Bass.

Glass, L., & M. C. Mackey. (1988). *From Clocks to Chaos: The Rhythms of Life*. Princeton, NJ: Princeton University Press.

Glasser, P., Sarri Rosemary, & Vinter Robert D. (1974). *Individual Change Through Small Groups*. New York: Free Press.

Glazer, N. (1974). The Schools of the Minor Professions. *Minerva* 12(3): 346–364.

Gleick, J. (1987). *Chaos: The Making of a New Science*. New York: Penguin Group, Viking Penguin.

Gleick, J. (1987). New Images of Chaos that are Stirring a Science Revolution. *Smithsonian* 18(9): 122–135.

Goffman, E. (1959). *The Presentation of Self in Everyday Life*. New York: Doubleday.

Goffman, E. (1974). *Frame Analysis*. New York: Harper & Row.

Goffman, I. (1961). *Asylum*. Harmondsworth: Penguin.

Goffman, I. (1965). *Stigma: Notes on the Management of Spoiled Identities*. Englewood Cliffs: Prentice Hall.

Goldfried, M. R., L. G. Castonguay, & J. D. Safran. (1992). Core Issues and Future Directions in Psychotherapy Directions. In J. C. Norcross, & M. R. Goldfried (Eds.), *Handbook of Psychotherapy Integration* (pp. 593–616). New York: Basic Books.

Goldfried, M. R., L. G. Castonguay, & J. D. Safran. (1992). In J. C. Norcross & M. R. Goldfried (Eds.), *Handbook of Psychotherapy Integration*. New York: Basic Books.

Goldstein, H. (1986). Toward the Integration of Theory and Practice: A Humanistic Approach. *Social Work* 31(5): 352–357.

Goleman, D. (August 31, 1987). Feelings of Inferiority Reported Common in Black Children. *New York Times*, pp. 1, 13.

Golinski, J. (1990). The Theory of Practice and the Practice of Theory: Sociological Approaches to the History of Science. *Isis* 81(306): 492–505.

Gomez, E. H., P. Ruiz, & J. Langrod. (1980). Multidisciplinary Team Malfunctioning on a State Hospital Unit: A Case Study. *Hospital and Community Psychiatry* 31(1): 38–40.

Gomory, T. (1994). Rule(d) Out: A Micro Review of J. Rule's *Insight and Social*

Betterment with a Spirited Defense of K. Popper. Unpublished manuscript, School of Social Welfare, University of California at Berkeley.

Goodman, H. G. (1990). *Deathwork: Staff Perspectives on the Care of Terminally Ill Patients in an Acute Care Hospital.* Unpublished doctoral dissertation, City University of New York.

Goodman, P. S., J. M. Pennings et al. (Eds.). (1977). *New Perspectives on Organizational Effectiveness.* San Francisco, CA: Jossey-Bass.

Gorz, A. (1980). *Farewell to the Working Class: An Essay on Post-Industrial Socialism.* London: Pluto Press.

Gottdiener, M. (1987). *The Decline of Urban Politics.* Newbury Park, CA: Sage Publications.

Gould, N. (1989). Students' Self-Evaluation on a Social Work Course. *Social Work Education .*

Gould, N. (1991). An Evaluation of Repertory Grid Technique in Social Work Education. *Social Work Education* 10(2): 38–49.

Gouldner, A. W. (1957). Theoretical Requirements of the Applied Social Sciences. *American Sociological Review* 22, 92–103.

Gouldner, A. W. (1971). *The Coming Crisis of Western Sociology.* London, England: Heinemann.

Graesser, A. C. (1981). *Prose Comprehension beyond the Work.* New York: Springer-Verlaf.

Graham, S. (1989). Motivation in Afro-Americans. In G. L. V. Berry & J. K. Asamen (Eds.), *Black Students: Psychosocial Issues and Academic Achievement.* Newbury Park, CA: Sage.

Gramick, J. (1983). Homophobia: A New Challenge. *Social Work* 28(2): 137–41.

Grasso, A. J., & I. Epstein. (1992). *Research Utilization in the Social Services.* New York: Haworth Press.

Grasso, A., & I. Epstein. (1988). Agency-Based Research Utilization in a Residential Child Care Setting. *Administration in Social Work* 12, 61–80.

Greenberger, E., W. Goldberg, R. Hamill, R. O'Neil, & C. Payne. (1989). Contributions of a Supportive Work Environment to Parents' Well-being and Orientation to Work. *American Journal of Community Psychology* 17, 755–783.

Greenwald, A. G., & M. R. Banaji. (1989). The Self as a Memory System: Powerful but Ordinary. *Journal of Personality and Social Psychology* 57, 41–54.

Greenwood, E. (1957). Social Work Research: A Decade of Reappraisal. *Social Service Review* 31(3): 311–320.

Greenwood, R., C. R. Hinnings, & J. Brown. (1994). Merging Professional Service Firms. *Organization Science* 5(2 May): 239–257.

Gresham, J. H. (July 24, 1989–July 31, 1989). The Politics of Family in America. *The Nation,* pp. 116–122.

Grinnell, R. M. Jr. (1985). *Social Work Research and Evaluation.* Itasca, IL: F. E. Peacock.

Gross, B. R., & N. Levitt. (1994). *Higher Superstition: The Academic Left and its Quarrels with Science.* Baltimore, MD: Johns Hopkins University Press.

Guess, D., & W. Sailor. (1993). Chaos Theory and the Study of Human Behavior: Implications for Special Education and Developmental Disabilities. *Journal of Special Education* 27(1): 16–34.

Gulick, D. (1992). *Encounters with Chaos.* New York: McGraw-Hill, Inc.

Gurin, P., A. Miller, & G. Gurin. (1980). Stratum Identification and Consciousness. *Social Psychology Quarterly* 43, 30–47.

Gutiérrez, L. (1989). Critical Consciousness and Chicano Identity: An Exploratory Analysis. In G. Romero (Ed.), *Estudios Chicanos and the Politics of Community.* Berkeley: NACS Press.

Gutiérrez, L. (1990). Working with Women of Color: An Empowerment Perspective. *Social Work* 35, 149–154.

Gutiérrez, L., L. GlenMaye, & K. DeLois. (1992). Improving the Human Condition through Empowerment Practice. Paper presented at *National Association of Social Work/International Federation of Social Work World Assembly.* 1992. Washington, DC

Gutman, H. G. (1976). *The Black Family in Slavery and Freedom, 1750–1925.* New York: Pantheon Press.

Gutman, H. G. (1983). Persistent Myths about the Afro-American Family. In M. Gordon (Ed.), *The American Family in Historical Perspective.* (pp. 459–481). New York: St. Martin's Press.

Hacker, A. (1992). *Two Nations: Black and White, Separate, Hostile and Unequal.* New York: Charles Scribner.

Hackman, J. R. (1987). The Design of Work Teams. In J. W. Lorsch (Ed.), *Handbook of Organizational Behavior.* (pp. 315–342). Englewood Cliffs, NJ: Prentice-Hall.

Hackman, J. R. et al. (1990). *Groups That Work and Those That Don't: Creating Conditions for Effective Teamwork.* San Francisco: Jossey-Bass.

Hambrick, D. C. (1983). High Profit Strategies in Mature Capital Goods Industries: A Contingency Approach. *Academy of Management Journal* 26, 687–707.

Hannan, M. T., & J. Freeman. (1989). *Organizational Ecology.* Cambridge, MA: Harvard University Press.

Hannan, M. T., & John Freeman. (1984). Structural Inertia and Organizational Change. *American Sociological Review* 49, 149–164.

Hardiker, P. (1981). Heart or Head - The Function and Role of Knowledge in Social Work. *Issues in Social Work Education* 1(2): 85–111.

Harding, S. (1987). *Feminism and Methodology.* Bloomington: Indiana University Press.

Hardy, S. (1926). What Measures Have We for Growth in Personality. *The Family* 7, 254–258.

Harragan, B. L. (1977). *Games Mother Never Taught You: Corporate Gamesmanship for Women.* New York: Warner Books.

Harry, J. (1990). A Probability Sample of Gay Males. *Journal of Homosexuality* 19(1): 89–104.

Hart, D., S. Fegley, & D. Brengelman. (1993). Perceptions of Past, Present, and Future Selves among Children and Adolescents. *British Journal of Developmental Psychology* 11, 265–282.

Hartman, A. (1992). In Praise of Subjugated Knowledge. Paper presented at the *First Annual Conference on The Integration of Social Work and Social Science.* October 29–November 1, 1992. Ann Arbor. School of Social Work, University of Michigan.

Hartmann, H. I. (1981). The Family as the Locus of Gender, Class, and Political Struggle: The Example of Housework. *Signs* 6, 366–394.

Harvey, D. (1989). *The Condition of Postmodernity.* Cambridge, MA: Basil Blackwell.

Hasenfeld, Y. (1987). Power in Social Work Practice. *Social Service Review* 61, 469–483.

Hasenfeld, Y. (1992). The Nature of Human Service Organizations. In Y. Hasenfeld (Ed.), *Human Services as Complex Organizations.* (pp. 3–23). Newbury Park, CA: Sage.

Hasenfeld, Y., & J. Leon. (1979). *A Profile of Doctoral Students in Social Work and Social Science at the University of Michigan* Unpublished paper. Ann Arbor: University of Michigan.

Hasenfeld, Y. (1972). People Processing Organizations: An Exchange Approach. *American Sociological Review* 37, 256–263.

Hasenfeld, Y., & R. English. (1974). *Human Service Organizations: A Book of Readings.* Ann Arbor: University of Michigan Press.

Hastie, R. (1981). Schematic Principles in Human Memory. In E. T. Higgins, C. P. Herman, & M. P. Zanna (Eds.), *Social Cognition: The Ontario Symposium.* Hillsdale, NJ: Lawrence Erlbaum.

Hatfield, A. (1987). The National Alliance for the Mentally Ill: The Meaning of a Movement. *International Journal of Mental Health* 15(4): 79–93.

Havelock, R. G. (1973). *Planning for Innovations through Dissemination and Utilization of Knowledge.* Ann Arbor: Institute for Social Research, University of Michigan.

Havens, L. L. (1973). *Approaches to the Mind: Movement of the Psychiatric Schools from Sects Toward Science.* Boston: Little, Brown and Company.

Hayek, F. A. (1960). *The Construction of Liberty.* Chicago, IL: University of Chicago Press.

Heidegger, J. (1962). *Being and Time.* Trans. J. Macquarrie & E. Robin. New York: Harper and Row.

Heiss, J., & S. Owens. (1972). Self-evaluation of Blacks and Whites. *American Journal of Sociology* 78, 360.

Held, V. (1985). Feminism and Epistemology: Recent Work on the Connections Between Gender and Knowledge. *Philosophy and Public Affairs* 14(3): 296–307.

Heller, K., R. W. Swindle, & L. Dusenbury. (1986). Component Social Support Processes: Comments and Integration. *Journal of Consulting and Clinical Psychology* 54, 466–470.

Henderson, R. F., A. Harcourt, & R. J. A. Harper. (1970). *People in Poverty: A Melbourne Survey.* Melbourne, Australia: Cheshire.

Hersen, M., & D. H. Barlow. (1976). *Single-Case Experimental Designs: Strategies for Studying Behavior Change.* New York: Pergamon Press.

Hershey, J. C., & P. J. Schoemaker. (1980). Prospect Theory's Reflection Hypothesis: A Critical Examination. *Organizational Behavior and Human Performance* 25(3): 395–418.

Hesse, M. (1986). Changing Concepts and Stable Order. *Social Studies of Science* 16(4 November): 714–726.

Hesse, M. (1988). Socializing Epistemology. *Construction and Constraint: The Shaping of Scientific Rationality.* ed. E. McMullin. Notre Dame.

Higginbothan, E. (1982). Two Representative Issues in Contemporary Sociological Work on Black Women. In G. Hull, R. B. Scott, & B. Smith (Eds.), *All the Women are White, All the Blacks are Men, But Some of Us Are Brave.* (pp. 93–98). Old Westbury, NY: Feminist Press.

Higgins, E. T., J. Vookles, & O. Tykocinski. (1992). Self and Health: How "Patterns" of Self-beliefs Predict Types of Emotional and Physical Problems. *Social Cognition* 10, 125–149.

Hill, C. W. L., & R. E. Hoskisson. (1987). Strategy and Structure in Multi-product Firms. *Academy of Management Review* 12, 331–341.

Hill, R. B. (1971). *The Strength of Black Families.* New York: Emerson Hill.

Hintzman, D. L. (1978). *The Psychology of Learning and Memory.* San Francisco: W. H. Freeman.

Hirsch, P., S. Michaels, & R. Friedman. (1987). "Dirty Hands" versus "Clean Models": Is Sociology in Danger of Being Seduced by Economics? *Theory and Society* 16, 317–336.

Hirschman, A. *The Rhetoric of Reason: Perversity, Futility, Jeopardy.* Cambridge, MA: Belknap.

Hodges, A., & D. Hutter. (1979). *With Downcast Gays: Aspects of Homosexual Self-Oppression.* Toronto: Pink Triangle Press.

Hokenstand, M. C., S. K. Khinduka, & J. Midgeley. (Eds.) (1992). *Profiles in International Social Work.* Washington, DC: National Association of Social Work Press.

Holland, S. (1990). Defining and Experimenting with Prevention. In S. Ramon (Ed.), *Psychiatry in Transition: British and Italian Experiences.* London: Pluto Press.

Holland, T. P., & A. K. Frost. (1987). *Doctoral Education in Social Work: Trends and Issues.* Austin: University of Texas.

Holland, T. P., & A. C. Kirkpatrick. (1991). Ethical Issues in Social Work: Toward a Grounded Theory of Professional Ethics. *Social Work* 36, 138–144.

Hollis, E. V., & A. L. Taylor. (1952). *Abridgment of Social Work Education in The United States.* New York: Council on Social Work Education by American Association of Social Workers.

Hong Kong Government. (1991). *White Paper: Social Welfare Into the 1990s and Beyond.* Hong Kong: Government of Hong Kong.

Hooijberg, R., & R. H. Price. (1989). The Great Disability Epidemic: Cultural Construction and Institutional Action. Paper presented at *Interdisciplinary Committee on Organizational Studies Seminar.* Winter, 1989. Ann Arbor. University of Michigan.

Hooker, E. (1957). The Adjustment of the Male Overt Homosexual. *Journal of Projective Techniques* 22, 33–54.

Hooker, E. (1965). An Empirical Study of Some Relations Between Sexual Patterns and Gender Identity in Male Homosexuals. In J. Money (Ed.), *Sex Research: New Developments.* New York: Holt, Rinehart & Winston.

hooks, b. (1981). *Ain't I a Woman: Black Women and Feminism.* Boston: South End Press.

Hopkins, J. (1969). The Lesbian Personality. *British Journal of Psychiatry* 115, 1433–1436.

Horner, M. S. (1972). Toward an Understanding of Achievement-Related Conflicts in Women. *Journal of Social Issues* 28(2).

Hornung, C. A. (1977). Social Status, Status Inconsistency and Psychological Distress. *American Sociological Review* 42, 623–628.

Howard, R. A., & J. E. Matheson. (1984). Influence Diagrams. In R. A. Howard & J. E. Matheson (Eds.), *The Principles and Applications of Decision Analysis.* (pp. 212–234). Menlo Park, CA: Strategic Decisions.

Howe, D. (1979). Agency Function and Social Work Principles. *British Journal of Social Work* 9, 29–47.

Hudson, W. W. (1982). *The Clinical Measure Package: A Field Manual.* Homewood, IL: Dorsey Press.

Hughes, D., & E. Galinsky. (1988). Balancing Work and Family Lives: Research and Corporate Applications. In A. E. Gottfried & A. Gottfried (Eds.), *Maternal Employment and Children's Development: Longitudinal Research.* (pp. 233–268). New York: Plenum Press.

Hyde, C. (1991). *Did the New Right Radicalize the Women's Movement? A Study of*

Change in Feminist Social Movement Organizations. Unpublished doctoral dissertation, University of Michigan, Ann Arbor.

Hyde, J. S., & B. G. Rosenberg. (1980). *Half the Human Experience: The Psychology of Women.* Lexington: D.C. Health and Company.

Igers, G. G. (1995). Historicism—The History and Meaning of the Term. *Journal of the History of Ideas* 56(1 January): 129–152.

Innes, J. et al. (1992). *Report of the Commission on the Doctorate in Planning to the Association of Collegiate Schools of Planning.* Association of Collegiate Schools of Planning.

Ironmonger, D. (1989). *Households Work: Productive Activities, Women and Income in the Household Economy.* Sydney, Australia: Allen & Unwin.

Isla, L. (1991). Chaos Theory: A New Paradigm for Psychotherapy? *Australian and New Zealand Journal of Psychiatry* 25(4): 548–560.

Jaccard, J., R. Turrisi, & C. K. Wan. (1990). *Interaction Effects in Multiple Regression.* Beverly Hills: Sage Publications.

Jackson, J. J. (1972). Black Women in a Racist Society. C. Jillie, B. Kramer, & B. Brown (Eds.), *Racism and Mental Health.* (pp. 185–267). Pittsburgh: University of Pittsburgh Press.

Jacobson, D. E. (1986). Types and Timing of Social Support. *Journal of Health and Social Behavior* 27, 250–264.

Jacobson, R. (1978). *Sound and Meaning.* Cambridge, MA: MIT Press.

Jacoby, R. (1987). *The Last Intellectual: American Culture in the Age of the Academe.* New York: Basic Books.

Jamrozik, A. (1986). Leisure as Social Consumption. In R. Castle, D. Lewis, & J. Mangen (Eds.), *Work, Leisure and Technology.* Melbourne, Australia: Longman Cheshire.

Jamrozik, A. (1989). The Household Economy and Social Class. In D. Ironmonger (Ed.), *Households Work: Productive Activities, Women and Income in the Household Economy.* Sydney, Australia: Allen & Unwin.

Jamrozik, A. (1991a). *Class, Inequality and the State: Social Change, Social Policy and the New Middle Class.* Melbourne, Australia: Macmillan.

Jamrozik, A. (1991b). The Roots of Unemployment. *Ethnic Spotlight* 21(May): 12–15.

Jamrozik, A. (1992). Challenges for the 21st Century. Comments delivered to the *Doctoral Conference in Social Work and Social Science.* November. University of Michigan, Ann Arbor.

Jamrozik, A., & C. Boland. (1991). *Human Resources in Community Services: Conceptual Issues and Empirical Evidence.* Sydney, Australia: University of New South Wales, Social Policy Research Centre.

Jamrozik, A., C. Boland, & D. Stewart. (1991). *Immigrants and Occupational Welfare: Industry Restructuring and Its Effects on the Occupational Welfare of Immigrants from Non-English Speaking Countries.* Canberra: Office of Multicultural Affairs.

Jamrozik, A., R. Urquhart, & M. Wearing. (1990). *Immigrants' Contributions to Skills Development and Occupational Structure.* Unpublished Report. Melbourne, Australia: Bureau of Immigration Research.

Janis, I. L., & L. Mann. (1977). *Decision Making: A Psychological Analysis of Conflict, Choice and Commitment.* New York: Free Press.

Janoff-Bulman, R. (1989). Assumptive Worlds and the Stress of Traumatic Events: Applications of the Schema Construct. *Social Cognition* 7, 113–136.

Jayaratne, S. (1979). Analysis of Selected Social Work Journals and Productivity Rankings among Schools of Social Work. *Journal of Social Work Education* 15, 72–

80.
Jayaratne, S., & R. Levy. (1979). *Empirical Clinical Practice*. New York: Columbia University Press.

Jeffrey, R. (1979). Normal Rubbish: Deviant Patients in Casualty Departments. *Sociology of Health and Illness* 1, 92–98.

Jencks, C. (1992). *Rethinking Social Policy: Race, Poverty and the Underclass*. New York: Harper Collins.

Jensen, D. D. (1989). Pathologies of Science, Precognition and Modern Psychophysics. *Skeptical Inquirer* 13, 147–160.

Johansson, I. (1991). Pluralism and Rationality in the Social Sciences. *Philosophy of the Social Sciences* 21(4 December): 427–443.

Johnson, A. (1908). *A Guide to Study of Charities and Correction by Means of the Proceedings of the National Conference of Charities and Corrections, 1874–1908*.

Johnston, W. (1987). *Workforce 2000: Work and Workers for the 21st Century*. Indianapolis, IN: Hudson Institute.

Jones, B. (1982). *Sleepers, Wake!: Technology and the Future of Work*. New York: Oxford University Press.

Jordanova, L. (1993). Gender and the Historiography of Science. *British Journal for the History of Science* 26(December): 469–483.

Josephson, J. R., B. Chandrasekaran, J. W. Smith, & M. C. Tanner. (1987). A Mechanism for Forming Composite Explanatory Hypotheses. *IEEE Transactions on Systems, Man, and Cybernetics* 17(3): 445–454.

Kahneman, D., & A. Tversky. (1979). Prospect Theory: An Analysis of Decision Under Risk. *Econometrica* 47, 263–291.

Kahnemann, D., & J. Snell. (1990). Predicting Utility. In R. M. Hogarth (Ed.), *Insights in Decision Making. A Tribute to Hillel J. Einhorn.* (pp. 295–310). Chicago: University of Chicago Press.

Katz, D., & R. Kahn. (1978). *The Social Psychology of Organizations*. 2nd ed. New York: John Wiley.

Katz, D. (1992). Information Flow, Social Structure and Behavior. Paper presented at the *First Annual Conference on The Integration of Social Work and Social Science*. October 29–November 1, 1992. Ann Arbor. School of Social Work, University of Michigan.

Katz, M. (1989). *The Undeserving Poor: From the War on Poverty to the War on Welfare*. New York: Pantheon.

Katz, M. B. (1986). *In the Shadow of the Poorhouse: A Social History of Welfare in America*. New York: Basic Books.

Katz, R. (1984). Empowerment and Synergy: Expanding the Community's Healing Resources. In H. Rappaport, C. Swift, & R. Hess (Eds.), *Studies in Empowerment: Toward Understanding and Action.* (pp. 201–226). New York: Haworth Press.

Kauffman, L. (June 30, 1992). The Left Attacks Identity Politics. *Village Voice*, p. 20.

Keidel, R. (1985). *Game Plans: Sports Strategies for Business*. New York: E. P. Dutton.

Keidel, R. (1988). *Game Plans: Designs for Working and Winning Together*. New York: John Wiley & Sons.

Keller, E. F. (1982). Feminism and Science. *Signs: A Journal of Women in Culture and Society* 7(2): 589–602.

Kellert, S. H. (1993). *In the Wake of Chaos*. Chicago: University of Chicago Press.

Kenniston, K. (1968). How Community Mental Health Stamped Out the Riots: 1968–78. *Transaction* 5(8): 21–29.

Kerlinger, F. N. (1973). *Foundations of Behavioral Research*. New York: Holt, Rinehart

& Winston.

Kerr, C., J. T. Dunlop, F. Harbison, & C. A. Myers. (1960). *Industrialism and Industrial Man: The Problems of Labor and Management*. Cambridge, MA: Harvard University Press.

Kessler, R. C. (1979). Stress, Social Status and Psychological Distress. *Journal of Health and Social Behavior* 20, 259–272.

Kessler, R. C., & P. D. Cleary. (1980). Social Class and Psychological Distress. *American Sociology Review* 45(June): 463–478.

Kessler, R. C., & J. A. McRae. (1981). Trends in the Relation between Sex and Psychological Distress: 1957–76. *American Sociological Review* 46(4): 443–452.

Khandwalla, P. N. (1974). Mass Output Orientation of Operations Technology and Organization Structure. *Administrative Science Quarterly* 19, 74–97.

Kieffer, C. (1984). Citizen Empowerment: A Developmental Perspective. In J. Rappaport, C. Swift, & Hess. R. (Eds.), *Studies in Empowerment: Toward Understanding and Action.* (pp. 9–36). New York: Haworth Press.

Kieser, A. (1994). Crossroads—Why Organization Theory Needs Historical Analyses and How They Should be Performed. *Organization Science* 5(4): 608–620.

Kieser, A. (1989). Organizational, Institutional, and Societal Evolution: Medieval Craft Guilds and the Genesis of Formal Organizations. *Administrative Science Quarterly* 34(4): 540–564.

Kihlstrom, J. F., N. Cantor, J. S. Albright, B. R. Chew, S. B. Klein, & P. M. Niedenthal. (1988). Information Processing and Study of the Self. *Advances in Experimental Social Psychology* 21, 145–178.

Kilty, K. M., & T. M. Meenaghan. (1995). Social Work and the Convergence of Politics and Science. *Social Work* 40(3): 445–453.

King, D. H. (1988). Multiple Jeopardy, Multiple Consciousness: The Context of a Black Feminist Ideology. *Signs: A Journal of Women in Culture and Society* 14(1): 42–72.

Kirk, S. (1979). Understanding Research Utilization in Social Work. In A. Rubin & A. Rosenblatt (Eds.), *Sourcebook on Research Utilization.* New York: Council on Social Work Education.

Kirk, S. A. (1990). Research Utilization: The Sub-structure of Belief. In L. Videka-Sherman & W. J. Reid (Eds.), *Advances in Clinical Social Work Research.* Washington, DC: National Association of Social Workers.

Kirk, S. A., & H. Kutchins. (1992). *The Selling of DSM: The Rhetoric of Science and Psychiatry*. New York: Aldine de Gruyter.

Kitzinger, C. (1987). *The Social Construction of Lesbianism*. London: Sage Publications.

Klein, E. (1984). *Gender Politics: From Consciousness to Mass Politics*. Cambridge, MA: Harvard University Press.

Klein, P. (1968). *From Philanthropy to Social Welfare*. San Francisco, CA: Jossey-Bass.

Kling, J., & P. Posner. (1990). *Dilemmas of Activism*. Philadelphia: Temple University Press.

Koch, S. (1981). The Nature and Limits of Psychological Knowledge. *American Psychologist* 36(3): 257–269.

Kogan, L. (Ed.) (1960). *Social Science Theory and Social Work Research*. New York: National Association of Social Work.

Kohn, M. (1977). *Class and Conformity: A Study in Values*. Chicago: The University of Chicago Press.

Kohn, M., & C. Schooler. (1973). Occupational Experience and Psychological Functional: An Assessment of Reciprocal Effects. *American Sociological Review* 38, 97–118.

Kolb, D. (1984). *Experiential Learning: Experience as the Source of Learning and Development.* Englewood Cliffs, NJ: Prentice Hall.

Kondrat, M. E. (1992). Reclaiming the Practical: Formal and Substantive Rationality in Social Work Practice. *Social Service Review* 66, 237–255.

Korda, J. (1975). *Power!: How to Get It, How to Use It.* New York: Random House.

Kronick, J. C., S. B. Kamerman, & C. Glisson. The Structure of Doctoral Programs in Social Work: A Critical Analysis. Paper presented at the *Group for the Advancement of Doctoral Education Conference.* 1989. Gatlinburg, TN.

Kubler-Ross, E. (1969). *On Death and Dying.* New York: Macmillan.

Kunkel, J. H. (1970). *Society and Economic Growth: A Behavioral Perspective of Social Change.* New York: Oxford University Press.

Laclau, E., & C. Mouffe. (1985). *Hegemony and Socialist Strategy: Towards a Radical Democratic Politics.* London: Verso.

Ladner, J. (1971). *Tomorrow's Tomorrow.* Garden City, NY: Doubleday.

Laird, J. (1992). An Anthropological Perspective for the Study of American Gay and Lesbian Families. Paper presented at the *First Annual Conference on The Integration of Social Work and Social Science.* October 29–November 1, 1992. Ann Arbor. School of Social Work, University of Michigan.

Lambert, S. (1990). Processes Linking Work and Family: A Critical Review and Research Agenda. *Human Relations* 43, 239–257.

Lambert, S. (1991). The Combined Effects of Job and Family Characteristics on the Job Satisfaction, Job Involvement, and Intrinsic Motivation of Men and Women Workers. *Journal of Organizational Behavior* 12, 341–363.

Lambert, S. (1993). Workplace Policies as Social Policy. *Social Service Review* 67, 237–260.

Lambert, S., K. Hopkins, G. Easton, J. Walker, H. McWilliams, & M. S. Chung. (1993). *Added Benefits: The Link Between Family-Responsive Policies and Work Performance at Fel-Pro, Inc.* Unpublished paper. Chicago: University of Chicago, School of Social Service Administration.

Langan-Fox, J. (1991). The Stability of Work, Self, and Interpersonal Goals in Young Women and Men. *European Journal of Social Psychology* 21, 419–428.

Langner, T. S., & S. T. Michael. (1963). *Life Stress and Mental Health.* New York: Free Press.

Lanzetta, J. T., & J. M. Driscoll. (1968). Effects of Uncertainty and Importance on Information Search in Decision Making. *Journal of Personality and Social Psychology* 10, 479–486.

Larsen, J. K. (1986). Local Mental Health Agencies in Transition. *American Behavioral Scientist* 30, 174–187.

Lash, S. (1990). *Sociology of Postmodernism.* New York: Routledge.

Lasson, K. (1990). Scholarship Amok: Excesses in the Pursuit of Truth and Tenure. *Harvard Law Review* 103, 926–950.

Latour, B. (1987). *Science in Action: How to Follow Scientists and Engineers through Society.* Cambridge, MA: Harvard University Press.

Latour, B. (1993). *We Have Never Been Modern.* New York: Harvester Wheatsheaf.

Lauer, R. H., & W. H. Handel. (1983). *Social Psychology. The Theory and Application of Symbolic Interactionism.* 2nd. ed. Englewood Cliffs, NJ: Prentice-Hall.

Lauffer, A. (1982). *Assessment Tools.* Newbury Park, CA: Sage

Lawler, E. E. (1976). Control Systems in Organizations. In M. D. Dunnette (Ed.), *Handbook of Industrial and Organizational Psychology.* (pp. 1247–1282). Chicago: Rand McNally.

Lawler, E. E., & J. G. Rhodes. (1976). *Information and Control in Organizations*. Pacific Palisades, CA: Goodyear.

Lawson, M. (1991). A Recipient's View. In Ramon. S. (Ed.), *Beyond Community Care: Normalisation and Integration Work*. London: Macmillan.

Lecca, P. J., & J. S. McNeil. (Eds.) (1985). *Interdisciplinary Team Practice: Issues and Trends*. New York: Praeger.

LeDoux, C. C. (1991). *Career Patterns of African American and Hispanic American Social Work Doctorates and ABD's*. Unpublished doctoral dissertation, University of Texas, Austin.

Lee, P. (1930). Social Work: Cause and Function. *Proceedings of the National Conference of Social Work, 1929*. (pp. 3–20). Chicago: University of Chicago Press.

Lefebvre, H. (1991). *The Production of Space*. Cambridge, MA: Blackwell.

Leighninger, L. (1987). *Social Work: Search for Identity*. New York: Greenwood Press.

Leiter, M. P. (1988). Burnout as a Function of Communication Patterns: A Study of a Multidisciplinary Mental Health Team. *Group & Organization Studies* 13(1): 111–128.

Lepenies, W. (1989). The Direction of the Disciplines: The Future of the Universities. *Comparative Criticism* 11, 51–70.

Lerner, G. (1974). Early Community Work of Black Club Women. *Journal of Negro History* 59(April): 112–117.

Lerner, M. (1986). *Surplus Powerlessness*. Oakland, CA: Institution for Labor and Mental Health.

Lerner, R., & C. Buehrig. (1975). The Development of Racial Attitudes in Young Black and White Children. *Journal of Genetic Psychology* 127(1): 45–54.

Levering, R., & M. Moskowitz. (1993). *The 100 Best Companies to Work For in America*. New York: Doubleday/Currency.

Levesque, G. H. (1951). Integrating the Social Work Curriculum into the Social Sciences. *Social Work Journal* 32(1): 63–69.

Levi-Strauss, C. (1963). *Structural Anthropology*. Vol. 1. New York: Basic Books.

Levine, M., & A. Levine. (1970). *A Social History of the Helping Professions*. NY: Appleton-Century-Crofts.

Levis, D. J. (1990). Behaviorism and Cognitivism in Behavior Therapy. Paper presented at the *24th Annual Convention of the Association for the Advancement of Behavior Therapy*. November 4, 1990. San Francisco.

Lewin, K. (1946). Action Research and Minority Problems. *Social Issues* 2(4): 34–46.

Lichtenberg, J. W., & P. L. Knox. (1991). Order out of Chaos: A Structural Analysis of Group Therapy. *Journal of Counseling Psychology* 38(3): 279–288.

Lichtenberg, P., & C. Roman. (1990). Psychological Contributions to Social Struggle. *Journal of Progressive Social Services* 1(2): 1–17.

Lieberman, M. A., & S. S. Tobin. (1983). *The Experience of Old Age*. New York: Basic Books.

Liederman, D. B., & J. Grisso. (1985). The Gomer Phenomenon. *Journal of Health and Social Behavior* 26, 224–227.

Lindon, J. A. (1991). Does Technique Require Theory? *Bulletin of the Menninger Clinic: A Journal of the Mental Health Professions* 55(1): 1–35.

Link, B. G., B. P. Dohrenwend, & A. E. Skodol. (1986). Socioeconomic Status and Schizophrenia: Noisome Occupational Characteristics as a Risk Factor. *American Sociological Review* 48, 228–239.

Linville, P. W., & L. F. Clark. (1989). Can Production Systems Cope with Coping?

Social Cognition 7, 195–236.

Lippit, R., & R. Havelock. (1968). *Research Implications for Educational Diffusion*. East Lansing, MI: Michigan State Department of Education.

Lipstiz, L. A., & A. L. Goldberg. (1992). Loss of "Complexity" and Aging: Potential Applications of Fractals and Chaos Theory to Senescence. *Journal of the American Medical Association* 267(13).

Lipton, J. P., & A. M. Hershaft. (1985). On the Widespread Acceptance of Dubious Medical Findings. *Journal of Health and Social Behavior* 26, 336–351.

Lister, L. (1982). Role Training for Interdisciplinary Health Teams. *Health and Social Work* 7(1): 19–25.

Litwak, E., & H. J. Meyer. (1974). *School, Family, Neighborhood: The Theory and Practice of School–Community Relations*. New York: Columbia University Press.

Lorber, J. (1975). Good Patients and Problem Patients: Conformity and Deviance in a General Hospital. *Journal of Health and Social Behavior* 16, 216–218.

Lorenz, E. (1963a). Deterministic Nonperiodic Flow. *Journal of the Atmospheric Sciences* 20, 130–141.

Lorenz, E. (1963b). The Mechanics of Vacillation. *Journal of the Atmospheric Sciences* 20, 448–464.

Lorenz, E. (1964). The Problem of Deducing the Climate from the Governing Equations. *Tellus* 16, 1–11.

Lowe, S. (1986). *Urban Social Movements: The City after Castells*. London: Macmillan.

Lubove, R. (1977). *The Professional Altruist: The Emergence of Social Work as a Career 1880–1930*. New York: Atheneum.

Lundberg, E. O. (1947). *Unto the Least of These: Services for Children*. New York: C. Appleton-Century.

Lynn, L. (1992). Public Management: A Survey. Paper prepared for the *Fourteenth Annual Research Conference of the Association for Public Policy Analysis and Management*. 1992. Denver, CO.

Lyotard, J. F. (1984). *The Postmodern Condition: A Report on Knowledge*. Minneapolis: University of Minnesota Press.

Maas, H. S. (1968). Social Work Knowledge and Social Responsibility. *Journal of Education for Social Work* 4(1).

Maas, H. (1950). Collaboration between Social Work and the Social Sciences. *Social Work Journal* 31(3): 104–109.

Maccoby, M. (1976). *The Gamesmen: The New Corporate Leaders*. New York: Simon and Schuster.

MacCrimmon, K., & R. Taylor. (1976). In M. D. Dunnette (Ed.), *Handbook of Industrial and Organizational Psychology*. Chicago, IL: Rand McNally.

Maciver, R. M. (1931). *The Contribution of Sociology to Social Work*. New York, NY: Columbia University Press.

MacNair, R. H. (1980). *Case Coordination: Designing Interagency Teamwork*. Athens, GA: Institute of Community and Area Development.

Mahoney, M. J. (1977). Publication Prejudices: An Experimental Study of Confirmatory Bias in the Peer Review System. *Cognitive Therapy and Research* 1, 161–175.

Mahoney, T. A. (1979). Organizational Hierarchy and Position Worth. *Academy of Management Journal* 22, 726–737.

Mahrer, A. R., & R. Gagnon. (1991). The Care and Feeding of a Psychotherapy Research Team. *Journal of Psychiatry and Neuroscience* 16(3): 188–192.

Malaka, D. W. (1992). The Use of Social Science in the Training of Social Work Students in Dealing with Rural Poverty. Paper presented at the *First Annual*

Conference on the Integration of Social Work and Social Science. October 29–November 1, 1992. Ann Arbor. School of Social Work, University of Michigan.

Malott, R. W., Whaley D.L., & M. E. Malott. (1993). *Elementary Principles of Behavior.* 2nd ed. Englewood Cliffs, NJ: Prentice Hall.

Mandelbrot, B. (1983). *The Fractal Geometry of Nature.* New York: W.H. Freeman and Company.

Mangel, M., & C. W. Clark. (1988). *Dynamic Modeling in Behavioral Ecology.* Princeton, NJ: Princeton University Press.

Mansbridge, J. (1980). *Beyond Adversary Democracy.* New York: Basic Books.

Manz, C. C., & H. P. Jr. Sims. (1987). Leading Workers to Lead Themselves: The External Leadership of Self-Managing Work Teams. *Administrative Science Quarterly* 32, 106–128.

March, J., & H. Simon. (1958). *Organizations.* New York: John Wiley.

March, J. (1972). Model Bias in Social Action. *Review of Educational Research* 42(4).

Marcus, G. (1989). *Lipstick Traces.* Cambridge, MA: Harvard University Press.

Markus, H., S. Cross, & E. Wurf. (1990). The Role of the Self-System in Competence. In R. J. Sternberg & J. Kolligan, Jr. (Eds.), *Competence Considered.* New Haven: Yale University Press.

Markus, H., & Z. Kunda. (1986). Stability and Malleability of the Self-Concept. *Journal of Personality and Social Psychology* 51, 858–866.

Markus, H., & P. S. Nurius. (1986). Possible Selves. *American Psychologist* 41, 954–969.

Marris, P., & M. Rein. (1972). *Dilemmas of Social Reform.* London: Routledge.

Marshall, E. (1980). Psychotherapy Works, but for Whom? *Science* 207(1 February): 506–508.

Marshall, N. (1991). *The Bottom Line: Impact of Employer Child Care Subsidies.* Wellesley, MA: Wellesley College, Center for Research on Women.

Marshall, T. H. (1981). *The Right to Welfare and Other Essays.* London: Heinemann.

Martin, R. (1991). The Problem of Other Cultures and Other Periods in Action Explanations. *Philosophy of the Social Sciences* 21(3 September): 345–366.

Marx, K., & F. Engels. (n.d.). *Basic Writings on Politics and Philosophy.* Ed. L. S. Feuer. Garden City, NY: Anchor.

Mathis, T., & D. Richan. (1986). Empowerment: Practice in Search of a Theory. Paper presented at *Annual Program Meeting of the Council on Social Work Education.* 1986. Miami, FL.

Mauksch, H. O. (1975). The Organizational Context of Dying. In E. Kubler-Ross (Ed.), *Death: The Final Stage of Growth.* Englewood Cliffs, NJ: Prentice-Hall.

Mayrl, W. (1973). Ethnomethodology: Sociology Without Society? *Catalyst* 7, 15–28.

McCall, M. W., Jr., & R. E. Kaplan. (1985). *Whatever It Takes: Decision Makers at Work.* Englewood Cliffs, NJ: Prentice-Hall.

McDonnell Douglas Corporation. (1989). *Employee Assistance Program Financial Offset Study: 1985–1989.* Seattle, WA: McDonnell Douglas Corporation and Alexander Consulting Group.

McLeod, J. D. (1990). Socioeconomic Status Differences in Vulnerability to Undesirable Life Events. *Journal of Health and Social Behavior* 31, 162–172.

Mead, G. H. (1938). *The Philosophy of the Act.* Chicago: University of Chicago Press.

Mead, L. (1992). *The New Politics of Poverty: The Non-Working Poor in America.* New York: Basic Books.

Melucci, A. (1989). *Nomads of the Present: Social Movements and Individual Needs in Contemporary Society.* Philadelphia: Temple University Press.

Menzies-Leith, I. (1970). *Anxiety in Institutions*. London: Tavistock.

Merton, R. K. (1968). *Social Theory and Social Structure*. New York: Free Press.

Merton, R. K. (1988). Foreword. In H. R. F. Ebaugh (Ed.), *Becoming an Ex: The Process of Role Exit* (p. ix–xi). Chicago: University of Chicago Press.

Merton, R. K., & R. Nisbett. (Eds.) (1971). *Contemporary Social Problems*. 3rd ed. New York: Harcourt, Brace & Jovanovich.

Meyer, H. J., E. Litwak, E. J. Thomas, & R. D. Vinter. (1967). Social Work and Social Welfare. In P. F. Lazarsfeld, W. H. Sewell, & H. L. Winensky (Eds.), *The Uses of Sociology*. New York: Basic Books.

Meyer, J. W., W. R. Scott, & D. Strang. (1987). Centralization, Fragmentation, and School District Complexity. *Administrative Science Quarterly* 32, 186–201.

Meyer, J. W., & B. Rowan. (1977). Institutional Organizations: Formal Structure as Myth and Ceremony. *American Journal of Sociology* 83, 340–363.

Michaels, M. D. (1989). The Chaos Paradigm. *Organizational Development Journal* Summer.

Midgley, J. (1986). *Community Participation, Social Development, and the State*. London: Methuen.

Mildred, J. (1992). Divorce Harms Kids: Reason or Rhetoric. Paper presented at the *First Annual Conference on The Integration of Social Work and Social Science*. October 29–November 1, 1992. Ann Arbor: School of Social Work, University of Michigan.

Milgrom, P., & J. Roberts. (1988). An Economic Approach to Influence Activities in Organizations. *American Journal of Sociology* 94(2): 154–179.

Miller, A. C., M. M. Merkhofer, R. A. Howard, J. E. Matheson, & T. R. Rice. (1976). *Development of Automated Aids for Decision Analysis*. Menlo Park, CA: Stanford Research Institute.

Miller, J. (1990). *Last One Over the Wall*. Columbus. Ohio State University Press.

Miller, J. D. (1987). The Scientifically Illiterate. *American Demographics* 9, 21–31.

Miller, J., C. Schooler, M. Kohn, & K. Miller. (1979). Women and Work: The Psychological Effects of Occupational Conditions. *American Journal of Sociology* 85, 66–94.

Mills, C. W. (1959). *The Sociological Imagination*. New York: Oxford.

Milroy, A., & R. Hennelly. (1989). Changing Our Professional Ways. In A. Brack & C. Grimshaw (Ed.), *Mental Health Care in Crisis*. London: Pluto Press.

Minkoff, D. C. (1994). From Service Provision to Institutional Advocacy: The Shifting Legitimacy of Organizational Forms. *Social Forces* 72(June): 943–969.

Minnich, E. K. (1990). *Transforming Knowledge*. Philadelphia: Temple University Press.

Mintz, S., & S. Kellog. (1988). *Domestic Revolutions: A Social History of American Family Life*. New York: Free Press.

Mintzberg, H. (1973). *The Nature of Managerial Work*. New York: Harper and Row.

Mirowsky, J., & C. E. Ross. (1983). Paranoia and the Structure of Powerlessness. *American Sociological Review* 48, 228–239.

Mirowsky, J., & C. E. Ross. (1989). *Social Causes of Psychological Distress*. New York: Aldine de Gruyter.

Mitchell, A. (October 4, 1992). On a Frontier of Hope, Building Homes for the Poor Proves Perilous. *New York Times*, p. 37.

Mitchell, J. (1975). *Psychoanalysis and Feminism*. New York: Vintage.

Mitchell, T. R., & L. R. Beach. (1990). ". . . Do I Love Thee? Let me Count. . ." Toward an Understanding of Intuitive and Automatic Decision Making. *Organizational Behavior and Human Decision Processes* 47(1): 1–20.

Moffitt, R. (1991). Incentive Effects of the U.S. Welfare System: A Review. *Special*

Report Series # 48. Madison: Institution for Research on Poverty, University of Wisconsin.

Mohan, B. (1992). *Global Development: Post Material Values and Social Praxis.* New York: Praeger.

Mooney, R. (1987). *A General Explanation-Based Learning Mechanism and Its Application to Narrative Understanding.* Unpublished doctoral dissertation, University of Illinois, Urbana-Champaign.

Moos, R. H. (1977). *Coping with Physical Illness.* New York: Plenum.

Moran, M. G. (1991). Chaos Theory and Psychoanalysis: The Fluidic Nature of the Mind. *International Review of Psychoanalysis* 18, 211–221.

Morgan, G. (1986). *Images of Organization.* Newbury Park, CA: Sage.

Morrison, F. (1991). *The Art of Modeling Dynamic Systems: Forecasting for Chaos, Randomness and Determinism.* New York: John Wiley and Sons.

Morrow-Bradley, C., & R. Elliot. (1986). Utilization of Psychotherapy Research by Practicing Psychotherapists. *American Psychologist* 41, 188–197.

Moynihan, D. P. (1986). *Family and Nation.* San Diego: Harcourt, Brace, & Jovanovich.

Mullen, E. J. (1981). Development of Personal Intervention Models. In R. M. Grinnell (Ed.), *Social Work Research and Evaluation.* Itasca, IL: F. E. Peacock.

Mullen, E. J. (1994). Design of Social Intervention. In J. Rothman & E. J. Thomas (Eds.), *Intervention Research: Design and Development for Human Service.* New York: Haworth Press.

Mullender, A., & D. Ward. (1991). *Self-Directed Groupwork: Users Take Action for Empowerment.* London: Whiting and Birch.

Muncy, R. (1991). *Creating a Female Dominion in American Reform 1890–1935.* New York: Oxford University Press.

Murphy, N. (1990). Scientific Realism and Postmodern Philosophy. *British Journal for the Philosophy of Science* 41(3): 291–303.

Murray, C. (1984). *Losing Ground: American Social Policy, 1950–1980.* New York: Basic Books.

Mutschler, E. (1979). Using Single-Case Evaluation Procedures in a Family and Children's Service Agency: Integration of Practice and Research. *Journal of Social Service Research* 3, 115–134.

Muzzio, D. (1982). *Watergate Games: Strategies, Choices, Outcomes.* New York: New York University Press.

Myerson, R. B. (1991). *Game Theory: Analysis of Conflict.* Cambridge, MA: Harvard University Press.

Myrtle, R. C., & J. P. Robertson. (1979). Developing Work Group Satisfaction: The Influence of Teams, Team Work and the Team Approach. *Long Term Care and Health Services Administration* 3(2): 149–164.

Nakamo-Glenn, E. (1985). Racial, Ethnic Women's Labor: The Intersection of Race, Gender, and Class Oppression. *Review of Radical Political Economics* 17(3): 86–108.

Neisser, U. (1976). *Cognition and Reality.* San Francisco: Freeman.

Newall, A., J. C. Shaw, & H. A. Simon. (1958). Elements of a Theory of Human Problem Solving. *Psychological Review* 65, 151–166.

Newmann, J. P. (1984). Sex Differences in Symptoms of Depression: Clinical Disorder or Normal Distress? *Journal of Health and Social Behavior* 25, 136–159.

Nickerson, R. S. (1986). *Reflections on Reasoning.* Hillsdale, NJ: Erlbaum.

Nisbett, R., & L. Ross. (1980). *Human Inference: Strategies and Shortcomings of Social Judgment.* Englewood Cliffs, NJ: Prentice Hall.

Nowotny, H., & J. Lambiri-Dimaki. (1985). *The Difficult Dialogue between Producers and Users of Social Science Research.* Vienna: European Centre for Social Welfare Training and Research.

Nurius, P. S. (1991). Possible Selves and Social Support: Social Cognitive Resources for Coping and Striving. In J. Howard & P. Collero (Eds.), *The Self-Society Dynamic: Cognition, Emotion, and Action.* New York: Cambridge University Press.

Nurius, P. S. (1993). Human Memory: A Basis for Better Understanding the Elusive Self-Concept. *Social Service Review* 67, 262–278.

Nurius, P. S. (1994a). Assessing and Changing Self-Concept: Guidelines from the Memory System. *Social Work* 39, 221–229.

Nurius, P. S. (1994b). Assumptive Worlds, Self-Definition, and Striving Among Women. *Basic and Applied Social Psychology* 15(3).

Nurius, P. S., & S. B. Berlin. (1993). Negative Self-Concept and Depression. In D. K. Granvold (Ed.), *Cognitive and Behavioral Social Work Treatment.* Belmont, CA: Wadsworth.

Nurius, P. S., & H. Markus. (1990). Situational Variability in the Self-Concept: Appraisals, Expectancies, and Asymmetries. *Journal of Social and Clinical Psychology* 9, 316–333.

Nye, J. L., & A. M. Brower. (1994). Social Cognition in Small Groups. *Small Group Research* 25(Special Issue).

O'Donohue, W., J. E. Fisher, J. J. Plaud, & S. D. Curtis. (1990). Treatment Decisions: Their Nature and Their Justification. *Psychotherapy* 27, 421–427.

O'Donohue, W., & J. Szymanski. (1994). How to Win Friends and Not Influence Clients: Popular but Problematic Ideas that Impair Treatment Decisions. *Behavior Therapist* 17, 29–33.

O'Leary, V (1981). Feminist Research: Problems and Perspectives. *Psychology of Women Quarterly* Special Issue, 595–653.

O'Reiley, C. A. (1982). Variations in Decision Makers' Use of Information Sources: The Impact of Quality and Accessibility of Information. *Academy of Management Journal* 25, 756–771.

O'Rourke, P., S. Morris, & S. Schulenburg. (1989). Abduction and World Model Revision. In *Proceedings of the Eleventh Annual Conference of the Cognitive Science Society.* (pp. 789–796). Hillsdale, NJ: Lawrence Erlbaum.

Oberstone, A., & H. Sukoneck. (1976). Psychological Adjustment and Lifestyle of Single Lesbians and Single Heterosexual Women. *Psychology of Women Quarterly* 1, 172–188.

Odum, H. (1910). *Social and Mental Traits of the Negro: Research into the Basic Conditions of the Negro Race in Southern Towns.* New York.

Offe, C. (1987). Challenging the Boundaries of Institutional Politics: Social Movements since the 1960s. In C. Maier (Ed.), *Changing Boundaries of the Political: Essays on the Evolving Balance between the State and Society, Public and Private in Europe.* Cambridge: Cambridge University Press.

Ohlin, L., R. B. Coates, & A. Miller. (1978). *Reforming Juvenile Corrections: The Massachusetts Experience.* Cambridge, MA: Ballinger.

Oliver, C. (1991). Strategic Responses to Institutional Processes. *Academy of Management Review* 16(1): 145–179.

Olmstead, S. M. (1983). *On Representing and Solving Decision Problems.* Unpublished doctoral dissertation, EES Department, Stanford University, Stanford, CA.

Omolade, B. (1987). The Unbroken Circle: A Historical and Contemporary Study of Black Single Mothers and Their Families. *Wisconsin Women's Law Journal* 249(3):

239–274.

Oosterwegel, A., & L. Oppenheimer. (1993). *Social-Cognitive Interplays of the Developing Self.* Hillsdale, NJ: Erlbaum.

Orcutt, B. A. (1990). *Science and Inquiry in Social Work Practice.* New York: Columbia University Press.

Osterman, P. (1992). Is There a Problem With the Labor Market and If So How Should We Fix It? Lessons for the US from American and European Experience. Sloan School, Massachusetts Institute of Technology.

Ouchi, W. G. (1977). The Relationship between Organizational Structure and Organizational Control. *Administrative Science Quarterly* 20(1): 95–113.

Ouchi, W. G., & M. A. Maguire. (1975). Organizational Control: Two Functions. *Administrative Science Quarterly* 20(4): 559–569.

Oyserman, D., & H. Markus. (1990). Possible Selves and Delinquency. *Journal of Personality and Social Psychology* 59, 112–125.

Ozawa, M. (1986). Nonwhites and the Demographic Imperative in Social Welfare Spending. *Social Work* 31, 440–445.

Pacey, A. (1986). *The Culture of Technology.* Cambridge, MA: MIT Press.

Packer, J. (1985). Hermeneutic Inquiry in the Study of Human Contact. *American Psychologist* 40(10): 1081–1093.

Paine, S. C., G. T. Bellamy, & B. Wilcox. (1984). *Human Services That Work: From Innovation to Standard Practice.* Baltimore, MD: Paul H. Brookes.

Parnell, M., & J. VanderKloot. (1991). Mental Health Services—2001: Serving a New America. *Journal of Independent Social Work* 5(3–4): 183–203.

Parsons, R. (1991). Empowerment: Purpose and Practice in Social Work. *Social Work With Groups* 14(2): 7–22.

Parsons, T. (1955). The American Family: Its Relations to Personality and Social Structure. In T. Parsons & R. Bales (Eds.), *Family Socialization and Interaction Process.* (pp. 3–33). New York: Free Press.

Parusnikova, Z. (1992). Is a Postmodern Philosophy of Science Possible? *Studies in History and Philosophy of Science* 23(1 March): 21–37.

Patterson, G. R., J. B. Reid, & T. J. Dishion. (1992). *A Social Learning Approach. Vol. 4. Antisocial Boys.* Eugene, OR: Castalia Press.

Patti, R. J., Poertner J., & C. A. Rapp. (Eds.) (1987). *Managing for Service Effectiveness in Social Welfare Organizations.* New York: Haworth Press.

Paul, R. (1993). *Critical Thinking: What Every Person Needs to Survive in a Rapidly Changing World.* Sonoma, CA: Foundation for Critical Thinking.

Payne, M. (1991). *Modern Social Work Theory: A Critical Introduction.* Chicago: Lyceum Books.

Payne, M. (1982). *Working in Teams.* London: British Association of Social Workers.

Pearlin, L. I., & J. S. Johnson. (1977). Marital Status, Life Stress and Depressions. *American Sociological Review* 42(5): 704–715.

Pecukonis, E., & S. Wenocur. (1994). Perceptions of Self and Collective Efficacy in Community Organization Theory and Practice. *Journal of Community Practice* 1(2): 5–22.

Peebles-Wilkins, W. (1989). Black Women and American Social Welfare: The Life of Fredericka Douglas Sprague Perry. *Affilia: Journal of Women and Social Work* 4(1): 22–44.

Peile, C. (1988). Research Paradigms in Social Work: From Stalemate to Creative Synthesis. *Social Service Review* 62(1): 1–19.

Peirce, C. S. Collected Papers of Charles Sanders Peirce, 1931–1958. In C. Hartchourne,

P. Weiss, & A. Burks (Eds.). Cambridge, MA: Harvard University Press.

Peitgen, H. O., & P. H. Richter. (1986). *The Beauty of Fractals: Images of Complex Dynamical Systems*. Berlin, GDR: Springer-Verlag.

Perlich, P. S. (1989). The Relation of Science to the Feminist Project. *Review of Radical Political Economics* 2(4): 113–138.

Perring, C. (1992). The Experiences and Perspectives of Patients and Care Staff on the Transition from Hospital to Community-based Care. In Ramon. S. (Ed.), *Psychiatric Hospital Closure: Myths and Realities*. London: Chapman Hall.

Perrow, C. (1967). A Framework for the Comparative Analysis of Organizations. *American Sociological Review* 32, 194–208.

Perrow, C. (1985). Review Essay: Overboard with Myth and Symbols. *American Journal of Sociology* 91, 151–155.

Petersen, I. (1988). *The Mathematical Tourist: Snapshots of Modern Mathematics*. New York: W.H. Freeman and Company.

Pettigrew, T. F. (1985). Can Social Scientists be Effective Actors in the Policy Arena? In R. L. Shotland & M. M. Mark (Eds.), *Social Science and Social Policy*. Newbury Park, CA: Sage.

Petzold, C. (1990). How to Create a Multithreaded Mandelbrot Program. *PC Magazine* 9(13).

Pfeffer, J., & G. R. Salancik. (1961). Organizational Decision Making as a Political Process: The Case of a University Budget. *Administrative Science Quarterly* 20, 135–151.

Pfeffer, J., & G. R. Salancik. (1978). *The External Control of Organizations: A Resource Dependence Perspective*. New York: Harper and Row.

Phillips, D. C. (1990a). Subjectivity and Objectivity: An Objective Inquiry. In E. W. Eisner & A. Peshkin (Eds.), *Qualitative Inquiry in Education: The Continuing Debate*. New York: Teachers College Press, Columbia University.

Phillips, D. C. (1990b). Post Positivistic Science: Myths and Realities. In E. G. Guba (Ed.), *The Paragon Dialogue*. Newbury Park, CA: Sage.

Phillips, D. C. (1992). *A Social Scientists' Bestiary: Fabled Threats to and Defenses of a Natural Science Approach*. New York: Pergamon.

Phillips, D. C., & T. F. Pettigrew. (1987). *Philosophy, Science, and Social Inquiry*. New York: Pergamon Press.

Pickover, C. A. (1990). *Computers Pattern Chaos and Beauty: Graphics from an Unseen World*. New York: St. Martin's Press.

Pickstone, J. V. (1993). Ways of Knowing: Towards a Historical Sociology of Science, Technology, and Medicine. *British Journal for the History of Science* 26(December): 433–458.

Pickstone, J. V. (1995). Past and Present Knowledges in the Practices of the History of Science. *History of Science* 33(100 June): 203–224.

Pieper, M. H. (1985). The Future of Social Work Research. *Social Work Research and Abstract* 21(4): 3–11.

Pieper, M. H. (1988). Comments on Research Paradigms in Social Work: From Stalemate to Creative Synthesis. *Social Service Review* 62, 535–536.

Pilatlis, J. (1986). The Integration of Theory and Practice: A Re-examination of Paradoxical Expectation. *British Journal of Social Work* 16, 79–96.

Pinderhughes, E. (1989). *Understanding Race, Ethnicity, and Power: The Key to Efficacy in Clinical Practice*. New York: Free Press.

Piven, F., & R. Cloward. (1982). *The New Class War: Reagan's Attack on the Welfare State and its Consequences*. New York: Pantheon.

Platt, A. M. (1977). *The Child Savers: The Invention of Delinquency.* 2nd ed. Chicago, Illinois: University of Chicago Press.

Pople, J. (1973). On the Mechanization of Adductive Logic. In *Proceedings of the Third International Joint Conference on Artificial Intelligence.* (pp. 147–152). Stanford, CA: Morgan Kaufman.

Popper, K. (1963). *The Open Society and Its Enemies.* Princeton, NJ: Princeton University Press.

Popper, K. (1992). *In Search of a Better World: Lectures and Essays from Thirty Years.* New York: Routledge.

Popper, K. R. (1961). *The Poverty of Historicism.* New York: Harper & Row.

Popper, K. R. (1963). *Conjecture and Refutations.* New York: Harper & Row.

Popper, K. R. (1994). *The Myth of the Framework: In Defense of Science and Rationality.* New York: Routledge.

Popple, P. (1985). The Social Work Profession: A Reconceptualization. *Social Service Review* 59(4): 560–577.

Population Council. (1994). *Report of the Conference on Population .* Washington, DC.

Porter, L. W., (1976). Communication in Organizations. (1976). In M. D. Dunnette (Ed.), *Handbook of Industrial and Organizational Psychology.* (pp. 1553–1590). Chicago: Rand McNally.

Powell, T. J., G. J. Meissen, & M. Warren. The Use of the Reasoned Action Model in Self-Help Research. Paper presented at the *First Annual Conference on The Integration of Social Work and Social Science.* October 29–November 1, 1992. Ann Arbor. School of Social Work, University of Michigan.

Powell, W. W. (1985). The Institutionalization of Rational Organizations. *Contemporary Sociology* 14, 564–566.

Powell, W. W. (1987). Institutional Effects on Organizational Structure and Performance. In L. G. Sucker (Ed.), *Institutional Patterns and Organizations: Culture and Environment.* (pp. 129–155). Beverly Hills, CA: Sage.

Powell, W. W., & P. J. DiMaggio. (1991). The New Institutionalism in Organizational Analysis. In W. W. Powell & P. J. DiMaggio (Eds.). *The New Institutionalism in Organizational Analyses.* (pp. 1–30). Chicago: The University of Chicago Press.

Pratkanis, A. R., & E. Aronson. (1991). *Age of Propaganda: The Everyday Use and Abuse of Persuasion.* New York: W.H. Freeman.

Price, R. H. (1978). *Abnormal behavior: Perspectives in conflict.* 2nd. ed. New York: Holt, Rinehart and Winston.

Price, R. H. (1989). Bearing Witness. *American Journal of Community Psychology* 17(2): 151–167.

Pugh, D. S., D. J. Hickson, C. R. Hinnings, & C. Turner. (1968). Dimensions of Organization Structure. *Administrative Science Quarterly* 13(2): 65–104.

Pusey, M. (1991). *Economic Rationalism in Canberra: A Nation Building State Changes Its Mind.* Cambridge, UK: Cambridge University Press.

Quadagno, J. (1994). *The Color of Welfare: How Racism Undermined the War on Poverty.*

Quinn, J. B. (1977). Strategic Goals: Process and Politics. *Sloan Management Review* 19(1): 21–37.

Quinn, R., & G. Staines. (1979). *The 1977 Quality of Employment Survey.* Ann Arbor, MI: Survey Research Center, Institute for Social Research.

Rackham, J., & J. Woodward. (1970). The Study of Managerial Controls. In J. Woodward (Ed.), *Industrial Organization: Behavior and Control.* (pp. 19–36). London: Oxford.

Radin, N. (1983). The Success of Graduates of Two Social Work Doctoral Programs and Implications for Comparable Programs. Paper presented at the *Group for the Advancement of Doctoral Education Conference.* 1983. Tuscaloosa, AL.

Radin, N. (1992). A Peer Feedback Approach to Assessing School Social Workers as Team Members. *Social Work in Education* 14, 57–62.

Radin, N., R. Benbenisty, & J. Leon. (1982). Predictors of Success in a Social Work Doctoral Program. *Social Service Review* 56, 641–658.

Ramon, S. (1985). *Psychiatry in Britain: Meaning and Policy.* London: Croom Helm.

Ramon, S. (1989). The Reactions of English-speaking Professionals to the Italian Psychiatric Reform. *International Journal of Social Psychiatry* 35(1): 120–128.

Ramon, S. (Ed.). (1992). *Psychiatric Hospital Closure: Myths and Realities.* London: Chapman Hall.

Random House. (1987). *Random House Dictionary of the English Language, 2nd Edition.* New York, NY: Random House.

Rappaport, J. (1981). In Praise of Paradox: A Social Policy of Empowerment Over Prevention. *American Journal of Community Psychology* 9(1): 1–25.

Reagan, M. D. (1969). *Science and The Federal Patron.* NY: Oxford University Press.

Reay, R. (1986). Bridging the Gap: A Model for Integrating Theory Y Practice. *British Journal of Social Work* 16, 49–64.

Reeves, T. K., & J. Woodward. (1970). The Study of Managerial Controls. In J. Woodward (Ed.), *Industrial Organization: Behavior and Control.* (pp. 19–36). London: Oxford.

Reggia, J. A., D. S. Nau, & C. Wanf. (1983). Diagnostic Expert Systems Based on a Set Covering Model. *International Journal of Man-Machine Studies* 19, 437–460.

Regier, D. A. et al. (1988). One Month Prevalence of Mental Disorders in the United States. *Archives of General Psychiatry* 45, 977–986.

Reid, W. J. (1979). The Model Development Dissertation. *Journal of Social Service Research* 3, 215–225.

Reid, W. J. (1987). Developing an Intervention in Developmental Research. *Journal of Social Service Research* 11, 17–39.

Reid, W. J. (1991). Reframing the Epistemological Debate. Paper presented at the *Conference on Qualitative Methods in Social Work Practice Research.* August, 1991. Albany, NY.

Reid, W. J. (1994). Field Testing and Data Gathering: Innovative Practice Interventions in Early Development. In J. Rothman & E. J. Thomas (Eds.), *Intervention Research: Design and Development for Human Service.* New York: Haworth Press.

Reid, W. J., & A. E. Fortune. (1982). Research Utilization in Direct Social Work Practice. In A. Grasso & I. Epstein (Eds.), *Research Utilization in the Social Services: Innovations for Practice and Administration.* New York: The Haworth Press.

Rein, M., & R. Weiss. The Evaluation of Broad-Aimed Programs. *Administrative Science Quarterly* .

Reingold, N. (1994). Science and Government in the United States Since 1945. *History of Science* 32(98 December): 361–386.

Reinharz, S. (1992). *Feminist Methods in Social Research.* New York: Oxford University Press.

Reitmeier, M. (1989). *The Impact of the Feminist Movement on the Profession of Social Work.* Unpublished doctoral dissertation, McMaster University, Hamilton, Ontario.

Rendell, R. (1988). *Interdisciplinary Collaboration, Communication Patterns and Personality Characteristics Within Milieu Teams in a Children's Psychiatric*

Hospital. Unpublished doctoral dissertation, University of Michigan, Ann Arbor.

Rickets, E. R., & I. V. Sawhill. (1988). Defining and Measuring the Underclass. *Journal of Policy Analysis and Management* 7(2): 316–325.

Riessman, C. K. (1994). Preface: Making Room for Diversity in Social Work Research. In C. K. Riessman (Ed.), *Qualitative Studies in Social Work Research.* (p. vii–xx). Thousand Oaks, CA: Sage.

Riessman, C. K. (Ed.). (1994). *Qualitative Studies in Social Work Research.* Thousand Oaks, CA: Sage.

Ripple, L. (1974). *Report of the Task Force on Structure and Quality in Social Work Education*. New York: Council on Social Work Education.

Roberts, R. E. (1987). An Epidemiologic Perspective on the Mental Health of People of Mexican Origin. In R. Rodriguez & M. T. Coleman (Eds.), *Mental Health Issues of the Mexican Origin Population in Texas.* Austin, TX: Hogg Foundation for Mental Health.

Robins, L. N., J. E. Helzer, M. M. Wiessman, H. Orvaschel, E. Gruenberg, J. D. Burke, & D. A. Regier. (1984). The NIMH Epidemiologic Catchment Area Program. *Archives of General Psychiatry* 41, 934–941.

Robinson, E. A. R. (1992). Applying a Stress and Coping Model to the Families of Those with Chronic Mental Illness. Paper presented at the *First Annual Conference on The Integration of Social Work and Social Science.* October 29–November 1, 1992. Ann Arbor. School of Social Work, University of Michigan.

Rodriguez, F. (1991). Social Work Education: A View from Portugal. *Issues in Social Work Education* 10(1 & 2): 146–155.

Rodwin, L. (1981). *Cities and City Planning*. New York: Plenum.

Roethlisberger, F. J., & W. T. Dickson. (1939). *Management of the Worker*. Cambridge, MA: Harvard University Press.

Rogers, A., & D. Pilgrim. (1991). Pulling Down Churches: Accounting for the British Mental Health Users Movement. *Sociology of Health and Illness* 13(2): 129–148.

Rogers, E., & F. Shoemaker. (1971). *Communication of Innovations*. New York: Free Press.

Rose, H. (1983). Hand, Brain, and Heart: A Feminist Epistemology for the Natural Sciences. *Signs: Journal of Women in Culture and Society* 9(11): 73–90.

Rose, S., & B. Black. (1985). *Advocacy and Empowerment: Mental Health Care in the Community*. Boston, MA: Routledge and Kegan Paul.

Rosen, A., & J. Stretch. (1982). *Doctoral Education in Social Work: Issues, Perspectives and Evaluation*. St. Louis: Washington University School of Social Work.

Rosenau, P. M. (1992). *Post-modernism and the Social Sciences: Insights, Inroads and Intrusions*. Princeton, NJ: Princeton University Press.

Rosenberg, M., & R. Simmons. (1972). *Black and White Self-Esteem: The Urban School Child*. Washington, DC: American Sociological Association.

Rosenthal, R. (1984). *Meta-Analytic Procedures for Social Research*. Beverly Hills, CA: Sage Publications.

Roth, P. A. (1987). *Meaning and Method in the Social Sciences: A Case for Methodological Pluralism*. Ithaca, NY: Cornell University Press.

Rothman, J. (1974). *Planning and Organizing for Social Change*. New York: Columbia University Press.

Rothman, J. (1980). *Social R & D: Research and Development in the Human Services*. Englewood Cliffs, NJ: Prentice-Hall.

Rothman, J. (1980). *Using Research in Organizations*. Newbury Park, CA: Sage.

Rothman, J., & E. J. Thomas (Eds.). (1994). *Intervention Research: Design and*

Development for Human Service. New York: Haworth Press.

Rothman, M. (1989). Myths About Science . . . and Belief in the Paranormal. *Skeptical Inquirer* 14, 25–34.

Rubin, A., & A. Rosenblatt. (1979). *Sourcebook on Research Utilization.* New York: Council on Social Work Education.

Rubin, H., L. Adamski, & S. R. Block. (1989). Toward a Discipline of Nonprofit Administration: Report from the Clarion Conference. *Nonprofit and Voluntary Sector Quarterly* 18(3): 279–286.

Rudwick, M. J. (1980). Social Order and the Natural World. *History of Science* 18(4 December): 269–285.

Ruelle, D. (1989). *Chaotic Evolution and Strange Attractors.* Cambridge, UK: Cambridge University Press.

Ruelle, D. (1989). *Elements of Differentiable Dynamics and Bifurcation Theory.* San Diego, CA: Academic Press, Inc.

Ruelle, D. (1991). *Chance and Chaos.* Princeton, NJ: Princeton University Press.

Rule, J. (1978). *Insight and Social Betterment: A Preface to Applied Social Science.* New York: Oxford University Press.

Ruvolo, A. P., & H. R. Markus. (1992). Possible Selves and Performance: The Power of Self-Relevant Imagery. *Social Cognition* 10, 95–124.

Sabel, C. (1992). Studied Trust: Building New Forms of Cooperation in a Volatile Economy. In F. Romo & R. Swedberg (Eds.), *Readings in Economic Sociology.* New York: Russell Sage.

Sabel, C. F. (1989). Flexible Specialisation and the Reemergence of Regional Economies. In P. Hirst & J. Seitlin (Eds.), *Reversing Industrial Decline? Industrial Structure and Policy in Britain and Her Competitors.* New York: Berg.

Sagan, C. (1987). The Burden of Skepticism. *Skeptical Inquirer* 12, 38–74.

Sanborn, F. B. (1876). The Work of Social Science, Past and Present. *Journal of Social Science* 8(May): 23–39.

Sanyal, B. (n.d.). Some Tentative Interpretations about Students' Comments on Ph.D.'s in Planning. Unpublished mimeograph. Department of Urban Planning, Massachusetts Institute of Technology.

Sarason, S. B. (1978). The Nature of Problem-Solving in Social Action. *American Psychologist* 33, 370–380.

Sarbin, T. R. (1967). On the Futility of the Proposition That Some People be Labeled "Mentally Ill." *Journal of Consulting Psychology* 31, 447–453.

Sarri, R. (1967). Self-Image Perspectives of Delinquents in Custodial and Treatment Institutions. In E. J. Thomas (Co-author and editor), *Behavioral Science for Social Workers.* New York: Free Press/Macmillan.

Sarri, R. (1971). The Rehabilitation Failure. *Trial* 7(5): 18–20.

Sarri, R. (1986). Organizational and Policy Practice in Social Work: Challenges for the Future. *Urban and Social Change Review* 19, 14–19.

Sarri, R. C., & F. F. Maple. (1972). *The School in the Community.* Washington, DC: National Association of Social Workers.

Sarri, R., & R. D. Vinter. (1965). Group Treatment Strategies in Juvenile Correctional Programs. *Crime and Delinquency* 11(October): 326–340.

Saunders, C. (1960). The Moment of Truth: Care of the Dying. In L. Pearson (Ed.), *Death and Dying.* Cleveland, OH: Case University Press.

Saunders, P., & P. Whiteford. (1989). *Measuring Poverty: A Review of Issues.* Canberra: Economic Planning Advisory Council.

Scanlon, T. J. (1982). Contractualism and Utilitarianism. In A. Sen & B. Williams (Eds.),

Utilitarianism and Beyond. Cambridge: Cambridge University Press.

Schachter, R. C. (1986). Language and Memory. *Cognitive Science* 4, 243–284.

Schachter, S. (1982). *Women and Male Violence.* Boston: South End Press.

Schank, R. C. (1980). Language and Memory. *Cognitive Science* 4, 243–284.

Schank, R. C. (1986). *Explanation Patterns: Understanding Mechanically and Creatively.* Hillsdale, NJ: Erlbaum Associates.

Schank, R. C., & R. P. Abelson. (1977). *Scripts, Plans, Goals, and Understanding.* Hillsdale, NJ: Erlbaum Associates.

Scheff, T. (1975). *Labeling Mental Illness.* Engelwood-Cliffs, NJ: Prentice Hall.

Schelling, T. C. (1984). Self Command in Practice, in Policy, and in a Theory of Rational Choice. *American Economic Review* 74(2).

Scheper-Hughes, N., & A. M. Lovell. (1987). *Psychiatry Inside Out: Selected Writings of Franco Basaglia.* New York: Columbia University Press.

Schinke, S. P. (1983). Data-Based Practice. In A. Rosenblatt & D. Waldfogel (Eds.), *Handbook of Clinical Social Work.* San Francisco, CA: Jossey-Bass.

Schmid, G. B. (1991). Chaos Theory and Schizophrenia: Elementary Aspects. *Psychopathology* 24, 185–198.

Schon, D. A. (1987). *Educating the Reflective Practitioner.* San Francisco: Jossey-Bass.

Schon, D. A. (1983). *The Reflective Practitioner: How Professionals Think in Action.* New York: Basic Books, Inc.

Schon, D. A. (1991). Causality and Causal Inference in the Study of Organizations. Department of Urban Studies and Planning. Mimeo. Department of Urban Studies and Planning, Massachusetts Institute of Technology.

Schon, D. A., & M. Rein. (1993). *Frame Reflection: Toward the Resolution of Intractable Policy Problems.* NY: Basic Books.

School of Social Work, University of Michigan. (n.d.). Mimeo. *School of Social Work Faculty Minutes, 1955-1970.* Archives of the School of Social Work and Bentley Historical Library.

Schorr, A. L. (1959). The Retreat to the Technician. *Social Work* 4(1): 29–33.

Schroeder, J. M., M. J. Driver, & S. Siegfried. (1967). *Human Information Processing: Individuals and Groups Function in Complex Social Situations.* New York: Holt, Rinehart and Winston, Inc.

Schroeder, M. (1991). *Fractals, Chaos and Power Laws: Minutes from an Infinite Paradise.* New York: W. H. Freeman and Company.

Schutz, A. (1967). Concept and Theory Formation in the Social Sciences. In M. Natanson (Ed.), *Collected Papers, Vol. I, The Problem of Social Reality.* The Hague: Martinus Nijhoff.

Schwab, D. P., J. D. Olian-Gottlieb, & H. G. Heneman. (1979). Between-Subjects Expectancy Theory Research: A Statistical Review of Studies Predicting Effect and Performance. *Psychological Bulletin* 86, 139–147.

Schwartz, E. (1977). Macro Social Work: A Practice in Search of Some Theory. *Social Service Review* 51(2): 201–227.

Scott, A. (1990). *Ideology and the New Social Movements.* London: Unwin Hyman.

Scott, A. F. (1990). Most Invisible of All: Black Women's Voluntary Associations. *Journal of Southern History* 56(1): 3–22.

Scott, W. R. (1987). *Organizations: Rational, Natural, and Open Systems.* Englewood Cliffs, NJ: Prentice-Hall.

Scott, W. R. (1987). The Adolescence of Institutional Theory: Problems and Potential for Organizational Analysis. *Administrative Science Quarterly* 32, 492–512.

Seeger, J. A. (1983). No Innate Phases in Group Problem Solving. *Academy of*

Management Review 8(4): 683–689.

Segal, Z. V. (1988). Appraisal of the Self-Schema Construct in Cognitive Models of Depression. *Psychological Bulletin* 103, 147–162.

Seidell, J. V., R. Kjolseth, & E. Seymour. (1988). *The Ethnograph (Version 3.0)*. Corvallis, OR: Qualis Research Associates.

Seidman, S. (1994). *Contested Knowledge: Social Theory in the Postmodern Era*. Cambridge, MA: Blackwell.

Selznick, P. (1957). *Leadership in Administration*. Evanston, IL: Row, Peterson.

Sen, A. (1974). Choice, Orderings, and Morality. In S. Korner (Ed.), *Practical Reason*. New Haven: Yale University Press.

Sennett, R., & J. Cobb. (1972). *Hidden Injuries of Class*. New York: Knopf.

Shachter, R. (1986). Evaluating Influence Diagrams. *Operations Research* 34, 871–882.

Shachter, R. (1988). Probabilistic Inference and Influence Diagrams. *Operations Research* 36(4): 589–604.

Shannon, C. E. (1949). *The Mathematical Theory of Communication*. Urbana, IL: University of Illinois Press.

Shapin, S. (1992). Discipline and Bounding: The History and Sociology of Science as Seen Through the Externalism-Internalism Debate. *History of Science* 30, 333–369.

Shapin, S. (1995). Here and Everywhere: Sociology of Scientific Knowledge. *Annual Review of Sociology* 21, 289–321.

Sheinfeld Gorin, S., & T. Weirich. (1981). Ideology and Performance: Service Delivery in a Community Mental Health Center. *Public Administration Review* 41(1): 63–72.

Sheinfeld Gorin, S., & T. Weirich. (1995). Innovation Use: Performance Assessment in a Community Mental Health Center. *Human Relations* 48(12): 1427–1453.

Sheinfeld Gorin, S., N. Viswanathan, & M. Arje. (1992). Putting Social Science to Work: The Use of Information in Management Decision-Making. Paper presented at the *First Annual Conference on The Integration of Social Work and Social Science*. October 29–November 1, 1992. Ann Arbor. School of Social Work, University of Michigan.

Shepard, R. N. (1964). On Subjectively Optimum Selection Among Multi-Attribute Alternatives. In M. W. I. Shelly & G. L. Poryan (Eds.), *Human Judgments and Optimality*. (pp. 257–281). New York: John Wiley.

Sherman, W., & S. Wenocur. (1983). Empowering Public Welfare Workers Through Mutual Support. *Social Work* 28(5): 275–79.

Shils, E. (1993). Do We Still Need Academic Freedom? *The American Scholar* 62(1 Spring): 187–209.

Sibeon, R. (1991). *Towards a New Sociology of Social Work*. Avebury: Gower Publishing.

Simmons, K. A., & L. E. Miller. (1992). Differences in Management Practices of Founding and Non-Founding Chief Executives of Human Service Organizations. *Entrepreneurship Theory and Practice* 16(Summer): 31–39.

Simmons, R. (1978). Blacks and High Self-Esteem: A Puzzle. *Social Psychology* 41(1): 58–61.

Simon, B. (1990). Rethinking Empowerment. *Journal of Progressive Human Services* 1(1): 27–40.

Simon, J. A. (1976a). *Administrative Behavior*. 3rd ed. New York: Free Press.

Simon, J. A. (1976b). Discussion: Cognition and Social Behavior. In J. Caroll & J. Payne (Eds.), *Cognition and Social Behavior*. (pp. 251–252). Hillsdale, NJ: Lawrence Erlbaum Associates.

Simpson, R. L. (1978). Is Research Utilization for Social Workers? *Journal of Social*

Service Research 2(2): 143–157.

Skeldon, R. Emigration, Immigration, and Fertility Decline: Demographic Integration or Disintegration?

Skinner, H. A. (1989). Butterfly Wings Flapping: Do We Need More 'Chaos' in Understanding Addictions. *British Journal of Addiction* 84, 353–356.

Skold, K. (1988). The Interests of Feminists and Children in Child Care. In S. M. Dornbusch & M. H. Strober (Eds.), *Feminism, Children, and the New Families.* (pp. 113–136). New York: Guilford Press.

Skrabanek, P. (1990). Reductionist Fallacies in the Theory and Treatment of Mental Disorders. *International Journal of Mental Health* 19, 1–18.

Slavin, S. (1980). A Theoretical Framework for Social Administration. In F. D. Perlmutter & S. Slavin (Eds.), *Leadership in Social Administration: Perspectives for the 1980's.* Philadelphia: Temple University Press.

Slovic, P., & D. MacPhillamy. (1974). Dimensional Commensurability and Cue Utilization in Comparative Judgment. *Organizational Behavior and Human Performance* 11(2): 172–194.

Smid, G., & R. V. Krieken. (1984). Notes on Theory and Practice in Social Work: A Comparative View. *British Journal of Social Work.* 14(1): 11-22.

Smith, B., & C. Noble-Spruell. (1986). An Overview of Feminist Research Perspectives. In H. Marchant & B. Waring (Eds.), *Gender Reclaimed.* Australia: Hale and Iremonger.

Smith, H. (1988). *Power Game: How Washington Works.* New York: Random House.

Snell, S. A. (1992). Control Theory in Strategic Human Resource Management: The Mediating Effect of Administrative Information. *Academy of Management Journal* 35(2): 292–327.

Snow, C. C., & L. G. Hrebiniak. (1980). Strategy, Distinctive Competence, and Organizational Performance. *Administrative Science Quarterly* 25, 317–335.

Snow, C. P. (1964). *The Two Cultures and a Second Look.* London, England: Cambridge University Press.

Snyder, M., & C. J. Thompson. (1988). Interactions between Therapists and Clients: Hypotheses Testing and Behavioral Confirmation. In D. C. Turk & P. Salovey (Eds.), *Reasoning, Inference and Judgment in Clinical Psychology.* New York: Free Press.

Soja, E. (1990). *Postmodern Geographies.* New York: Verso.

Solinger, R. (1990). The Girl Nobody Loved: Psychological Explanations for White Single Pregnancy in the pre-Roe v. Wade Era, 1945–1965. *Frontiers* 2(3): 45–55.

Solinger, R. (1992). *Wake Up Little Susie: Single Pregnancy and Race Before Roe v. Wade.* New York: Routledge.

Solinger, R. (July 6, 1992). Boris, In Trouble Deep. *The Nation*, pp. 24–26.

Solomon, B. (1976). *Black Empowerment.* New York: Columbia University Press.

Specht, H. (1986). Review of S. Taylor and R. Roberts, Eds., *Theory and Practice of Community Social Work. Social Work* 31(2): 154–155.

Specht, H., & M. E. Courtney. (1994). *Unfaithful Angels.* New York: Free Press.

Spendlove, D. C., J. R. Gavelek, & V. MacMurray. (1981). Learned Helplessness and the Depressed Housewife. *Social Work* 26(6): 474–82.

Sperber, I. (1990). *Fashions in Science: Opinion Leaders and Collective Behavior Sciences.* Minneapolis: University of Minnesota Press.

Spretnak, C., & F. Capra. (1985). *Green Politics.* London: Grafton.

Springbett, B. M. (1958). Factors Affecting the Final Decision in the Employment Interview. *Canadian Journal of Psychology* 12, 13–22.

Staats, A. W. (1981). Paradigmatic Behaviorism, Unified Theory, Unified Theory Construction Methods, and the Zeitgeist of Separatism. *American Psychologist* 36(3 March): 239–256.

Staats, A. W. (1991). Unified Positivism and Unification Psychology: Fad or New Field. *American Psychologist* 46(9): 899–912.

Stack, C. B. (1974). *All Our Kin: Strategies for Survival in a Black Community.* New York: Harper and Row.

Staples, L. (1990). Powerful Ideas About Empowerment. *Administration in Social Work: Empowerment Issues in Administrative and Community Practice* 14(1): 29–42.

Starr, S. L. (1991). The Sociology of the Invisible: The Primacy of Work in the Writings of Anselm Strauss. In D. R. Maines (Ed.), *Social Organization and Social Process: Essays in Honor of Anselm Strauss.* (pp. 265–283). New York: Aldine de Gruyter.

Stauch, M. (1992). Natural Science, Social Science, and Democratic Practice: Some Political Implications of the Distinction between the Natural and the Human Sciences. *Philosophy of the Social Sciences* 22(3): 337–356.

Steenberg, D. (1991). Chaos at the Marriage of Heaven and Hell. *Harvard Theological Review* 84(4): 447–466.

Steil, J. M. (1989). Marital Relationships and Mental Health: The Psychic Costs of Inequality. In J. Freeman (Ed.), *Women: A Feminist Perspective.* 4th ed. (pp. 138–149). Mountain View, CA: Mayfield Publishing.

Stevens, R. T. (1989). *Fractal Programming in C.* Redwood City, CA: M & T Books.

Stevenson, G. S. (1934). *Child Guidance Clinics: A Quarter Century of Development.* NY: The Commonwealth Fund.

Stevenson, O., & P. Parsloe. (1978). *Social Service Teams: The Practitioner's View.* London: HMSO.

Stewart, I. (1989). *Does God Play Dice?: The Mathematics of Chaos.* Oxford, UK: Basil Blackwell.

Strauss, A. L. (1987). *Qualitative Analysis for Social Scientists.* Cambridge, MA: Cambridge University Press.

Strauss, A. L., & J. Corbin. (1990). *Basics of Qualitative Research: Grounded Theory Procedure and Techniques.* Newbury Park, CA: Sage Publications.

Strauss, J. S. (1989). Subjective Experiences of Schizophrenia: Toward a New Dynamic Psychiatry—II. *Schizophrenia Bulletin* 15, 179–187.

Street, D., R. D. Vinter, & C. Perrow. (1966). *Organization for Treatment.* New York: Free Press.

Stretton, H. (1976). *Capitalism, Socialism and Environment.* Cambridge, UK: Cambridge University Press.

Streufert, S. (1987). Decision Making Research and Theory: Challenges for Applied Social Psychology. *Journal of Applied Social Psychology* 17(7): 609–621.

Sundstrom, E., & I. Altman. (1989). Physical Environments and Work-Group Effectiveness. *Research in Organizational Behavior* 11, 175–209.

Sundstrom, E., K. P. DeMeuse, & D. Futrell. (1990). Work Teams: Applications and Effectiveness. *American Psychologist* 45(2): 120–133.

Sutton, J. (1985). The Juvenile Court and Social Welfare: Dynamics of Progressive Reform. *Law and Society Review* 19(1): 107–144.

Sutton, J. R. (1988). *Stubborn Children: Controlling Delinquency in the United States, 1640–1981.* Berkeley, California: University of California Press.

Swift, C., & G. Levin. (1987). Empowerment: An Emerging Mental Health Technology. *Journal of Primary Prevention* 8(1&2): 71–94.

Swindler, A., & J. Arditi. (1994). The New Sociology of Knowledge. *Annual Review of*

Sociology 20, 305–329.

Szasz, T. (1994). *Cruel Compassion: Psychiatric Control of Society's Unwanted.* New York: John Wiley.

Talyigas, K., & G. Hegesyi. (1992). Social Work in Hungary: New Opportunities in a Changing Society. In M. C. Hoskenstad, S. K. Khinduka, & J. Midgeley (Eds.), *Profiles in International Social Work.* Washington: National Association of Social Work Press.

Tannenbaum, A. S. (1968). *The Social Psychology of Work Organization.* Belmont, CA: Brooks/Cole Publishing.

Tannenbaum, S. I., R. L. Beard, & E. Salas. (1992). Team Building and its Influence on Team Effectiveness: An Examination of Conceptual and Empirical Developments. In K. Kelley (Ed.), *Issues, Theory and Research in Industrial/Organizational Psychology.* (pp. 117–151). Amsterdam: Elsevier Science Publishers.

Taylor, E. H. (1989). Schizophrenia: Fire in the Brain. *Social Work* 34(3): 258–261.

Taylor, M. C., & E. J. Walsh. (1979). Explanations of Black Self-Esteem: Some Empirical Tests. *Social Psychology* 42(3): 242–253.

Taylor, S. E. (1983). Adjustment to Threatening Events: A Theory of Cognitive Adaptation. *American Psychologist* 38, 1161–1173.

Taylor, S. E., & J. D. Brown. (1988). Illusion and Well-being: A Social Psychological Perspective on Mental Health. *Psychological Bulletin* 103, 193–210.

Taylor, S., & R. Roberts. (1985). *Theory and Practice of Community Social Work.* New York: Columbia University Press.

Terem, E. (1991). Interdisciplinary Teams and the Control of Clients: A Sociotechnical Perspective. *Human Relations* 44(4): 342–356.

Test, A. M., & L. Stein. (1980). Alternatives to Mental Hospital Treatment. *Archives of General Psychiatry* 37.

Thagard, P. (1988). *Computational Philosophy of Science.* Cambridge, MA: The MIT Press.

Theobald, R. (1965). *Free Men and Free Markets.* New York: Doubleday.

Therborn, G. (1976). *Science, Class and Society: On the Formation of Sociology and Historical Materialism.* London, England: New Left Books.

Thomas, E. J. (1960). Theory and Research on the Small Group: Selected Themes and Problems. In L. S. Kogan (Ed.), *Social Science Theory and Social Work Research.* New York: National Association of Social Work.

Thomas, E. J. (1964). Selecting Knowledge from Behavioral Science. *Building Social Work Knowledge: Report of a Conference.* (pp. 38–48). New York: National Association of Social Work.

Thomas, E. J. (1967). Types of Contributions Behavioral Science Makes to Social Work. In E. J. Thomas (Ed.), *Behavioral Science for Social Workers.* New York: Free Press.

Thomas, E. J. (1967). *The Socio-behavioral Approach and Applications to Social Work.* New York: Council on Social Work Education.

Thomas, E. J. (1967). *Behavioral Science for Social Workers.* New York: Free Press.

Thomas, E. J. (1970). Behavioral Modification and Casework. In R. W. Roberts & R. H. Nee (Eds.), *Theories of Social Casework.* Chicago: Chicago University Press.

Thomas, E. J. (1975). Uses of Research Methods in Interpersonal Practice. In N. A. Polansky (Ed.), *Social Work Research: Methods for the Helping Professions.* Rev. ed. Chicago: University of Chicago Press.

Thomas, E. J. (1978). Generating Innovation in Social Work: The Paradigm of Developmental Research. *Journal of Social Service Research* 2, 95–116.

Thomas, E. J. (1984). *Designing Interventions for the Helping Professions.* Beverly Hills: Sage.

Thomas, E. J. (1990). Modes of Practice in Developmental Research. In L. Videka-Sherman & W. J. Reid (Eds.), *Advances in Clinical Social Work Research.* Silver Spring, MD: National Assocation of Social Work Press.

Thomas, E. J., & E. Goodman. (1965). *Socio-behavioral Theory and Interpersonal Helping in Social Work.* Ann Arbor, MI: Campus Publishers.

Thomas, E. J., D. McLeod et al. (1960). *In-Service Training and Reduced Workload— Experiments in the State Welfare Department.* New York: Russell Sage.

Thomas, J. B., & R. R. McDaniel. (1990). Strategic Issue Interpretation: The Effects of Strategy and Information Processing on Top Management Teams. *Academy of Management Journal* 33, 286–306.

Thomas, M. E., & M. Hughes. (1986). The Continuing Significance of Race: A Study of Race, Class, and Quality of Life in America, 1972–1985. *American Sociological Review* 51, 830–841.

Thompson, J. D. (1967). Organization in Action. In J. Shafritz & J. Ott (Eds.), *Classics of Organization Theory.* Belmont, CA: Brooks/Cole Publishing.

Thorne, B. (1982). Feminist Rethinking of the Family: An Overview. In B. Thorne & M. Yalom (Eds.), *Rethinking the Family: Some Feminist Questions.* (pp. 1–24). New York: Longman.

Thyer, B. A., & K. E. Thyer. (1990). Single-System Research Designs in Social Work Practice: A Bibliography from 1965 to 1990. *Research on Social Work Practice* 2, 99–116.

Thyer, B., & K. Bentley. (1986). Academic Affiliation of Social Work Authors: A Citation Analysis of Six Major Journals. *Journal of Social Work Education* 22, 67–73.

Todd, J. T., & E. K. Morris. (1983). Misconceptions and Miseducation: Presentations of Radical Behaviorism in Psychology Textbooks. *Behavior Analyst* 6, 153–160.

Tomlinson, D. (1991). *Utopia, Community Care and the Retreat from the Asylum.* Buckingham, UK: Open University Press.

Toseland, R. W., J. Palmer-Ganeles, & D. Chapman. (1986). Teamwork in Psychiatric Settings. *Social Work* 31(1): 46–52.

Touraine, A. (1985). An Introduction to the Study of Social Movements. *Social Research* 52, 749–787.

Towle, C. (1958 October). [Letter to Kathleen Woodroofe]. Charlotte Towle Papers. Regenstein Library, Department of Special Collections, University of Chicago.

Trattner, W. I. (1968). *Homer Folks: Pioneer in Social Welfare.* New York: Columbia University Press.

Trice, H. M., & W. Sonnenstuhl. (1988). Drinking Behavior and Risk Factors Related to the Work Place: Implications for Research and Prevention. *The Journal of Applied Behavioral Science* 24, 327–346.

Tripodi, T. (1974). *Uses and Abuses of Social Research in Social Work.* New York: Columbia University Press.

Tripodi, T. (1981). The Logic of Research Design. In R. M. Grinnell (Ed.), *Social Work Research and Evaluation.* (pp. 198–225). Itasca, IL: F.E. Peacock.

Tripodi, T. (1983). *Evaluative Research for Social Workers.* Englewood Cliffs, NJ: Prentice-Hall.

Tripodi, T., & I. Epstein. (1980). *Research Techniques for Clinical Social Workers.* New York: Columbia University Press.

Tripodi, T., P. Fellin, & I. Epstein. (1971). *Social Program Evaluation: Guidelines for*

Health, Education, and Welfare Administrators. Itasca, IL: F.E. Peacock.

Tripodi, T., P. Fellin, & H. J. Meyer. (1969). *Assessment of Social Research: Guidelines for Use in Research in Social Work and Social Science*. Itasca, IL: F. E. Peacock.

Tropman, J. (1987). *Effective Meetings*. Newbury, CA: Sage.

Tsang, N. M. (1992). From Learning Styles to Learning Strategies. *Issues in Social Work Education* 12(2).

Tucker, D. J. (1996). Eclecticism is Not a Free Good: Barriers to Knowledge Development in Social Work. *Social Service Review* 70(3): 400–434.

Tuckman, B. W., & M. A. C. Jensen. (1977). Stages in Small Group Development Revisited. *Group and Organizational Studies* 2, 419–427.

Tufillaro, N. B., T. Abbott, & J. Reilly. (1992). *An Experimental Approach to Nonlinear Dynamics and Chaos*. Redwood City, CA: Addison-Wesley.

Turcotte, W. E. (1974). Control Systems, Performance, and Satisfaction in Two State Agencies. *Administrative Science Quarterly* 19(1): 60–73.

Turk, D. C., & P. Salovey. (1988). *Reasoning, Inference and Judgment in Clinical Psychology*. New York: Free Press.

Turner, B. (1986). *Equality*. Chichester: Ellis Horwood.

Turner, F. J. (1986). *Social Work Treatment: Interlocking Theoretical Approaches*. New York: Free Press.

Turner, V. (1967). *The Forest of Symbols*. Ithaca, NY: Cornell University.

Tyson, K. (1995). *New Foundations for Social and Behavioral Research: The Heuristic Approach*. Newbury Park, CA: Sage.

Tyson, K. B. (1992). A New Approach to Relevant Scientific Research for Practical Practitioners: The Heuristic Paradigm. *Social Work* 37, 541–556.

United Nations Development Program. (1994). *Human Development*. New York: Oxford University Press.

Vinokur-Kaplan, D. (1992). *Pre- and Post-Training Team-Building Assessment: Final Report to Michigan Department of Mental Health*. Unpublished Manuscript. University of Michigan School of Social Work, Ann Arbor.

Vinokur-Kaplan, D. (1995a). Integrating Work Team Effectiveness into Mental Health Practice in Psychiatric Hospitals. *Administration and Policy in Mental Health* 22(5): 521–530.

Vinokur-Kaplan, D. (1995b). Treatment Teams That Work (and Those That Don't): An Application of Hackman's Group Effectiveness Model to Interdisciplinary Teams in Psychiatric Hospitals. *Journal of Applied Behavioral Science* 31(3): 303–327.

Vinokur-Kaplan, D., & G. Walker-Burt. (1994). Meeting Professionals' Training Needs During Retrenchment: An Example of Federal, State and University Collaboration with Public Psychiatric Hospitals. *Administration and Policy in Mental Health* 21(6): 525–530.

Vinter, R. D. (1959). The Social Structure of Service. In A. J. Kahn (Ed.), *Issues in American Social Work*. New York: Columbia University Press.

Vinter, R. D. (1960). Small Group Theory and Research: Implications for Group Work. In L. Kogan (Ed.), *Social Science Theory and Social Work Research*. New York: National Association of Social Workers.

Vinter, R. D. (1963). The Analysis of Treatment Organizations. *Social Work* 8(2): 3–15.

Vinter, R. D. (1967). The Juvenile Court as an Institution. in *Juvenile Delinquency and Youth Crime*. Washington, DC: Government Printing Office for the President's Commission on Law Enforcement.

Vinter, R. D., R. Sarri et al. (1967). *Readings in Group Work Practice*. Ann Arbor, MI: Campus Publishers.

Wakefield, J. C. (1988). Psychotherapy, Distributive Justice, and Social Work. Part 1. Distributive Justice as a Conceptual Framework for Social Work. *Social Service Review* 62(2): 187–210.

Walker, S. (1994). *Sense and Nonsense about Crime and Drugs: A Policy Guide.* Belmont, CA: Wadsworth.

Wallerstein, I. (1990). Anti-systemic Movements: History and Dilemmas. In S. Amin et al. (Eds.), *Transforming the Revolution: Social Movements and the World-System.* New York: Monthly Review Press.

Wallerstein, N. (1992). Powerlessness, Empowerment and Health: Implications for Health Promotion Programs. *American Journal of Health Promotion* 6(3): 197–205.

Wamsley, G. L., & M. N. Zald. (1973). *The Political Economy of Public Organizations: A Critique and Approach to the Study of Public Administration.* Lexington, MA: Lexington Books.

Warheit, G., C. E. Holzer, & S. A. Avery. (1975). Race and Mental Illness: An Epidemiological Update. *Journal of Health and Social Behavior* 16, 243–256.

Warner, R. (1985). *Recovery from Schizophrenia.* London: Routledge.

Warren, R. (1971). *The Community in America.* 2nd ed. Chicago: Rand McNally.

Waterhouse, L. (1987). The Relationship Between Theory and Practice in Social Work Training. *Issues in Social Work Education* 7(1).

Weber, M. (1947). *The Theory of Social and Economic Organization.* New York: Free Press.

Weick, A. (1987). Reconceptualizing the Philosophical Perspective of Social Work. *Social Service Review* 61(2 June): 218–230.

Weick, K. E. (1976). Educational Organizations as Loosely Coupled Systems. *Administrative Science Quarterly* 21, 1–19.

Weick, K. E. (1984). Small Wins: Redefining the Scale of Social Problems. *American Psychologist* 39, 40–49.

Weil, M. (1986). Women, Community, and Organizing. In N. Van DenBergh & L. Cooper (Eds.), *Feminist Visions for Social Work.* (pp. 187–210). Silver Springs: National Association of Social Work.

Weinberg, M. S., & C. J. Williams. (1975). *Male Homosexuals: Their Problems and Adaptations.* New York: Oxford University Press.

Weingarten, H. R. (1992). Crisis and Competency: A Participatory Action Research Approach to Late Life Divorce. Paper presented at the *First Annual Conference on The Integration of Social Work and Social Science.* October 29–November 1, 1992. Ann Arbor. School of Social Work, University of Michigan.

Weiss, C. H. (1986). Research and Policy-Making: A Limited Partnership. P. Heller (Ed.), *The Use and Abuse of Social Science.* London: Sage.

Weiss, J. A., & D. K. Cohen. (1991). The Interplay of Social Science and Prior Knowledge in Policy and Practice.

Weissman, H., I. Epstein, & A. Savage. (1983). *Agency-based Social Work: Neglected Aspects of Clinical Practice.* Philadelphia, PA: Temple University Press.

Wenocur, S., & M. Reisch. (1989). *From Charity to Enterprise: The Development of American Social Work in a Market Economy.* Chicago, Illinois: University of Illinois Press.

Wernet, S. P., & D. M. Austin. (1991). Decision Making Styles and Leadership Patterns in Nonprofit Human Service Organizations. *Administration in Social Work* 15(3): 1–17.

Westcott, M. (1990). Feminist Criticisms of the Social Sciences. J. M. Nielson (Ed.), *Feminist Research Methods: Exemplary Readings in Social Sciences.* Boulder, CO:

Westview Press.

Whan, M. (1983). Tricks of the Trade: Questionable Theory and Practice in Family Therapy. *British Journal of Social Work* 13, 321–337.

Whan, M. (1986). On the Nature of Practice. *British Journal of Social Work* 16, 243–250.

Wheelan, S. A. (1994). *Group Process: A Development Perspective*. Boston: Allyn and Bacon.

White, S. H. (1979). Old and New Routes from Theory to Practice. In L. B. Resnick & P. A. Weaver (Eds.), *Theory and Practice of Early Reading*. Hillsdale, NJ: Lawrence Erlbaum Associates.

White, S. H. (1994). The Relationships of Developmental Psychology to Social Policy. In E. F. Zigler, S. L. Kagan, & N. Hall (Eds.), *Children, Families and Government: Preparing for the 21st Century*. New York: Cambridge University Press.

Whitley, R. (1982). The Establishment and Structure of Science as Reputational Organizations. N. Elias, H. Martin, & R. Whitley (Eds.), *Scientific Establishments and Hierarchies*. Dordrecht, Holland: D. Reidel Publishing.

Whittaker, J. K., & P. Pecora. (1981). The Social "R&D" Paradigm in Child and Youth Services. *Children and Youth Services Review* 3, 305–317.

Wicken, A. J. (May 3, 1991). AVCC Copyright Advice. *Uniken* No. 6, p. 12.

Wiebe, R. H. (1967). *The Search for Order 1877–1920*. New York: Hill and Wang.

Wierson, M., & R. Forehand. (1994). Parent Behavioral Training for Child Noncompliance: Rationale, Concepts and Effectiveness. *Current Directions in Psychological Science* 3, 146–149.

Wilensky, H., & C. Lebeaux. (1958). *Industrial Society and Social Welfare*. New York: Russell Sage Foundation.

Williams, L. (1990). The Challenge of Education to Social Work: The Case of Minority Children. *Social Work* 35, 236–242.

Williamson, O. E. (1963). A Model of Rational Managerial Behavior. In R. M. Cyert & J. G. March (Eds.), *A Behavioral Theory of the Firm*. (pp. 237–252). Englewood Cliffs, NJ: Prentice-Hall.

Wilshire, B. (1988). *The Moral Collapse of the University*. Albany: State University of New York Press.

Wilson, W. J. (1987). *The Truly Disadvantaged: The Inner City, The Underclass and Public Policy*. Chicago: University of Chicago Press.

Wilson, W. J., & K. M. Neckerman. (1986). Poverty and Family Structure: The Widening Gap between Evidence and Public Policy Issues. In S. H. Danziger & D. H. Weinberg (Eds.), *Fighting Poverty: What Works and What Doesn't*. (pp. 232–282). Cambridge, MA: Harvard University Press.

Winerip, M. (September 27, 1992). Some People Taking Back Their Power. *New York Times*, p. 1.

Wodarski, J. S. (1981). *The Role of Research in Clinical Practice: A Practical Approach for the Human Services*. Baltimore, MD: University Park Press.

Wolfe, A. (1989). *Whose Keeper? Social Science and Moral Obligation*. Berkeley, CA: University of California Press.

Woodroffe, K. (1962). *From Charity to Social Work in England and the United States*. Toronto, Canada: University of Toronto Press.

Yonay, Y. P. (1994). When Black Boxes Clash: Competing Ideas of What Science is in Economics. *Social Studies of Science* 24(1): 39–80.

Young, K. (1993). Marriages Under Stress. *Research Report Series, Hong Kong University* December.

Young, L., J. Baker, & T. Monnone. (1989). Poverty and Child Abuse in the Sydney Metropolitan Area. *Child Abuse and Neglect Program: Paper No. 9.* Sydney, Australia: Department of Family and Community Services.

Young, T. R. (1991). Chaos and Social Change: Metaphorics of the Postmodern. *Science Journal* 28(3): 289–305.

Young, T. R. (1991). Chaos Theory and Symbolic Interaction Theory: Poetics for the Post Modern Sociologist. *Symbolic Interaction* 14(3): 321–334.

Zald, M. (1993). Organization Studies as a Scientific and Humanistic Enterprise: Towards a Reconceptualization of the Foundation of the Field. *Organization Science* 4(4 November): 513–528.

Zander, A. (1979). Psychology of Group Process. *Annual Review of Psychology.*

Zaretsky, E. (1982). The Place of the Family in the Origins of the Welfare State. In B. Thorne & M. Yalom (Eds.), *Rethinking the Family: Some Feminist Questions.* (pp. 188–224). New York: Longman.

Zaslavsky, G. M., R. Z. Sagdeev, D. A. Usikov, & A. A. Chernikov. (1991). *Weak Chaos and Quasi-Regular Patterns.* Cambridge: Cambridge University Press.

Zeelen, J., & J. Weeghel. (1993). *Vocational Rehabilitation in a Changing Psychiatry.* The Netherlands: Department of Anthropology, Groningen University.

Zimakova, T. (1992). Presentation at Panel on International Perspectives on Social Work and Social Science in the 1990s. Paper presented at the *First Annual Conference on The Integration of Social Work and Social Science.* October 29–November 1, 1992. Ann Arbor. School of Social Work, University of Michigan.

Zimmerman, M., B. Israel, & Amy Schulz (1992). Further Explorations in Empowerment Theory: An Empirical Analysis of Psychological Empowerment. *American Journal of Community Psychology* 20, 707–727.

Zinn, M. B. (1990a). Family, Feminism and Race in America. *Gender & Society* 4(1): 68–82.

Zinn, M. B. (1990b). Minority Families in Crisis. In K. V. Hansen & I. J. Philipson (Eds.), *Women, Class and the Feminist Imagination.* Philadelphia: Temple University Press.

Zucker, L. G. (1987). Institutional Theories of Organization. *Annual Review of Sociology* 13, 443–464.

Index

About the Contributors

MIMI ABRAMOVITZ, Hunter College School of Social Work, City University of New York

SUSAN BERNSTEIN, Department of Social Work Services, The Mount Sinai Medical Center

RICHARD E. BOETTCHER, College of Social Work, Ohio State University

AARON M. BROWER, School of Social Work, University of Wisconsin, Madison

IRWIN EPSTEIN, Hunter College School of Social Work, City University of New York

ROBERT FISHER, Graduate School of Social Work, University of Houston

EILEEN GAMBRILL, School of Social Welfare, University of California, Berkeley

CHARLES GARVIN, School of Social Work, University of Michigan

HARRIET GOODMAN, Hunter College School of Social Work, University of New York

LORRAINE GUTIÉRREZ, School of Social Work, University of Michigan

ADAM JAMROZIK, Social Policy Research Center of the University of New South Wales

JOSEPH KLING, Government Department, St. Lawrence University, New York

SUSAN LAMBERT, School of Social Service Administration, University of Chicago

ARMAND LAUFFER, School of Social Work, University of Michigan

DAVID LAWS, Department of Urban Studies and Planning, Massachusetts Institute of Technology

JOHN F. LONGRES, School of Social Work, University of Washington

JAMES PATRICK MACE, Faculty of Social Science, Hong Kong Shue Yan College

DIANA MAK, Department of Applied Social Studies, Hong Kong Polytechnic

TSANG NAI-MING, Department of Applied Social Studies, Hong Kong Polytechnic

PAULA S. NURIUS, School of Social Work, University of Washington

RICHARD H. PRICE, Institute for Social Research, University of Michigan

SHULAMIT RAMON, London School of Economics

MARTIN REIN, Department of Urban Studies and Planning, Massachusetts Institute of Technology

ROSEMARY SARRI, School of Social Work, University of Michigan

SHERRI SHEINFELD-GORIN, School of Public Health, Columbia University, and Health Sciences Center, SUNY, Stony Brook, New York

EDWIN J. THOMAS, School of Social Work, University of Michigan

DAVID J. TUCKER, School of Social Work, University of Michigan

DIANE VINOKUR-KAPLAN, School of Social Work, University of Michigan

ROBERT D. VINTER, School of Social Work, University of Michigan

NARAYAN VISWANATHAN, Aldephi University School of Social Work, New York